All You Can Eat!

chinese and thai cooking

Over 600 easy and exotic recipes from the Far East!

Rhonda Lauret Parkinson & Jennifer Malott Kotylo

Published by Adams Media, an F+W Publications Company
57 Littlefield Street, Avon, MA 02322 U.S.A.
www.adamsmedia.com

ISBN: 1-59337-740-1
Printed in the United States of America.

J I H G F E D C B A

Previously published as the Everything® Chinese Cookbook and the Everything® Thai Cookbook.

Contents

Introduction

▶ Asian cooking has never been more popular. *All You Can Eat: Chinese and Thai Cookbook* brings these two types of exciting cuisine together, so now you can have your crab rangoons—and eat your pad thai too.

Gone are the days when Chinese food meant greasy pork fried rice in a takeout container. Today, you can cook Chinese at home—without having to visit specialty stores. A search for ingredients often takes you no farther than your local supermarket, where chili paste and hoisin sauce are readily available, and vegetables with exotic names such as amaranth share space with cabbage in the produce section. With a little practice, it's easy to prepare home-cooked Chinese dishes that are tasty and healthful. The first half of this book features the best in sauces, rice, noodles, soups, and more. The recipes will provide you with a helpful introduction to the fascinating world of Chinese cuisine.

Harmony is the name of the game when it comes to Thai cooking. The balance of sweet, salty, sour, bitter, and hot flavors is essential, not only within most dishes, but also within the context of the overall Thai meal. And you don't have to visit you favorite Thai restaurant to enjoy the best Thailand has to offer. Like the ingredients in Chinese cooking, the ingredients are readily available, and provide an array of healthy choices to satisfy the palate. Packed with wide varieties of fish, vegetables, fruits, and rice, Thai cuisine is just what the doctor ordered.

So put your wok to good use, and use your kitchen to celebrate the rich flavors that make up the *All You Can Eat: Chinese and Thai Cookbook*.

Introduction to Chinese Cooking

WHAT MAKES CHINESE CUISINE SO APPEALING? Restaurant classics such as Mu Shu Pork and Kung Pao Chicken captivate our senses. Even an order of the ubiquitous Chicken Balls with Sweet-and-Sour Sauce from the local Chinese takeout has its own special appeal.

What is it that makes Chinese food so special? It's not the exotic vegetables and seasonings—a skilled chef can prepare a meal that epitomizes the best of Chinese cooking using only native ingredients. It's not the equipment, either. Many tasty stir-fries have been born in a frying pan instead of a wok.

The true secret to Chinese cuisine lies in a harmonious blending of flavors, textures, and colors. Take Basic Sweet-and-Sour Pork (page 141), for example. The sweet and sour flavors balance each other nicely, and the reddish sauce provides a nice contrast to the pineapple and green bell peppers.

This characteristic isn't limited to entrées, either. The same satisfying balance can be found in many Chinese dishes, such as Wonton Soup (page 56), where pork-filled wonton wrappers are swimming in a rich broth.

So, why aren't more people stir-frying noodles and boiling dumplings? A common misconception is that it takes a skilled chef working with state-of-the-art equipment to prepare good Chinese food. Fortunately, that's not true. Stir-frying, steaming, and deep-frying—the three primary Chinese cooking techniques—are all easily mastered with practice.

What are the pluses of cooking Chinese food at home? Besides the obvious advantage to your wallet, it's often healthier than restaurant fare, since you control the fat and calorie count. You can let your own creativity come into play, adjusting a recipe to add favorite foods or seasonal local ingredients. Cooking Chinese food at home also allows you to modify a recipe to suit your family's tastes; substituting parsley for cilantro, for example.

An added bonus is that there is something about cooking Chinese food that brings families together. Many pleasurable evenings can be spent filling dumplings or making pancakes. Appetizers such as egg rolls can often be baked as well as deep-fried, making it easier to involve young children.

This book is designed to help you incorporate home-cooked Chinese meals into your daily life. Tips on purchasing equipment, cooking techniques, and stocking the pantry are all here. Recipes include popular favorites such as Mu Shu Pork, and less well-known dishes such as MaPo Dofu, a tofu dish. Information on cooking with more exotic ingredients such as Szechwan peppercorns and fermented black beans is provided, along with suggestions for substitutes where possible.

Chapter 1

Let's Get Started

Chinese cuisine can seem very exotic after a dim sum brunch or dinner at a Chinatown restaurant, but it's easy to prepare many Chinese recipes at home. All it takes is a good wok, mastery of a few simple cooking skills, and stocking the pantry with basic ingredients, many of which are available on local supermarket shelves.

At the Asian Market

To supplement your regular shopping, you may want to visit the local Asian grocery store. When you enter, you'll be hit with the pungent aromas of exotic ingredients. Then, you'll note the profusion of unusual sights and sounds. Live lobster and crab swim in tanks, competing for your attention with strange fruits and vegetables. You wander past, taking note of the brightly decorated red lanterns hanging from the ceiling and the pleasant sounds of Oriental music in the background.

To the uninitiated, a visit to the Asian market can seem like a trip to a foreign land, minus a map or guidebook. But structure and organization do exist. Unlike the typical large supermarket, Asian groceries share much in common with the shops of days gone by, when several businesses shared the same general space. Most groceries have a butcher shop, where slabs of glazed barbequed pork hang from hooks. A fishmonger sells the freshest fish possible, preferably caught earlier that day. Most stores have a bakery that offers fresh-baked bread and buns. All of these businesses normally operate independently from the main grocery store.

What about monosodium glutamate (MSG)?
You don't need to add MSG to home-cooked dishes; fresh ingredients will provide plenty of flavor. However, since many restaurants use MSG, you may find it difficult to reproduce the taste of your favorite restaurant dish without it.

As for the main grocery area, the most important thing to remember is that the space allocation for various products is different from that in Western supermarkets. One aisle may be set aside for the myriad sauces and seasonings used in Chinese cooking, while another contains a varied assortment of noodles, flour, and starch. And where else would you find an entire aisle devoted to tea, China's national drink?

Two areas that may prove challenging are spices and fresh vegetables. It is very common for grocers to provide only the Cantonese names for produce. Similarly, bags of spices may have Chinese writing on the label, leaving you unsure of their English equivalent. At this point you may notice another difference in Asian markets; there tends to be fewer staff on the floor to ask for help. Don't worry. The checkout cashier will gladly assist you, even if it means temporarily leaving the till.

An added plus to shopping at the Asian market is that you can stock up on ingredients and purchase the tools you need to begin cooking Chinese food at the same time. While most supermarkets carry a few cooking tools, in Chinese markets it is very common for several aisles to be set aside for everything from woks to harder-to-find accessories such as cooking chopsticks.

In Chinese cooking, the fresher the better! It is quite possible that the fish you see on a slab of ice was killed mere hours before being delivered to the market. Freshness is particularly important in Cantonese cuisine. It is a point of pride with Cantonese cooks to create dishes that retain as much of the natural flavor and texture of the food as possible.

Staple Ingredients

Certain flavors such as ginger and garlic feature prominently in Chinese cooking. While on occasion you may find yourself scouring Chinatown for a seldom-used ingredient such as shark's fin, keeping the pantry stocked with the items below will allow you to whip up a stir-fry any night of the week, using whatever combination of meat and vegetables you have on hand.

In southern China the day begins and ends with a bowl of steaming rice. While noodles are the grain of choice in China's colder northern regions, rice is consumed there as well. Long grain rice is favored for main dishes, but medium grain rice is an acceptable substitute. Short grain rice is used primarily in desserts.

Chinese noodles are not much different from Italian pasta. Most types of noodles are very user-friendly, often requiring only a quick soaking to soften before use. A chart of Chinese noodles and cooking times is included on the following page.

Cooking Chinese Noodles		
Noodle Type	**Cooking Method**	**Cooking Time**
Cellophane/Bean Thread Noodles	Soak in Hot Water	15 minutes
Egg Noodles, Fresh	Boil	3–5 minutes
Egg Noodles, Dried	Boil	4–5½ minutes
Rice Noodles	Soak in Hot Water	15–20 minutes
Rice Paper	Soak in Hot Water	1 minute
Wheat Flour, Fresh	Boil	3–5 minutes
Wheat Flour, Dried	Boil	4–5 minutes

Fresh Is Best

Always use the freshest ingredients possible; nothing can replace the bite of freshly ground white pepper, or ginger that has gone straight from garden to kitchen, bypassing the market.

- *Ginger:* Used for everything from seasoning oil to masking fishy odors in seafood dishes. Be sure to use fresh instead of powdered.
- *Garlic:* The mainstay of northern Chinese dishes, where cooks rely on hardy vegetables that can tolerate cold winters and a short growing season. Like ginger, it is also used to flavor hot oil before stir-frying.
- *Green onions:* Also called spring onions and scallions, these are used in cooked dishes and as a garnish.
- *Celery:* Celery's crisp texture makes a nice contrast with other vegetables in stir-fries.
- *White pepper:* Freshly ground white pepper lends a sharp bite to soups and stir-fries. Use sparingly at first or according to taste.

The Chinese also use hundreds of dried ingredients, from tangerine peel to lily buds. The most commonly used are dried black mushrooms—you'll frequently find these stacked in bins at the entrance to Asian markets. Don't worry about purchasing the most expensive brands, but do look for mushrooms with a nice curl to them.

Sauces and Oils

A good sauce is a key component in Chinese cooking. Savory sauces like oyster and hoisin sauce add their own intriguing blend of flavors to a sauce or marinade, while soy sauce is used both to flavor and color the food. Here are some of the sauces most commonly used in Chinese cooking:

- *Dark soy sauce:* This sauce is used primarily to lend a darker color to marinades, sauces, and heavier dishes. The recipe will state if dark soy sauce is required.
- *Light soy sauce:* Saltier and aged for a shorter period of time, light soy sauce makes a frequent appearance in soups, stir-fries, and deep-fries. When a recipe calls for soy or soya sauce, use light soy sauce.
- *Oyster sauce:* This rich sauce adds a savory flavor to dishes such as Broccoli with Oyster Sauce (page 242).
- *Hoisin sauce:* Made from seasoned soybean paste, the sweet and savory flavor of hoisin sauce is an indispensable tool of northern Chinese cooks.
- *Chili paste and chili sauce:* Fiery Szechuan cuisine wouldn't be the same without hot chilies. Just remember that a little goes a long way!

Versatile cornstarch has many uses, from binding liquid ingredients in meat marinades to coating food during deep-frying. Mixed with water, it's frequently used to thicken sauces during the final stages of cooking.

Both stir-frying and deep-frying require oils with a high smoking point. While Chinese cooks favor peanut oil, it can go rancid if there is too long a period between stir-fries. Vegetable oils such as canola and corn oil are an acceptable substitute. Sesame oil is used to add a unique nutty flavor to soups and fried dishes—just drizzle a few drops into the dish in the final stages of cooking.

You will also need to get Chinese rice wine, which is valued for its sweet flavor and ability to mask strong odors in marinades and stir-fries.

(Generally, pale dry sherry is an acceptable substitute.) In marinades and special sauces where the flavor of each ingredient counts more, stick with Chinese rice wine or make sure to use a higher quality pale dry sherry.

Cooking Equipment

You don't need to splurge on a bunch of fancy gadgets to cook Chinese food. All it takes is a wok and a few basic utensils. The versatile wok is a steamer, frying pan, deep-fryer, and roasting pan all rolled into one. A good chef's knife can be used instead of a Chinese cleaver, and you don't need a rice cooker to boil rice, but a wok is the one piece of equipment that you should definitely consider purchasing before you begin cooking Chinese food.

It would be stretching the truth to say that you absolutely must have a wok to cook Chinese food. Many satisfactory meals of chop suey and chow mein have been born in a frying pan. The main thing is to use a heavy skillet that can take the high heats required for stir-frying. Cast iron and Calphalon hard anodized pans are both good choices. Still, if it's possible, a wok is preferable. Here are a few tips on choosing a good wok.

Material Matters

Originally, woks were large round vessels made of cast iron, with handles on either side for easy lifting in and out of the conventional Chinese oven. Over the centuries, woks have evolved to meet changing needs. Today, most Asian cooks favor woks made of carbon steel. Inexpensive and easy to handle, carbon steel woks can take the high heat needed for stir-frying and deep-frying. Properly seasoned and cleaned, they will last for years.

Still, modern technology has provided other options. It's now possible to purchase woks made with a nonstick coating. There are several advantages to cooking with a nonstick wok. For one thing, it's healthier since you don't need to use as much oil. For another, there is less cleanup. It can be frustrating to interrupt cooking dinner to wash the remains of a meat marinade from the wok before starting to stir-fry the vegetables. A nonstick coating means less fuss and muss.

The one potential drawback with nonstick woks is that the coating may warp under higher temperatures. Be prepared to pay extra for hard-anodized aluminum or carbon steel woks with a nonstick coating that can take the high heats needed for stir-frying.

Wok Design

As a general rule, the type of stove you have will influence your choice of wok design. Traditional round-bottomed woks don't sit properly on an electric stove element. Originally, wok manufacturers tried to solve the problem by devising a round "collar" to sit on the burner and hold the wok in place. However, a better solution for an electric stove is a wok with a flat bottom. In addition to being safer, flat-bottomed woks ensure that the food cooks quickly and evenly. Both round and flat-bottomed woks work on gas stoves.

Purchase a wok that is too small, and you'll be spending extra time in the kitchen, stir-frying and deep-frying in batches. While fascinating to look at, the mammoth woks favored by Chinese restaurant chefs are designed to feed a crowd, and aren't necessary for home cooking. For most families, a 14-inch wok is a good choice.

Pay Attention to the Cover

Be sure that the wok you purchase comes with a lid. Unlike the conventional frying pan cover, wok lids are bowl-shaped, with a handle on top. Use them to cover foods during braising and steaming, and as a large bowl for tossing food prior to cooking.

Other Kitchen Accessories

Just because you're learning an ancient cuisine doesn't mean you can't take advantage of modern technology. Here are a number of handy tools and gadgets that will make your cooking go more smoothly.

- *Cleaver or chef's knife:* It doesn't need to be a Chinese cleaver, but it must be sharp and able to cut everything from meat to mushrooms.
- *Mandoline:* Great for cutting potatoes and other root vegetables julienne style. There are also miniature mandolines that do a nifty job of shredding garlic and ginger.
- *Food processor:* Invaluable for mixing sauces and crushing ingredients.
- *Wire mesh skimmer:* A large wire mesh spoon that makes transferring deep-fried food from wok to plate much easier.
- *Cooking chopsticks:* Longer than regular chopsticks, these are great for lightly beating eggs, mixing marinade ingredients, and maneuvering individual pieces of food in the wok.
- *Cutting board:* Chinese chefs favor thick, round wooden cutting boards, but acrylic is also acceptable. Avoid plastic, as it can damage your knife.
- *Chinese spatula:* With a wide handle shaped like a child's toy shovel, this utensil is the perfect size and shape for moving large quantities of food through the wok while stir-frying, ensuring that the food lands back in the pan and not on the stove or floor.

Peeling garlic is easy with a Chinese cleaver. Use the edge of the cleaver to separate one clove from the rest, then smash the clove using the side of the cleaver. Peel the garlic and chop or mince according to the directions in the recipe.

Cooking Techniques

While anyone can learn to prepare Chinese food, it helps to master a few basic techniques. Whether you're stir-frying chicken for four or making egg rolls for twenty, here are a few general tips to keep in mind when cooking Chinese food:

- *Start small.* Try preparing a stir-fry entrée accompanied by steamed rice, or a vegetable side dish to serve with your main meal. Later, you can work up to an entire Chinese meal complete with appetizer, soup, and dessert.

- *Try to create meals that provide an interesting variety of textures, colors, and flavors.* The goal of Chinese cooking is to strike a pleasing balance, with no one ingredient overpowering the others.
- *Use fresh ingredients wherever possible.* If a recipe calls for a certain ingredient that is out of season, substitute whatever is available locally.
- *Think about texture as well as color when making substitutions.* Zucchini stands in nicely for a Chinese gourd, while crisp broccoli makes a good substitute for bok choy.
- *Be creative with leftovers.* Leftover vegetables can liven up a dish of fried rice, while chicken bones can be used to make chicken stock.
- *Leaving the meat partially frozen will make it easier to cut.*
- *Always marinate fresh meat before cooking.* Use the time while the meat is marinating to cut vegetables and mix sauces.
- *Keep a supply of paper towels on hand to drain stir-fried and deep-fried food.*
- *Don't use dark soy sauce unless the recipe specifically calls for it.* Light soy sauce has a higher salt content than dark; substituting one for the other will affect the flavor of the dish.
- *Never use more cornstarch than the recipe calls for; a little goes a long way.*
- *Trust your judgment.* Something as minor as varying salt levels between different brands of soy sauce can affect the flavor of a dish. Always do a taste test at the end of cooking and adjust the seasonings if you think it is necessary.

Stir-frying

It may look daunting when we watch a television chef skillfully maneuvering food in a wok, but anyone can learn to stir-fry. The key to successful stir-frying is high heat combined with vigorous stirring.

Make sure all your ingredients are prepared ahead of time. The average stir-fry takes less than seven minutes, leaving little time for last minute slicing and dicing. Always leave stir-frying until the end of cooking. Stir-fries are meant to go straight from wok to table.

Cut all the ingredients to a uniform size, to ensure that they cook at the same rate. If you're improvising instead of following a recipe, a good rule of thumb is to cut everything into bite-sized pieces.

If you are using a carbon steel wok, preheat the wok for 1 minute before adding oil. If you are using a wok made out of a different type of material, or a wok or frying pan with a nonstick coating, check the manufacturer's instructions first to ensure that preheating will not cause any damage.

Stir-frying may be China's most famous cooking technique, but it was not the first. Stir-frying came into vogue during the Han dynasty, when fuel shortages forced people to adopt a speedy cooking method that used oil sparingly.

When adding oil, pour it so that it swirls around the sides of the wok before reaching the bottom. Test to see if the oil is hot by standing a cooking chopstick straight up in the wok's center. If the oil sizzles all the way around the chopstick, you can start cooking. If you don't have a chopstick, a small piece of bread works also.

Before adding other ingredients, try flavoring the oil with a few slices of ginger and/or garlic. Stir-fry until they are aromatic. Then, add other ingredients. To stir-fry, simply move the spatula through the wok and stir the ingredients every few seconds.

When you cook meat, sear it briefly before stir-frying. To make sure all of it comes into contact with the pan, it's important not to overcrowd the wok. Cook meat in batches, if necessary.

When it comes to cooking temperatures for stir-frying, be prepared to do a bit of experimenting. Every stove is different, and it may take a few attempts before you find the optimum temperature for stir-frying on your make and model.

Never pour a cornstarch-and-water mixture directly over the food in the wok. Instead, push the food up to the sides of the wok and add the cornstarch and water in the middle. Turn up the heat and stir vigorously to thicken. Once it has thickened you can mix it with the other ingredients.

Most importantly, don't panic. If you feel things are moving too fast, just take the wok or frying pan off the heat and give yourself a moment to relax and refocus. Stir-frying is a very forgiving art.

Deep-frying

Deep-frying has gotten a bad rap in recent years, thanks to visions of oil-splattered stoves and concern over high cholesterol levels. But there is nothing like deep-frying for sealing in meat's juices and adding a crispy coating to dishes such as Ginger Beef (page 129).

The trick to deep-frying is keeping the temperature constant during cooking. Too low temperatures will lead to greasy food loaded with extra fat and calories. The following tips will help you prepare deep-fried dishes that are crisp and full of flavor.

First of all, make sure the wok is securely attached to the stand. Next, pour in enough oil to completely cover the food being cooked, while leaving a couple of inches of room at the top of the wok. Unless the recipe states otherwise, the temperature of the oil should rise to about 350–375°F.

Slide the food in carefully, so that it doesn't splatter when it meets the hot oil. Leave plenty of room in the wok for the food to move around. Deep-fry in batches, if necessary. As soon as the food is added, check the temperature of the oil. Turn and separate the individual pieces of food while they are cooking.

> Continue to monitor the oil temperature while deep-frying. The easiest way to do this is with a deep-fry thermometer with a clamp that can attach to the side of the wok. That way, your hands remain free for cooking while you're checking the temperature.

Use a slotted spoon or a mesh skimmer to carefully remove the deep-fried food from the wok. Drain the deep-fried food on paper towels. If the recipe calls for food to be deep-fried twice, retest the temperature and make sure the oil is hot enough before you begin deep-frying the second time.

To reuse cooked oil, let it cool and then strain and store in a sealed container in the refrigerator. Cooked oil can be reused up to five times. Throw it out if the color darkens or it begins to smell rancid.

Even with these tips, you may find that using a wok to deep-fry is not for you. Wok deep-frying demands your undivided attention. If you have small children at home, or frequent interruptions are the norm, consider using a deep-fat fryer instead.

Steaming

Steaming, or cooking food by placing it over boiling or simmering water, is the third and the simplest Chinese cooking technique. The key to successful steaming lies in ensuring that the hot water never touches the food.

When it comes to equipment, a set of bamboo steamers is ideal. Bamboo steamers allow you to prepare multiple layers of food at the same time. In contrast to aluminum steamers, the natural texture of bamboo acts to prevent condensation from getting into the food. The cooked food can move straight from wok to table, with the steaming baskets doing double duty as cooking utensil and serving dish.

> Steaming is the least intrusive cooking technique; the flavor, color, and texture of the steamed food remain closer to what nature intended. Nutritionally speaking, steamed food retains more nutrients and vitamins, and is generally lower in fat and calories, than food cooked by other methods.

Steaming with bamboo is easy if you keep the following tips in mind:

- Before placing the food in the bamboo steamer, line the steamer with cabbage leaves, bamboo or banana leaves, or cheesecloth. This prevents the food from sticking.
- Be sure to leave approximately an inch between the water and food to be steamed.

- For smaller items such as dumplings, place the bamboo base or trivet in the water, with the steaming basket on top. Place the food in the basket, cover, and cook. For larger items such as meat and seafood dishes, either move to a larger set of bamboo steamers or substitute a heatproof dish. Also placed on the bamboo base, the heatproof dish can be anything from a dinner plate to an aluminum pie plate. The wok lid makes an ideal cover.
- When choosing a bamboo steamer, inspect it carefully to make sure none of the parts are connected with staples. If you find staples, choose another brand.
- Prior to its first use, give the steamer a thorough washing with soap and hot water. Dry completely before using.
- For best results, always use the freshest ingredients possible.

Tea Time

Dine at a Chinese restaurant, and chances are that before you've placed your order, the waitress will appear at your table with a steaming pot of tea. In China, tea is more than merely a hot drink. Over centuries, tea drinking has gone from being a refined pastime stretching several hours to an essential part of every meal.

A Brief History of Tea in China

According to a charming legend, tea was discovered when an Emperor fell asleep underneath a tea bush and awoke to find that a brown leaf had drifted into his cup of boiled water. This legend places the discovery of tea to 2737 B.C. Whether or not the story is true, there is no doubt that the Chinese were cultivating tea by A.D. 350.

However, it took the publication of a scholarly work to transform tea from merely a hot brew into China's national drink. Late in the eighth century, Lu Yu published *The Classic Art of Tea Drinking*. A poet and performer who had been educated by Buddhist monks, Lu Yu attempted to provide a complete overview of the history, cultivation, processing, and drinking of tea. The result was a definitive tome that is still consulted by tea experts today.

Brewing the perfect cup of green tea is a tricky process. With improper handling, those same polyphenols that protect the body against cancer and other diseases can ruin the tea's flavor. Allow boiled water to cool to a temperature of no more than 175°F before pouring over the tea. Steep for 2 to 3 minutes before drinking. Plan on using 1–2 teaspoons of green tea per cup.

Tea's popularity skyrocketed following the publication of Lu Yu's work. Buddhist monks introduced tea to the Japanese, although its use in Japan didn't become widespread until the 1200s. Today, teahouses are scattered throughout cities in China. Each has its own atmosphere; you can play chess at one, listen to music played on ancient Chinese instruments at another. The one thing that remains constant is the quality of the tea.

Tea Tapping

When dining at a Chinese restaurant, you may have noticed diners tapping the table each time their teacup is refilled. "Tea tapping" is a charming custom that originated during the Qing dynasty. According to legend, one of the emperors during this period was fond of traveling throughout the country incognito with his servants. During one trip they stopped at a teahouse. In order to preserve his disguise, the emperor took a turn at pouring the tea.

His traveling companions wanted to thank the emperor by bowing. However, this would have revealed the emperor's true identity. Instead, the emperor asked his companions to show their appreciation by tapping their fingers on the table each time he poured the tea. He suggested they tap the table three times, with one tap representing their bowed head and the two remaining taps their outstretched arms.

The custom has survived to this day. It's an easy way to thank someone for refilling your teacup without disrupting the conversation at the table.

Types of Tea Available

When you consider the different types of teas available, it's easy to believe that they come from different plants. In fact, all tea comes from the *Camellia sinensis* plant. In general, tea is categorized both by the way it is processed and its country of origin.

When it comes to tea, not all water is created equal. Tea just won't taste the same if it is made with water that contains impurities or has been treated with chlorine. A good water filter helps here, and bottled water is always preferable. According to the sage of Chinese tea, Lu Yu, pure water from natural springs is best for making tea, followed by river water and well water, in that order.

There are literally hundreds of varieties of Chinese teas, many named after the region where they were first cultivated. However, the majority fall into one of these five categories:

- *Green tea:* Probably the most famous Chinese tea due to its reputed health benefits, green tea is made from unfermented tea leaves. The leaves are dried immediately after picking. This prevents oxidation, leaving the chemical properties of the tea intact.
- *Oolong tea:* Made from larger tea leaves, this is a tea that has been partially fermented, so that full oxidization of the leaves does not take place. After drying in the sun, the leaves are heated to stop the oxidation process. This gives them a greenish-black color. Because fermentation can be stopped at any point, the flavor of different types of oolong tea vary.
- *Black tea:* Black tea consists of tea leaves that have been rolled and then fully dried and fermented, giving them a darker color. Black tea is more popular in the west than in Asia. It is often used in cooking dishes, such as Tea Smoked Chicken (page 177).
- *Scented teas:* These are made by adding flowers to the tea leaves during the fermentation process. The most popular scented teas are jasmine and chrysanthemum.

- *White tea:* Like green tea, white teas are unfermented. However, instead of steam drying, the tea leaves are dried naturally in the sun. White tea is believed to have even more health benefits than green tea.

Health Benefits of Tea

In recent years, scientists have been paying a great deal of attention to the health benefits of drinking green tea. What sets green tea apart from other teas? Green teas contain a polyphenol called epigallocatechin gallate (EGCG), which is known to be a powerful antioxidant.

Since antioxidants inhibit the growth of free radicals found in cancer cells, it's not surprising that most of the research on green tea has focused on its ability to prevent cancer. However, EGCG has other health benefits as well. Green tea has been shown to lower blood pressure and reduce high cholesterol levels. It is also believed to lower the risk of stroke.

Which is better, tea bags or loose-leaf tea?
Loose-leaf teas are preferable to bagged tea. Made with a lower grade of tea leaves known as "fannings," bagged teas tend to have less flavor. Many higher quality teas aren't available in bags. Still, bagged tea does have its advantages if you're in a hurry or want a quick cup of tea at the office.

While most of the research has focused on green tea, scientists are discovering that there are also health benefits to be derived from drinking black tea. Black teas contain another type of polyphenol called theaflavin-3'-monogallate (TF-2). Like EGCG, TF-2 is believed to inhibit the growth of cancer cells. Research is also being conducted on the use of black tea to treat arthritis.

Chapter 2

Common Dipping Sauces

Hot Mustard Dip

Yields 1/3 cup

Hot mustard's bite makes a great combination with Egg Rolls (page 34) and less highly spiced appetizers such as Gow Gees (page 47).

3 tablespoons hot mustard
3 tablespoons water
1 teaspoon rice vinegar
½ teaspoon sugar

Combine all the ingredients. Use immediately.

What Makes Hot Mustard Hot?

A better question would be, why aren't all mustards hot? The secret behind hot mustard's fiery flavor lies in the chemical reaction that occurs when mustard seeds come in contact with a liquid such as water or salad oil. Commercially prepared mustards tone down the reaction by adding ingredients such as flour. The strength and flavor of mustard also depends on the type of mustard seeds used.

Hot Mustard Sauce

Yields about 1/4 cup

This is a little runnier than a paste. Use in a salad like Chinese Potato Salad (page 71).

2 tablespoons mustard powder
2 tablespoons rice vinegar
1 teaspoon brown sugar
1 tablespoon vegetable oil
3 drops sesame oil

Mix all the ingredients and use immediately.

Plum Sauce

1 12-ounce can prune plums, drained
2 tablespoons brown sugar
4 tablespoons rice vinegar
1 slice ginger
1 clove garlic
½ cup canned juice from the drained plums
½ cup water

1. Remove the plum pits. In a medium saucepan, bring all ingredients to a boil. Simmer, covered, for about 2 hours, or until the plums are soft.
2. Remove the ginger and garlic. Process the sauce in a blender or food processor until smooth. Cool and chill in the refrigerator. Use within a few days.

Yields ⅔ cup

For best results, prepare the plum sauce several hours ahead of time to give the flavors a chance to blend.

Brown Sauce

1 tablespoon plus 1 teaspoon oyster sauce
3 teaspoons hoisin sauce
1 teaspoon sherry
1 teaspoon soy sauce
½ teaspoon sugar
½ cup beef broth or juices from cooked meat
2 tablespoons water
1 tablespoon cornstarch

1. Combine all the ingredients, adding the cornstarch last. Bring to a boil.
2. Cook on medium to medium-low heat, stirring constantly to thicken mixture. The sauce should be neither too thin nor too runny, but thick enough to use as a dip, if desired.

Yields about ⅔ cup

Out of cornstarch? You can substitute flour as a thickener in this recipe—just double the amount to 2 tablespoons.

Peanut Sauce

Yields 1 cup

Use this spicy sauce with Gado Gado Salad (page 72) or to liven up a plain garden salad.

½ cup chicken broth
½ cup peanut butter
2 garlic cloves, minced
2 tablespoons red onion, minced
2 teaspoons brown sugar
4 tablespoons soy sauce
½ teaspoon chili sauce
2 tablespoons plus 2 teaspoons rice vinegar
2 tablespoons water
1 teaspoon chopped cilantro (optional)

1. Combine all the ingredients except for the cilantro and purée in a food processor.
2. Bring to a boil in a small saucepan. Stir in the cilantro. Use immediately.

Szechwan Salt and Pepper Mix

Yields about ⅓ cup

For variety, try using this flavorful mix in place of plain salt and pepper, even when you're not eating Chinese food.

2 tablespoons Szechwan peppercorns
1 teaspoon black peppercorns
½ teaspoon white peppercorns
¼ cup salt

1. Brown the peppercorns and salt in a heavy skillet on medium to medium-low heat, shaking the pan occasionally, until the Szechwan peppercorns are fragrant and the salt turns a light brown color.
2. Grind the cooled mixture in a blender. Store in a sealed jar and use as a dip or condiment.

Don't Let the Name Fool You

Szechwan peppers aren't peppers at all! They are distinctive reddish brown berries that come from the prickly ash native to Szechwan province.

Sweet-and-Sour Worcestershire Sauce

¼ cup white rice vinegar
2 tablespoons black rice vinegar
½ cup brown sugar
1 tablespoon Worcestershire sauce
¼ cup ketchup
½ cup pineapple juice
¼ cup water
2 teaspoons cornstarch mixed with 4 teaspoons water

1. In a medium saucepan, bring the white rice vinegar, black rice vinegar, brown sugar, Worcestershire sauce, ketchup, pineapple juice, and water to a boil.
2. Add the cornstarch-and-water mixture, stirring vigorously to thicken.

Yields about 1¼ cups

Use this flavorful sauce wherever you might normally use a sweet-and-sour sauce.

Hoisin Satay Sauce

3 tablespoons hoisin sauce
2 teaspoons dark soy sauce
1 teaspoon rice vinegar
1 teaspoon orange marmalade
Up to ¼ teaspoon cayenne pepper flakes
1 clove garlic, chopped
¼ cup peanuts, crushed

Combine all the ingredients. Serve with Beef Satay (page 118).

Yields ⅓ cup

Orange marmalade lends flavor to a traditional hoisin-based sauce in this fusion recipe. For a different taste, substitute 1 tablespoon of honey.

Quick and Easy Sweet-and-Sour Sauce

Yields ½ cup

This simple sauce adds flavor to Egg Rolls (page 34). Adjust the thickness by increasing or reducing the amount of cornstarch.

½ cup vinegar
1 tablespoon and 1 teaspoon sugar
1 large clove garlic, minced
1 teaspoon cornstarch
4 teaspoons water

In a medium saucepan, bring all the ingredients to a boil, stirring to thicken.

Sweet-and-Sour Sauce with Ketchup

Yields about ¾ cup

For extra flavor, add red and green bell pepper and pineapple chunks to the sauce after stirring in the cornstarch.

⅓ cup rice vinegar
¼ cup brown sugar
2 tablespoons ketchup
1 tablespoon soy sauce
¼ cup water
4 teaspoons cornstarch mixed with 4 teaspoons water

1. In a small saucepan, combine the rice vinegar, brown sugar, ketchup, soy sauce, and water and bring to a boil.
2. Stir in the cornstarch-and-water mixture, stirring vigorously to thicken.

Hot Chili Oil

6 red chili peppers
1 tablespoon sesame oil
1 cup vegetable oil

1. Cut the chili peppers in half and remove the seeds. Chop coarsely.
2. Mix the oils and heat in a wok or heavy skillet.
3. Add the chopped chili peppers and cook over low heat for about 5 minutes, or until the oil turns red.
4. Cool the oil and strain into a sealed jar. Store in the refrigerator.

Yields ⅞ cup

Chili Oil makes an excellent dipping sauce for Potstickers with Rice Wine (page 43). Use it whenever you want to add heat to your meal.

Handling Hot Chilies

When handling chili peppers, it's important to make sure that none of the chemical gets in your eyes. For extra safety, wear rubber gloves.

Spicy Szechwan Peanut Sauce

3 tablespoons peanut butter
3 tablespoons soy sauce
4 teaspoons sugar
3 tablespoons black rice vinegar
1 tablespoon sesame oil
1 clove garlic, chopped
1–2 tablespoons Hot Chili Oil (page 25)

Process all the ingredients in a food processor.

Yields ½ cup

Use as a dipping sauce or in Szechwan dishes such as Bang Bang Chicken (page 165). For best results, use within a few days.

Mild Szechwan Peanut Sauce

Yields ⅓ cup

Want to enjoy Szechwan cooking without experiencing the extreme heat? Use this sauce instead of Spicy Szechwan Peanut Sauce (page 25).

3 tablespoons peanut butter
3 tablespoons soy sauce
4 teaspoons sugar
3 teaspoons black rice vinegar
1 teaspoon sesame oil
1 clove garlic, chopped
2 teaspoons chili sauce

Process all the ingredients in a food processor.

Hot Food Antidote

Tempted to reach for a glass of water after tasting fiery Szechwan food? Try a forkful of rice instead. Oil and water don't mix, and a glass of water will roll right over the chili oils that add heat to Szechwan cooking. Rice, milk, or even beer all provide more immediate relief than a glass of water.

Soy Hoisin Dressing

Yields about ⅓ cup

This savory dressing makes a great dip and adds flavor to vegetable and noodle salads.

2 teaspoons Chinese rice wine or dry sherry
1 teaspoon minced ginger
2 teaspoons hoisin sauce
2 tablespoons soy sauce
2 tablespoons dark soy sauce

Combine all the ingredients.

Storing Homemade Dips

Unlike their store-bought counterparts, homemade dipping sauces have a relatively short life span. Store them in a sealed container in the refrigerator, and use within a few days. Waiting a few hours or even overnight (refrigerated) before using a sauce gives the flavors a chance to blend.

Soy Ginger Dressing

2 tablespoons soy sauce
2 teaspoons rice vinegar
1 teaspoon grated ginger
A few drops sesame oil (about 1/8 teaspoon)

Combine all the ingredients.

Yields about 1/3 cup

The clean flavor of ginger gives this dressing a sharp bite. Use as a dip with Chinese dumplings such as Gow Gees (page 47).

Worcestershire Sauce

It may have been invented by two British chemists in the 1800s, but Worcestershire sauce wouldn't be the same without an Asian influence. The secret ingredient in Worcestershire sauce is tamarind, an acid-tasting fruit that gives many Thai sauces their sharp bite. Today, Worcestershire sauce makes a frequent appearance in Chinese dipping sauces.

Soy Vinegar Dressing

3 tablespoons soy sauce
2 teaspoons rice vinegar
1/4 teaspoon minced ginger

Combine all the ingredients in a small bowl.

Yields about 1/4 cup

This dressing takes mere minutes to make. Drizzle over vegetables and rice, or use as a dipping sauce for Mini Spring Onion Pancakes (page 50).

Asian Vinaigrette

Yields about ½ cup

This dressing nicely complements a simple tossed green salad. Stored in a sealed container and refrigerated, it will keep for a few days.

4 tablespoons salad oil
2 tablespoons black rice vinegar
2 teaspoons soy sauce
½ teaspoon sugar
A few drops sesame oil

Combine all the ingredients in a jar and shake to mix thoroughly. Drizzle over the salad.

Stocking Up on Asian Ingredients

If the local grocery store doesn't carry a certain ingredient, and there is no Asian market nearby, try the Internet. Several online grocery stores carry a broad range of Asian ingredients and cooking equipment. Just be sure to check out availability and shipping rates for your area before ordering.

Speedy Sweet Chili Sauce

Yields ½ cup

A quick and easy recipe for those days when you don't have any chili peppers on hand.

¼ cup rice vinegar
4 tablespoons sugar
1½ teaspoons chili sauce, or to taste
1 teaspoon cornstarch mixed with 4 teaspoons water

1. In a small saucepan, bring the rice vinegar, sugar, and chili sauce to a boil.
2. Add the cornstarch-and-water mixture, stirring vigorously to thicken.

Sweet Green and Red Chili Sauce

3 jalapeno peppers
1/4 red bell pepper
1/4 cup rice vinegar
4 tablespoons sugar
1 teaspoon cornstarch
4 teaspoons water

1. Cut the jalapeno peppers in half lengthwise. Remove the seeds and chop. Wash the red bell pepper and cut into squares.
2. Process the rice vinegar, sugar, jalapeno peppers, and red pepper in a blender or food processor.
3. In a small saucepan, bring the liquid to a boil. As it simmers for a few minutes, mix the cornstarch and water.
4. Stir in the cornstarch mixture, until the sauce thickens.

Yields 2/3 cup

This dip will give a burning sensation in the back of your mouth, but without the sweating and watery eyes associated with hotter peppers.

Northern Noodle Sauce

1 small clove garlic, chopped
1/2 green onion, mainly white part, thinly sliced
1/4 cup dark soy sauce
2 teaspoons black rice vinegar
1 teaspoon Hot Chili Oil (page 25)
1/2 teaspoon sugar
1/4 teaspoon sesame oil
1 teaspoon cornstarch mixed with 4 teaspoons water

1. Combine garlic clove and green onion with the dark soy sauce, black rice vinegar, Hot Chili Oil, sugar, and sesame oil. Process in a blender or food processor until smooth.
2. In a small saucepan, bring the sauce to a boil. Give the cornstarch-and-water mixture a quick stir. Add to the sauce, stirring vigorously to thicken. Cool and serve as a dip or serve hot with noodles.

Yields 1/3 cup

This spicy sauce adds bite to noodle and tofu dishes. For a milder sauce, leave out the chili oil.

Potsticker Dipping Sauce

Yields ⅓ cup

Feel free to serve this spicy sauce with other Chinese dumplings besides Potstickers (page 43).

2 tablespoons dark soy sauce
2 tablespoons light soy sauce
¼ teaspoon sesame oil
1 teaspoon oyster sauce
2 teaspoons black rice vinegar
1 teaspoon sugar
1 teaspoon Hot Chili Oil (page 25)
1 teaspoon cilantro leaves, finely chopped

Combine all the ingredients.

Intriguing XO Sauce

For an exotic twist, try adding a teaspoon of XO sauce to your favorite dipping sauce recipe. First served at Hong Kong Chinese restaurants, this flavorful sauce is an intriguing mix of seafood and spicy seasonings such as hot chilies and garlic.

Jazzed Up Black Bean Sauce

Yields about ¾ cup

This is a savory sauce that can be used with pancakes, noodles, and steamed buns.

1½ tablespoons black bean sauce
2 teaspoons sugar
1 tablespoon oyster sauce
1 teaspoon Chinese rice wine or dry sherry
¼ teaspoon chili sauce with garlic
½ cup water

Combine all the ingredients.

Jazzed Up Hoisin Sauce

½ cup hoisin sauce
1 clove garlic, finely chopped
1 teaspoon finely chopped ginger
1 teaspoon black rice vinegar, or to taste
½ teaspoon sesame oil

Combine all the ingredients.

Yields about ½ cup

Serve as a dipping sauce with dumplings, or snacks such as Mandarin Pancakes (page 270) or Mini Spring Onion Pancakes (page 50).

What about Duck Sauce?

Not sure whether to serve duck sauce or plum sauce with your mandarin pancakes? Actually, both terms refer to the same sweet and spicy sauce. Plum sauce was nicknamed "duck sauce" after Western Chinese restaurants began serving it with Peking Duck, under the mistaken impression that this was an authentic practice. In reality, Peking Duck is traditionally served with hoisin sauce. But whatever name it goes by, the thick reddish sauce makes an excellent dipping sauce for Egg Rolls (page 34) and goes well with sparerib and chicken dishes.

CHAPTER 3

Asian Appetizers and Dim Sum

Egg Rolls

Yields 15 egg rolls

This wrapping method allows you to add more filling than the traditional "envelope" method. Firmly sealing the edges prevents oil from entering during deep-frying.

¼ cup canned bamboo shoots, sliced
1 tablespoon oyster sauce
1 tablespoon chicken broth or stock
½ teaspoon sugar
2 tablespoons oil for stir-frying
6 large fresh mushrooms, thinly sliced
1 stalk celery, thinly sliced on the diagonal
¼ cup water chestnuts, thinly sliced
1 cup fresh mung bean sprouts, drained
2 green onions, thinly sliced on the diagonal
½ pound barbecued pork
15 egg roll wrappers
3 tablespoons cornstarch mixed with 2 tablespoons water
4–6 cups oil for frying

1. Thinly slice the bamboo shoots. Combine the oyster sauce, chicken broth, and sugar. Set aside.
2. Add 2 tablespoons oil to a preheated wok or skillet. When oil is hot, add the mushrooms and stir-fry for about 1 minute. Add the celery, then the water chestnuts, then bamboo shoots, stir-frying each for about 1 minute in the middle of the wok before adding the next vegetable. (If the wok is too crowded, stir-fry each vegetable separately.) Add more oil as necessary, pushing the vegetables up to the side of the wok until the oil is hot. Add the bean sprouts and the green onions.
3. Add the sauce to the middle of the wok and bring to a boil. Add the barbequed pork. Heat everything through. Cool.
4. Heat 4–6 cups oil to 375°F. While the oil is heating, prepare the wrappers. To wrap, spread a heaping tablespoon of filling in the middle of the wrapper, evenly spread out but not too close to the edges. Coat the top edge and the sides with the cornstarch/water mixture. Fold the bottom half over the filling. Fold the top half over, making sure the 2 sides overlap. Press down to seal all the edges. Continue with the remainder of the egg rolls. (Prepare more cornstarch and water if necessary.)
5. Deep-fry the egg rolls until they turn golden brown (2–3 minutes). Drain on paper towels.

Deep-fried Wontons

3 medium dried mushrooms
1½ cups ground pork
½ cup canned bamboo shoots, shredded
1½ green onions, thinly sliced
1 slice ginger
2 teaspoons black rice vinegar
2 teaspoons soy sauce
1 teaspoon sugar
1 teaspoon sesame oil
1 package wonton wrappers
4–6 cups oil for deep-frying

1. Soak the dried mushrooms in hot water for at least 20 minutes to soften. Drain, remove the stems, and slice finely. Shred the bamboo shoots.
2. Combine the ground pork, bamboo shoots, green onions, dried mushrooms, ginger, black rice vinegar, soy sauce, sugar, and sesame oil.
3. Add oil to a preheated wok and heat to 375°F. While waiting for the oil to heat, wrap the wontons. Lay the wrapper in a square shape in front of you. Place 1 teaspoon of filling in the middle of the wrapper. Fold the wonton wrapper in half lengthwise, making sure the ends meet. Roll the wonton wrapper over again, being sure to keep the filling centered. Wet the ends. Bring the corners together so that one overlaps the other, and seal. Continue with the remainder of the wontons. Cover the completed wontons with a damp towel to prevent drying.
4. Carefully slide a few wontons at a time into the wok. Deep-fry until they turn golden (about 2 minutes). Remove with a slotted spoon and drain on paper towels.

Yields 30–35 wontons

Have more filled wontons than you need? Freeze and use the next time you're making Wonton Soup (page 56). Thaw before adding to the soup.

Maintaining Oil Temperature During Deep-frying

To prevent greasy food, it's important to keep the oil temperature from dropping substantially during deep-frying. This can be tricky, since it is normal for the temperature to drop when food is first added to the wok. One solution is to heat the oil to a higher temperature than called for in the recipe. For example, if the instructions state the food should be deep-fried at 350°F, wait until the oil temperature reaches 355–360°F before starting to deep-fry.

Wonton Wrappers

Yields 24–28 wrappers

Stuffed wonton wrappers feature prominently in soups and dim sum dishes. They can even replace egg roll wrappers in the recipe for Bowties (page 274-275).

½ teaspoon salt
2¼ cups flour
⅔ cup water
1 medium egg
1 teaspoon vegetable oil

1. Sift the salt into the flour. Add the remaining ingredients, adding the water slowly and not using more than necessary. Form the batter into a dough and knead until smooth. Cover the dough and let it rest for 30 minutes.
2. Cut the dough in half. Form each half into a cylinder. Lightly score the dough into ½-inch pieces and cut (you should have 12–14 pieces). Repeat with the other half of the dough.
3. On a lightly floured surface, roll each piece out into a 3½-inch square. Store wrapped in plastic in the refrigerator or freeze until ready to use.

Water Chestnut Appetizer

Yields 20 appetizers

This simple but tasty appetizer works best with fresh chestnuts. For quicker cooking, broil the water chestnuts for 5–6 minutes instead of baking.

20 fresh water chestnuts
½ cup soy sauce
10 slices raw bacon
½ cup brown sugar
20 toothpicks

1. Peel the water chestnuts. Rinse and drain well. Place the soy sauce in a plastic bag. Add the water chestnuts and seal. Marinate for 3 hours, turning occasionally to cover completely.
2. Preheat the oven to 350°F. Cut each slice of bacon in half. Spread the brown sugar out on a piece of waxed paper.
3. Remove the water chestnuts from the bag, reserving the marinade. Roll each water chestnut in the brown sugar. Wrap a slice of bacon around each water chestnut and secure with a toothpick.
4. Bake the water chestnuts at 350°F for 45 minutes. After 20 minutes, turn the water chestnuts over and pour the reserved marinade over. Continue baking.

Spring Rolls

½ pound pork tenderloin, shredded
2 tablespoons oyster sauce, divided
½ teaspoon baking soda
6 dried mushrooms
1 carrot
1 tablespoon chicken broth or stock
½ teaspoon sugar
1 cup mung bean sprouts, rinsed and drained
2 green onions, thinly sliced on the diagonal
¼ teaspoon sesame oil
12 spring roll wrappers
2 tablespoons cornstarch mixed with 1 tablespoon water
4–6 cups oil for frying

Yields 12 Spring Rolls

Both barbecued pork and chicken marinated in oyster sauce also work well in this recipe.

1. Marinate the pork in 1 tablespoon oyster sauce and baking soda for 30 minutes.
2. Soak the dried mushrooms in hot water to soften; drain and thinly slice. Wash and grate the carrot until you have ¼ cup.
3. Combine the remaining 1 tablespoon oyster sauce, chicken broth, and sugar. Set aside.
4. Add 2 tablespoons oil to a preheated wok or skillet. When oil is hot, add the pork. Stir-fry briefly until it changes color and is nearly cooked through. Remove from the wok.
5. Add 1½ tablespoons oil. When oil is hot, add the dried mushrooms. Stir-fry for 1 minute, then add the bean sprouts, grated carrot, and the green onion. Add the sauce in the middle of the wok and bring to a boil. Add the pork and mix through. Drizzle with the sesame oil. Cool.
6. Heat 4–6 cups oil to 375°F. While oil is heating, prepare the spring rolls. To wrap, lay the wrapper in a diamond shape. Place a tablespoon of filling in the middle. Coat all the edges with the cornstarch-and-water mixture. Roll up the wrapper and tuck in the edges. Seal the tucked-in edges with cornstarch and water. Continue with the remainder of the Spring Rolls. (Prepare more cornstarch and water as necessary.)
7. Deep-fry the spring rolls, 2 at a time, until they turn golden. Drain on paper towels.

Crab Rangoon

Yields 44–48 Crab Rangoon

Guests love this popular party appetizer that combines the sweet, delicate flavor of crab with the crunchy texture of deep-fried wonton.

48 wonton wrappers
1 cup fresh or canned crabmeat
1 cup cream cheese
½ teaspoon Worcestershire sauce
½ teaspoon soy sauce
⅛ teaspoon freshly ground white pepper, or to taste
2 teaspoons minced onion
1½ green onions, thinly sliced
1 large clove garlic, minced
Water for wetting wontons
4 cups oil for deep-frying

1. Cover the wonton wrappers with a damp towel to prevent drying. Set aside.
2. If using canned crabmeat, drain thoroughly. Flake the crabmeat with a fork. Add the cream cheese, then mix in the Worcestershire sauce, soy sauce, white pepper, onion, green onion, and garlic.
3. To prepare the Crab Rangoon: lay a wrapper in a diamond shape or circle, depending on the shape of wonton wrappers you are using. Add a heaping teaspoon of filling in the middle, spread out evenly but not too near the edges. Spread the water along all 4 sides. Fold the bottom over the top to form a triangle (round wrappers will form a half moon). Seal the edges, adding more water if needed. Cover filled wontons with a damp towel to prevent drying.
4. Heat 4 cups oil in a preheated wok to 375°F. Slide in the wonton wrappers a few at a time, and deep-fry for 2–3 minutes, until they turn golden brown. Remove with a slotted spoon and drain on paper towels. Cool and serve.

Make-Ahead Crab Rangoon

Want to get a head start on making cocktail appetizers? Crab Rangoon can be prepared ahead of time up to the deep-frying stage and frozen. Thaw the filled wontons before deep-frying.

Lettuce Wraps

1 pound boneless, skinless chicken breasts
1 head iceberg lettuce
1 red bell pepper
½ 8-ounce can water chestnuts, rinsed and drained
½ 8-ounce can bamboo shoots, rinsed and drained
1 tablespoon soy sauce
2 tablespoons oyster sauce
1 tablespoon Chinese rice wine
1 teaspoon sugar
4 tablespoons oil for stir-frying
1 teaspoon minced garlic clove
1 teaspoon minced ginger
1 stalk celery, thinly sliced on the diagonal
1 tablespoon cornstarch mixed with 2 tablespoons water
2 green onions, thinly sliced on the diagonal
1 teaspoon sesame oil

Yields 12 wraps

Serve lettuce wraps as an appetizer, or as a main course with stir-fried rice vermicelli.

1. Wash the chicken and pat dry. Pound lightly to tenderize. Cut the chicken into thin slices approximately 2½ inches long.
2. Wash the lettuce, and dry and separate the leaves. Remove the seeds from the red pepper and chop into bite-sized pieces. Slice the water chestnuts and bamboo shoots into 1-inch pieces.
3. Mix together the soy sauce, oyster sauce, Chinese rice wine, and sugar. Set aside.
4. Add 2 tablespoons oil in a preheated wok or heavy skillet. When oil is hot, add the garlic and ginger. Stir-fry briefly, then add the chicken. Stir-fry until it is browned and nearly cooked through. Remove from the wok and drain on paper towels.
5. Add 2 tablespoons oil. When oil is hot, add the water chestnuts and celery. Stir-fry for about 1 minute, then add the red pepper. Add the bamboo shoots. Stir-fry until the vegetables are brightly colored and tender. Add the sauce. Give the cornstarch/water mixture a quick stir and add in the middle, stirring quickly to thicken. Stir in the green onions. Drizzle with sesame oil.
6. To prepare lettuce wrap, lay a lettuce leaf flat. Place one-twelfth of the chicken combined with the vegetable/sauce mixture into the middle and roll up the lettuce leaf.

Paper Wrapped Chicken

24 chicken packages

This popular appetizer also makes a satisfying meal when served with green salad. Cooking parchment or cellophane paper can be used instead of aluminum foil.

2 large boneless, skinless chicken breasts, 6–8 ounces each
4 large Chinese dried mushrooms
1½ green onions
2 tablespoons oyster sauce
2 tablespoons soy sauce
1 slice ginger, shredded
1 teaspoon sesame oil
1 tablespoon Chinese rice wine or dry sherry
2 teaspoons sugar
Salt and pepper to taste
24 6-inch squares of aluminum foil

1. Wash the chicken and pat dry. Cut the chicken into thin slices approximately 2½ inches long. You want to have 48 strips, or 2 strips for each packet. (With a larger breast you may have more chicken than you need, so you can make more packets.)
2. Soak the dried mushrooms in hot water for 20 minutes, or until they are softened. Squeeze gently to remove excess water, and cut into 24 thin slices, or 6 slices per mushroom. Thinly slice the green onions on the diagonal, so that you have 48 pieces, or 2 slices per packet.
3. In a small bowl, combine the oyster sauce, soy sauce, shredded ginger, sesame oil, Chinese rice wine, sugar, salt and pepper, and green onions. Add to the chicken and marinate for 45 minutes. Add the mushrooms and marinate for another 15 minutes.
4. Preheat oven to 350°F.
5. To wrap the chicken, lay out a square of foil so that the lower corner is pointing toward you. Place 2 chicken slices, 1 mushroom slice, and 2 green onion slices in the middle. Bring the bottom corner up over the chicken. Roll this corner once. Fold the right corner over toward the middle, and then the left corner, so that one is overlapping the other. Tuck the triangle at the top into the flap.
6. Place the wrapped parcels on a baking sheet and bake at 350°F for 15 minutes. Allow to cool before serving.
7. To serve, do not unwrap the chicken packets, but serve heaped on a large platter for guests to open.

Gift Wrapped Beef

½ pound flank steak
1 teaspoon oyster sauce
¼ teaspoon baking soda
6 large dried mushrooms
1 bok choy
2 tablespoons hoisin sauce
2 tablespoons water
½ teaspoon sugar
1 bunch cilantro
2 tablespoons sesame oil
12 6-inch squares of aluminum foil

24 beef packages

Serve the beef packets piled on a serving dish with a cilantro garnish. Like Paper Wrapped Chicken, Gift Wrapped Beef can be deep-fried instead of baked.

1. Preheat oven to 350°F.
2. Cut the beef into thin slices 2–3 inches long. You want to have about 3 slices for each packet. Add the oyster sauce and baking soda. Marinate the beef for 30 minutes.
3. Soak the dried mushrooms in hot water for 20 minutes, or until they are softened. Squeeze gently to remove any water, and cut into 48 thin slices, or 8 slices per mushroom. Wash the bok choy, drain thoroughly, and shred. You want to have 3–4 pieces for each packet.
4. Mix the hoisin sauce, water, and sugar and set aside.
5. To wrap the beef, lay out a square of foil so that it forms a diamond shape. Add 3 of the beef slices, 2–3 slices of mushroom, a few shreds of bok choy, and a few sprigs of cilantro in the middle, being sure to keep the filling in the center and not near the edges. Mix in ¼ teaspoon of sesame oil and ½ teaspoon of the hoisin and water mixture.
6. Bring the bottom corner up over the beef. Roll this corner once. Fold the right corner over toward the middle, and then the left corner, so that one is overlapping the other. Tuck the triangle at the top into the flap.
7. Place the wrapped parcels on a baking sheet and bake at 350°F for 15 minutes. Allow to cool before serving. Serve wrapped on a platter, unopened.

Shrimp Stuffed Mushrooms

Yields 20 mushrooms

Large portobello mushrooms work well in this recipe. Garnish with cilantro or parsley sprigs before serving.

20 large fresh mushrooms
1 teaspoon baking powder
¾ cup flour
½ teaspoon sugar
¼ teaspoon salt
2 tablespoons vegetable oil
¾ cup water
½ batch Shrimp Paste (page 216)
¼ cup cornstarch
4–6 cups oil for deep-frying

1. Wash the mushrooms, dry thoroughly, and remove the stems.
2. Sift the baking powder into the flour. Stir in the sugar, salt, and vegetable oil. Add the water slowly, adding more or less as necessary to make a smooth batter.
3. Add oil to a preheated wok and heat to 350°F. While oil is heating, spread up to ½ teaspoon of the Shrimp Paste on the inside of the mushroom. Lightly dust the outside of the cap with cornstarch. Use your fingers to coat the outside with the batter.
4. When oil is hot, deep-fry the mushrooms, adding a few at a time. Deep-fry until the batter turns a golden brown. Drain on paper towels.

How to Use Chopsticks

It may look tricky, but chopsticks are really quite easy to use. Hold the chopsticks slightly above the middle, making sure that the ends don't cross. Position them so that the top chopstick is between your thumb and index finger, and the lower chopstick between your middle and fourth fingers. To pick up food, use your thumb and index finger to raise and lower the upper chopstick. Think of it as a type of lever, and you've got the idea. One final tip: Stick to wood or bamboo chopsticks if possible, as food can slide off chopsticks made of plastic.

Potstickers with Rice Wine

1½ cups ground pork
3 teaspoons Chinese rice wine or dry sherry
3 teaspoons soy sauce
1½ teaspoons sesame oil
1½ tablespoons chopped onion
1 package round wonton (gyoza) wrappers
½ cup water for boiling potstickers
Oil for frying as needed

Yields 30–35 potstickers

For a different flavor, try steaming the potsticker dumplings in chicken broth instead of water.

1. Combine the ground pork, rice wine, soy sauce, sesame oil, and chopped onion.
2. To make the potstickers: Place 1 teaspoon of filling in the middle of the wrapper. Wet the edges of the wrapper, fold over the filling, and seal, crimping the edges. Continue with the remainder of the potstickers. Cover the completed potstickers with a damp towel to prevent drying.
3. Add 2 tablespoons of oil to a preheated wok or skillet (1 tablespoon if using a nonstick pan). When oil is hot, add a few of the potstickers, smooth side down. Do not stir-fry, but let cook for about 1 minute.
4. Add ½ cup of water. Do not turn the potstickers over. Cook, covered, until most of the liquid is absorbed. Uncover, and cook until the liquid has evaporated.
5. Loosen the potstickers with a spatula and serve with the burnt side facing up. Serve with Potsticker Dipping Sauce (page 30).

Potsticker Origins

Potstickers are dumplings that are pan-fried on the bottom and steamed on top. According to legend, they were invented by a imperial court chef who panicked after realizing he'd accidentally burnt a batch of dumplings. With no time to make more, he served them anyway, and the rest is history. When cooking potstickers, it's important to add enough steaming water. While a crispy brown bottom is desirable, potstickers aren't supposed to stick too firmly to the bottom of the pot!

Sticky Rice in Cabbage Leaves

Serves 4

Don't like cabbage? You can also wrap the sticky rice in aluminum foil or waxed paper before steaming.

1 cup short grain (sticky) rice
4 large cabbage leaves
4 dried mushrooms
4 Chinese sausages
2 tablespoons oyster sauce
2 tablespoons Chinese rice wine or dry sherry
2 tablespoons chicken broth or stock
2 tablespoons oil for stir-frying
1 garlic clove, finely chopped
2 slices ginger, finely chopped
2 green onions, finely chopped

1. Cover the sticky rice in warm water and let soak for at least 2 hours, preferably overnight. Drain well. In a medium-sized saucepan, bring the sticky rice and 2 cups of water to a boil. Simmer, covered, for 20 minutes or until rice is cooked. Remove from the element and let cool for 15 minutes. Fluff up the rice before removing from the pot. Split the rice into 4 equal portions and set aside.
2. Blanch the cabbage leaves in boiling water. Drain thoroughly. Soak the dried mushrooms in hot water for at least 20 minutes to soften. Drain, giving them a gentle squeeze to remove any excess water. Cut into thin slices.
3. Chop the Chinese sausages into small pieces. Combine the oyster sauce, rice wine, and chicken broth.
4. Add the oil to a preheated wok or skillet. When oil is hot, add the garlic and ginger. Stir-fry briefly until aromatic. Add the sausage. Stir-fry for about 2 minutes, then add the mushrooms. Stir in the green onion. Make a well in the middle of the wok and add the sauce, bringing to a boil. Mix everything together, then remove from the heat and allow to cool.
5. Split the filling into 4 equal portions. Take a cabbage leaf and add a quarter of the rice and the filling, layering it so that there is rice at the top and bottom, with the meat and vegetable filling in the middle. Roll up the cabbage leaf as in cabbage rolls. Repeat with the remaining 3 cabbage leaves.
6. Steam the cabbage wraps, covered, on a heatproof plate in a bamboo steamer for 15 minutes, or until they are done.

Sticky Rice in Lotus Leaves

1 cup short grain (sticky) rice
4 lotus leaves
4 dried mushrooms
2 Chinese sausages
½ cup chicken meat
2 tablespoons oyster sauce
2 tablespoons rice wine
2 tablespoons chicken broth or stock
2 tablespoons oil for stir-frying
1 garlic clove, finely chopped
2 slices ginger, finely chopped
2 green onions, finely chopped

Serves 4

Steaming imparts the delicate flavor of lotus leaves to the sticky rice in this popular dim sum dish.

1. Cover the sticky rice in warm water and let soak for at least 2 hours, preferably overnight. Drain well. In a medium-sized saucepan, bring the sticky rice and 2 cups of water to a boil. Simmer, covered, for 20 minutes or until rice is cooked. Let cool for 15 minutes. Fluff up the rice before removing from the pot. Split the rice into 4 equal portions.
2. Blanch the lotus leaves in boiling water and drain. Soak the dried mushrooms in hot water for at least 20 minutes to soften. Drain, giving them a gentle squeeze to remove any excess water. Cut into thin slices.
3. Chop the sausages into small pieces. Thinly slice the chicken. Combine the oyster sauce, rice wine, and chicken broth and set aside.
4. Add the oil to a preheated wok or skillet. When oil is hot, add the garlic and ginger. Stir-fry briefly until aromatic. Add the chicken, and then the sausage. Stir-fry for about 2 minutes, then add the mushrooms. Stir in the green onion. Make a well in the middle of the wok and add the sauce, bringing to a boil. Mix everything together, then remove from the heat and allow to cool.
5. Take a lotus leaf and add a quarter of the rice and the filling, layering it so that there is rice at the top and bottom, with the meat and vegetable filling in the middle. Form a square parcel with the lotus leaf and tie it up with twine. Repeat with the remaining lotus leaves.
6. Steam the lotus leaf wraps, covered, on a heatproof plate in a bamboo steamer for 15 minutes, or until they are done.

Spicy Potstickers

Yields 30–35 potstickers

Out of round wonton wrappers? Cut square wonton wrappers into a circular shape.

¼ pound (4 ounces) fresh shrimp
½ cup canned bamboo shoots, shredded
3 medium dried mushrooms
1 cup ground pork
1½ green onions, thinly sliced
2 teaspoons Worcestershire sauce
2 teaspoons soy sauce
1 teaspoon sugar
1 teaspoon sesame oil
1 package round wonton (gyoza) wrappers
½ cup water for boiling potstickers
Oil for frying as needed

1. Wash and devein the shrimp, and chop finely. Shred the bamboo shoots. Soak the dried mushrooms in hot water for at least 20 minutes to soften. Drain, remove the stems, and slice finely.
2. Combine the ground pork, shrimp, bamboo shoots, green onions, dried mushrooms, Worcestershire sauce, soy sauce, sugar, and sesame oil.
3. To make the potstickers: Place 1 teaspoon of filling in the middle of the wrapper. Wet the edges, fold the wrapper over the filling and seal, crimping the edges. Continue with the remainder of the wontons. Cover the completed wontons with a damp towel to prevent drying.
4. Add 2 tablespoons oil to a preheated wok or skillet (1 tablespoon if using a nonstick pan). When oil is hot, add a few of the potstickers, smooth side down. Do not stir-fry, but let cook for about 1 minute. Add ½ cup of water. Do not turn the dumplings over.
5. Cook, covered, until most of the liquid is absorbed. Uncover, and cook until the liquid has evaporated. Loosen the potstickers with a spatula and serve with the burnt side facing up. Serve with Potsticker Dipping Sauce (page 30).

Traditional Gow Gees

¼ pound (4 ounces) shrimp
3 medium dried mushrooms
1 cup ground pork
1 napa cabbage leaf, shredded
1½ green onions, thinly sliced
¼ teaspoon minced ginger
2 teaspoons Chinese rice wine or dry sherry
2 teaspoons soy sauce
1 teaspoon sugar
1 teaspoon sesame oil
1 package round wonton (gyoza) wrappers
4–6 cups oil for deep-frying

Yields 30–35 gow gees

Serve with soy sauce or a dipping sauce such as Sweet-and-Sour Worcestershire Sauce (page 23).

1. Wash, devein, and finely chop the shrimp. Soak the dried mushrooms in hot water for at least 20 minutes to soften. Drain, remove the stems, and slice finely.
2. Combine the ground pork, shrimp, cabbage, green onions, dried mushrooms, ginger, rice wine, soy sauce, sugar, and sesame oil.
3. Add oil to a preheated wok and heat to 375°F. Wrap the gow gees while waiting for the oil to heat. Place 1 teaspoon of filling in the middle of the wrapper. Wet the edges of the wrapper, fold over the filling and seal, crimping the edges. Continue with the remainder of the wontons. Cover the completed wontons with a damp towel to prevent drying.
4. Carefully slide gow gees into the wok, a few at a time. Deep-fry until they turn golden (about 2 minutes). Remove with a slotted spoon and drain on paper towels.

Avoid Drying Out the Wrappers

It's important to cover filled wontons with a damp towel while preparing the rest, as they have a tendency to dry out quickly. For extra protection, also cover wrappers that haven't been used yet.

Crisp Chinese "Seaweed"

Serves 4

The trick to making this popular restaurant dish is to use thoroughly dried bok choy, and to stop deep-frying the moment it turns crispy.

¼ pound bok choy
¼ cup unblanched almonds
¼ teaspoon salt
1 teaspoon brown sugar
2 cups oil for deep-frying

1. Wash the bok choy and drain well. While the bok choy is drying, crush the unblanched almonds in a food processor and set aside.
2. Separate the bok choy leaves from the stalks. Roll the leaves up like a cigar or sausage, and cut into thin shreds. Discard the stalks or save for another dish.
3. Heat wok and add oil. When the oil is heated to between 300°F and 320°F, add the bok choy shreds. Fry them very briefly, until they turn crispy but do not brown. (This will take only a few seconds.) Remove from the wok with a slotted spoon and drain on paper towels.
4. Toss the salt and brown sugar over the "seaweed" and add the crushed almonds.

Chinese "Seaweed"

People are often surprised to discover that this elegant dish is made from everyday Chinese greens! Crisp Chinese "Seaweed" takes its name from the crisp texture and bright green color of the bok choy, which resembles dried seaweed after deep-frying. Serve as an appetizer, or as a colorful side dish with fish.

Deep-fried Mushrooms

20 fresh mushrooms
1 teaspoon baking powder
¾ cup flour
½ teaspoon sugar
¼ teaspoon salt
2 tablespoons vegetable oil
¾ cup water
¼ cup cornstarch
4 cups oil for deep-frying

Yields 20 mushrooms

For best results, don't begin heating the oil for deep-frying until you've applied the batter. This gives the batter time to dry on the mushrooms.

1. Wipe the mushrooms with a damp cloth and cut off the stems.
2. To make the batter: In a medium bowl, sift the baking powder into the flour. Add the sugar, salt, and vegetable oil, stirring. Add the water, and stir into a smooth batter. Add a bit more water if the batter is too dry, or flour if it is too wet. Use a wooden spoon to test the batter—it should drop slowly, and be able to coat the back of the spoon.
3. Lightly dust the mushrooms with cornstarch and coat with the batter, using your fingers.
4. Add the oil to a preheated wok and heat to 350°F. When the oil is ready, add about 5 mushrooms at a time, and deep-fry until golden brown. Drain on paper towels. Cool and serve.

Flavorful Mushrooms

If you normally enjoy mushrooms raw in a salad, try adding a little heat. A little known fact is that many varieties of mushrooms contain over 90 percent water. Deep-frying causes the water to evaporate and seals in the mushroom's natural juices.

Mini Spring Onion Pancakes

Yields 12 pancakes

Serve the pancakes alone or with a soy-based sauce such as Soy Vinegar Dressing (page 27).

1 cup flour
2½ teaspoons salt, divided
½ cup boiling water
2 teaspoons sesame oil
4 green onions, thinly sliced
4–6 tablespoons oil for frying

1. Place the flour in a medium bowl. Sift ½ teaspoon salt into the flour. Stir in a small amount of the boiling water. Add more water and begin forming into a dough. Add the rest of the water and mix in. Cover the dough with a damp towel and let it rest for 30 minutes.
2. Knead the dough until it is smooth. Cut the dough in half.
3. Roll one-half of the dough out until it is no more ¼ inch thick. Spread 1 teaspoon of sesame oil over the dough. Sprinkle with half the green onion slices.
4. Roll the dough up like a jelly roll and cut into 6 pieces. Take a piece of cut dough, use your fingers to lengthen it a bit, and then form it into an *L* shape. Push down on the top of the *L* with the palm of your hand to form a circle. The pancake should be about 2–3 inches in diameter. Continue with the remainder of the dough.
5. Add 2 tablespoons oil to a preheated wok or skillet. Add half the pancakes and fry until brown on both sides. Sprinkle with the remainder of the salt while cooking. Add more oil as needed.

Gow Gees with Ground Turkey

1½ cups ground turkey
1½ tablespoons oyster sauce
¾ teaspoon sugar
2 teaspoons soy sauce
1 teaspoon sesame oil
1½ green onions, minced
1 tablespoon minced ginger
1 package round wonton (gyoza) wrappers
4–6 cups oil for deep-frying

Yields 30–35 gow gees

These dumplings taste delicious served with Hot Mustard Dip (page 20), Soy Ginger Dressing (page 27), or chili paste.

1. Combine the ground turkey, oyster sauce, sugar, soy sauce, sesame oil, green onions, and ginger.
2. Add oil to a preheated wok and heat to 375°F. Wrap the gow gees while waiting for the oil to heat. Place 1 teaspoon of filling in the middle of the wrapper. Wet the edges of the wrapper, fold over the filling, and seal, crimping the edges. Continue with the remainder of the wontons. Cover the completed wontons with a damp towel to prevent drying.
3. Carefully slide gow gees into the wok, a few at a time. Deep-fry until they turn golden (about 2 minutes). Remove with a slotted spoon and drain on paper towels.

Dim Sum Isn't Always Dim Sum

Australians refer to dumplings cooked in the Chinese style as "dim sim." Meanwhile, at Chinese-American restaurants you can order a pu pu platter filled with juicy spareribs, fried wontons, and other Chinese finger foods. In Hawaii, pu pu platters also feature local ingredients such as taro and pineapple.

Siu Mai (Cook and Sell) Dumplings

Yields 15–18 dumplings

Adding oil before steaming helps prevent the Siu Mai from sticking to the heatproof plate.

¼ pound (4 ounces) fresh shrimp
3 medium dried mushrooms
1 cup ground pork
1½ green onions, thinly sliced
½ cup canned bamboo shoots, shredded
2 teaspoons oyster sauce
2 teaspoons soy sauce
1 teaspoon sugar
1 teaspoon sesame oil
1 package Siu Mai or wonton wrappers
Oil for coating heatproof plate

1. Wash and devein the shrimp, and chop finely. Soak the dried mushrooms in hot water for at least 20 minutes to soften. Drain, remove the stems, and slice finely.
2. Combine the ground pork, shrimp, green onions, dried mushrooms, bamboo shoots, oyster sauce, soy sauce, sugar, and sesame oil.
3. To wrap the Siu Mai: Place 2 teaspoons of filling in the middle of the wrapper. **Do not** fold the wrapper over the filling. Gather up the edges of the wrapper and gently pleat the sides so that it forms a basket shape, with the top open.
4. Lightly coat a heatproof plate with oil. Place the dumplings on the plate. Place the plate on a bamboo steamer in a wok set up for steaming. Steam the dumplings for 5–10 minutes or until they are cooked.

Mix and Match

Feel free to experiment by trying the different fillings with any of the dumplings. For example, potsticker fans could use this recipe to make potstickers instead of siu mai. The sticky rice recipes also work well in dumplings or with other wrappers such as banana leaves.

Turkey Fried Wontons

1½ cups ground turkey
2 teaspoons dark soy sauce
1½ tablespoons oyster sauce
1 large garlic clove, minced
½ cup chopped spinach leaves
1 package wonton wrappers
4 cups oil for deep-frying

1. Combine the ground turkey, dark soy sauce, oyster sauce, garlic, and spinach leaves.
2. Add oil to a preheated wok and heat to 375°F. While waiting for the oil to heat, wrap the wontons (see the Deep-fried Wontons recipe on page 33 for instructions).
3. Carefully slide a few wontons at a time into the wok. Deep-fry until they turn golden (about 2 minutes). Remove with a slotted spoon and drain on paper towels.

Yields 30–35 wontons

For this recipe, there is no need to blanch the spinach leaves prior to cooking. You can substitute chopped bok choy leaves for the spinach.

Translucent Dumpling Dough

1 cup wheat starch
¼ teaspoon salt
1 cup boiling water
1 tablespoon lard

1. Place the wheat starch in a medium-sized bowl. Sift in the salt.
2. Slowly pour in the boiling water. Pour in only as much as you need. Stir with a wooden spoon or chopsticks until you have a sticky dough. Let the dough rest and cool for 30 minutes.
3. Add 1 tablespoon lard to the dough, a portion at a time, gradually working it in. Knead the dough until it is smooth and satiny. Make sure the lard is fully mixed in. Use as called for in the recipe.

Yields 22–24 dumplings

This dough is used for Har Gow Dumplings (page 52). Vegetable oil can be substituted for the lard.

Har Gow Dumplings

Yields 22–24 dumplings

These taste delicious with Hot Chili Oil (page 23). For variety, replace half the bamboo shoots with 2 tablespoons minced water chestnuts.

Translucent Dumpling Dough (page 51)
6 ounces raw shrimp
4 tablespoons shredded canned bamboo shoots
1 teaspoon oyster sauce
1 teaspoon sugar
¾ teaspoon Chinese rice wine or dry sherry
¼ teaspoon sesame oil

1. Peel and devein the shrimp. Mince finely. Rinse the bamboo shoots in warm water. Drain well. Combine the shrimp and bamboo shoots with the oyster sauce, sugar, rice wine, and sesame oil. Chill.
2. Work the rested dough if necessary. Cut into quarters. Roll each quarter into a cylinder. Cut into 6 equal pieces (each piece should be approximately 1 inch thick and 1 inch wide). You should now have 24 pieces.
3. On wax paper, roll each piece of dough into a circle 2½–3 inches in size. Cover with a towel while rolling out the remainder to prevent drying.
4. Prepare the wok for steaming. Place up to 1 teaspoon of the filling in each dumpling. Carefully fold the dough over the filling and pleat the edges.
5. Place the dumplings 1 inch apart for steaming. Steam, covered, on medium heat for 15–20 minutes, or until the dumplings are done.

CHAPTER 4

Soups and Salads

Wonton Soup

Serves 4

This recipe calls for ready-made wontons you can buy at your local Asian grocery store, but you can also try making your own.

Water for boiling wontons
24 filled wonton dumplings
6 cups chicken broth or stock
½ cup shredded napa cabbage
Salt and pepper, to taste
1 green onion, thinly sliced

1. Bring a large pot of water to a boil. Add the wonton dumplings, making sure there is enough room for them to move about freely. Boil for at least 5 minutes, until the wontons rise to the top and the filling is cooked through. Remove from the pot with a slotted spoon.
2. Bring the chicken stock to a boil. Add the cabbage and cook until tender. Season the broth with salt and pepper. Add the cooked wontons and bring the soup back to a boil. Remove the pot from the heat and add the green onion. When serving, allow 6 wontons per person.

Watercress Soup

Serves 4

If you don't have time to prepare the chicken stock, you may substitute 2 cups of canned chicken broth mixed with 2 cups of water.

1 bunch watercress
4 cups chicken stock
1 pinch salt
¼ teaspoon sugar
⅜ teaspoon white pepper

1. Wash the watercress and drain thoroughly. In a large saucepan, add the chicken stock and bring to a boil.
2. Add the salt, sugar, and white pepper. Add the watercress, and cook for another 2–3 minutes. Serve hot.

Canned Broth or Homemade Stock?

Many recipes in the book call for chicken broth. Nothing beats a good homemade stock, but canned chicken broth is an acceptable alternative. If possible, choose brands labeled "reduced sodium."

Hot and Sour Soup

6 dried mushrooms
¼ cup dried lily buds
1 cake firm tofu
6 cups chicken stock, or 5 cups stock and 1 cup mushroom soaking liquid
¼ cup ground pork
1 teaspoon salt
2 tablespoons soy sauce
2 tablespoons mildly sweetened rice vinegar
½ teaspoon white pepper, or to taste
1 tablespoon tapioca starch
¼ cup water
1 egg white, lightly beaten
1 green onion, minced
A few drops of sesame oil

Serves 4–6

This popular soup is reputed to be good for colds. Serve with Kung Pao Stir-fry (page 168) or Restaurant-Style Mu Shu Pork (page 146).

1. Soak the dried mushrooms in hot water for 20 minutes to soften. Give the mushrooms a little squeeze to remove excess water and cut into thin slices. Reserve the soaking liquid if desired. Soak the dried lily buds in hot water for 20 minutes. Drain.
2. Cut the tofu into cubes.
3. In a large saucepan, bring the chicken stock or stock and mushroom liquid mixture to a boil. When it is boiling, add the mushrooms, lily buds, tofu, and the ground pork.
4. Bring back to a boil and add the salt, soy sauce, rice vinegar, and white pepper.
5. Mix the tapioca starch and water and slowly pour it into the soup, stirring. When the soup thickens, turn off the heat.
6. Pour in the egg white and stir quickly to form thin shreds. Stir in the green onion. Drizzle with sesame oil. Give a final stir.

Freezing Instructions

This dish can be prepared ahead of time and frozen. Prepare the soup, leaving out the tofu and egg. When ready to serve, thaw the soup, add the tofu, and bring to a boil. When the soup is boiling, add the beaten egg white.

Quick and Easy Hot and Sour Soup

Serves 4–6

This modified version of the famous Szechwan soup contains ingredients that are all available at the local supermarket.

1 cup chicken broth
6 cups water
1 teaspoon salt
1 teaspoon sugar
2 tablespoons soy sauce
½ cup canned bamboo shoots, rinsed and drained
2 shiitake mushrooms, sliced
½ cup cooked pork or chicken, cut as desired
3 tablespoons rice vinegar
White pepper to taste
1 tablespoon cornstarch
¼ cup water
1 egg, lightly beaten
1 green onion, minced
A few drops sesame oil

1. In a large saucepan, bring the chicken broth and water to a boil. When it is boiling, add the salt, sugar, soy sauce, bamboo shoots, mushrooms, and cooked meat.
2. Bring back to a boil and add the rice vinegar and white pepper. Test the broth and adjust the taste if required. Mix the cornstarch and water and slowly pour it into the soup, stirring. When the soup thickens, turn off the heat.
3. Pour in the beaten egg and stir quickly to form thin shreds. Stir in the green onion. Drizzle with the sesame oil. Give a final stir and serve hot.

How Do You Drop?

The most challenging part of preparing Egg Drop Soup is streaming the egg into the soup. First, turn off the heat: this prevents the eggs from developing a rubbery texture. Next, hold a fork twelve inches above the pot and slowly pour the beaten egg through the tines. Stir rapidly in a clockwise direction to form thin shreds; gently to form long streams.

Egg Drop Soup

4 cups chicken broth or stock
1/8 teaspoon white pepper
1/4 teaspoon salt
1/4 teaspoon sugar
1 teaspoon Chinese rice wine or dry sherry
2 eggs, lightly beaten
2 green onions, minced
A few drops of sesame oil

1. Bring the chicken stock or broth to a boil.
2. When the broth is boiling, add the white pepper, salt, sugar, and rice wine. Cook for another minute.
3. Turn off the heat and pour the eggs into the soup in a steady stream, stirring rapidly in a clockwise direction until they form thin strands.
4. Add the green onions and sesame oil. Give the soup a final stir. Serve hot.

Serves 4

For contrast, serve Egg Drop Soup with a more strongly spiced main dish and a colorful stir-fried vegetable.

Walnut Soup

6 whole walnuts
4 cups water
2 slices ginger
2 tablespoons plus 1 teaspoon sugar

1. In a medium saucepan, bring to a boil the walnuts and 4 cups water. Turn down the heat and simmer for 30 minutes.
2. Add the ginger slices. Simmer for at least another 30 minutes. Stir in the sugar. Remove the walnuts. Leave in the ginger or remove as desired.

Serves 4

This soup does double duty as a nourishing hot broth, or chilled and served as a dessert soup.

Cream Corn Soup

Serves 4

This soup tastes delicious served with Beef with Broccoli (page 115) and cooked rice.

4 cups chicken stock or broth
¼ teaspoon salt
¼ teaspoon sugar
¼ teaspoon white pepper, or to taste
1 teaspoon Chinese rice wine or dry sherry
1 can creamed corn
2 slices cooked ham, diced
1 tablespoon cornstarch
4 tablespoons water
2 egg whites, lightly beaten
2 green onions, minced
A few drops of sesame oil

1. Bring the broth or stock to a boil.
2. Add the salt, sugar, white pepper, rice wine, corn, and cooked ham. Bring the broth back to a boil.
3. Mix the cornstarch and water and pour into the soup, stirring to thicken. When the soup has thickened, turn off the heat.
4. Pour the egg whites into the soup in a steady stream, and quickly stir in a clockwise direction until they form thin shreds.
5. Add the green onions and sesame oil. Give the soup a final stir.

Make Your Own Stock

It's easy! Bring 2½–3 pounds of chicken bones, a sliced green onion, and a few slices of ginger to a boil in a large pot of water (about 8 cups). Skim off the foam that rises to the top. Reduce the heat and simmer the stock, uncovered, for at least 2 hours. Cool before using.

Chicken Velvet Soup

4 ounces skinless, boneless chicken breast
1 tablespoon water
2 teaspoons Chinese rice wine or dry sherry, divided
4 cups chicken stock or broth
¼ teaspoon salt
⅛ teaspoon white pepper
1 can creamed corn
1 tablespoon cornstarch mixed with 4 tablespoons water
2 eggs whites, lightly beaten
2 green onions, sliced

1. Cut the chicken into chunks and place in a food processor. Add the water and 1 teaspoon rice wine, and mince the chicken into a fine paste.
2. Bring the broth or stock to a boil. Add the salt, white pepper, 1 teaspoon rice wine, and creamed corn. Add the chicken paste, stirring so that the chicken breaks up into small pieces. Cook until the chicken turns white.
3. Mix the cornstarch and water, and pour the mixture into the soup, stirring to thicken. Turn off the heat.
4. Pour the eggs into the soup in a steady stream, and quickly stir in a clockwise direction until they form thin shreds.
5. Add the green onions and give the soup a final stir.

Serves 4

In a pinch, you can make chicken stock from chicken bones that have been boiled for as little as thirty minutes, but the flavor won't be as strong.

Tomato Egg Flower Soup

Serves 4

Beef and tomato are a natural combination. For a heartier soup, add ½ cup of ground beef or lean beef.

4 cups beef broth
2 medium tomatoes
⅛ teaspoon white pepper
¼ teaspoon salt
½ teaspoon sugar
1 teaspoon Chinese rice wine or dry sherry
1 tablespoon cornstarch
4 tablespoons water
1 egg white, lightly beaten
2 green onions, minced
A few drops of sesame oil

1. Bring the 4 cups of beef broth to a boil.
2. Bring a large pot of water to a boil. Blanch the tomatoes briefly in the boiling water. (This will make it easier to remove the peel.) Peel the tomatoes and cut each into 6 equal pieces.
3. When the beef broth comes to a boil, add the white pepper, salt, sugar, rice wine, and tomatoes. Bring the broth back to boiling.
4. Mix the cornstarch and water, and pour it into the soup, stirring to thicken. Turn off the heat.
5. Pour the egg white into the soup and quickly stir in a clockwise direction to form thin shreds.
6. Add the green onions and a few drops of sesame oil. Give the soup a final stir.

Cholesterol Concerns

Using egg whites instead of eggs in the Egg Drop Soup–type recipes helps reduce the amount of cholesterol. Another option is to forego the egg altogether—heartier soups such as Chicken Velvet Soup taste fine without it.

Winter Melon Soup

2 Chinese dried mushrooms
1 pound winter melon
3½ cups water
2½ cups chicken stock or 1 cup chicken broth mixed with 1½ cups water
½ cup barbequed pork, diced
2 slices ginger
1 teaspoon Chinese rice wine or dry sherry
1 pinch salt

Serves 4

For a more impressive presentation, purchase a whole winter melon and steam the soup inside the melon.

1. Cut the stems off the dried mushrooms and soak in hot water for 20 minutes. Give the mushrooms a little squeeze to remove excess water and cut into thin slices.
2. Wash the winter melon and remove the green rind, seeds, and the pulp. Cut into slices approximately 2 inches long and ½ inch thick. In a large saucepan, add the winter melon to 3½ cups water and bring to a boil. Simmer for 20 minutes or until the melon is tender.
3. Add the chicken stock or chicken broth and water mixture, barbequed pork, dried mushrooms, and ginger.
4. Add the rice wine and salt. Simmer for another 15 minutes. Serve hot. Leave the ginger slices in or remove as desired.

Drink Your Soup!

The Chinese believe that cold drinks and hot food don't mix, so soup normally takes the place of a beverage at meals. It's customary in Chinese restaurants for the waitress to bring a steaming pot of tea as soon as you're seated, but traditionally tea was looked upon as a digestive aid, to be consumed at the conclusion of a meal.

Cucumber and Carrot Soup

Serves 4

This modified version of Winter Melon Soup uses easy-to-find ingredients. Serve hot, or leave out the ham and chill.

1 cucumber
4 shiitake mushrooms
1 carrot, diced
½ cup cooked ham, diced
1 teaspoon Chinese rice wine or dry sherry
⅛ teaspoon salt
4 cups chicken broth
1 green onion, minced
A few drops sesame oil

1. Peel the cucumber, remove the seeds, and dice. Wash the shiitake mushrooms and cut into thin slices.
2. In a large saucepan, add the cucumber, mushrooms, diced carrot, diced ham, rice wine, and salt to the chicken broth.
3. Bring the soup to a boil and cook over low heat for about 20 minutes.
4. Turn off the heat and add the green onion. Drizzle with the sesame oil.

Pork and Spinach Soup

Serves 4

Ground pork is used more frequently than ground beef in Chinese cooking. For a heartier soup, add a cup of Chinese noodles.

1 tablespoon soy sauce
1 teaspoon Chinese rice wine or dry sherry
1 tablespoon cornstarch
½ cup ground pork
¾ cup spinach leaves
5 cups chicken stock or 4 cups canned broth mixed with 1 cup water
½ teaspoon sugar
¼ teaspoon salt

1. Add the soy sauce, rice wine, and cornstarch to the ground pork. Marinate the pork for 15 minutes.
2. Blanch the spinach in boiling water briefly, just until the leaves begin to wilt. Drain well.
3. Bring the chicken stock or broth to a boil. Add the marinated pork and simmer for about 10 minutes. Add the sugar, salt, and spinach. Heat through and serve hot.

Emerald Soup

15 leaves of spinach
1 boneless, skinless chicken breast
1 slice ginger
1 tablespoon oil for stir-frying
¼ teaspoon salt
¼ teaspoon sugar
4½ cups chicken stock or broth
1 teaspoon soy sauce
1 teaspoon Chinese rice wine or dry sherry

Serves 4

Made with spinach, ginger, and chicken broth, this soup is great for fighting colds. Blanching the spinach before stir-frying preserves its brilliant green color.

1. Wash the spinach leaves and cut off the ends. Blanch the leaves briefly in boiling water, just until the leaves begin to wilt. Remove and sprinkle with cold water.
2. Cut the chicken into thin slices. Blanch briefly in boiling water with the ginger until it turns white. Remove from the water and set aside.
3. Heat a wok or frying pan and add oil for stir-frying. When the oil is ready, stir-fry the spinach very briefly (under 1 minute), adding the salt and sugar.
4. Add the chicken broth to the spinach. Add the soy sauce and rice wine and bring to a boil.
5. Add the chicken and bring back to a boil. Serve hot.

Cilantro

Also called Chinese parsley, cilantro is the common name for the leaves of the coriander plant. Indispensable in Chinese cooking, cilantro leaves lend a pleasantly musky odor to soups, salads, and stir-fries. Just remember that, like garlic, a little goes a long way. Substitute parsley leaves if you find the flavor too overpowering.

Sizzling Rice Soup

Serves 4

Success lies in keeping the soup hot while deep-frying the rice, so that the rice crackles and pops when it meets the heated broth.

10 squares Rice Crisps (page 84)
6 large dried black mushrooms
⅓ pound cooked shrimp
1 large chicken breast
6 cups chicken stock or 5 cups broth with 1 cup water
½ 8-ounce can water chestnuts, drained and sliced
½ cup frozen peas
1 teaspoon salt
1 tablespoon Chinese rice wine or dry sherry
White pepper to taste (optional)
1 teaspoon sesame oil
4–6 cups oil for deep-frying

1. Two hours ahead of time, begin preparing the Rice Crisps.
2. Soak the mushrooms in hot water for 20 minutes to soften. Give a gentle squeeze to remove any excess liquid. Cut into thin slices. Rinse the shrimp in warm water and pat dry.
3. Bring a large pan of water to a boil and poach the chicken very briefly in the boiling water. Drain. Cut the chicken into thin slices.
4. Bring the chicken stock or broth and water mixture to a boil. Add the chicken, water chestnuts, mushrooms, shrimp, and peas. Bring the soup back to a boil.
5. While waiting for the soup to boil, begin heating oil for deep-frying the Rice Crisps.
6. Add the salt, rice wine, and white pepper to the soup, if desired. Drizzle with sesame oil. Pour the soup into a large tureen or serving bowl. Keep warm.
7. When the oil is hot, add the Rice Crisps. Deep-fry until the pieces puff up and turn brown. Remove from the wok and drain on paper towels.
8. At the table, slide the sizzling rice into the soup. The rice will make crackling sounds.

West Lake Beef Soup

1 tablespoon soy sauce
1 teaspoon Chinese rice wine or dry sherry
½ teaspoon salt, divided
1 tablespoon cornstarch
½ cup lean ground beef
5 cups chicken or beef broth
1 teaspoon sugar
1½ tablespoons cornstarch mixed with ⅓ cup water
2 egg whites, lightly beaten
¼ teaspoon sesame oil

Serves 4

Pair this dish with Beef and Bean Sprouts in Black Bean Sauce (page 117) and steamed rice for a quick and easy dinner.

1. Add the soy sauce, rice wine, ¼ teaspoon salt, and cornstarch to the ground beef, adding the cornstarch last. Marinate for 15 minutes.
2. Bring the chicken or beef broth to a boil. Stir in the marinated ground beef. Bring back to a boil and add the sugar and ¼ teaspoon salt.
3. Boil for 5 more minutes and add the cornstarch mixed with water, stirring to thicken. When the soup has thickened, turn off the heat.
4. Pour the egg whites into the soup in a steady stream, and quickly stir in a clockwise direction until they form thin shreds.
5. Drizzle with the sesame oil. Give the soup a final stir. Serve hot.

Thick or Thin?

In Chinese cooking, thin soups are soups in which the meat and vegetables are added to the heated broth during the final stages of cooking. With thick soups, the ingredients are all added together and the soup is slowly simmered, giving the flavors time to blend.

Bean Curd Soup

Serves 4

Use firm tofu for this soup so that it will hold its shape during cooking. Vegetarians can substitute vegetable stock for the chicken.

2 cakes firm tofu
1 green onion
4 fresh water chestnuts
1 tablespoon oil
1 teaspoon shredded ginger
5½ cups chicken stock or broth
¼ teaspoon salt
1 teaspoon Chinese rice wine or dry sherry

1. Drain the tofu, and cut into 1-inch cubes. Slice the green onion on the diagonal into thirds. Cut the top off the water chestnuts, peel the skin, and chop.
2. In a large saucepan heat the oil on medium-low heat. Add the ginger and cook briefly until aromatic.
3. Add the chicken stock or broth and bring to a boil. Add the salt, rice wine, tofu, and water chestnuts. Bring back up to a boil and simmer for about 10 minutes. Stir in the sliced green onion.

Creamy Fruit Salad

Serves 1

Don't feel like cooking? Serve with Chinese-Style Gado Gado Salad (page 72) for a convenient summer meal.

½ cup plain yogurt
¼ teaspoon cinnamon
2½ teaspoons honey
1 half section of cantaloupe or other melon

Process the yogurt, cinnamon, and honey until smooth. Spoon into the middle of the cantaloupe.

Bird's Nest Soup

4 ounces bird's nest
Basic Chicken Velvet (page 162), use the amounts specified in the recipe
6 cups stock or broth
1½ teaspoons Chinese rice wine or dry sherry
½ teaspoon salt
½ teaspoon sugar
⅛ teaspoon white pepper, or to taste
2 green onions, minced
¼ cup ham, chopped

Serves 6

Be sure to take extra care when preparing this expensive delicacy. Combine bird's nest with rock sugar and water for a sweet dessert soup.

1. To prepare the bird's nest, soak overnight in water. Drain thoroughly. Spread out the bird's nest and use tweezers to carefully remove any foreign materials or dirt. Bring a large pot of water to a boil and simmer the bird's nest for 5 minutes. Drain thoroughly and check again for any foreign material.
2. Prepare the Basic Chicken Velvet.
3. Bring stock or broth to a boil. Add the bird's nest and simmer for 30 minutes. Add the rice wine, salt, and sugar.
4. Fold in the Basic Chicken Velvet and bring the soup back up to a boil. Add the white pepper. Stir in the green onions and ham or add after serving as a garnish.

Exotic Bird's Nest

Not keen to try a soup filled with twigs and branches? Actually, bird's nest isn't made from traditional nesting materials. Instead, the swiftlet—a type of swallow—makes a nest using its own saliva, which hardens upon exposure to air. The swiftlet inhabits remote caves in China and Southeast Asia. Retrieving the nests can be hazardous; the men who perform this task often come from families that have been earning their living in this manner for generations.

Sweet Red Bean Paste Soup

Serves 3

This simplified version of a famous Chinese wedding soup can be served as a snack or as a sweet dessert soup.

4 cups water
1 piece dried tangerine peel, 2–3 inches wide
½ cup Sweet Red Bean Paste (page 271)
⅓ cup sugar

1. In a medium saucepan, add the 4 cups water and the dried tangerine peel. Bring to a boil and simmer for about 30 minutes.
2. Add the Sweet Red Bean Paste. Continue simmering for another 30 minutes. Add the sugar, stirring to dissolve. Chill before serving.

Chinese Wedding Soup

Traditionally, sweet red bean paste soup is made with raw adzuki beans and contains lotus seeds, a symbol of fertility in Chinese culture.

Sweet Almond Soup

Serves 4

Traditionally this dessert would be made with Chinese almonds, which are actually apricot pits.

½ cup unblanched almonds
3 tablespoons long grain rice
2 tablespoons Chinese dates
2 tablespoons vegetable oil
2½ cups milk
2 tablespoons sugar

1. Process the almonds in a blender or food processor into a fine powder. Combine 3 tablespoons of the processed almonds with the white rice and process again. Add water, a few drops at a time, to form a paste.
2. Process the Chinese dates into small pieces and set aside.
3. Add oil to a preheated wok or heavy skillet. When oil is hot, add the milk and heat until it is almost, but not quite, boiling. Add the almond and rice paste and cook for 10 minutes at a near boil, stirring frequently.
4. Bring the milk to a boil. Add the sugar, stirring. Add the Chinese date pieces. Serve chilled.

Chinese Potato Salad

4 potatoes
2 eggs
3 tablespoons mayonnaise
1½ tablespoons soy sauce
1½ teaspoons chopped cilantro leaves
¾ teaspoon Hot Mustard Sauce (page 18)
¾ teaspoon sugar
¼ teaspoon plus a few drops of sesame oil
1 cup shredded napa cabbage
⅓ cup chopped red onion

Serves 6–8

For extra bite, add up to ½ teaspoon of curry paste to the potato salad before serving.

1. Boil the potatoes and hard-boil the eggs. Drain and peel the potatoes, and cut them into bite-sized squares. Slice the hard-boiled eggs.
2. Mix together the mayonnaise, soy sauce, cilantro leaves, Hot Mustard Sauce, and sugar. Stir in the sesame oil.
3. Mix the potatoes, eggs, shredded cabbage, and chopped red onion together in a large bowl. Mix in the mayonnaise sauce. Keep in a sealed container in the refrigerator until ready to serve.

Main Dish Salad

The common tossed green salad is unknown in Chinese cuisine. A salad can be hot or cold, an appetizer or part of the main meal. It may even take the place of a sorbet when served between courses.

Chinese-Style Gado Gado Salad

Serves 4

This Chinese take on the popular Indonesian salad features peanut sauce without the lime juice. Serve with scented rice for a light supper.

Peanut Sauce (page 22)
2 red potatoes
2 hard-boiled eggs
½ English cucumber
½ cup snow peas
½ cup cauliflower
½ cup spinach leaves
½ cup carrots, chopped
½ cup mung bean sprouts

1. Boil the potatoes with their skins on and slice. Boil the eggs and cut into thin slices. Peel the cucumber and cut into thin slices. String the snow peas. Chop the cauliflower.
2. Blanch the snow peas, spinach leaves, carrots, and bean sprouts.
3. Arrange the vegetables on a platter, working from the outside in. You can arrange the vegetables in any order, but the boiled egg slices should be placed on top.
4. Pour the Peanut Sauce over the salad. Serve immediately.

Steamed Beef Salad

Serves 6

This is an excellent dish to serve on summer days when you want something more substantial than chicken wings or potato salad.

Spicy Steamed Beef (page 126)
1 bunch Romaine lettuce leaves
1 carrot, shredded
1 cup raw cherry tomatoes, halved
2 tablespoons red rice vinegar
2 teaspoons soy sauce
1 teaspoon sugar
A few drops sesame oil

1. Prepare the steamed beef. Place the cooked beef in a sealed container in the refrigerator and leave overnight.
2. Place the vegetables in a medium-sized bowl and toss with the red rice vinegar, soy sauce, sugar, and sesame oil.
3. Serve the steamed beef on a plate with the salad arranged around it.

Watermelon and Watercress Salad

¼ cup rice vinegar
½ teaspoon lemon juice
¼ teaspoon chili sauce
¼ teaspoon sesame oil
1 tablespoon sesame paste or peanut butter
2 tablespoons water
2 cups watercress
1 small tomato
1 leaf Romaine lettuce, shredded
10 1-inch cubes of watermelon, green peel and seeds removed

Serves 2

For extra flavor, add a few Spicy Roasted Peanuts (page 276) to the dressing before processing. The dressing yields ⅓ cup.

1. For the dressing, place the rice vinegar, lemon juice, chili sauce, sesame oil, sesame paste, and water in a blender and process until smooth. Place in a bowl and set aside.
2. Wash the watercress. Drain thoroughly, and remove the stems. Cut the tomato into thin slices.
3. Toss the watercress with the Romaine lettuce and tomato. Place in a serving bowl and add the watermelon cubes. Drizzle the dressing over. Refrigerate leftover dressing in a sealed jar. It will keep for 3–4 days.

Peanut Butter Is a Substitute

The more authentic version of this dish uses sesame paste. Made from toasted sesame seeds, sesame paste has a sweet flavor similar to peanut butter, which makes a convenient substitute. Although it is also made from ground sesame seeds, the Middle Eastern tahini is not a good substitute for sesame paste: It is made with untoasted sesame seeds, giving it a very different flavor.

Hot Spiced Cucumbers

Serves 2

Rice vinegar and rice wine vinegar both mean the same thing. Rice vinegar is simply rice wine that has been allowed to ferment.

½ English cucumber
½ teaspoon salt
1 teaspoon grated ginger
1 garlic clove, finely minced
1 tablespoon plus 1 teaspoon red rice vinegar
1 tablespoon sugar
¼ teaspoon chili paste

1. Peel the cucumber and cut into thin slices. Place in a bowl and toss with the salt and leave for 15 minutes.
2. Combine the remaining ingredients in a bowl. Place the cucumber in a clean bowl and pour the sauce mixture over. Serve immediately or chill.

Creamy Cucumber Salad

Serves 2

This is a wonderful picnic dish. For a less spicy version, leave out the chili paste.

1 English cucumber
¼ teaspoon salt
1 clove garlic, minced
½ cup plain yogurt
½ teaspoon cilantro leaves
1 teaspoon honey
1 teaspoon freshly squeezed lemon juice
¼ teaspoon chili paste
1 Asian pear

1. Peel the cucumber and slice. Place in a bowl and toss with salt, allowing to stand for 15 minutes.
2. Place the garlic, yogurt, cilantro leaves, honey, lemon juice, and chili paste in the blender and process until smooth. Makes ⅓ cup.
3. Serve the cucumber slices on a plate with the dressing on the side. Garnish with Asian pear slices.

Bean Sprout and Carrot Salad

2 cups mung bean sprouts, rinsed and drained
½ carrot, shredded
1 tablespoon red rice vinegar
1 teaspoon sugar
1 tablespoon soy sauce
1 teaspoon chili with garlic sauce
¼ teaspoon sesame oil

1. Trim the ends of the bean sprouts if desired. Combine with the shredded carrot.
2. Mix together the red rice vinegar, sugar, soy sauce, chili with garlic sauce, and sesame oil. Drizzle over the mixture of bean sprouts and carrot, and refrigerate for at least 2 hours before serving.

Serves 3–4

For an attractive presentation, trim the ends of the bean sprouts and serve on a plate of Romaine lettuce leaves decorated with green onion brushes.

Green Onion Brushes

This attractive garnish is easy to make. Simply slice a green onion into 1½-inch pieces, then, starting in the middle and going left, cut several slits with a pin. Repeat in the other direction. (Leave a small section in the middle untouched so that the green onion doesn't fall apart.)

Cold Asparagus Salad with Garlic

Serves 4

This dish tastes excellent refrigerated and served the next day with a beef stir-fry and rice.

1 pound fresh asparagus
1 clove garlic, chopped
2 tablespoons black rice vinegar
2 teaspoons white sugar
1 tablespoon soy sauce
⅛ teaspoon sesame oil

1. Wash the asparagus and drain well. Cut off the ends and cut diagonally into 1½-inch pieces.
2. Bring a large pot of water to a boil. Parboil the asparagus, and plunge into cold water. Drain well.
3. Mix together the garlic clove, black rice vinegar, sugar, soy sauce, and sesame oil. Toss with the asparagus.

Black Rice Vinegar

With its intriguing combination of tart and sweet, black rice vinegar is the crème de la crème of the rice vinegars. The most famous comes from southern China's Chinkiang region. If you enjoy black rice vinegar's distinctive smoky flavor, try substituting it in any recipe where rice vinegar is called for.

Hot Chicken Salad

4 boneless, skinless chicken breasts
½ cup soy sauce, divided
1 head Romaine lettuce
1 red bell pepper
4 tablespoons red rice vinegar
3 teaspoons sesame oil
2 green onions, minced
2 teaspoons sugar
½ teaspoon chili paste
2 tablespoons toasted sesame seeds

Serves 4

For an interesting contrast in taste and texture, serve this dish with hard Chinese noodles such as Chow Mein or Deep-fried Vermicelli (page 101).

1. Marinate the chicken in ¼ cup soy sauce for 1 hour. Steam the chicken in a bamboo steamer in a wok until it is cooked through. Cool. Shred the cooked chicken meat.
2. Wash the Romaine lettuce leaves and drain well. Wash the red bell pepper and cut into thin slices.
3. Mix together ¼ cup soy sauce, the red rice vinegar, sesame oil, green onions, sugar, and chili paste.
4. Arrange the lettuce and red bell pepper on a plate. Add the shredded cooked chicken. Drizzle with the red rice vinegar dressing and top with toasted sesame seeds.

How to Shred Meat

Hold the cleaver parallel to the cutting board and slice the meat horizontally into thin sections. Lay the cut pieces on top of each other, position the cleaver perpendicular to the board, and cut the meat lengthwise into thin slices, from ¼- to ⅛-inch thick. For easier shredding, partially freeze the meat ahead of time.

CHAPTER 5

Rice and Noodles

Basic Cooked Rice

Serves 4–6

Most Chinese recipes call for long grain rice, although medium grain rice is also acceptable. Short grain rice is reserved for desserts.

2 cups long grain rice
3¼ cups water

1. If necessary, rinse the rice to remove any excess starch.
2. In a large saucepan, bring the rice and water to a boil on medium heat.
3. Once the rice is boiling, turn down the heat to medium low. Put the lid at an angle on the pot, so that the pot is partially covered but some steam can escape.
4. When the water has evaporated to the point where you can see holes in the rice, put the lid fully on.
5. Simmer the rice on low heat for 15 more minutes.

The Knuckle Method of Measuring Water

This really works! Stick your finger on the top of the rice and begin adding water. You know you've added enough when the water reaches your first knuckle.

Basic Fried Rice

3 medium or large eggs
2½ tablespoons oyster sauce, divided
⅛ teaspoon salt, divided
⅛ teaspoon pepper, divided
3–4 tablespoons oil for frying, divided
4 cups cold cooked rice

1. Lightly beat the eggs and add 1 tablespoon oyster sauce and a small amount of salt and pepper to taste.
2. Add 2 tablespoons oil to a preheated wok or heavy skillet and turn the heat on high. When oil is hot, add the egg mixture. Scramble gently until the eggs are almost cooked but still moist. Remove from the heat and let sit for 1 minute before removing from the pan.
3. Wipe the wok clean and add 2 tablespoons oil. When oil is hot, add the rice, stirring to separate the grains. Stir-fry for 2–3 minutes, then blend in the scrambled egg. Add 1½ tablespoons oyster sauce, and salt and pepper to taste. Mix through and serve hot.

Serves 4

This recipe is very adaptable—enjoy as is, or add your favorite meat and vegetable combinations.

Eggs and Rice

There are many ways to cook the beaten egg in fried rice. You can scramble it, or fry it whole and cut into strips to serve on top of the fried rice. For added variety, try scrambling half the beaten egg and frying the other half.

Basic Scented Rice

Serves 4–6

The trick to making scented rice is to reduce the amount of water used, so that the rice is steamed rather than boiled.

2 cups jasmine or balsamic scented rice
3 cups water

1. Rinse the rice thoroughly to remove any excess starch. The water should be clear and not milky.
2. In a large saucepan, bring the rice and water to a boil.
3. When the rice has boiled, turn down the heat to very low. Cover and simmer for about 20 minutes, or until the rice is cooked.
4. Remove the pot from heat. Let the rice cool for 15 minutes before removing from the pot. Fluff and serve.

Fried Glutinous Rice

Serves 4

Serve this fragrant dish where you would normally serve Thai scented rice. The sauce is similar to the sauce for Beef with Broccoli (page 115).

2 cups glutinous rice
2 tablespoons oil for stir-frying
½ cup beef broth
2 tablespoons oyster sauce
1 teaspoon brown sugar
2 tablespoons water

1. Rinse the rice several times, and soak for several hours or overnight, if possible. Drain well.
2. Add oil to a preheated heavy skillet or wok. When the oil is hot, add the rice and stir-fry for 2–3 minutes. Add the remaining ingredients and mix through.

Pork-filled Rice Balls

½ cup glutinous rice
1 green onion
2 dried mushrooms
1 green leaf from Stir-fried Bok Choy (page 237), optional
¼ teaspoon salt
1 tablespoon soy sauce
1 tablespoon soaking liquid from the mushrooms
1 tablespoon Chinese rice wine or dry sherry
¼ teaspoon sugar
1 tablespoon cornstarch
1 cup ground pork

1. Rinse the rice several times, and soak for several hours or overnight, if possible. Drain well.
2. Chop the green onion very thinly into small rounds. Reconstitute the dried mushrooms by soaking in hot water for at least 20 minutes. Reserve the soaking liquid. Cut the mushrooms into thin slices. Thinly slice the bok choy leaf, if desired.
3. Combine the salt, soy sauce, mushroom liquid, rice wine, sugar, and cornstarch in a small bowl. Set aside.
4. In a medium bowl, mix the ground pork with the mushrooms, green onion, and bok choy leaf. Add the cornstarch mixture, 1 tablespoon at a time, and work it into the pork with your hands.
5. Place a piece of waxed paper on the counter and spread out the dried glutinous rice. Use your hands to shape the pork mixture into a ball roughly the size of a golf ball. Roll the ball over the rice, making sure it is covered with rice. Repeat with the remainder of the pork.
6. Steam the pork balls for about 30 minutes, or until they are firm and cooked through. Serve warm or cold.

Yields 12 rice balls

Serve this delicate appetizer to guests with Crisp Chinese "Seaweed" (page 48) for an interesting contrast of colors, textures, and flavors.

Fungus Fun

The Chinese believe dried mushrooms can lower blood pressure and they are also thought to be an aphrodisiac! Meanwhile, cloud ear, strange-looking fungus that does vaguely resemble a human ear, is thought to improve blood circulation. Any kind of mushroom will add texture to a variety of dishes, from soups to stir-fries.

Rice Crisps

Yields 8–10 squares

Crispy rice is used to make Wor Wonton Soup, a popular restaurant dish with seafood and vegetables swimming in a rich broth.

1 cup short grain rice
1 cup water

1. Bring rice and water to boil, uncovered, in a medium saucepan.
2. Cover and simmer on low heat for 30 minutes. Remove from the burner and allow to cool.
3. Spread the rice out on a baking sheet, making sure it is no more than ¼ inch thick.
4. Bake at 300°F for 50 minutes or until dry. When cooled, cut into 2-inch squares and store in a canister to use as needed.

Rinsing Rice

In the past, cooks always rinsed the rice to remove impurities and to soften it, making the grains easier to separate. Today, raw rice is cleaner, and rinsing does remove some of the nutrients. If you're uncertain about whether or not to rinse, check the directions on the bag or box. (Thai scented rice and glutinous rice should always be rinsed.) To rinse, place the rice in a large bowl and cover with cold water. Use your fingers to swirl the rice around, then drain. Repeat this process 2 or 3 times, until the water comes out clear and is not cloudy.

Beef Fried Rice

2 large eggs
2½ tablespoons oyster sauce
⅛ teaspoon salt
⅛ teaspoon pepper
½ red bell pepper
1 green onion
6–7 tablespoons oil for stir-frying
2 garlic cloves, minced
½ onion, chopped
4 mushrooms, sliced
4 cups cold cooked rice
1 pound cooked beef, cut as desired
1 tablespoon mushroom soy sauce
½ teaspoon sugar

Serves 4–6

Concerned about cholesterol? Serve the fried rice without the strips of cooked egg on top.

1. Lightly beat the eggs. Stir in the oyster sauce and salt and pepper to taste.
2. Remove the seeds from the red pepper and cut into bite-sized cubes. Cut the green onion into 1-inch slices on the diagonal.
3. Add 2 tablespoons oil to a preheated wok or skillet. When oil is hot, pour the egg mixture into the pan. Cook on medium to medium-high heat, using 2 spatulas to turn it over once. Don't scramble. Remove and cut into thin strips. Set aside.
4. Clean out wok, if necessary. Add 2–3 tablespoons oil. When oil is hot, add the garlic cloves and stir-fry until aromatic. Add the onion. Stir-fry for 1 minute, then add the mushrooms, and then the red pepper. Stir-fry the vegetables until they are tender. Remove.
5. Add 2 tablespoons oil to the wok. When oil is hot, add the rice, stirring to separate the grains. Stir-fry on medium heat for 2–3 minutes, then blend in the vegetables and beef. Stir in the mushroom soy sauce and sugar. Stir in the green onion. Serve hot, topped with the egg strips.

Chicken Fried Rice

Serves 4

Thick soy sauce is thickened with molasses. Restaurants frequently rely on it to add flavor to fried rice and noodle dishes.

2 large eggs
2½ tablespoons oyster sauce, divided
⅛ teaspoon salt
⅛ teaspoon pepper
5–6 tablespoons oil for stir-frying
2 stalks celery, diced
½ cup chopped onion
4 cups cold cooked rice
1½ cups cooked chicken, chopped
2 teaspoons thick soy sauce
2 green onions, minced

1. Lightly beat the eggs. Stir in 1 tablespoon oyster sauce and salt and pepper to taste.
2. Add 2 tablespoons oil to a preheated wok or skillet. When oil is hot, pour the egg mixture into the pan. Cook on medium to medium-high heat, using 2 spatulas to turn it over once. Don't scramble. Remove and cut into thin strips. Set aside.
3. Clean out wok, if necessary. Add 1–2 tablespoons oil. When oil is hot, add the celery. Stir-fry for 1 minute, then add the onion. Stir-fry the vegetables until they are tender. Remove.
4. Add 2 tablespoons oil. When oil is hot, add the rice. Stir-fry on medium heat, stirring to separate the grains. Add 1½ tablespoons oyster sauce, and a small amount of salt and pepper. Blend in the chicken, onion, and celery. Stir in the thick soy sauce. Add extra salt and sugar if desired. To serve, garnish the chicken with the strips of fried egg and green onions.

Flavorful Fried Rice

Instead of serving fried rice immediately, try storing it in the refrigerator in a sealed container to use another day. This gives the flavors more time to blend. Just be sure to allow the fried rice to cool completely before storing.

Fried Rice with Ham

2 large eggs
Salt and pepper to taste
6 tablespoons oil for stir-frying
½ cup chopped onion
½ cup frozen peas
4 cups cold cooked rice
1 tablespoon dark soy sauce
1 tablespoon oyster sauce
1 cup cooked ham
1 green onion, minced

1. Lightly beat the eggs and add a small amount of salt and pepper to taste.
2. Add 2 tablespoons oil to a preheated wok or heavy skillet and turn the heat on high. When oil is hot, add the egg mixture. Scramble gently until the eggs are almost cooked but still moist. Remove from the heat and let sit for 1 minute before removing from the pan.
3. Clean out the wok and add 2 tablespoons oil. When oil is hot, add the onion. Stir-fry for 1 minute, then add the peas. Stir-fry until the peas are bright green and the onion tender. Remove.
4. Wipe the wok clean and add 2 tablespoons oil. When oil is hot, add the rice, stirring to separate the grains. Stir-fry for 2–3 minutes, then add the dark soy sauce and oyster sauce. Add the ham, green peas, and onion. Blend in the scrambled egg. Stir in the green onion and serve hot.

Serves 4

Fried rice dishes can be prepared ahead of time and frozen. Thaw completely before reheating.

Lumpy Leftovers

Fried rice tastes best when you use previously cooked rice instead of fresh, but leftover rice can get a bit lumpy. To remove any lumps, just sprinkle a bit of cold water on the rice and break them up with your fingers. Another trick is to add the lightly beaten egg to the cold rice before stir-frying, instead of cooking the egg separately. This makes the rice grains much easier to separate.

Yangchow Fried Rice

Serves 4

This colorful dish flecked with yellow, orange, green, and pink is named for the city of Yangchow in Jiangsu province, famous for its rice dishes.

2 large eggs
2 tablespoons oyster sauce, divided
Salt and pepper to taste
4 cups cold cooked rice
1 green onion
6 tablespoons oil for stir-frying
¼ pound (4 ounces) fresh shrimp, peeled and deveined
½ cup baby carrots, halved
½ cup peas
½ teaspoon sugar
1 cup barbequed pork, cubed

1. Lightly beat the eggs. Stir in 1 tablespoon oyster sauce, and a small amount of salt and pepper to taste. Mix the egg in with the rice, stirring to separate the grains.
2. Cut the green onion into 1-inch pieces on the diagonal.
3. Add 2 tablespoons oil to a preheated wok or heavy skillet. When oil is hot, add the shrimp. Stir-fry briefly until they turn pink. Remove and drain on paper towels.
4. Clean out wok and add 2 tablespoons oil. When oil is hot, add the baby carrots. Stir-fry for 1 minute, then add the green peas. Stir-fry until the peas are bright green. Remove.
5. Wipe the wok clean and add 2 tablespoons oil. When oil is hot, add the rice and egg mixture. Stir-fry for 2–3 minutes, then add 1 tablespoon oyster sauce and the sugar. Add the barbequed pork and shrimp. Add the vegetables. Stir in the green onion and serve hot.

Pineapple Fried Rice

2 whole, fresh pineapples
2 eggs
⅛ teaspoon salt
Pepper to taste
4 cups cold cooked rice
3–4 tablespoons oil for stir-frying
½ cup chopped onion
½ cup peas
2 tablespoons oyster sauce
1 cup diced cooked ham

Serves 4

Serving the fried rice inside the pineapple skins adds glamour to a fairly simple dish. You can substitute cooked shrimp for the ham.

1. Cut the pineapples in half lengthwise, cutting through the crown. Cut out the fruit in the middle, without cutting through the skins. Turn the skins inside out to drain. Dice the pineapple fruit.
2. Lightly beat the eggs and add a small amount of salt and pepper to taste. Add the beaten eggs to the rice, stirring to separate the grains.
3. Add 2 tablespoons oil to a preheated wok or skillet. When oil is hot, add the onion. Stir-fry for 1 minute, then add the peas. Stir-fry until the peas are bright green and the onion tender. Remove.
4. Wipe the wok clean and add 2 tablespoons oil. When oil is hot, add the rice/egg mixture. Stir-fry for 2–3 minutes, then add the oyster sauce. Add the ham, peas, and onion. Stir in the diced pineapple.
5. Place 1 cup of the fried rice inside each of the pineapple half shells and serve.

Basic Congee

Serves 6–8

Feel free to adjust the proportion of chicken broth to water to suit your own tastes.

1 cup long grain rice
7 cups water
1 cup chicken stock or broth

Rinse the rice and drain. In a large saucepan, bring the rice, water, and chicken broth to a boil. Simmer, covered, for 1½ hours.

Versatile Congee

Congee does double duty as a nutritious meal and a beverage replacement. Just as the Chinese frequently serve a thin soup instead of a beverage at the main meal, a bowl of creamy congee takes the place of a beverage at the breakfast table.

Speedy Congee

Serves 4–6

Leftover fried rice comes is handy on days when there is no time to prepare fresh congee. Feel free to add other seasonings.

3 cups cold fried rice
6 cups chicken broth or water
Salt and pepper to taste

1. Make sure the fried rice is at room temperature.
2. Bring the broth or water to a boil. Add the fried rice. Bring the broth back up to a boil. Add the salt and pepper. Serve hot.

Congee with Beef

½ pound beef
2 teaspoons oyster sauce
1 cup long grain rice
6 cups water
2 cups chicken broth
2 green onions
2 tablespoons oil for stir-frying
2 slices ginger, minced
1 clove garlic, minced
2 tablespoons dark soy sauce
1 tablespoon Chinese rice wine or dry sherry
½ teaspoon sesame oil
Salt and pepper to taste

Serves 6–8

Serve this hearty dish for breakfast, or as a midday meal. Be sure to add bread for dipping!

1. Cut the beef into thin slices. Marinate with the oyster sauce for 30 minutes.
2. Bring the rice, water, and chicken broth to a boil. Simmer, covered, for 30 minutes.
3. Cut the green onions into 1-inch pieces on the diagonal.
4. Add oil to a preheated wok or skillet. When oil is hot, add the ginger and garlic. Stir-fry briefly until aromatic. Add the beef and stir-fry until it changes color and is nearly cooked through. Remove and drain on paper towels.
5. Add the ginger, garlic, and beef to the congee. Stir in the dark soy sauce and rice wine. Continue simmering for another 30 minutes, or until the congee has a creamy texture. Stir in the green onions. Drizzle with the sesame oil. Add salt to taste.

Congee—More Than a Chinese Porridge

At its simplest, congee consists of rice cooked in water until it has a creamy texture. However, it would be a mistake to view congee as merely the Chinese version of porridge. Congee can be savory or sweet; a bland, watery "soup" for a sick patient, or a hearty meal swimming in a richly seasoned broth. It all depends on the length of cooking time and which ingredients are added to the basic rice and water mix. Congee is frequently accompanied by Chinese crullers: thick, deep-fried strips of dough approximately twelve inches in length.

Rice and Sausage Dinner

Serves 4

If you can't find dried mushrooms at the local supermarket, use fresh mushrooms. For extra flavor, add ¼ cup of chopped onion.

4 Chinese sausages
1 cup baby carrots
4 dried mushrooms
2 green onions
¾ cup beef broth
2 teaspoons hoisin sauce
1 teaspoon sugar
3 tablespoons oil for stir-frying
1 teaspoon minced shallot
3 cups cooked long grain rice

1. Cut the Chinese sausage into bite-sized pieces.
2. Blanch the baby carrots by plunging briefly into boiling water. Cut in half. Soak the dried mushrooms in hot water for at least 20 minutes to soften. Cut into thin slices. Cut the green onions on the diagonal into ½-inch pieces.
3. Combine the beef broth, hoisin sauce, and sugar; set aside.
4. Add 2 tablespoons oil to a preheated wok or skillet. When oil is hot, add the sausages. Stir-fry for 2–3 minutes, and remove from the wok.
5. Add 1 tablespoon oil to the wok. When oil is hot, add the shallot and stir-fry briefly until aromatic. Add the carrots, stir-fry for about 1 minute, and add the mushrooms. Make a well in the middle of the wok. Add the sauce in the middle and bring to a boil. Mix in the cooked rice. Add the sausages back to the wok. Stir in the green onions. Mix everything through and serve hot.

Hot, Sour, and Spicy Rice Noodles

¼ pound rice stick noodles
¼ cup dark soy sauce
1 teaspoon sugar
¼ teaspoon Hot Chili Oil (page 25)
¼ teaspoon Szechwan Salt and Pepper Mix (page 22)
¼ teaspoon chili paste
1 teaspoon black rice vinegar
½ cup water
1½ tablespoons oil for stir-frying
¼ cup chopped onion

Serves 4–6

Rice stick noodles come in many intriguing shapes and sizes. They can be nearly as thin as strands of human hair.

1. Soak the rice stick noodles in hot water for 15 minutes or until they are softened. Drain thoroughly.
2. Combine the dark soy sauce, sugar, Hot Chili Oil, Szechwan Salt and Pepper Mix, chili paste, black rice vinegar, and water; set aside.
3. Add oil to a preheated wok or skillet. When oil is hot, add the chopped onion. Stir-fry until it is soft and translucent.
4. Add the rice noodles and stir-fry for 2–3 minutes. Add the sauce in the middle of the wok. Mix in with the noodles and stir-fry until the noodles have absorbed all the sauce.

How to Make Toasted Szechwan Peppercorns

Toast the peppercorns on low heat in a heavy pan, shaking occasionally, until the peppercorns turn fragrant and begin to smoke. Remove and cool. Grind the peppercorns in a pepper mill or with a mortar and pestle before using.

Cellophane Noodles with Beef and Oyster Sauce

Serves 2–4

Not a fan of canned baby corn? Try substituting canned or fresh bamboo shoots instead.

½ pound flank steak
2 tablespoons soy sauce
1½ teaspoons Chinese rice wine or dry sherry, divided
1½ teaspoons sugar, divided
½ teaspoon baking soda
2-ounce bag cellophane noodles
1 can baby corn
½ cup beef broth
2 tablespoons oyster sauce
2 tablespoons dark soy sauce
1 tablespoon light soy sauce
2–4 tablespoons oil for stir-frying

1. Cut the beef into thin slices. Add the soy sauce, 1 teaspoon rice wine, ½ teaspoon sugar, and baking soda. Marinate the beef for 30 minutes.
2. Without removing the string wrapping, soak the cellophane noodles in hot water to soften. Cut the noodles along the string wrapping into thirds. Drain thoroughly. Rinse the baby corn in warm water and drain.
3. Combine the beef broth, oyster sauce, dark soy sauce, light soy sauce, ½ teaspoon rice wine, and 1 teaspoon sugar, and set aside.
4. Add 2 tablespoons oil to a preheated wok or skillet. When oil is hot, add the beef. Stir-fry until it changes color and is nearly cooked through. Remove from the wok and set aside.
5. Add more oil, if necessary. Stir-fry the baby corn for 1–2 minutes. Add the sauce to the middle of the wok and bring to a boil. Add the noodles, stirring quickly to mix in with the sauce. Add the beef. Mix everything through and serve hot.

Mad about Mein!

Mein is the Chinese word for noodles. When it comes to important staple foods, noodles rank second only to rice in the Chinese diet. Noodles are steamed, stir-fried, added to soups, and used to make dumplings. Although noodles are enjoyed throughout China, they are particularly important in the north, where a harsher climate prohibits the cultivation of rice crops.

Beef Chow Fun

4 ounces wide rice noodles
1 cup mung bean sprouts
½ cup chicken stock or broth
1 teaspoon soy sauce
2 tablespoons oil for stir-frying
1 cup cooked beef, shredded
¼ teaspoon chili paste

1. Soak the rice noodles in hot water for at least 15 minutes to soften. Drain well. Blanch the mung bean sprouts by plunging briefly into boiling water. Drain well.
2. Combine the chicken broth and soy sauce. Set aside.
3. Add oil to a preheated wok or skillet. When oil is hot, add the noodles. Stir-fry briefly, then add the sauce. Mix with the noodles and add the shredded beef. Stir in the chili paste. Add the mung bean sprouts. Mix through and serve hot.

Serves 4

Barbequed pork also works well in this dish. For an interesting juxtaposition of color and texture, serve with Braised Baby Bok Choy (page 258).

Noodle Pancake

8 ounces steamed egg noodles
2 teaspoons sesame oil
5 tablespoons oil

1. Cook the noodles until they are tender. Drain thoroughly and toss with the sesame oil.
2. Add 3 tablespoons oil to a preheated wok or skillet. When oil is hot, add noodles. Use a spatula to press down on the noodles and form into a pancake shape. Cook until a thin brown crust forms on the bottom—this will take at least 5 minutes. Slide the pancake out of the pan onto a plate.
3. Add 2 tablespoons oil to the wok. Turn the noodle pancake over, put back in the wok, and cook until the other side is browned. Remove from the wok. To serve, cut into quarters.

Serves 4

Noodle Pancake makes a nice alternative to rice in stir-fries, and tastes great topped with any Egg Foo Yung sauce (see Chapter 9).

Pork Chow Mein

Serves 4–6

The mushroom soaking liquid adds an earthy flavor to this dish. You can also use fresh mushrooms and ¼ cup water instead.

1 pound fresh egg noodles
¼ teaspoon sesame oil
1 pound pork tenderloin, cubed
1 tablespoon Chinese rice wine
¼ teaspoon salt
2½ cups shredded napa cabbage
4 large dried mushrooms
½ green or red bell pepper
⅓ cup chicken broth
⅛ cup water
⅛ cup reserved mushroom soaking liquid
4 teaspoons oyster sauce
⅛ teaspoon salt
4–6 tablespoons oil for stir-frying
2 garlic cloves, minced
1 carrot, diced
1 stalk celery, thinly sliced on the diagonal
1 cup mung bean sprouts, rinsed and drained
1 teaspoon cornstarch mixed with 4 teaspoons water
1 teaspoon sugar

1. Boil the noodles. Drain and toss with sesame oil.
2. Marinate pork in rice wine and ¼ teaspoon salt for 30 minutes.
3. Soak the dried mushrooms for at least 20 minutes to soften. Thinly slice them. Remove the seeds from the pepper and cut into cubes.
4. Combine chicken broth, water, mushroom soaking liquid, oyster sauce, and ⅛ teaspoon salt. Set aside.
5. Add 2 tablespoons oil to a preheated wok or skillet. Add the pork and stir-fry until it is nearly cooked. Remove and drain on paper towels.
6. Add 2 tablespoons oil. When oil is hot, add the noodles and stir-fry until light brown. Remove and keep warm. Clean out the wok.
7. Add 2 tablespoons oil. When oil is hot, add the garlic and stir-fry briefly until aromatic. Either stir-fry the carrot, celery, pepper, dried mushrooms, cabbage, and bean sprouts together or separately, adding one at a time and adding more oil as needed. (Move the vegetables up to the side of the wok and wait until oil is heated.)
8. Add the sauce to the middle of the wok and bring to a boil. Add the cornstarch-and-water mixture, stirring quickly to thicken. Add the sugar. Add the pork and heat through. Serve hot over the noodles.

Chicken Chow Mein

1 pound fresh egg noodles
¼ teaspoon sesame oil
1 pound boneless, skinless chicken breasts
10 teaspoons oyster sauce, divided
¼ teaspoon salt
½ red bell pepper
1 bunch (about 2½ cups after cutting) bok choy
⅓ cup chicken broth
¼ cup water
⅛ teaspoon salt
6–8 tablespoons oil for stir-frying
2 garlic cloves, minced
6–8 large mushrooms, thinly sliced
2 stalks celery, thinly sliced on the diagonal
1 cup mung bean sprouts, rinsed and drained
1 teaspoon cornstarch mixed with 4 teaspoons water
1 teaspoon sugar

Serves 4–6

Like chop suey, this is a great one-dish meal to make when it's time to clean out the vegetable section of the refrigerator.

1. Boil the noodles. Drain thoroughly and toss with sesame oil.
2. Cut the chicken breasts into thin strips. Marinate in 6 teaspoons oyster sauce and ¼ teaspoon salt for 30 minutes.
3. Remove the seeds from the red pepper and cut into thin slices. Cut the bok choy leaves across and thinly slice the stalks on the diagonal.
4. Combine chicken broth, water, 4 teaspoons oyster sauce, and ⅛ teaspoon salt. Set aside.
5. Add 2 tablespoons oil to a preheated wok or skillet. Add the chicken and stir-fry until it is nearly cooked. Drain on paper towels.
6. Add 2 tablespoons oil. Add the noodles and stir-fry until they turn light brown. Remove and keep warm. Clean out the wok.
7. Add 2 tablespoons oil. Add the garlic and stir-fry briefly until aromatic. Stir-fry the mushrooms, bok choy stalks, celery, pepper, bok choy leaves, and bean sprouts, adding one at a time and adding more oil as needed.
8. Add the sauce to the middle of the wok and bring to a boil. Add the cornstarch/water mixture, stirring quickly to thicken. Add the sugar. Add the chicken and heat through. Serve hot over the noodles.

Beef Chow Mein

Serves 4–6

Feel free to add seasonal vegetables such as tomatoes and green beans in this recipe.

1 pound wonton noodles
1 pound beef flank steak
1 tablespoon soy sauce
½ teaspoon baking soda
½ red bell pepper
½ cup snow peas
⅓ cup beef broth
¼ cup water
1 tablespoon plus 1 teaspoon oyster sauce
1 teaspoon sugar
⅛ teaspoon salt
4–6 tablespoons oil for stir-frying
2 garlic cloves, minced
½ cup carrots, thinly sliced
1 cup mung bean sprouts, rinsed and drained
1 teaspoon cornstarch
4 teaspoons water
½ teaspoon sesame oil

1. Boil the wonton noodles until they are soft. Drain thoroughly.
2. Cut the beef into thin strips. Marinate in the soy sauce and baking soda for 30 minutes.
3. Remove the seeds from the pepper and cut into thin slices. String the snow peas. Combine the beef broth, water, oyster sauce, sugar, and salt. Set aside.
4. Add 2 tablespoons oil to the wok. When oil is hot, add the beef. Stir-fry until it changes color and is nearly cooked. Remove and drain on paper towels.
5. Add 1–2 tablespoons oil. When oil is hot, add the wonton noodles. Stir-fry until they are golden but still soft. Remove.
6. Add 2 tablespoons oil to the wok. When oil is hot, add the garlic. Stir-fry until aromatic. Add the carrots. Stir-fry for 1 minute, then add the snow peas, red pepper, and bean sprouts. Stir-fry until the vegetables are colorful and tender.
7. Make a well in the middle of the wok. Add the sauce and bring to a boil. Add mixed cornstarch and water, stirring to thicken. Add the beef. Drizzle with sesame oil. Mix everything through and serve over the wonton noodles.

Post-Thanksgiving Turkey Chow Mein

4 cups dry chow mein noodles
4 mushrooms, sliced
1 cup bean sprouts
2 stalks celery
2 cups snow peas
4½ tablespoons oil for stir-frying
1 tablespoon soy sauce
½ cup cashews
2 cups cooked turkey
2 tablespoons oyster sauce
1 tablespoon cornstarch mixed with 4 tablespoons water

Serves 4

A great way to make use of leftover Thanksgiving turkey. Serve with Egg Drop Soup (page 59) for a nourishing fall meal.

1. Boil the chow mein noodles according to the directions on the package. Drain well. Keep warm.
2. Wash and slice the mushrooms. Parboil the bean sprouts and celery by briefly plunging into boiling water; drain thoroughly. Wash and cut the celery on the diagonal into thin slices. String the snow peas.
3. Add 2 tablespoons of oil to a preheated wok or skillet. Stir-fry the celery on medium-high heat. Add the mushrooms, bean sprouts, and soy sauce. Stir-fry, remove, and set aside.
4. Add the snow peas and fry as in the recipe for Snow Pea Stir-fry (page 235). Remove and set aside.
5. Add 1½ tablespoons oil to the wok or frying pan. Add the cashews and stir-fry on medium heat very briefly. Remove and set aside.
6. Add 1 tablespoon oil to the wok. Add the cooked turkey and the oyster sauce. Add the vegetables and mix through.
7. Make a well in the middle of the pan and add the cornstarch-and-water mixture, stirring to thicken. Mix with the other ingredients. Stir in the cashews. Serve over the chow mein noodles.

Beefy Fried Rice Noodles

Serves 4–6

For a different flavor, replace the oyster sauce in the chicken broth mixture with 1 tablespoon of hoisin sauce.

½ pound beef flank or sirloin steak
1½ teaspoons oyster sauce
⅛ teaspoon salt
¼ teaspoon baking soda
4–5 ounces medium-width rice stick noodles
1 red bell pepper
1 tablespoon oyster sauce
2 tablespoons dark soy sauce
1 teaspoon sugar
½ cup chicken stock or broth
4–5 cups oil for frying
¼ cup cornstarch
1 teaspoon finely chopped ginger
2 garlic cloves, finely chopped
1 cup mung bean sprouts, rinsed and drained

1. Cut the beef across the grain into thin strips about 2 inches long. Add the oyster sauce, salt, and baking soda. Marinate the beef for 30 minutes.
2. Soak the rice noodles in hot water for 20 minutes or until they are softened. Wash the pepper, remove the seeds, and cut into thin strips about 2 inches long.
3. Combine the oyster sauce, dark soy sauce, sugar, and chicken stock. Set aside.
4. Heat 4 cups of oil in the wok to 375°F. Lightly dust the marinated beef with the cornstarch. Deep-fry the beef in the hot oil for a few minutes, until it turns light brown. Drain on paper towels.
5. Remove all but 3 tablespoons oil from the wok or heat 3 tablespoons oil in a second wok or heavy skillet. When oil is hot, add the ginger and garlic and stir-fry until aromatic. Add the red pepper and stir-fry until it is tender and has a bright color (stir-fry in 2 batches, if necessary). Add the bean sprouts. Push the vegetables up to the side, add the sauce, and bring to a boil.
6. Turn down the heat slightly and add the noodles. Stir-fry briefly and add the beef. If necessary, add a bit of water. Mix everything through and serve hot.

Cold Szechwan Sesame Noodles

8 ounces egg noodles
Spicy Szechwan Peanut Sauce (page 25)
1 cucumber
½ teaspoon salt
1 tablespoon toasted sesame seeds

1. Prepare the egg noodles according to the instructions on the package.
2. Peel the cucumber, toss with salt, and leave for 15 minutes. Toast the sesame seeds.
3. Allow the noodles to cool. When cold, toss with the Spicy Szechwan Peanut Sauce. Sprinkle with sesame seeds. Serve over the cucumber slices.

Serves 4

Italian pasta can be substituted for Chinese egg noodles in this recipe. For added flair, garnish with cilantro leaves.

Deep-fried Vermicelli

4 ounces vermicelli noodles
4 cups oil for deep-frying

1. Heat oil in preheated wok or heavy saucepan to 375°F. If the noodles come with string wrappings, cut them off. Do not soak the noodles.
2. Drop one 2-ounce package of noodles into the wok. It should puff up immediately. Remove and drain on paper towels. Repeat with the other package. Cut the noodles into serving portions or serve as is.

Serves 6–8

Top these noodles with dishes that have a lot of sauce, such as Mongolian Beef with Vegetables (page 111).

Singapore Fried Rice Noodles

Serves 2–4

For a different taste and texture, try substituting chicken for the pork and experimenting with rice noodles of different thickness.

4 ounces rice vermicelli
½ red bell pepper
2 teaspoons mild curry powder
¼ teaspoon turmeric
½ teaspoon grated ginger
½ cup chicken stock or broth
2 tablespoons plus 1 teaspoon soy sauce
½ teaspoon sugar
4–5 tablespoons oil for stir-frying
2 ounces shrimp, peeled and deveined
1 cup mung bean sprouts, rinsed and drained
4 ounces barbequed pork, cut into very thin slices
⅛ teaspoon freshly ground pepper

1. Soak the rice noodles in hot water for 20 minutes or until softened. Drain thoroughly. Wash the red pepper and remove the seeds.
2. Combine the curry powder, turmeric, and ginger. Set aside. Combine the chicken broth, soy sauce, and sugar. Set aside.
3. Add 2 tablespoons oil to a preheated wok or skillet. When oil is hot, add the shrimp and stir-fry briefly until they turn pink. Remove and set aside.
4. Add 2–3 tablespoons oil. When oil is hot, add the curry powder mixture and stir-fry until aromatic. Add the red pepper and bean sprouts. Add the noodles and stir-fry for a few minutes, adding water if necessary.
5. Add the sauce in the middle of the wok. Bring to a boil. Add the barbequed pork and mix through. Add the stir-fried shrimp. Sprinkle with the freshly ground pepper and serve hot.

Dan Dan Noodles

8 ounces fresh egg noodles
2 teaspoons plus 1 tablespoon sesame oil, divided
3 tablespoons peanut butter
2 tablespoons dark soy sauce
1 tablespoon light soy sauce
3 tablespoons rice vinegar
4 teaspoons sugar
1 tablespoon Hot Chili Oil (page 25)
1½ tablespoons toasted sesame seeds
3 green onions, cut into 1-inch pieces

Serves 4

A mild, sweetened rice vinegar works very well in this recipe. If you want to add a vegetable, try 1 cup blanched bean sprouts.

1. Bring a pot of water to boil, and cook the noodles al dente. Drain thoroughly and toss with 2 teaspoons sesame oil. Cool.
2. Combine the peanut butter, dark soy sauce, light soy sauce, rice vinegar, sugar, 1 tablespoon sesame oil, and Hot Chili Oil. Process in a blender or food processor.
3. Mix the sauce in with the noodles. Sprinkle the toasted sesame seeds over. Garnish with the green onion.

How to Toast Sesame Seeds

Spread the sesame seeds out on a pan and cook at low heat, shaking the pan occasionally. Toast the sesame seeds until they turn a light brown. Remove from the pan, cool, and use as called for in recipes. When cooking the seeds, be sure not to overcook and let them burn.

Beef Lo Mein

Serves 4

To cook noodles al dente, boil until they are tender, but still firm and not mushy.

1 pound flank steak
2 teaspoons oyster sauce
1½ teaspoons sugar, divided
½ teaspoon baking soda
6 dried mushrooms
8 ounces fresh egg noodles
2 tablespoons dark soy sauce
1 tablespoon light soy sauce
1 teaspoon Chinese rice wine or dry sherry
¼ cup water
3 tablespoons oil for stir-frying
6 cabbage leaves, shredded

1. Cut the steak into thin slices, about 2 inches in length. Add the oyster sauce, ½ teaspoon sugar, and baking soda. Marinate the steak for 30 minutes.
2. Soak the dried mushrooms in hot water for at least 20 minutes to soften.
3. In a large pot of water, boil the noodles until the flour is removed but they are still firm. Drain thoroughly.
4. Cut the mushrooms into thin slices. Combine the dark soy sauce, light soy sauce, 1 teaspoon sugar, rice wine, and water, and set aside.
5. Add 2 tablespoons oil to a preheated wok or skillet. When oil is hot, add the steak. Stir-fry until it changes color and is nearly cooked through. Remove and drain on paper towels.
6. Add 1 tablespoon oil to the wok. When oil is hot, add the cabbage leaves. Stir-fry until they are bright green and tender. Season with ¼ teaspoon salt if desired. Add the mushrooms. Stir-fry briefly. Add the sauce in the middle of the wok, and bring to a boil. Turn down the heat slightly and add the beef. Add the noodles. Mix everything through and serve hot.

Chow Mein or Lo Mein?

People are often surprised to learn that the difference between these popular dishes has more to do with cooking styles than specific ingredients. Chow Mein are fried noodles cooked separately from the meat and vegetables. Lo Mein dishes feature boiled noodles that are combined with the other ingredients during the final stages of cooking.

Chicken Lo Mein

1 cup cooked chicken
8 ounces fresh egg noodles
½ cup mushrooms, fresh or dried
2 tablespoons oyster sauce
1 tablespoon soy sauce
1 teaspoon sugar
1 teaspoon Chinese rice wine or dry sherry
½ cup water
2–3 tablespoons oil for stir-frying
4 cabbage leaves, shredded
¼ teaspoon salt, optional
½ cup mung bean sprouts, rinsed and drained

Serves 4

Leftover Tea Smoked Chicken (page 177) works very well in this recipe, imparting a lovely smoky flavor.

1. Cut the cooked chicken into thin slices. In a large pot of water, boil the noodles until the flour is removed and they are tender. Drain thoroughly.
2. If using dried mushrooms, soak in hot water for at least 20 minutes to soften. Slice mushrooms.
3. Combine the oyster sauce, soy sauce, sugar, rice wine, and water, and set aside.
4. Add 2 tablespoons oil to a preheated wok or skillet. When oil is hot, add the cabbage leaves. Stir-fry until they turn bright green and are tender. Season with salt, if desired. Add 1 tablespoon oil, if necessary.
5. Add the mushrooms. Stir-fry briefly, then add the bean sprouts. Add the sauce in the middle of the wok. Bring to a boil. Turn down the heat slightly and add the chicken. Add the noodles. Mix everything through and serve hot.

Savory Shanghai Noodles

Serves 2–4

Frying the shrimp briefly in 1 cup of hot oil gives it a soft, velvety texture.

½ pound (8 ounces) fresh cooked shrimp, tails and vein removed
½ teaspoon sugar
½ teaspoon cornstarch
1 bunch spinach
¾ cup chicken broth
¼ cup water
2 tablespoons plus 2 teaspoons oyster sauce
1 teaspoon Chinese rice wine or dry sherry
1 garlic clove, finely chopped
2 slices ginger, finely chopped
½ pound fresh Shanghai noodles
½ teaspoon sesame oil
1¼ cups oil for frying

1. Rinse the shrimp in warm water and pat dry. Marinate the shrimp in the sugar and cornstarch for 15 minutes.
2. Wash the spinach and drain thoroughly. Mix together the chicken broth, water, oyster sauce, and rice wine, and set aside.
3. Add 1 cup oil to a preheated wok or skillet. When oil is hot, add the shrimp and fry briefly for 1 minute (if using raw shrimp, fry longer until the shrimp turn pink and firm up around the edges). Remove the shrimp from the wok with a slotted spoon and drain on paper towels.
4. Remove all but 2 tablespoons oil from the wok. Add the spinach and fry until it changes color. Add seasonings such as salt or soy sauce, if desired. Remove from the wok and set aside.
5. Add the garlic and ginger and stir-fry briefly until aromatic. Add the noodles. Stir-fry and toss with the sesame oil. Make a well in the middle of the wok and add the sauce. Bring to a boil. Add the spinach and the shrimp back into the wok. Mix everything through and serve hot.

Noodle Lore

The Chinese have been enjoying noodles since ancient times. Symbolizing a long life in Chinese culture, noodles occupy an important place in festive celebrations such as Chinese New Year. And birthday celebrations wouldn't be complete without a heaping bowl of longevity noodles.

Oyster Sauce Pork with Cellophane Noodles

1 pound pork
1 green onion, cut in thirds
3 tablespoons soy sauce, divided
2 stalks celery
2 tablespoons oyster sauce
1 teaspoon sugar
¼ teaspoon Chinese rice wine or dry sherry
½ cup chicken broth
1 2-ounce package cellophane noodles
4 cups oil for frying

Serves 2–4

Because it resembles a bird's nest, a packet of deep-fried cellophane noodles is sometimes used to replace authentic bird's nest in mock bird's nest soup.

1. Cut the pork into cubes. Marinate the pork in 1 tablespoon soy sauce and green onion for 30 minutes.
2. Blanch the celery by plunging briefly into boiling water. Drain well. Cut into thin slices along the diagonal.
3. Combine the oyster sauce, 2 tablespoons soy sauce, sugar, rice wine, and chicken broth. Set aside.
4. Add 4 cups oil to a preheated wok and heat to at least 350°F. While oil is heating, remove the string wrappings from the cellophane noodles. When oil is hot add the noodles. Deep-fry briefly until it puffs up and forms a "nest." Remove and drain on paper towels. Leave as is or cut into individual servings.
5. Drain all but 2 tablespoons oil from the wok. Add the pork and stir-fry until it changes color and is almost cooked through. Remove and drain on paper towels.
6. Add the celery and stir-fry until it turns shiny and is tender. Add the sauce to the middle of the wok and bring to a boil. Add the pork. Mix everything through. Serve over the noodles.

Cellophane Noodles

Made from mung bean starch, cellophane noodles are also called bean thread or glass noodles. After soaking they became very absorbent, picking up the flavors of the foods they are cooked with. Deep-frying without soaking first causes them to puff up immediately. Use cellophane noodles in dishes with lots of flavorful sauce.

Chapter 6

Beef Dishes

Basic Beef Stir-fry

Serves 2–4

This is a good basic recipe for marinating and stir-frying beef that you can adapt according to your tastes and the ingredients you have on hand.

½ pound beef
2 teaspoons soy sauce
1 teaspoon cornstarch
¼ teaspoon baking soda
1 tablespoon vegetable oil
2 tablespoons oil for stir-frying
1 clove garlic, smashed
1 tablespoon Chinese rice wine or dry sherry
½ teaspoon sugar

1. Cut the beef across the grain into thin strips. Add the soy sauce, cornstarch, and baking soda to the meat, in that order. Use your hands to mix in the cornstarch and baking soda. Marinate the meat for 30 minutes, add the vegetable oil, and marinate for another 30 minutes.
2. Add oil to a preheated wok or skillet. When oil is hot, add the garlic and stir-fry briefly until aromatic. Add the beef, laying it flat on the wok. Let the meat cook for a minute, turn over and brown on the other side, and then begin stir-frying. When it is nearly cooked through, add the rice wine and sugar. When the meat is cooked, remove from the wok and drain on paper towels.

Searing Meat

While stir-frying is normally a hands-on process, when cooking meat it's best to give the spatula a brief rest. Lay the meat out flat in the wok and brown for about thirty seconds before stir-frying.

Mongolian Beef with Vegetables

1 pound sirloin or flank steak
1 egg white
Pinch of salt
1½ teaspoons sesame oil, divided
1 tablespoon cornstarch
1½ tablespoons oil
2 green onions
2 garlic cloves, minced
½ teaspoon chili sauce
1 can baby corn, rinsed and drained
1 tablespoon Chinese rice wine or dry sherry
2 tablespoons hoisin sauce
1 tablespoon dark soy sauce
½ teaspoon sugar
1½ teaspoons cornstarch
2 tablespoons water
1 cup oil for frying beef

Serves 4

This northern Chinese favorite makes a complete meal when served with rice. For a more authentic dish, use bamboo shoots instead of baby corn.

1. Slice the beef across the grain into thin strips. Add the egg white, salt, 1 teaspoon sesame oil, and cornstarch to the beef, adding the cornstarch last. Marinate the beef for thirty minutes. Add 1½ tablespoons oil and marinate for another thirty minutes.
2. While beef is marinating, cut the green onions into thirds on the diagonal.
3. Add 1 cup oil to a preheated wok or skillet. When oil is hot, carefully slide the beef into the wok, a few pieces at a time. Fry the beef until it changes color. Remove from the wok with a slotted spoon and drain on paper towels.
4. Remove all but 2 tablespoons of oil. When oil is hot, add the garlic and chili sauce. Stir-fry briefly until the garlic is aromatic. Add the baby corn.
5. Add the beef back into the wok. Add the rice wine, hoisin sauce, dark soy sauce, and sugar. Mix the cornstarch and water, and add to the middle of the wok, stirring vigorously to thicken. Mix all the ingredients together thoroughly. Stir in the green onion. Drizzle with ½ teaspoon sesame oil and serve hot.

Mongolian Beef with Rice Noodles

Serves 4–6

Leeks are a popular vegetable in northern China, where cooks rely on hardy vegetables that can survive cold winters and a short growing season.

1 pound sirloin or flank steak
3 tablespoons dark soy sauce, divided
1 tablespoon Chinese rice wine or dry sherry
1 teaspoon sesame oil
1 tablespoon cornstarch
8 ounces rice vermicelli noodles
1 bunch leeks
2 tablespoons hoisin sauce
½ teaspoon sugar
½ teaspoon chili sauce
2 garlic cloves, minced
1½ teaspoons cornstarch
2 tablespoons water
1½ cups oil for frying

1. Slice the beef across the grain into thin slices. Add 2 tablespoons dark soy sauce, sherry, sesame oil, and cornstarch, adding the cornstarch last. Marinate the beef for 30 minutes. Soak the rice vermicelli in hot water for 15–20 minutes to soften. Drain thoroughly.
2. Wash the leek bunch, and cut into slices about 1½ inches long. Mix together the hoisin sauce, sugar, chili sauce, and 1 tablespoon dark soy sauce. Set aside.
3. Heat 1½ cups oil to 350°F in a preheated wok. When the oil is hot, add the rice vermicelli. Deep-fry until they puff up and turn crispy. Remove and drain on paper towels.
4. Remove all but 2 tablespoons oil. When oil is hot, add the garlic and stir-fry until aromatic. Add the beef and stir-fry until it changes color and is nearly cooked through. Remove and drain on paper towels.
5. Add more oil, if necessary. Add the leeks to the wok. Stir-fry for about 1 minute. Add the sauce to the middle of the wok. Mix the cornstarch and water and add to the sauce, stirring to thicken. Bring to a boil. Add the beef back into the wok and mix all the ingredients together. Serve over the rice noodles.

Beef with Peppers

1½ pounds beef, such as eye of round
2 tablespoons dark soy sauce
2 tablespoons Chinese rice wine or dry sherry, divided
1 teaspoon sesame oil
1 tablespoon cornstarch
½ red bell pepper
½ green bell pepper
½ cup canned bamboo shoots
¼ cup water
2 tablespoons soy sauce
2 teaspoons sugar
4½ tablespoons oil
2 garlic cloves, chopped
2 slices ginger, chopped

Serves 4–6

Eye of round is a good cut to use in this dish—it is one of the leanest cuts of beef and is also very tender.

1. Cut the beef in thin slices, across the grain. Mix in the dark soy sauce, 1 tablespoon rice wine, sesame oil, and cornstarch, adding the cornstarch last. Marinate the beef for 30 minutes.
2. Remove the seeds from the peppers and cut into thin strips, about 2½ inches in length. Wash the bamboo shoots.
3. Mix together the water, 1 tablespoon rice wine, soy sauce, and sugar.
4. Add 3 tablespoons oil to a preheated wok or skillet. Add the garlic and ginger and stir-fry briefly until aromatic. Add the beef and stir-fry in batches until it changes color. Remove and set aside.
5. Wipe the wok with a paper towel. Add 1½ tablespoons oil. When the oil is hot, add the red and green peppers. Stir-fry briefly and add the bamboo shoots. Add the sauce and bring to a boil. Add the beef. Mix everything through and serve hot.

Why Cut Meat Across the Grain?

The "grains" running across a piece of flank steak are muscle fibers. Since the muscle is the part of the body that does all the work, these fibers are tough. Cutting the meat across—instead of along with—the grain shortens the muscle fibers, giving the meat a more tender texture. This technique is not as important with pork and chicken, as the meat is more tender to begin with.

Beef with Tomatoes

Serves 4–6

Blanching tomatoes makes the skin easy to peel off. Serve this dish with Sweet-and-Sour Celery (page 254) for an interesting combination of flavors.

1 pound beef steak, round or flank
2 tablespoons dark soy sauce
½ teaspoon salt
⅛ teaspoon pepper or to taste
2 teaspoons cornstarch
½ teaspoon baking soda
4 large tomatoes
3–4 tablespoons oil for stir-frying
3 slices ginger, minced
½ cup beef broth
1 tablespoon oyster sauce
1 teaspoon sugar
1 tablespoon cornstarch
4 tablespoons water
¼ teaspoon sesame oil

1. Cut the beef across the grain into slices that are approximately 1½–2 inches long. Add the dark soy sauce, salt, pepper, cornstarch, and baking soda to the beef. Marinate the beef for 20 minutes.
2. Bring a large pot of water to a boil. Blanch the tomatoes. Peel off the skin and cut each into 6 equal pieces. (Be sure to remove the tomatoes from the boiling water before they soften.)
3. Add 2 tablespoons oil to a preheated wok or skillet. Add the beef. Fry until it changes color and it is nearly cooked through, turning it over once. Fry in batches if necessary. Remove the beef from the wok.
4. Wipe the wok if necessary and add 1–2 tablespoons oil. When the oil is hot, add the ginger and stir-fry briefly until aromatic. Add the tomatoes and stir-fry briefly, making sure they don't soften too much.
5. Add the beef broth, oyster sauce, and sugar, and bring to a boil. Add the cornstarch mixed with water to the middle of the wok, stirring to thicken. Add the beef back into the wok. Cover and simmer until everything is cooked through. Drizzle with the sesame oil.

Baking Soda—The Secret Tenderizer

A general rule of thumb is to use ½ teaspoon of baking soda per pound of meat. When cooking with a very tough cut of meat, add the baking soda alone first. Use your fingers to rub it over the meat. Wait 20 minutes and then rinse thoroughly to remove any baking soda flavor before adding the other marinade ingredients.

Beef with Broccoli

¾ pound beef steak, such as inside round
3 teaspoons Chinese rice wine or dry sherry
1½ teaspoons cornstarch
½ teaspoon baking soda
Brown Sauce (page 21)
6–8 broccoli stalks with flowerets
¼ red onion
1½ cups oil for frying
2 garlic cloves, minced

Serves 3–4

Serve this restaurant favorite on a bed of white rice or cooked noodles, accompanied by a few fortune cookies.

1. Cut the beef across the grain into thin strips about 2 inches long. Add the rice wine, cornstarch, and baking soda. Marinate the beef for 1 hour.
2. Blanch the broccoli by plunging into boiling water for about 3 minutes. Drain thoroughly. Separate the flowers and the stalks, and cut the stalks into spears along the diagonal. Chop the red onion.
3. Add 1½ cups oil to a preheated wok or skillet. When oil is hot, velvet the beef by adding it to the hot oil just until it changes color, and quickly removing from the wok. Drain the velveted beef on paper towels.
4. Remove all but 2 tablespoons oil from the wok. Add the garlic and stir-fry briefly until aromatic. Add the broccoli. Stir-fry for a minute and then add the red onion. Stir-fry the broccoli until it turns bright green and the red onion until it is soft and translucent.
5. Give the Brown Sauce a quick stir. Push the vegetables up to the sides and add the sauce into the middle of the wok. Turn up the heat and bring the sauce to a boil, stirring vigorously to thicken. Add the beef back into the wok. Mix everything through and serve hot.

Beef with Snow Peas

Serves 2–4

Feel free to follow the recipe for Mangetout and Bean Sprouts (page 239) in step 5, then add the sauce and beef and mix through.

¾ pound beef flank steak
2 teaspoons soy sauce
1 teaspoon cornstarch
¼ teaspoon baking soda
½ cup snow peas
1 cup mung bean sprouts
1 tablespoon dark soy sauce
1 tablespoon oyster sauce
1 tablespoon Chinese rice wine or dry sherry
1 teaspoon sugar
¼ teaspoon sesame oil
2 tablespoons water
3 tablespoons oil for stir-frying
2 garlic cloves, minced

1. Cut the beef across the grain into thin strips about 2 inches long. Add the soy sauce, cornstarch, and baking soda. Marinate the beef for 30 minutes.
2. Trim the snow peas. Blanch the bean sprouts and snow peas by plunging them briefly into boiling water. Drain well.
3. In a small bowl, combine the dark soy sauce, oyster sauce, rice wine, sugar, sesame oil, and water and set aside.
4. Add 2 tablespoons oil to a preheated wok or skillet. When oil is hot, add the beef and stir-fry until it changes color. Remove from the wok and drain on paper towels.
5. Add another tablespoon of oil to the wok. When oil is hot, add the garlic and stir-fry briefly until aromatic. Add the snow peas and bean sprouts and stir-fry briefly. Add the sauce in the middle of the wok and bring to a boil. Mix with the vegetables. Add the beef. Add 1–2 more tablespoons water if desired. Mix everything together and serve hot.

Beef and Bean Sprouts in Black Bean Sauce

½ pound beef steak
2 teaspoons soy sauce
¼ teaspoon salt
½ teaspoon sugar
1 teaspoon cornstarch
¼ teaspoon baking soda
1 cup mung bean sprouts
1 teaspoon fermented black beans
¼ teaspoon chili paste
½ cup chicken stock or broth
1 tablespoon dark soy sauce
1 teaspoon sugar
1 teaspoon red rice vinegar
3 tablespoons oil for stir-frying
1 garlic clove, minced

Serves 2–4

This dish can also be made with green jalapeno peppers—chop 3 jalapeno peppers, remove the seeds, and stir-fry with the chili paste.

1. Cut the beef across the grain into thin strips about 2 inches long. Add the soy sauce, salt, sugar, cornstarch, and baking soda. Marinate the beef for 30 minutes.
2. Blanch the bean sprouts by plunging very briefly into boiling water. Drain thoroughly. Soak the black beans, mash, and mix with the chili paste.
3. Mix together the chicken broth, dark soy sauce, and sugar.
4. Add 2 tablespoons oil to a preheated wok or skillet. When oil is hot, add the beef and stir-fry until it changes color and is nearly cooked through. Remove from the wok and drain on paper towels.
5. Add 1 tablespoon oil to the wok. When oil is hot, add the garlic and chili paste mixture. Stir-fry briefly until aromatic. Add the bean sprouts. Stir-fry briefly, and then add the red rice vinegar.
6. Add the sauce in the middle of the wok and bring to a boil. Add the beef. Simmer until everything is cooked through.

Do You Need to Buy a Chinese Cleaver?

Strictly speaking, no. Successful stir-frying demands food that is evenly cut, but many types of knives will do the job. Still, a Chinese cleaver has many advantages. The cleaver's wide rectangular shape makes it handy for cutting beef, pounding chicken, smashing garlic, and using its thicker-side blade to separate individual garlic cloves.

Dry Fried Beef

Serves 4

This dish tastes great combined with mustard in a sandwich or smoked in tea leaves and spices, a process described in the Tea Smoked Chicken recipe (page 177).

2 tablespoons soy sauce
1 teaspoon Chinese rice wine or dry sherry
½ teaspoon sugar
½ teaspoon baking soda
1 pound flank steak, shredded
5–6 tablespoons oil for frying

1. Add the soy sauce, rice wine, sugar, and baking soda to the beef. Marinate the beef for 30 minutes.
2. Add 3 tablespoons oil to a preheated wok or skillet. When oil is hot, add half the beef. Lay flat and fry for 2 minutes, then turn over and fry for another 2 minutes. Stir-fry the beef until it turns a dark brown (this will take about 8 minutes). Remove from the wok and drain on paper towels. Repeat with the remainder of the beef.

Beef Satay

Serves 6–8

For an authentic touch, thread the meat onto bamboo skewers that have been soaked in cold water for 30 minutes (to ensure that they don't burn).

½ pound beef sirloin steak
¼ cup dark soy sauce
¼ teaspoon chili paste
1 tablespoon hoisin sauce
1 teaspoon sugar
1 teaspoon orange marmalade
1 clove garlic, minced
1 slice ginger, minced

1. Cut the beef across the grain into very thin strips, about 1 inch long.
2. Combine the remaining ingredients. Marinate the beef in the refrigerator overnight or for at least 2 hours. Drain the beef, reserving the marinade.
3. Thread at least 2 slices of the marinated beef onto each skewer, weaving them in and out like an accordion. Brush with the reserved marinade.
4. Grill the beef on both sides. Serve with Hoisin Satay Sauce (page 23).

Beef Curry

½ pound beef sirloin
2 teaspoons Chinese rice wine or dry sherry
1 teaspoon cornstarch
¼ teaspoon baking soda
2 ounces rice stick noodles
1 tablespoon curry paste
¼ teaspoon turmeric
¼ teaspoon ground cumin
3 tablespoons oil for stir-frying
2 teaspoons minced ginger
1 teaspoon minced garlic
2 tablespoons chopped red onion
1 tablespoon plain yogurt

Serves 2–4

Yogurt helps take the edge off a hot curry—add more than 1 tablespoon, if desired.

1. Cut the beef across the grain into thin strips about 1½ inches in length. Add the rice wine, cornstarch, and baking soda (in that order). Marinate the beef for 1 hour.
2. Soak the rice noodles in hot water for 15 minutes or until they are softened. Drain thoroughly.
3. Mix together the curry paste, turmeric, and ground cumin.
4. Add 2 tablespoons oil to a preheated wok or skillet. When oil is hot, add the ginger and garlic and stir-fry briefly until aromatic. Add the beef. Stir-fry until it changes color and is nearly cooked through. Remove from the wok and drain on paper towels.
5. Add 1 tablespoon oil to the wok. When oil is hot, add the curry paste mixture and stir-fry briefly until it is aromatic. Add the onion and stir-fry until it is soft and translucent. Add the rice stick noodles and mix with the onion. Add 2 tablespoons water if necessary. Add the meat and the yogurt. Mix everything together and cook until the meat is cooked through.

Tangy Turmeric

Indian cooks have been relying on turmeric's distinctive yellow color and strong taste to lend flavor to curries since early times. It took China a bit longer to discover turmeric's possibilities. Today, turmeric is frequently found in Chinese curry recipes—a small amount mixed with curry powder or paste adds a lovely yellowish hue to the dish.

Basic Red-Cooked Beef

Serves 4–6

Don't have any stewing beef? Red cooking is a nice way to add flavor to less popular cuts of meat, such as liver.

6 dried mushrooms
1 large daikon
2 slices ginger
1 cup light soy sauce
4 tablespoons dark soy sauce
4 tablespoons Chinese rice wine or dry sherry
4 teaspoons sugar
4 tablespoons plus 2 teaspoons brown sugar
½ teaspoon five-spice powder
2 tablespoons oil for stir-frying
2 garlic cloves, minced
1½ pounds boneless stewing beef, cut into chunks
2 cups water

1. Soak the dried mushrooms in hot water for at least 20 minutes to soften. Gently squeeze to remove any excess water, and slice. Peel the daikon and cut into ½-inch slices. Peel the ginger, if desired.
2. Combine the light soy sauce, dark soy sauce, rice wine, white sugar, brown sugar, and five-spice powder; set aside.
3. Add oil to a preheated wok or skillet. When oil is hot, add the ginger and garlic and stir-fry briefly until aromatic. Add the beef and cook until browned.
4. Add the sauce and 2 cups water. Bring to a boil, then turn down the heat and simmer. After 1 hour, add the daikon and dried mushrooms. Simmer for 30 minutes, or until the liquid is reduced.

Make Your Own Sauce for Red Cooking

In red cooking, previously browned meat is stewed in a combination of soy sauce and other ingredients. To make your own red cooking sauce, experiment with different combinations of light and dark soy sauce, rice wine, and other liquid ingredients until you find one you like. For extra flavor, add stronger seasonings such as star anise and dried tangerine peel (see Spicy Red-Cooked Beef, page 121, for ideas).

Spicy Red-Cooked Beef

6 dried mushrooms
1 large daikon
2–3 tablespoons oil for stir-frying
2 slices ginger
3 small garlic cloves, minced
2 pounds boneless stewing beef, cut into chunks
3 cups water
½ cup dark soy sauce
¼ cup light soy sauce
1 piece dried tangerine peel, 2–3 inches wide
1 star anise
1 piece (about 1 ounce) yellow rock sugar

Serves 4–6

Star anise is a star-shaped seed pod with a strong flavor reminiscent of licorice, used to flavor meat dishes.

1. Soak the dried mushrooms in hot water for at least 20 minutes to soften. Gently squeeze to remove any excess water and slice. Peel the daikon and cut into ½-inch slices. Peel the ginger if desired.
2. Add oil to a preheated wok or skillet. When oil is hot, add the ginger and garlic and stir-fry briefly until aromatic. Add the beef and cook until browned.
3. Add the water, ¼ cup of dark soy sauce, 2 tablespoons of light soy sauce, and the tangerine peel and star anise, and bring to a boil. Reduce the heat and simmer for 45 minutes. Add the remaining dark and light soy sauce, the rock sugar, the daikon, and the dried mushrooms. Simmer for another 45 minutes, or until liquid is reduced.

Shopping for a Chinese Cleaver

When choosing a Chinese cleaver, look for one made of stainless steel or a combination of stainless and carbon steel, with a handle that attaches firmly to the blade. Try out several to find one that you're comfortable holding.

Beef with Red Onions

Serves 4–6

Red onions add a distinctive flavor to this simple dish. Serve on a bed of steamed rice.

1 pound beef steak, flank or sirloin, shredded
1 tablespoon soy sauce
½ teaspoon baking soda
1 tablespoon vegetable or peanut oil
2 green onions
3 tablespoons oil for stir-frying
1 clove garlic, minced
1 teaspoon minced ginger
1 large red onion, chopped
2 tablespoons dark soy sauce
2 teaspoons sugar
1 tablespoon Chinese rice wine or dry sherry
¼ teaspoon chili paste with garlic

1. With the beef, mix in the soy sauce and baking soda in that order, using your fingers to mix in the baking soda. Marinate the beef for 30 minutes. Add 1 tablespoon of oil and marinate the beef for another 30 minutes.
2. Cut the green onions into 1½-inch slices along the diagonal.
3. Add 2 tablespoons oil to a preheated wok or skillet. When oil is hot, add the beef. Stir-fry until it changes color and is nearly cooked through. Remove from the wok and drain on paper towels.
4. Add 1 tablespoon oil to the wok. When oil is hot, add the garlic and ginger and stir-fry briefly until aromatic. Add the red onion, and stir-fry until soft and translucent. Stir in the dark soy sauce, sugar, rice wine, and chili paste with garlic. Add the beef. Stir in the green onions. Mix everything together and cook for a few more minutes on medium heat, making sure the beef is cooked through, and serve hot.

Mu Shu Beef

½ pound beef
½ cup water
1 tablespoon dark soy sauce
1 tablespoon plus 1 teaspoon hoisin sauce
1 teaspoon sugar
1 teaspoon oyster sauce
¼ teaspoon sesame oil
2 eggs, lightly beaten
¼ teaspoon salt
3–4 tablespoons oil for stir-frying
1 slice ginger, minced
½ cup mung bean sprouts, rinsed and drained

Serves 2–3

For a more flavorful dish, try marinating the beef in oyster sauce, sugar, and cornstarch, adding the cornstarch last.

1. Cut the beef into thin slices. Marinate if desired.
2. Combine the water, dark soy sauce, hoisin sauce, sugar, oyster sauce, and sesame oil, and set aside.
3. Mix the eggs with ¼ teaspoon salt. Add 1 tablespoon oil to a preheated wok or skillet. When oil is hot, scramble the eggs and remove from the wok.
4. Add 2 more tablespoons oil. When oil is hot, add the beef and stir-fry until it changes color and is nearly cooked through. Remove from the wok and set aside.
5. Add more oil if necessary. Add the ginger and stir-fry briefly until aromatic. Add the bean sprouts. Add the sauce and bring to a boil. Add the beef and the scrambled egg. Mix everything together and serve hot.

Carrot Flowers

Although the Chinese rarely eat raw vegetables, they are a popular ingredient for garnishes. To make a quick and easy garnish, take a 3-inch-long slice of carrot and cut 4 V-shaped notches at 90° intervals. To finish, slice the carrot into thin "flowers."

Peppery Beef

Serves 2–4

For a less biting dish, forego the chili paste and substitute black pepper for the Szechwan peppercorn.

1 tablespoon soy sauce
½ teaspoon Chinese rice wine or dry sherry
1¼ teaspoons sugar, divided
¼ teaspoon baking soda
½ pound flank steak, shredded
½ green bell pepper
½ red bell pepper
½ cup chicken stock
2 tablespoons dark soy sauce
3 tablespoons oil for stir-frying
1 clove garlic, minced
1 teaspoon minced ginger
¼ teaspoon chili paste
¼ teaspoon sesame oil
⅛ teaspoon Szechwan peppercorns, roasted and ground

1. Add the soy sauce, rice wine, ¼ teaspoon sugar, and baking soda to the beef. Marinate the beef for 30 minutes.
2. Remove the seeds from the peppers and cut into thin slices. Combine the chicken stock, dark soy sauce, and 1 teaspoon sugar and set aside.
3. Add 2 tablespoons oil to a preheated wok or skillet. When oil is hot, add the beef and stir-fry until it changes color and is nearly cooked through. Remove from the wok and drain on paper towels.
4. Add 1 tablespoon oil if necessary. Add the garlic, ginger, and chili paste. Stir-fry briefly until aromatic. Add the green peppers, stir-fry briefly, and add the red peppers. Stir-fry the peppers until they have a bright color and are tender.
5. Add the sauce to the middle of the wok and bring to a boil. Stir in the sesame oil. Add the beef. Sprinkle the Szechwan peppercorns over. Mix everything through and serve hot.

Stir-fried Orange Beef

2 teaspoons Chinese rice wine or dry sherry, divided
½ teaspoon baking soda
1 pound sirloin or flank steak, shredded
⅓ cup dried orange peel
1 green onion
2 tablespoons soy sauce
1 teaspoon sugar
¼ teaspoon chili paste
3 tablespoons oil for stir-frying
2 slices ginger, minced
1 clove garlic, minced

Serves 4–6

Leftovers can be used to make sandwiches—purée the beef with a bit of water and spread on buttered bread.

1. Add 1 teaspoon rice wine and baking soda, using your fingers to add the baking soda, to the beef. Marinate the beef for 30 minutes.
2. Cut the dried orange peel into thin slices. Cut the green onion into 1½-inch slices on the diagonal.
3. Combine the soy sauce, sugar, chili paste, and 1 teaspoon rice wine. Set aside.
4. Add 2 tablespoons oil to a preheated wok or skillet. When oil is hot, add the beef. Stir-fry until it is nearly cooked through. Remove from the wok and drain on paper towels.
5. Add 1 tablespoon oil. Add the ginger, garlic, green onion, and dried orange peel. Stir-fry until the orange peel is aromatic. Add the sauce in the middle and bring to a boil. Add the beef back in. Mix everything and stir-fry until the beef is cooked through, and serve hot.

Orange Peel Cold Cure

Have a cold? Why not try an orange peel cure? For centuries, Chinese medical practitioners have recommended dried orange peel to treat everything from colds to insomnia. Whatever their medicinal value, there is no doubt that the peel contains more vitamin C than any other part of the orange.

Spicy Steamed Beef

Serves 4–6

This dish tastes good served hot or cold. For a tasty appetizer, deep-fry the steamed beef twice in a flour, cornstarch, and egg batter. See Spicy Orange Beef (page 128) for an example of this technique.

1 pound sirloin or flank steak
1 tablespoon soy sauce
½ teaspoon baking soda
2 tablespoons dark soy sauce
½ teaspoon sugar
¼ teaspoon dried crushed chili flakes
1 tablespoon dried orange peel
1 tablespoon Toasted Szechwan Peppercorns (see sidebar on page 93)

1. Cut the beef across the grain into thin slices about 1½ inches long. Add the soy sauce and baking soda, using your fingers to mix it in the baking soda. Marinate the beef for 30 minutes.
2. Combine the dark soy sauce, sugar, and crushed chili flakes. Cut the dried orange peel into thin slices.
3. Prepare the wok for steaming. Place the beef on a heatproof plate on a bamboo steamer. Rub the roasted peppercorn mixture over the beef. Brush on half of the sauce. Place the orange peel slices around the beef.
4. Steam the beef for 20 minutes or until it is cooked through. Brush on the remainder of the sauce during steaming.

Make Your Own Orange Peel

To make dried orange peel, remove the skin from an orange. Use a paring knife to remove the white pith inside. Leave the peel to dry in the sun or dry quickly by placing in a previously warmed oven. Remove the peel before it hardens.

Beef with String Beans

1 pound flank or sirloin steak
1 tablespoon soy sauce
1 green onion, cut into 1-inch pieces
1 tablespoon cornstarch
1 cup string beans
¼ cup chicken stock or broth
1 tablespoon Chinese rice wine or dry sherry
1 teaspoon sugar
¼ teaspoon salt
3 tablespoons oil for stir-frying
1 clove garlic, minced
¼ teaspoon chili paste with garlic
1 teaspoon cornstarch
4 teaspoons water

Serves 4–6

When choosing string beans, look for younger ones with a firm texture and bright color.

1. Cut the beef across the grain into thin slices, about 1½ inches long. Add the soy sauce, green onion, and cornstarch, using your fingers to mix in the cornstarch. Marinate the beef for 30 minutes.
2. Trim the string beans and parboil by plunging briefly into boiling water. Drain thoroughly and cut lengthwise into thin slices.
3. Combine the chicken broth, rice wine, sugar, and salt. Set aside.
4. Add 2 tablespoons oil to a preheated wok or skillet. When oil is hot, add the beef. Stir-fry until it changes color and is nearly cooked. Remove and set aside.
5. Add 1 tablespoon oil. When oil is hot, add the garlic and the chili paste with garlic. Stir-fry briefly until aromatic. Add the string beans. Stir-fry for 3–4 minutes. Push the string beans up to the side of the wok and add the sauce in the middle. Bring to a boil. Mix the cornstarch and water and add to the sauce, stirring quickly to thicken. Add the beef. Mix everything through and cook on medium heat for a few more minutes until the beef is cooked. Serve hot.

Spicy Orange Beef

Serves 4–6

This recipe shows fiery Szechwan cuisine at its finest—for a less spicy dish, leave out the dried chili.

1 pound flank steak
4–6 cups oil for frying
2 garlic cloves, minced
3 slices ginger, minced
1 dried chili
4 tablespoons soy sauce
2 teaspoons Chinese rice wine or dry sherry
2 teaspoons sugar
½ teaspoon chili paste
2 medium eggs
3 tablespoons flour
2 tablespoons cornstarch
1 teaspoon dried orange peel or 1 small piece dried tangerine peel

1. Cut the beef across the grain into thin slices about 2 inches in length. Remove the seeds from the chili and chop.
2. Combine the soy sauce, rice wine, sugar, and chili paste, and set aside.
3. Beat the eggs and mix with the flour and cornstarch into a batter. Coat the beef slices with the batter, using your fingers.
4. Heat 4–5 cups of oil to 350°F. When oil is hot, add a few pieces of beef into the hot oil and deep-fry until they turn light brown. Remove with a slotted spoon and drain on paper towels. Continue with the rest of the beef.
5. Raise the oil temperature to 400°F. Deep-fry the beef pieces a second time, until they turn brown and crispy. Remove and drain.
6. Remove all but 2 tablespoons of oil from the wok or add 2 tablespoons oil to a second wok or skillet. Add the garlic, ginger, chili, and orange peel. Stir-fry until aromatic. Add the sauce and bring to a boil. Add the beef. Mix everything through and serve hot.

Ginger Beef

¾ pound flank or sirloin steak
8 tablespoons soy sauce, divided
4 teaspoons Chinese rice wine or dry sherry, divided
5½ teaspoons sugar, divided
2 teaspoons freshly squeezed ginger juice, divided
2 teaspoons sesame oil
Up to ¼ teaspoon chili flakes
½ cup water
3 tablespoons flour
2 tablespoons cornstarch
2 medium eggs
4–6 cups oil for frying
1 clove garlic, minced
1 slice ginger, minced
1 teaspoon cornstarch mixed with 4 teaspoons water

Serves 4–6

Ginger juice is easy to make—just grate the ginger and squeeze out the fresh juice.

1. Cut the beef along the grain into matchstick strips. Add 2 tablespoons soy sauce, 1 teaspoon rice wine, ½ teaspoon sugar, and 1 teaspoon ginger juice to the beef. Marinate for 30 minutes.
2. Combine 6 tablespoons soy sauce, 3 teaspoons rice wine, 5 teaspoons sugar, 1 teaspoon ginger juice, sesame oil, chili flakes, and water. Set aside.
3. Combine the flour, cornstarch, and eggs into a batter. Coat the beef in the batter, using your fingers to spread it. Add 4–5 cups oil to the wok and heat to 350°F. When oil is ready, deep-fry the beef in batches, turning occasionally, until they turn golden. Remove and drain on paper towels.
4. Raise the oil temperature to 400°F. Deep-fry the beef a second time, until it turns brown and crispy. Drain on paper towels.
5. Remove all but 2 tablespoons of oil from the wok, or add 2 tablespoons oil to a second wok or skillet. When oil is hot, add the garlic and ginger and stir-fry briefly until aromatic.
6. Add the sauce and bring to a boil. Add the cornstarch-and-water mixture, stirring quickly to thicken. Add the meat. Mix everything together and serve hot.

Dry Ginger Beef

Serves 2

For an added touch, top with a few slices of preserved red ginger before serving.

1 tablespoon soy sauce
½ teaspoon Chinese rice wine or dry sherry
¼ teaspoon sugar
¼ teaspoon baking soda
½ pound flank steak, shredded
½ red bell pepper
2 tablespoons dark soy sauce
1 tablespoon plus 1 teaspoon oyster sauce
1½ teaspoons sugar
½ cup water
4–5 tablespoons oil for frying
2 slices ginger, minced
½ cup mushrooms, sliced

1. Add the soy sauce, rice wine, sugar, and baking soda to the beef. Marinate the beef for 30 minutes.
2. Wash the red pepper, remove the seeds, and cut into thin slices.
3. Combine the dark soy sauce, oyster sauce, sugar, and water and set aside.
4. Add 3 tablespoons oil to a preheated wok or skillet. When oil is hot, add the beef. Lay flat and fry for 2 minutes, then turn over and fry for another 2 minutes. Stir-fry the beef until it turns a dark brown (this will take about 8 minutes). Remove from the wok and drain on paper towels.
5. Add 1–2 tablespoons oil to the wok. When oil is hot, add the ginger and stir-fry briefly until aromatic. Add the mushrooms and red pepper and stir-fry until tender. Add the sauce to the middle of the wok and bring to a boil. Add the beef. Mix everything through and serve hot.

Ginger Beef Origins

According to rumor, Ginger Beef originated in Alberta, the beef capital of Canada. However, it is based on an authentic Chinese dish. Authentic ginger beef is much dryer, and lacks the sweet sauce found in the Alberta version. It is frequently made with preserved red ginger.

Oriental Meatballs

½ pound ground beef
1 tablespoon dark soy sauce
1 teaspoon Chinese rice wine or dry sherry
1 teaspoon oyster sauce
½ teaspoon sugar
¼ teaspoon sesame oil

1. In a medium-sized bowl, mix the beef with the remaining 5 ingredients. Prepare the wok for steaming.
2. Form the beef into 6 medium-sized meatballs. Place in a heatproof bowl on a bamboo steamer in the wok and steam, covered, for about 15 minutes or until the meatballs are cooked through.

Yields 6 meatballs

Need a quick and easy appetizer recipe? Serve guests these tasty meatballs with Potsticker Dipping Sauce (page 30).

Beef Toast

Spicy Orange Beef (page 128)
1 cup plus 3 teaspoons water
4–6 slices bread
3 cups oil for deep-frying

1. Cool Spicy Orange Beef. Cut into thin pieces. Purée in a blender or food processor with 3 teaspoons water.
2. Cut each slice of bread into 4 equal squares. Dip into the 1 cup of water briefly and squeeze to soak out excess water. Spread the beef purée onto each square.
3. Heat oil to 375°F. When oil is ready, add 2–3 squares into the oil. Cook the top side for about 1 minute. Turn over and briefly cook the other side, until the squares turn golden brown. Drain on paper towels.

Serves 4

Instead of a wok or heavy skillet, smaller items like Beef Toast can be deep-fried in a medium-sized saucepan with a heavy bottom.

Beef and Lotus Root with Oyster Sauce

Serves 2

In Buddhist religion the beautiful white lotus flower is a symbol of purity. Lotus root can be boiled, stir-fried, or deep-fried. Always peel before using.

1 piece lotus root (about 2–3 inches)
½ pound beef
6 teaspoons oyster sauce, divided
2 teaspoons cornstarch
¼ cup chicken broth
1 teaspoon sugar
½ teaspoon sesame oil
3 tablespoons oil for stir-frying
1 slice ginger

1. Peel the lotus root. Cut into 6 thin rounds, about ¼ inch wide. Blanch the lotus root rounds briefly in boiling water.
2. Cut the beef in thin slices. Marinate in 2 teaspoons oyster sauce and the cornstarch for 30 minutes.
3. Combine 4 teaspoons oyster sauce, chicken broth, sugar, and sesame oil. Set aside.
4. Add 2 tablespoons oil to a preheated wok or skillet. When oil is hot, add the beef. Stir-fry until it changes color and is nearly cooked through. Remove and drain on paper towels.
5. Add 1 tablespoon oil. When oil is hot, add the ginger. Stir-fry briefly until aromatic. Add the lotus root. Stir-fry for 1–2 minutes. Add the sauce in the middle of the wok and bring to a boil. Add the beef. Cook for 1–2 more minutes, and serve hot.

Chapter 7

Pork Entrées

Ants Climbing a Tree

Serves 4

For easier handling of the noodles, don't remove the string wrapping until the noodles have been soaked and drained.

4 ounces rice vermicelli noodles
4 Chinese dried mushrooms
1 bunch spinach leaves
3 tablespoons oil for stir-frying
2 slices ginger, finely chopped
½ pound ground pork
1 tablespoon soy sauce
1 tablespoon Chinese rice wine or dry sherry
½ teaspoon sesame oil, divided
¼ teaspoon sugar
¼ teaspoon salt
1 tablespoon chili sauce
¼ cup chicken broth or reserved mushroom liquid
2 green onions, chopped

1. Soak the noodles in hot water for 5 minutes or until they are softened. Cut the noodles into 2-inch lengths. Soak the dried mushrooms in hot water for at least 20 minutes to soften. Reserve the soaking liquid if desired. Remove the stems from the mushrooms and cut into thin slices.
2. Wash the spinach leaves. Blanch the spinach in boiling water briefly, just until the leaves begin to wilt. Drain well and chop finely.
3. Add 2 tablespoons oil to a preheated wok or skillet. When oil is hot, add the ginger and stir-fry briefly until aromatic. Add the ground pork. Mix in the soy sauce, rice wine, and ¼ teaspoon sesame oil. Stir-fry the ground pork until it loses its pink color. Remove from the wok and set aside.
4. Wipe the wok clean with a paper towel and add 1 tablespoon oil. When the oil is hot, add the spinach. Add the sugar and salt and stir-fry briefly, for less than a minute. Add the mushrooms. Push the spinach up to the sides of the wok and add the pork. Stir in the chili sauce, and then the noodles. Add the chicken broth or reserved mushroom liquid and continue to cook until most of the liquid is absorbed. Stir in the green onions. Drizzle with ¼ teaspoon sesame oil and serve.

Lion's Head Meatball Stew

1 pound ground pork
1 tablespoon soy sauce
1 teaspoon sugar
½ teaspoon sesame oil
2 tablespoons Chinese rice wine or dry sherry, divided
2 bunches spinach leaves
3 tablespoons oil for stir-frying
1 cup chicken broth or stock
¼ teaspoon salt
White pepper to taste

Serves 2–4

Lion's Head Meatballs can be made in advance and frozen. Bring the meatballs back to room temperature before reheating.

1. Place the pork in a medium-sized bowl. Mix in the soy sauce, sugar, sesame oil, and 1 tablespoon rice wine. Marinate the pork for 20 minutes.
2. Wash the spinach leaves. Blanch the spinach in boiling water briefly, just until the leaves begin to wilt. Drain thoroughly.
3. Form the marinated pork into 4 large meatballs, each roughly the size of a tennis ball. (Alternately, you can make the meatballs the size of golf balls, which will give you more meatballs.)
4. Add oil to a preheated wok or skillet. Pan-fry the meatballs on medium heat for 4–5 minutes on each side, until they brown. (The meatballs will not be cooked through.) Remove and drain on paper towels.
5. While the meatballs are frying, preheat the oven to 375°F.
6. Bring the chicken broth or stock to a boil. Stir in the salt, white pepper, and 1 tablespoon rice wine. Remove from the heat.
7. Line the bottom of a casserole dish with the spinach leaves. Add the meatballs and pour the chicken stock mixture over. Bake at 375°F for 30 minutes, or until the meatballs are cooked through.

Intriguing Recipe Names

Like most cooking styles, Chinese cuisine has its share of intriguing recipe names. According to legend, Mapo Dofu, or "Pockmarked Tofu" (page 198), is named in honor of the elderly woman rumored to have invented the dish. In Ants Climbing a Tree, the tiny flecks of marinated pork are meant to resemble ants, while the fried noodles are the bark of the tree. This dish is also known as Ants Creeping up a Tree and Ants Climbing a Log.

Honey Roasted Pork

Serves 4–6

Roasted pork makes a tasty addition to stir-fries and noodle dishes. For a quick and easy lunch, try roast pork sandwiches.

1½ pound spareribs
2 tablespoons honey
4 tablespoons hoisin sauce
4 tablespoons dark soy sauce
2 tablespoons Chinese rice wine or dry sherry

1. Separate the pork into pieces about 2 by 6 inches. Combine the honey, hoisin sauce, dark soy sauce, and rice wine. Add to the pork ribs and marinate in the refrigerator for at least 2 hours, preferably overnight.
2. Preheat oven to 375°F.
3. Drain the pork, reserving the marinade. Fill a shallow pan with boiling water and place at the bottom of the oven. Place the pork on a roasting rack, cover with half the reserved marinade and roast the pork for 15 minutes. Brush the pork with the remaining marinade and roast for another 15 minutes, or until the pork turns golden brown and is cooked. Cool.

Curry Spareribs

Serves 2–4

Commonly associated with Southeast Asian cooking, spicy curry is also featured in southern Chinese dishes.

1 pound pork ribs
4 tablespoons soy sauce
2 tablespoons Chinese rice wine or dry sherry
2 teaspoons sugar
2 teaspoons curry paste
1 teaspoon turmeric
1 large clove garlic, chopped
2–4 cups oil for deep-frying

1. Cut the ribs into bite-sized pieces. Add the soy sauce, rice wine, sugar, curry paste, turmeric, and chopped garlic. Marinate the ribs for 30 minutes.
2. Heat the oil in the wok to 350°F. When oil is hot, deep-fry the spareribs until they turn a deep brown and rise to the surface.

Braised Spareribs in Black Bean Sauce

1–1½ pounds spareribs
1 tablespoon fermented black beans
1 garlic clove, minced
2 green onions
3 tablespoons hoisin sauce
3 tablespoons soy sauce
1½ teaspoons sugar
½ cup water
2 tablespoons oil for stir-frying

Serves 2–4

Savory fermented black beans nicely complement the delicate sweet flavor of pork in this recipe.

1. Wash the spareribs, pat dry, and separate. Mash the black beans with the back edge of a knife or cleaver. Mix with the garlic and a bit of water. Cut the green onions into 1-inch pieces.
2. Combine the hoisin sauce, soy sauce, sugar, and water.
3. Add oil to a preheated wok or skillet. Stir-fry the pork for 2–3 minutes. Add the fermented bean and garlic mixture and stir-fry until aromatic.
4. Add the sauce and bring to a boil. Turn down the heat, cover, and simmer for 20–25 minutes, until the spareribs are cooked. Stir in the green onions or serve as a garnish.

Fermented Black Beans

These are not the dried black beans that enliven many Mexican dishes. Instead, fermented black beans (also called salted black beans) are made with black soybeans that have been fermented in salt, garlic, and a number of spices. Fermented black beans are sold in cans and plastic bags in Asian markets. In a pinch, black bean sauce can be used as a substitute, but the dish won't have the same flavor.

Sweet-and-Sour Spareribs

Serves 2–4

This recipe can easily be doubled to serve as a main dish for 4 to 6 people.

1½ pounds spareribs
4 teaspoons sugar, divided
2 tablespoons plus 1 teaspoon rice vinegar, divided
2 tablespoons ketchup
2 tablespoons Worcestershire sauce
4 tablespoons soy sauce
2 tablespoons oil for stir-frying

1. Wash spareribs and pat dry. Separate into serving-sized pieces. Marinate the ribs in 1 teaspoon sugar and 1 teaspoon rice vinegar for 30 minutes.
2. Mix together 3 teaspoons sugar, 2 tablespoons rice vinegar, ketchup, Worcestershire sauce, and soy sauce, and set aside.
3. Add oil to a preheated wok or skillet. When oil is hot, add the ribs and stir-fry for about 5 minutes, until they brown.
4. Add the sauce, turn down the heat, cover, and simmer the ribs for 45 minutes to 1 hour.

Five-Spice Spareribs

Serves 2–4

These spicy ribs nicely complement a less highly seasoned dish such as Three Vegetable Stir-fry (page 252).

1½ pounds spareribs
2 garlic cloves, smashed and peeled
3 tablespoons soy sauce
1 teaspoon sesame oil
1 tablespoon Chinese rice wine or dry sherry
2 teaspoons brown sugar
1 teaspoon Hot Chili Oil (page 25)
½ teaspoon Szechwan Salt and Pepper Mix (page 22)
½ teaspoon five-spice powder, or to taste
2 tablespoons water

1. Mix together all the ingredients except for the spareribs. Marinate the spareribs for 30 minutes. Reserve the marinade.
2. Preheat oven to 350°F. Brush half of the reserved marinade on the spareribs and roast for 15 minutes. Brush on the rest of marinade and roast the spareribs for another 15 minutes or until they are cooked.

Deep-fried Garlic Spareribs

2 pounds spareribs
1 cup brown sugar
1 cup water
3 tablespoons soy sauce
1 tablespoon dry mustard
3 garlic cloves, minced
3 eggs
1 cup flour
4–6 cups oil for deep-frying

Serves 4–6

Deep-frying the spareribs twice gives them a crispy coating and seals in the juicy flavors.

1. Cut the ribs into bite-sized pieces.
2. Combine the brown sugar, water, soy sauce, mustard, and garlic cloves. Add to the ribs and marinate for 1 hour.
3. Lightly beat the eggs and add to the flour to make a batter, adding water or more flour as needed. Use a wooden spoon to test the batter—it should drop slowly and be able to coat the back of the spoon.
4. Add the oil to a wok and heat to 350°F. While waiting for the oil to heat, coat the ribs in the batter. When oil is hot, carefully add the spareribs into the wok. Deep-fry in batches for about 5 minutes. Remove and drain on paper towels.
5. Raise the oil temperature to 400°F. Deep-fry the ribs briefly a second time, until they turn brown. Remove and drain.

Recycled Deep-frying Oil

Start deep-frying regularly, and you'll quickly find your stock of vegetable oil running low. Fortunately, deep-frying oil can be reused up to 5 times. To save the oil, simply cool and store in a sealed container. Discard the oil when it starts to smell bad, changes color, or smokes at lower temperatures.

Pork with Young Bamboo Shoots

Serves 2–4

Due to their strong flavor, young bamboo shoots are considered to be a great delicacy in China.

½ pound pork tenderloin
3 teaspoons Chinese rice wine or dry sherry, divided
½ teaspoon sugar
1½ teaspoons cornstarch
8 ounces canned or fresh peeled young bamboo shoots
½ cup chicken stock or broth
1 teaspoon rice vinegar
3 tablespoons oil for stir-frying

1. Cut the pork into thin slices. Add 2 teaspoons of the rice wine, the sugar, and the cornstarch. Marinate the pork for 30 minutes.
2. Blanch the bamboo shoots in boiling water for at least 5 minutes. Drain thoroughly and chop.
3. Combine the chicken stock, 1 teaspoon rice wine, and the rice vinegar, and set aside.
4. Add 2 tablespoons oil to a preheated wok or skillet. When oil is hot, add the pork and stir-fry until it changes color and is nearly cooked. Remove and drain on paper towels.
5. Add 1 tablespoon oil to the wok. Add the bamboo shoots and stir-fry. Add the sauce in the middle of the wok and bring to a boil. Add the pork. Turn down the heat and simmer for 5 minutes. Serve hot.

Why Waste a Wok?

Don't hide your wok in the cupboard when you're not cooking Chinese food. A wok's unusual shape makes it useful for everything from mixing batter to tossing a salad. And nothing beats a wok for turning out scrambled eggs and omelets that don't stick to the bottom of the pan.

Basic Sweet-and-Sour Pork

1 pound pork loin, center cut, bone in
1 tablespoon soy sauce
1 tablespoon cornstarch
1 teaspoon baking soda
2/3 cup canned pineapple chunks
1/2 cup reserved pineapple juice
1/2 red bell pepper
1/2 green bell pepper
1/4 pound baby carrots
1/3 cup rice vinegar
1/2 cup brown sugar
1 tablespoon Worcestershire sauce
1/4 cup ketchup
1/4 cup water
3 tablespoons oil for stir-frying
2 teaspoons cornstarch mixed with 4 teaspoons water

Serves 2–4

For extra flavor, use 2 tablespoons black rice vinegar and 1/4 cup white rice vinegar when making the sauce.

1. Cut away the bone from the pork and remove any fat. Cut the pork into cubes. Add the soy sauce, cornstarch, and baking soda to the pork. Marinate the pork in the refrigerator for 1½ hours.
2. Open a can of pineapple chunks and remove 2/3 cup pineapple and 1/2 cup juice. Blanch the peppers and carrots by plunging briefly into boiling water. Remove the seeds from the green and red peppers, and cut into cubes. Cut the carrots in half.
3. Bring the rice vinegar, brown sugar, Worcestershire sauce, ketchup, reserved pineapple juice, and water to a boil. Turn down the heat to low and keep warm.
4. Add 2 tablespoons oil to a preheated wok or skillet. When oil is hot, add the pork. Stir-fry until it changes color and is nearly cooked through. Remove from the wok and drain on paper towels.
5. Add 1 tablespoon oil. When oil is hot, add the carrots. Stir-fry for a minute and add the red and green peppers.
6. Bring the sauce back up to a boil. Add the cornstarch-and-water mixture, stirring vigorously to thicken. Mix the pineapple in with the sauce. Push the vegetables up to the sides of the wok and add the sauce in the middle. Add the pork back into the wok. Mix through and serve hot.

Deep-fried Sweet-and-Sour Pork

Serves 2–4

This is one of the most popular dishes served at Chinese restaurants. The sweet-and-sour sauce works well with pork, spareribs, and chicken.

1 pound pork loin, center cut, deboned and cubed
1 tablespoon soy sauce
3 tablespoons cornstarch, divided
1 teaspoon baking soda
½ red bell pepper
½ green bell pepper
¼ pound baby carrots
3 tablespoons flour
2 medium eggs
⅓ cup rice vinegar
½ cup brown sugar
1 tablespoon Worcestershire sauce
¼ cup ketchup
½ cup reserved pineapple juice
¼ cup water
2 teaspoons cornstarch mixed with 4 teaspoons water
4–6 cups oil for frying
⅔ cup canned pineapple chunks

1. Take the pork cubes and add the soy sauce, 1 tablespoon cornstarch, and baking soda. Marinate in the refrigerator for 1½ hours.
2. Blanch the peppers and carrots in boiling water. Deseed and cube the green and red pepper. Cut the carrots in half.
3. Combine the flour, cornstarch, and eggs into a batter. Coat the pork in the batter. Add 4–5 cups oil to the wok and heat to at least 350°F. Deep-fry the pork cubes in batches, turning occasionally, until they turn golden. Remove and drain on paper towels.
4. Increase the oil temperature to 400°F. While waiting for the oil to heat, bring the rice vinegar, brown sugar, Worcestershire sauce, ketchup, reserved pineapple juice, and water to boil in a small saucepan. Turn the heat down to low and keep the sauce warm.
5. When the oil is ready, add the pork cubes. Deep-fry a second time until they turn brown and crispy. Remove and drain on paper towels.
6. Remove all but 2 tablespoons oil from the wok. When oil is hot, add the carrots. Stir-fry for a minute and add the red and green peppers.
7. Bring the sauce back up to a boil. Add the cornstarch-and-water mixture, stirring vigorously to thicken. Add the pineapple.
8. Push the vegetables up to the sides of the wok and add the sauce in the middle. Add the pork back into the wok. Mix through and serve hot.

Twice Cooked Pork

½ pound boneless pork
½ red bell pepper
½ green bell pepper
1 clove garlic, chopped
2 slices ginger, chopped
3 tablespoons oil for stir-frying
1 teaspoon hot bean paste
2 tablespoons dark soy sauce
1 teaspoon sugar

1. Boil the pork in water for 20–25 minutes. Remove and cool. Cut into thin strips.
2. Blanch the peppers by plunging briefly into boiling water. Cut into thin slices.
3. Add 3 tablespoons oil to a preheated wok or skillet. When oil is hot, add the ginger, garlic, and hot bean paste with garlic. Stir-fry briefly until the garlic and ginger are aromatic. Add the peppers and stir-fry. Mix in the dark soy sauce and sugar. Add the pork. Combine all the ingredients thoroughly and stir-fry for about 1 more minute. Serve hot.

Serves 2–4

Pork is cooked twice in this simple but popular Szechwan dish. Serve on a bed of steamed rice or noodles.

Pork—Not the "Other White Meat"

Pork may be the "other white meat" in the West, but in China the words pork and meat are virtually synonymous. When it comes to beef, cows and oxen have traditionally been valued more as work animals than as the main source of protein at the dinner table. By contrast, economical pigs are cheaper to feed, requiring less grazing space. While beef is now widely enjoyed in northern China, it is still not uncommon for southern Chinese families to rely primarily on pork as their main source of meat.

Pork in Plum Sauce

Serves 4

For best results, make the Plum Sauce (page 21) ahead of time so that the flavors have a chance to blend. Serve with steamed rice.

1 pound boneless pork loin chops
1 tablespoon soy sauce
1 tablespoon cornstarch
1 teaspoon baking soda
2 carrots
2 slices ginger
½ cup Plum Sauce (page 19)
3 tablespoons oil for stir-frying
2 green onions, thinly sliced on the diagonal

1. Cut the pork into cubes. Add the soy sauce, cornstarch, and baking soda. Marinate the pork in the refrigerator for 90 minutes.
2. Peel the carrots and cut into slices about ½ inch thick. Blanch by plunging into boiling water and draining.
3. Add 2 tablespoons oil to a preheated wok or skillet. When oil is hot, add the pork. Stir-fry until it changes color and is nearly cooked through. Remove from the wok and drain on paper towels.
4. Add 1 tablespoon oil. When oil is hot, add the ginger slices and stir-fry briefly until aromatic. Add the carrots and stir-fry for about 1 minute. Add the Plum Sauce and bring to a boil.
5. Add the pork. Stir in the green onions. Mix everything through and serve hot.

Eastern and Northern China

The cuisine of eastern China features red-cooked dishes—stews that have been slowly cooked in soy sauce and seasonings. And northern China is famous for noodle-based dishes and festive specialties such as Mu Shu Pork and Peking Duck with pancakes. The influence of the Mongol warriors can be seen in dishes such as Mongolian Beef.

Pork in Bean Sauce

1 pound pork tenderloin chops, boneless
1 tablespoon oyster sauce
½ teaspoon sugar
1½ teaspoons cornstarch
2 tablespoons black bean sauce
2 tablespoons dark soy sauce
2 teaspoons Chinese rice wine or dry sherry
2 teaspoons sugar
¼ teaspoon salt
¼ cup water
¼ teaspoon sesame oil
2 tablespoons oil for stir-frying
¼ teaspoon chili paste

Serves 4

Serve with Glazed Carrots (page 236) for a nutritious meal with an interesting combination of flavors.

1. Cut the pork into thin strips. Add the oyster sauce, sugar, and cornstarch, adding the cornstarch last. Marinate the pork for 30 minutes.
2. Combine the black bean sauce, dark soy sauce, rice wine, sugar, salt, water, and sesame oil, and set aside.
3. Add oil to a preheated wok or skillet. When oil is hot, add the chili paste and stir-fry briefly until aromatic. Add the pork. Stir-fry until it changes color and is nearly cooked through.
4. Push the pork up to the side of the wok and add the sauce in the middle. Bring to a boil. Mix the sauce with the pork. Cover and simmer for a few minutes until the pork is cooked through.

Szechwan and Cantonese Cooking

Fiery Szechwan cuisine is famous for its "mouthburners"—dishes such as Kung Pao Chicken and Mapo Tofu made with hot chilies and Toasted Szechwan Peppercorns. Reputed to represent the best of Chinese cooking, Cantonese cuisine features fresh ingredients that are subtly seasoned and not overcooked. Cantonese cooks pride themselves on allowing the natural flavors of the ingredients to come through in dishes such as Sweet-and-Sour Pork and Lobster Cantonese.

Restaurant-Style Mu Shu Pork

Serves 2–4

Softened dried mushrooms absorb the hoisin sauce and other seasonings in this simplified version of a traditional Beijing dish.

½ pound boneless pork chops
3 green onions, divided
1 tablespoon soy sauce
2½ teaspoons sugar, divided
2 teaspoons cornstarch
½ teaspoon baking soda
4 dried mushrooms
½ cup reserved mushroom liquid
1 tablespoon dark soy sauce
1 tablespoon hoisin sauce
¼ teaspoon sesame oil
2 eggs
¼ teaspoon salt
3–5 tablespoons oil for stir-frying
1 slice ginger
1 cup canned bamboo shoots, rinsed
1 cup canned water chestnuts, rinsed

1. Trim any fat from the pork and cut into thin strips. Add 1 chopped green onion, soy sauce, ½ teaspoon sugar, cornstarch, and baking soda. Marinate the pork for 30 minutes.
2. Soak the dried mushrooms in hot water for at least 20 minutes to soften. Reserve the soaking liquid. Give the mushrooms a gentle squeeze to remove any excess water and thinly slice. Cut the remaining 2 green onions into 1-inch pieces.
3. Combine the reserved mushroom liquid, dark soy sauce, 2 teaspoons sugar, hoisin sauce, and sesame oil, and set aside.
4. Lightly beat the eggs and stir in ¼ teaspoon salt. Add 1 tablespoon oil to a preheated wok or skillet. When oil is hot, turn down the heat and add the eggs. Scramble quickly and remove from the wok. Wipe the wok clean if necessary.
5. Add 2 more tablespoons oil. When oil is hot, add the pork strips and stir-fry until they turn white and are nearly cooked through. Remove from the wok and set aside. Add more oil if needed. Add the ginger and green onion and stir-fry briefly. Add the mushrooms, bamboo shoots, and water chestnuts. Add the sauce and bring to a boil. Add the pork and the scrambled egg. Mix everything through and serve hot.

Traditional Mu Shu Pork

½ pound boneless pork chops
3 green onions, divided
1 tablespoon soy sauce
½ teaspoon sesame oil
2 teaspoons cornstarch
½ teaspoon baking soda
4 dried mushrooms
15 dried lily buds
4 tablespoons wood fungus
10 fresh water chestnuts
½ cup reserved mushroom liquid
2 tablespoons dark soy sauce
2 teaspoons sugar
¼ teaspoon sesame oil
2 eggs
¼ teaspoon salt
3–5 tablespoons oil for stir-frying
1 slice ginger
½ cup canned bamboo shoots, rinsed
Mandarin Pancakes (page 270)
½ cup hoisin sauce

Serves 4

For an authentic touch, use Green Onion Brushes (page 75) to brush the hoisin sauce onto the Mandarin Pancakes.

1. Trim any fat from the pork and cut into thin strips. Add 1 chopped green onion, soy sauce, sesame oil, cornstarch, and baking soda. Marinate the pork for 30 minutes.
2. Soak the dried mushrooms, dried lily buds, and wood fungus in hot water for at least 20 minutes to soften. Reserve the mushroom soaking liquid. Give the mushrooms a gentle squeeze to remove any excess water and thinly slice. Cut the remaining 2 green onions into 1-inch pieces. Peel the fresh water chestnuts and cut in half.
3. Combine the reserved mushroom liquid, dark soy sauce, sugar, and sesame oil and set aside.
4. Lightly beat the eggs and stir in ¼ teaspoon salt. Add 1 tablespoon oil to a preheated wok or skillet. When oil is hot, scramble the eggs. Remove from the wok and set aside.
5. Add 2 more tablespoons oil. When oil is hot, add the pork strips and stir-fry until they turn white and are nearly cooked through. Add the ginger and green onions and stir-fry briefly. Add the mushrooms, lily buds, wood fungus, bamboo shoots, and water chestnuts. Add the sauce and bring to a boil. Add the pork and the scrambled egg. Mix everything through.
6. To serve, brush a pancake with the hoisin sauce, add a generous helping of Mu Shu Pork, and roll up the pancake.

Pork Chop Suey

Serves 4

Vegetables take center stage in this dish; the meat is there only to add a bit of flavor.

½ pound pork tenderloin
2 teaspoons Chinese rice wine or dry sherry
2 teaspoons soy sauce
2 teaspoons baking soda
2 green onions, thinly sliced on the diagonal
2 tablespoons oyster sauce
2 tablespoons chicken broth or stock
1 teaspoon sugar
4–6 tablespoons oil for stir-frying
6 fresh mushrooms, thinly sliced
1 stalk celery, thinly sliced on the diagonal
2 stalks bok choy including leaves, thinly sliced on the diagonal
1 8-ounce can bamboo shoots, drained

1. Cut the pork into thin slices. Marinate the pork with the rice wine, soy sauce, and baking soda for 30 minutes.
2. Combine the oyster sauce, chicken broth, and sugar. Set aside.
3. Add 2 tablespoons oil to a preheated wok or skillet. When oil is hot, add the pork. Stir-fry until it changes color and is nearly cooked through. Remove from the wok.
4. Add 1–2 tablespoons oil. When oil is hot, add the mushrooms and stir-fry for about 1 minute. Add the celery and the bok choy stalks, then the bamboo shoots, stir-frying each for about 1 minute in the middle of the wok before adding the next vegetable. (If the wok is too crowded, stir-fry each vegetable separately.) Add more oil as necessary, pushing the vegetables up to the side of the wok until the oil is heated. Add the bok choy leaves and the green onion.
5. Add the sauce to the middle of the wok and bring to a boil. Add the pork. Mix everything through and serve hot.

Spicy Hoisin Pork

¾ pound pork tenderloin
1 tablespoon soy sauce
2 teaspoons baking soda
1 bunch spinach
2 tablespoons hoisin sauce
1 tablespoon dark soy sauce
¼ cup water
3 tablespoons oil for stir-frying
¼ teaspoon chili paste

Serves 4

For a less spicy dish, substitute ¼ teaspoon chili sauce with garlic for the chili paste.

1. Cut the pork into thin slices. Marinate in the soy sauce and baking soda for 30 minutes.
2. Blanch the spinach briefly in boiling water and drain thoroughly.
3. Combine the hoisin sauce, dark soy sauce, and water. Set aside.
4. Add 2 tablespoons oil to a preheated wok or skillet. When oil is hot, add the pork and stir-fry until it changes color and is nearly cooked through. Remove and drain on paper towels.
5. Add 1 tablespoon oil. When oil is hot, add the chili paste and stir-fry until aromatic. Add the spinach. Stir-fry for a minute, adding sugar or soy sauce to season if desired. Add the sauce in the middle of the wok and bring to a boil. Add the pork. Turn down the heat, mix everything through, and serve hot.

How to Season a Carbon Steel Wok

It's important to properly season a wok before using it for the first time. First, wash the wok in soapy water. Dry thoroughly, then lightly coat the inside surface with vegetable oil, using a paper towel and tilting the wok to ensure even coverage. Heat the wok on low-medium heat for 10 minutes. Remove to a cool burner and wipe off the inside with a paper towel. Repeat this process several times. The wok is ready to use when the paper towel doesn't pick up any black residue.

Ham with Asian Pear

Serves 4–6

Although China's Yunnan hams are famous throughout Europe, they are hard to find in the West. Smithfield hams are a good substitute.

1½ pounds ham, thinly sliced
2 teaspoons sesame oil
2 teaspoons cornstarch
2 tablespoons soy sauce
2 tablespoons dark soy sauce
2 tablespoons honey
1 green onion
2 tablespoons oil for frying
2 Asian pears, sliced

1. Marinate the ham for 30 minutes in the sesame oil and cornstarch.
2. Combine the soy sauce, dark soy sauce, and honey. Set aside. Cut the green onion into 1-inch slices on the diagonal.
3. Add 2 tablespoons oil to a preheated wok or skillet. When oil is hot, add the sliced ham and brown briefly. Remove and drain on paper towels.
4. Prepare the wok for steaming. Place the sliced ham on a heatproof dish on a bamboo steamer. Brush half of the sauce over. Cover and steam, adding more boiling water as necessary.
5. After 25 minutes, drain the ham juices, combine with the remaining half of the sauce, and bring to a boil in a small saucepan. Arrange the pear slices with the ham. Steam the ham for another 5 minutes, or until it is cooked. Pour the cooked sauce over the ham before serving. Garnish with the green onion.

Asian Pears

In ancient times, Chinese nobles dined on Asian pears poached in wine and honey. Today, thanks to their delicate sweetness, Asian pears are becoming a familiar sight in local supermarkets. Try them in stir-fries and salads.

Chinese Sausage and Cabbage Stir-fry

3 Chinese sausages
2 tablespoons oil for stir-frying
1 teaspoon minced shallot
6 large cabbage leaves, shredded
½ cup chicken broth
1 teaspoon Chinese rice wine or dry sherry
2 green onions, finely chopped on the diagonal

1. Cut the sausage on the diagonal into bite-sized pieces.
2. Add oil to a preheated wok or skillet. When oil is hot, add the shallot and stir-fry briefly. Add the sausages. Stir-fry for about 2 minutes, then push the sausages up to the side of the wok. Add the cabbage. Stir-fry for about 2 minutes. Add the chicken broth and rice wine in the middle of the wok and bring to a boil.
3. Simmer, covered, for 3–4 minutes, stir in the green onions, and serve hot.

Serves 2–4

Shallot makes an interesting change from garlic and ginger in this simple recipe. Add 4 softened, dried mushrooms for a complete, one-dish meal.

How to Clean a Carbon Steel Wok

Never scrub the wok with an abrasive cleanser. Instead, remove stubborn food particles with a nonmetallic scrubber. Wash the wok in soapy water. To ensure it dries completely, leave for a few minutes on the stove with the heat turned low. Add a light coating of oil before storing in the cupboard. (You can skip this last step if the wok sees a lot of use.)

CHAPTER 8

Chicken and Other Poultry

Basic Chicken Stir-fry

Serves 4–6

Simmering the chicken in broth and seasonings brings out its natural flavors. Serve with Stir-fried Bok Choy (page 237) for a quick and easy meal.

1 pound chicken meat
2 tablespoons oil for stir-frying
1 garlic clove, minced
2 thin slices ginger
½ cup chicken stock or broth
1 tablespoon Chinese rice wine or dry sherry
1 teaspoon sugar
¼ teaspoon salt

1. Wash the chicken meat, pat dry, and cut into cubes or thin slices.
2. Add oil to a preheated wok or skillet. When oil is hot, add the garlic and ginger. Stir-fry briefly until aromatic. Add the chicken and stir-fry until it changes color.
3. Add the chicken stock, rice wine, sugar, and salt and bring to a boil. Simmer, covered, until the chicken is cooked.

The Base of Many Chicken Recipes

Basic Chicken Stir-fry is a skeleton recipe that you can adapt according to your tastes and the ingredients you have on hand. Add a marinade and experiment with different seasonings such as chili paste. To make a one-dish meal that includes vegetables, stir-fry the chicken first and remove it from the wok. Stir-fry the vegetables and add the sauce. Add the chicken back and simmer until the meat is cooked. For longer-cooking pieces of meat such as chicken legs, increase the amount of broth and simmer the chicken for 20–30 minutes or until the meat is cooked through.

Moo Goo Gai Pan

2 large boneless, skinless chicken breasts
4 tablespoons oyster sauce, divided
2 teaspoons cornstarch, divided
½ cup chicken stock or broth
1 teaspoon sugar
⅛ teaspoon white pepper
½ cup fresh mushrooms
4 tablespoons oil for stir-frying
1 clove garlic, minced
½ 8-ounce can bamboo shoots, rinsed

1. Wash the chicken and cut into thin slices. Mix in 2 tablespoons oyster sauce and 1 teaspoon cornstarch. Marinate the chicken for 30 minutes.
2. Mix together the chicken stock, sugar, white pepper, 2 tablespoons oyster sauce, and 1 teaspoon cornstarch. Set aside. Wipe the mushrooms clean with a damp cloth and thinly slice.
3. Add 2 tablespoons oil to a preheated wok or skillet. When oil is hot, add the garlic and stir-fry briefly until aromatic. Add the chicken and stir-fry until it changes color and is nearly cooked through. Remove the chicken from the wok and set aside.
4. Wipe the wok clean and add 2 more tablespoons oil. When the oil is hot, add the mushrooms and stir-fry for about 1 minute. Add the bamboo shoots.
5. Give the sauce a quick stir. Make a well in the middle of the wok by pushing the vegetables up to the sides. Add the sauce in the middle, stirring vigorously to thicken. Add the chicken and mix through.

Serves 4

The marriage of chicken and mushrooms is central to this dish, but feel free to substitute other vegetables for the bamboo shoots.

Chicken Glazed in Bean Sauce

Serves 2–4

This recipe produces a tender chicken lightly glazed with savory bean sauce. For added protein, try stirring in cashews or peanuts before serving.

2 large boneless, skinless chicken breasts (12–14 ounces)
2 tablespoons Chinese rice wine or dry sherry
1 tablespoon soy sauce
2½ green onions, thinly sliced on the diagonal
½ cup chicken stock or broth
1 tablespoon dark soy sauce
1 tablespoon bean sauce
2 tablespoons brown sugar
1 clove garlic, chopped
2 tablespoons oil for stir-frying
1 teaspoon cornstarch mixed with 4 teaspoons water

1. Wash the chicken breasts, pat dry, and dice.
2. Mix together the rice wine, soy sauce, and half of a green onion. Marinate the chicken for 1 hour.
3. In a small bowl, combine the chicken stock, dark soy sauce, bean sauce, brown sugar, and garlic. Set aside.
4. Add oil to a preheated wok or skillet. When oil is hot, add the chicken and stir-fry until it is nearly cooked through. Remove from the wok and set aside.
5. Add the sauce into the wok. Add the cornstarch-and-water mixture in the middle, stirring vigorously to thicken. Add the chicken, mixing in and letting the sauce reduce until it is a glaze. Stir in the 2 sliced green onions.

Baked Oyster Sauce Chicken

1½ pounds chicken thighs
1 tablespoon dark soy sauce
2 tablespoons oyster sauce
1 tablespoon Chinese rice wine or dry sherry
1½ teaspoons sugar
4 tablespoons water
½ teaspoon sesame oil
2 garlic cloves, minced
1 teaspoon minced ginger

1. Wash the chicken thighs and pat dry. Remove the skin and make 2 diagonal cuts on each side of the thigh.
2. Mix together the dark soy sauce, oyster sauce, rice wine, sugar, water, and sesame oil. Place the sauce in a plastic bag. Add the chicken, shaking the bag lightly to make sure the sauce coats all the chicken. Seal the bag and place in the refrigerator. Marinate the chicken for 2–3 hours, turning the bag occasionally.
3. Preheat the oven to 400°F.
4. Remove the chicken thighs from the bag, reserving the sauce. Place the chicken thighs on a baking sheet sprayed with cooking spray. Pour half of the sauce over, making sure both sides of the thighs are covered. Add the minced garlic and ginger. Bake the thighs for 15 minutes. Add the remaining half of the sauce and cook for another 15 minutes, or until the thighs are cooked.

Serves 4–6

Scoring the chicken thighs makes it easier for the marinade to penetrate the meat. This dish tastes delicious served with Snow Pea Stir-fry (page 235).

Bagging It

Don't have a large enough bag to hold the chicken thighs? Place them on a plate and rub the marinade over, making sure to coat all the chicken. Cover with plastic wrap and refrigerate for 2–3 hours. Reserve any leftover marinade to pour over the chicken while baking.

Soy Sauce Chicken

Serves 2

For a fancier presentation, chop the chicken legs into pieces and place on a platter. Pour the sauce over the chopped chicken.

2 chicken legs
1 teaspoon five-spice powder
1 tablespoon cornstarch
½ cup soy sauce
¾ cup water
2 tablespoons Chinese rice wine or dry sherry
4 teaspoons brown sugar
1 large clove garlic, minced
1 slice ginger, minced
3–4 cups oil for deep-frying

1. Rinse the chicken legs and pat dry. Mix the five-spice powder and the cornstarch. Mix in with the chicken and marinate for 30 minutes.
2. In a medium bowl, mix together the soy sauce, water, rice wine, and brown sugar, and set aside.
3. Heat the oil in a wok. When the oil reaches 325°F, deep-fry the chicken legs until they are browned. Remove with a slotted spoon and drain on paper towels.
4. Drain all but 2 tablespoons oil out of the wok. Add the garlic and ginger and stir-fry briefly until aromatic. Add the sauce. Add the chicken, cover and simmer for 15–20 minutes, until the chicken is cooked.

From Marinade to Sauce

When a marinade does double duty as a sauce, it's important to ensure that it is thoroughly cooked. As an added precaution, you can bring the marinade to boil in a saucepan before adding it to the wok.

Curry Chicken Thighs

6 chicken thighs
2 green onions, divided
5 tablespoons soy sauce, divided
1½ tablespoons cornstarch
¼ cup chicken broth
½ cup water
¾ cup plain yogurt
1 tablespoon Chinese rice wine or dry sherry
1 teaspoon honey
1½ tablespoons oil for stir-frying
2 slices ginger, minced
1 large red onion, cut into wedges
1 large potato, cubed
1 tablespoon curry paste

Serves 4

This one-dish meal is great for cold winter nights. Serve with baked bread for a hearty meal.

1. Place the chicken thighs in a medium-sized bowl. Cut the green onions into 1-inch pieces on the diagonal. Mix 1 green onion, 4 tablespoons soy sauce, and cornstarch with the chicken, adding the cornstarch last. Marinate the chicken for 15 minutes.
2. Combine the chicken broth, water, yogurt, rice wine, honey, and 1 tablespoon soy sauce. Set aside.
3. Add oil to a preheated wok or skillet. When oil is hot, add the ginger and curry paste. Stir-fry briefly until aromatic. Add the chicken and stir-fry for 3 minutes. Add the onion and stir-fry for another 2 minutes, making sure to brown the chicken on both sides.
4. Give the sauce a quick stir and add it to the wok. Add the potato, reduce the heat to low or medium low, and simmer for 30 minutes or until the chicken thighs are cooked through. Stir in the remaining green onion and serve.

Hoisin Chicken

Serves 2–4

To ward off fears about bacteria, always refrigerate any dish while it is marinating.

1½ pounds chicken thighs, bone in
2 tablespoons hoisin sauce
1 tablespoon dark soy sauce
4 tablespoons water
1 teaspoon sugar
⅛ teaspoon white pepper, or to taste
1 large garlic clove, chopped

1. Wash the chicken thighs and pat dry. Remove the skin and make 2 diagonal cuts on each side of the thigh.
2. Mix together the hoisin sauce, dark soy sauce, water, sugar, white pepper, and garlic. Place the sauce in a large, zipper-lock plastic bag. Add the chicken, shaking the bag slightly to make sure the sauce coats all the chicken. Seal the bag and place in the refrigerator. Marinate the chicken for 2–3 hours, turning the bag occasionally.
3. Preheat the oven to 400°F.
4. Remove the chicken thighs from the bag, reserving the sauce. Place the thighs on a baking sheet sprayed with cooking spray. Brush on half of the sauce, making sure both sides of the thighs are covered. Bake the thighs for 15 minutes. Brush on the remainder of the sauce, and bake for another 15 minutes, or until the thighs are cooked.

Lemony Chicken Stir-fry

2 large skinless, boneless chicken breasts
2 tablespoons Chinese rice wine or dry sherry, divided
3 teaspoons soy sauce, divided
3 tablespoons plus ½ teaspoon freshly squeezed lemon juice, divided
1 teaspoon cornstarch
½ cup water
2 tablespoons brown sugar
1 teaspoon honey
3–4 tablespoons oil for stir-frying
1 clove garlic, minced
1 teaspoon minced ginger
1 teaspoon cornstarch mixed with 4 teaspoons water

Serves 2–4

Sweet brown sugar nicely balances tart lemon juice in this recipe. Serve with Tomato Egg Flower Soup (page 62) for an interesting flavor combination.

1. Cut the chicken into thin strips. Add 1 tablespoon rice wine, 1 teaspoon soy sauce, ½ teaspoon lemon juice, and 1 teaspoon cornstarch to the chicken, adding the cornstarch last. Marinate the chicken for 30 minutes.
2. Mix together 3 tablespoons freshly squeezed lemon juice, water, 1 tablespoon rice wine, 2 teaspoons soy sauce, brown sugar, and honey. Set aside.
3. Add 2 tablespoons oil to a preheated wok or skillet. When oil is hot, add the chicken and stir-fry until it changes color and is nearly cooked. Remove from the wok and set aside.
4. Clean out the wok with a paper towel. Preheat and add 1½ tablespoons oil. When oil is hot, add the garlic and ginger. Stir-fry briefly until aromatic. Add the sauce, bringing to a boil.
5. Give the cornstarch-and-water mixture a quick stir. Add to the sauce, stirring vigorously to thicken. Add the chicken and heat through.

Why Marinate?

Although it can seem time consuming, never forego marinating meat if a recipe calls for it. Besides lending flavor, a good marinade tenderizes the meat as well. It's rare to find a Chinese recipe that doesn't call for marinating meat prior to stir-frying.

Steamed Lemon Chicken

Serves 1–2

This recipe provides a generous helping of sauce to mix with rice and other vegetables.

1 chicken breast
1 tablespoon minced ginger
1½ tablespoons freshly squeezed lemon juice
¼ cup water
2 teaspoons Chinese rice wine or dry sherry
1 teaspoon soy sauce
1½ teaspoons sugar
½ teaspoon black rice vinegar
1 teaspoon cornstarch

1. Place the chicken in a heatproof plate on a bamboo steamer. Add the minced ginger. Steam for 20 minutes, or until the chicken turns white and is cooked.
2. While the chicken is steaming, mix together the lemon juice, water, rice wine, soy sauce, sugar, black rice vinegar, and cornstarch. In a small saucepan, heat the sauce to boiling. Pour over the steamed chicken.

Basic Chicken Velvet

Serves 2

To make sure the raw chicken does not contaminate other foods, prepare it in a separate work area and wash your hands thoroughly afterward.

2 boneless, skinless chicken breasts
2 tablespoons rice vinegar
¼ teaspoon five-spice powder
2 teaspoons cornstarch
1 egg white

1. Using a sharp knife or a food processor, mince the chicken.
2. Mix together the rice vinegar, five-spice powder, and cornstarch. Add to the minced chicken, separating the individual chicken pieces.
3. Beat the egg white until creamy but not stiff. Fold into the chicken mixture.

Chicken Velvet Soup

Basic Chicken Velvet's delicate flavor inspired the creation of Chicken Velvet Soup (page 61). For best results, add the Basic Chicken Velvet to the boiling broth before adding seasonings and stir.

Deep-fried Chicken Velvet

½ cup chicken stock
2 tablespoons Chinese rice wine or dry sherry
½ teaspoon salt (or to taste)
2 leeks, cut diagonally into 1-inch sections
1 tablespoon soy sauce
Basic Chicken Velvet (page 162)
2 teaspoons cornstarch
4 teaspoons water
4¼ cups oil for frying

Serves 2–4

Deep-fried Chicken Velvet nearly does melt in your mouth. The possibilities for pairing this dish are endless—look for contrasts in texture and color.

1. Mix together the chicken stock, rice wine, and salt. Set aside.
2. In a preheated wok, heat 4 cups oil to 350°F. While the oil is heating, use a second skillet or wok to stir-fry the leeks. Add 1–2 tablespoons of oil. When oil is hot, add the leeks. Stir-fry for about 1 minute, then add 1 tablespoon of soy sauce. Stir-fry until the leeks turn a bright green, and remove from the pan. Wipe out the pan with a paper towel if using to heat the chicken stock (see step 4).
3. When the oil for deep-frying is ready, carefully slide in the Basic Chicken Velvet pieces and deep-fry until the chicken turns white and is cooked. (This will take a minute at most.) Remove from the wok and drain on paper towels.
4. Heat the chicken broth mixture. When it is boiling, add the Basic Chicken Velvet and mix. If necessary, break up the chicken with chopsticks or a spatula. Push the chicken up to the sides of the pan. Mix the cornstarch and water and add to the middle of the pan, stirring vigorously to thicken. Mix through with the chicken. Serve the chicken with the leeks.

Chicken with Red and Green Peppers

Serves 2–4

Serve with a sweet-and-sour vegetable dish such as Sweet-and-Sour Celery (page 254) for an interesting juxtaposition of flavors.

2 boneless, skinless chicken breasts
1 tablespoon soy sauce
1 egg white
1½ teaspoons cornstarch
1 green bell pepper
1 red bell pepper
¼ cup water
1½ teaspoons sugar
1 tablespoon black bean sauce
¼ teaspoon chili paste
1 tablespoon cornstarch
3–4 tablespoons oil for stir-frying
2 garlic cloves, chopped
½ cup chopped red onion

1. Chop the chicken into 1½-inch cubes. Mix in the soy sauce, egg white, and cornstarch, being sure to add the cornstarch last. Marinate the chicken for 30 minutes.
2. Wash the green and red peppers, remove the seeds, and cut into chunks.
3. To make the sauce, mix together the water, sugar, black bean sauce, chili paste, and cornstarch, and set aside.
4. Add 2 tablespoons oil to a preheated wok or skillet. When the oil is hot, add the chopped garlic and stir-fry briefly until aromatic. Add the marinated chicken to the wok. Stir-fry until the chicken turns white and is nearly cooked through. Remove from the wok and set aside.
5. Add 2 tablespoons oil. When oil is hot, add the green pepper and onion. Stir-fry for about 1 minute, and then add the red pepper. Stir-fry until the peppers turn a bright color and the onion is softened.
6. Give the sauce a quick stir. Push the vegetables to the side of the wok and add the sauce in the middle, stirring vigorously to thicken. Mix with the vegetables. Add the chicken. Mix all the ingredients and serve hot.

Quick Red Bell Peppers

Although they are both members of the capsicum family, red peppers have a shorter cooking time than green peppers. For best results, add them at a later stage in stir-frying.

Bang Bang Chicken

1 pound boneless, skinless chicken breasts
Spicy Szechwan Peanut Sauce (page 25)
1 large dried bean curd sheet
2 small cucumbers
½ teaspoon salt

1. Boil chicken breasts in water for 15–20 minutes. Drain well.
2. Cut the bean curd sheet into 4 squares. Soak the sheet in cold water to soften. Peel the cucumbers and slice, toss with salt, and leave for 15 minutes.
3. Chop the chicken meat into thin slices. Lay the cucumber slices on a plate and top with a bean curd sheet. Top with the chicken and the sauce. Serve the remainder of the sauce in a dipping bowl so guests can help themselves.

Serves 4

To use Chinese noodles instead of bean curd sheets, cook the noodles according to instructions, drain well, and lay over the cucumber slices.

Spicy Chicken with Cashews

2 boneless, skinless chicken breasts
2 tablespoons dark soy sauce
1 tablespoon Chinese rice wine or dry sherry
1 teaspoon sugar
¼ teaspoon sesame oil
¼ teaspoon chili paste
3 tablespoons oil for stir-frying
½ cup cashews

1. Cut the chicken into 1-inch cubes. Mix together the dark soy sauce, rice wine, sugar, sesame oil, and chili paste, and set aside.
2. Add 2 tablespoons oil to a preheated wok or skillet. Stir-fry the chicken until it is nearly cooked through. Remove, and drain on paper towels.
3. Wipe the wok clean with a paper towel and add 1 tablespoon of oil. Stir-fry the cashews very briefly, until they are golden.
4. Add the sauce to the wok and bring to a boil. Turn down the heat and add the chicken back into the wok. Mix through and serve hot.

Serves 2–4

Native to Brazil, cashews made their way east via seventeenth-century Portuguese explorers and are now commonly featured in Asian dishes.

General Tso's Chicken

Serves 4

To serve a vegetable with this dish, stir-fry while you are waiting for the oil to heat up for deep-frying.

1 pound dark chicken meat
2 tablespoons soy sauce
3 teaspoons Chinese rice wine or dry sherry, divided
1/8 teaspoon white pepper
1 tablespoon cornstarch
4 tablespoons dark soy sauce
2 teaspoons sugar
1/2 teaspoon sesame oil
6 dried red chilies
4–6 cups oil for deep-frying
1 large clove garlic, minced
1 teaspoon minced ginger
2 green onions, thinly sliced

1. Cut the chicken into cubes. Mix in the soy sauce, 2 teaspoons of the rice wine, white pepper, and the cornstarch, adding the cornstarch last. Marinate the chicken for 30 minutes.
2. Combine the dark soy sauce, sugar, sesame oil, and 1 teaspoon rice wine. Set aside. Cut the red chilies in half and remove the seeds. Chop and set aside.
3. Heat the oil to 350°F. When the oil is hot, add the chicken cubes and deep-fry until they are lightly browned. Remove from the wok and drain on paper towels.
4. Raise the temperature of the wok to 400°F. Deep-fry the chicken a second time briefly, until the chicken turns golden brown. Remove from the wok and drain on paper towels.
5. Drain the wok, leaving 2 tablespoons of oil for stir-frying. When the oil is hot, add the garlic, ginger, and green onions. Stir-fry briefly until aromatic. Add the chilies and cook for 1 minute. Add the sauce in the middle of the wok and bring to a boil. Add the chicken and mix through.

Food Fit for a General

General Tso's Chicken is named after a famous military leader who helped quash China's Taipeng rebellion in the mid-1800s. How the dish came to be named after General Tso is lost to history, although he was rumored to have a penchant for fiery foods.

Quick and Easy Orange Chicken

2 large boneless, skinless chicken breasts, about 7 ounces each
2 tablespoons Chinese rice wine or dry sherry
1 egg white
5 teaspoons cornstarch, divided
¼ cup water
5 teaspoons freshly squeezed orange juice
1 tablespoon soy sauce
1½ teaspoons brown sugar
¼ teaspoon chili paste
¼ teaspoon sesame oil
2 tablespoons oil for stir-frying
1 teaspoon minced ginger
1 clove garlic, minced

Serves 4

Serve with rice and a steamed vegetable for a quick and easy dish on busy weeknights.

1. Cut the chicken into 1-inch cubes. Mix in the rice wine, egg white, and 3 teaspoons cornstarch, adding the cornstarch last. Marinate the chicken for 15 minutes.
2. Mix together the water, orange juice, soy sauce, brown sugar, chili paste, sesame oil, and 2 teaspoons cornstarch.
3. Add oil to a preheated wok or skillet. When the oil is ready, add the ginger and garlic. Stir-fry briefly until aromatic.
4. Add the chicken and stir-fry until the chicken changes color and is nearly cooked through.
5. Give the sauce a quick stir. Push the chicken up the sides of the wok and add the sauce, stirring vigorously to thicken. Mix the sauce with the chicken and cook the chicken for another minute.

Kung Pao Stir-fry

Serves 2–4

This healthier version of Kung Pao Chicken uses less oil but still contains protein-rich peanuts.

2 boneless, skinless chicken breasts
1 tablespoon soy sauce
2 tablespoons Chinese rice wine or dry sherry, divided
1 tablespoon cornstarch
2 tablespoons dark soy sauce
1 teaspoon sugar
¼ teaspoon sesame oil
4 tablespoons oil for stir-frying
1 clove garlic, minced
¼ teaspoon chili paste
½ cup unsalted, roasted peanuts

1. Cut the chicken into 1-inch cubes. Add the soy sauce, 1 tablespoon rice wine, and the cornstarch to the chicken, adding the cornstarch last. Marinate the chicken for 30 minutes.
2. Mix together the dark soy sauce, 1 tablespoon rice wine, sugar, and sesame oil.
3. Add 2 tablespoons oil to a preheated wok or skillet. When oil is hot, add the chicken cubes and stir-fry until they turn golden. Remove the chicken from the wok and drain on paper towels.
4. Add 2 tablespoons oil. When oil is hot, add the garlic clove and chili paste. Stir-fry briefly until aromatic. Add the peanuts and stir-fry very briefly, taking care not to burn.
5. Add the sauce to the wok and bring to a boil. Turn down the heat and add the chicken. Mix everything and simmer for a few minutes until the chicken is cooked through.

Sweet-and-Sour Chicken

1½ cups chicken meat
¾ cup pineapple juice
2 tablespoons rice vinegar
1 teaspoon black rice vinegar
1 tablespoon soy sauce
½ green bell pepper
½ red bell pepper
2 tablespoons oil for stir-frying
2 tablespoons plus 1 teaspoon sugar
¼ cup pineapple chunks
1 tablespoon cornstarch mixed with 4 tablespoons water

Serves 4

This is a variation on traditional Chinese Pineapple Chicken, where the chicken is deep-fried in batter before mixing with the sauce.

1. Cut the chicken meat into bite-sized pieces. Mix together the pineapple juice, rice vinegar, black rice vinegar, and soy sauce, and set aside. Cut the green and red peppers into bite-sized cubes.
2. Add oil to a preheated wok or skillet. When oil is hot, add the chicken. Stir-fry until it changes color and is nearly cooked through.
3. In a medium saucepan, bring the pineapple juice mixture to a boil. Stir in the sugar, stirring to dissolve. Add the green and red peppers and the pineapple chunks. Bring back to a boil and add the cornstarch-and-water mixture, stirring quickly to thicken.
4. Pour the sauce over the stir-fried chicken and heat through.

Or Make It Pineapple-Orange Chicken

To transform the sweet-and-sour sauce into a pineapple-orange sauce, just decrease the amount of pineapple juice to ½ cup and add 1 tablespoon plus 1 teaspoon of orange juice. Include or leave out the peppers and pineapple chunks as desired.

Sesame Hoisin Surprise

Serves 4

Hoisin sauce, chili paste, and brown sugar make an intriguing taste combination. Serve with steamed vegetables and rice or noodles.

3 boneless, skinless chicken breasts
2 tablespoons soy sauce
1 tablespoon Chinese rice wine or dry sherry
3 tablespoons cornstarch, divided
1 cup water
2 teaspoons hoisin sauce
2 tablespoons brown sugar
4 teaspoons dark soy sauce
Up to 2 teaspoons chili paste
2 teaspoons vegetable oil
2 garlic cloves, minced
2 tablespoons oil for stir-frying
1 green onion, thinly sliced
2 tablespoons toasted sesame seeds

1. Cut the chicken into 1-inch cubes. Mix in the soy sauce, rice wine, and 1 tablespoon cornstarch, adding the cornstarch last. Marinate the chicken for 30 minutes.
2. In a small saucepan, bring the water, hoisin sauce, brown sugar, dark soy sauce, chili paste, vegetable oil, garlic cloves, and 2 tablespoons cornstarch to a boil. Turn down the heat to low and keep warm while stir-frying the chicken.
3. Add the oil to a preheated wok or skillet. When oil is hot, add the marinated chicken pieces and stir-fry until they change color and are nearly cooked through. Remove the chicken from the wok and set aside.
4. As you finish stir-frying the chicken, bring the sauce back up to a boil. Mix in the green onion. Pour the sauce over the chicken and mix through. Garnish with the toasted sesame seeds.

Garlic Chicken

4 boneless, skinless, chicken breasts
2 egg whites
¼ teaspoon salt
2 teaspoons cornstarch
2 tablespoons oil for stir-frying
3 large garlic cloves, chopped
½ tablespoon chili paste
¼ cup soy sauce
2 tablespoons Chinese rice wine or dry sherry
½ teaspoon sesame oil
2 green onions, cut into 1½-inch pieces
1 tomato, cut into wedges

Serves 4

This dish is a garlic lover's delight. To increase its potent aroma, add more cloves or mince them instead of chopping.

1. Wash the chicken, pat dry, and cut into cubes. Add the egg whites, salt, and cornstarch, adding the cornstarch last. Marinate the chicken for 1 hour.
2. Bring a large pot of water to a very low boil. Add the chicken, stirring to separate the pieces, and remove as soon as it is just turning white (about 60–90 seconds). Drain immediately.
3. Add oil to a preheated wok or skillet. When oil is hot, add the garlic and chili paste and stir-fry until the garlic is aromatic. Add the chicken and stir-fry briefly. Add the soy sauce and rice wine. Bring to a boil and cook for a few minutes until everything is heated through. Stir in the green onions and drizzle with the sesame oil. Serve on a bed of white rice, garnished with the tomato wedges.

Water-Poached Chicken

Poaching poultry in water gives it a soft and tender texture. For best results keep the water at a low simmer and not strongly bubbling. It helps to have a colander set up before you poach the chicken, since it should be drained immediately. On its own, the whitish color of water-poached chicken can be a little disconcerting. This technique works best when you have a darker cut of meat or plan to cook the chicken in a dark-colored sauce.

Chicken with Walnuts

Serves 4–6

The crunchy texture of walnuts goes well with velvety chicken cooked in a savory sauce.

2 boneless, skinless chicken breasts
1 egg white
¼ teaspoon salt
2 teaspoons cornstarch
1½ tablespoons dark soy sauce
3 tablespoons oyster sauce
1½ tablespoons Chinese rice wine or dry sherry
2¼ teaspoons sugar
⅓ cup water
½ cup walnut halves
1 garlic clove, smashed
1 teaspoon cornstarch mixed with 4 teaspoons water
1¼ cups oil for frying

1. Cut the chicken into 1-inch cubes. Mix in the egg white, salt, and cornstarch, adding the cornstarch last. Marinate the chicken for 30 minutes.
2. Combine the dark soy sauce, oyster sauce, rice wine, sugar, and water, and set aside.
3. Boil the walnuts in water for at least 5 minutes. Drain and dry.
4. Add 1 cup oil to a preheated wok or skillet. When oil is hot, add the chicken cubes. Velvet the chicken cubes by submerging them in the hot oil just until they change color. Remove immediately and drain on paper towels.
5. Remove all but 1 tablespoon oil. When oil is hot, add the garlic and stir-fry until aromatic. Add the walnuts and stir-fry for about 1 minute. Push up to the side of the wok and add the sauce in the middle. Bring to a boil.
6. Give the cornstarch-and-water mixture a quick stir. Add in the middle of the wok, stirring quickly to thicken. Add the chicken. Mix everything together. Cover and simmer for a few minutes until the chicken is cooked through.

Chengdu Chicken

Serves 4

Chengdu Chicken is named after Chengdu, the capital city of Szechuan province in western China.

4 boneless, skinless chicken breasts
2 stalks celery
3 teaspoons red or black rice vinegar
1 teaspoon sugar
¾ teaspoon salt, divided
½ cup hot water
1 teaspoon Chinese rice wine or dry sherry
3 tablespoons oil for stir-frying
1 tablespoon chopped ginger
2 garlic cloves, chopped
2 tablespoons hot bean sauce
2 teaspoons cornstarch
¼ cup water

1. Rinse the chicken breasts and cut into cubes. Cut the celery into 1-inch slices on the diagonal. Blanch or parboil the celery in a pot of boiling water for 2–3 minutes.
2. Combine the rice vinegar, sugar, ½ teaspoon salt, hot water, and rice wine. Set aside.
3. Add 1 tablespoon oil to a preheated wok or skillet. When the oil is hot, add the celery. Stir-fry briefly and add ¼ teaspoon salt. Stir-fry until the celery changes color and is tender but still firm. Remove from the wok.
4. Wipe the wok clean with a paper towel. Add 2 tablespoons oil. When the oil is hot, add the ginger and garlic and stir-fry briefly until aromatic. Add the chicken cubes. Stir-fry for 2–3 minutes, then add the hot bean sauce. Stir-fry until the chicken changes color and is nearly cooked through.
5. Add the sauce and bring to a boil. Mix the cornstarch and water and add to the middle of the wok, stirring vigorously to thicken. Add the celery. Mix everything through and serve hot.

Mango Chicken

Serves 4

Turmeric is a distant relative of ginger. In this recipe it gives the chicken a nice yellow color.

4 boneless, skinless chicken breasts
1 egg white
1 tablespoon Chinese rice wine or dry sherry
¼ teaspoon salt
2 teaspoons cornstarch
2 tablespoons rice vinegar
2 tablespoons plus 1 teaspoon brown sugar
1 can mango slices with reserved juice
1 tablespoon minced ginger
1 teaspoon curry paste
½ teaspoon turmeric
1 cup oil for frying

1. Cut the chicken into cubes. Mix in the egg white, rice wine, salt, and cornstarch. Marinate the chicken for 30 minutes.
2. In a small saucepan, bring the rice vinegar, brown sugar, and ¾ cup of reserved mango juice to a boil. Keep warm on low heat.
3. Add 1 cup oil to a preheated wok or skillet. When the oil is hot, velvet the chicken by cooking very briefly in the hot oil, until it changes color and is nearly cooked through (about 30 seconds). Use tongs or cooking chopsticks to separate the individual pieces of chicken while it is cooking.
4. Remove all but 2 tablespoons oil from the wok. (Wipe out the wok with a paper towel if necessary.) When oil is hot, add the ginger, curry paste, and turmeric. Stir-fry for about 1 minute until aromatic. Add the chicken and mix with the curry paste.
5. Add the sauce and bring to a boil. Stir in the mango slices. Mix all the ingredients and serve hot.

Velveting Meat

Velveting meat is a handy trick restaurants use to tenderize meat such as chicken, pork, or beef. Why does it work? The initial contact with hot oil shocks the muscles, causing them to relax. The muscles remain relaxed when they are stir- or deep-fried according to the recipe instructions. The result is a piece of meat that is both firm and juicy.

Quick and Easy Curry Chicken

2 boneless, skinless chicken breasts
2 green onions, minced
1 heaping teaspoon minced ginger
1 clove garlic, minced
1 tablespoon mild curry powder, or to taste
Stir-fried Water Chestnuts and Bamboo Shoots (page 234)
¼ cup chicken broth
4 tablespoons oil, or as needed

Serves 2

Worried your curry powder is too strong? Add 1–2 teaspoons while stir-frying the ginger and garlic, and then add more with the chicken, if desired.

1. Wash the chicken breasts, pat dry, and cut into cubes. Cut the green onions into thin slices.
2. Add 2 tablespoons oil to a preheated wok or skillet. When oil is hot, add the ginger, garlic, and curry powder and stir-fry until there is a strong odor of curry. Add the chicken and stir-fry for about 5 minutes, until the chicken is well mixed with the curry powder. Remove and set aside.
3. Add the Stir-fried Water Chestnuts and Bamboo Shoots to the wok. If making from scratch, follow the directions in the recipe. If previously made, bring to a boil. Add oil as required.
4. Add the chicken back into the wok. Add the chicken broth. Bring to a boil, cover and simmer until the dish is cooked through. Stir in the green onions or add as a garnish.

Curry—More Than a Powder

Although we tend to think of curry as a spice or blend of spices, the word has its origins in the Tamil word kahri, a spicy sauce. We have a British official to thank for the association of curry with a dry powder. The story is that, when leaving India, the official ordered his servant to prepare a compilation of spices so that he could enjoy his favorite Indian dishes upon returning home to Britain. Freshly made curry powder is preferable to commercially prepared brands. Still, in today's busy world it's not always possible to find time for chopping herbs and grinding fresh spices. Although this recipe uses a mild curry powder, the hotter Madras curry powders generally work best in Chinese dishes.

Princess Chicken

Serves 4

Princess Chicken is a variation on General Tso's Chicken, made with light instead of dark chicken meat.

1 pound light chicken meat
6 tablespoons soy sauce, divided
4 teaspoons Chinese rice wine or dry sherry, divided
1 tablespoon cornstarch
2 teaspoons sugar
¼ teaspoon sesame oil
6 dried red chilies
3 tablespoons oil for stir-frying
1 large clove garlic, minced
1 teaspoon minced ginger
2 green onions, thinly sliced

1. Cut the chicken into cubes. Mix in 2 tablespoons soy sauce, 3 teaspoons rice wine, and the cornstarch, adding the cornstarch last. Marinate the chicken for 30 minutes.
2. Combine the 4 tablespoons soy sauce, 1 teaspoon rice wine, sugar, and the sesame oil, and set aside. Cut the red chilies in half and remove the seeds. Chop and set aside.
3. Add 2 tablespoons oil to a preheated wok or skillet. When the oil is hot, add the chicken cubes and stir-fry until they are nearly cooked through. Remove from the wok and drain on paper towels.
4. Add 1 tablespoon oil to the wok. When the oil is hot, add the garlic, ginger, and green onions. Stir-fry briefly until aromatic. Add the chilies and cook for 1 minute. Add the sauce in the middle of the wok and bring to a boil. Add the chicken and mix through.

Tea Smoked Chicken

3-pound fryer chicken
2 tablespoons dark soy sauce
1 teaspoon sugar
1½ teaspoons Chinese rice wine or dry sherry
½ green onion, minced
3 tablespoons black tea leaves
½ cup brown sugar
¼ teaspoon Szechwan Salt and Pepper Mix (page 22)
½ cup uncooked rice

Serves 6

For a different flavor, try simmering the chicken prior to steaming in the black tea leaves.

1. Wash the chicken and pat dry. Mix together the dark soy sauce, sugar, rice wine, and green onion. Rub over the chicken and marinate for 1 hour. Mix together the tea leaves, brown sugar, Szechwan Salt and Pepper Mix, and rice. Set aside.
2. Prepare a bamboo steamer and steam the chicken for about 45 minutes, until it is cooked.
3. Cover the bottom of the wok and the inside of the wok with several layers of aluminum foil. Place the smoking spices at the bottom of the wok. Place a cake rack inside the wok and place the chicken on the rack. Turn the heat up. When smoke appears in a few places (about 10–15 minutes), cover the chicken with the lid and adjust the heat so that the stream of smoke remains steady. Continue smoking until the chicken turns a deep brown (about 15 minutes).

Tea-Smoked Food

There is no need to purchase a wood smoker to make Chinese favorites such as tea smoked duck or chicken. Along with steaming and stir-frying, the versatile wok also functions as a smoker. Chinese cooks make a further departure from traditional smoking methods by using smoking solely to impart flavor to the food, not to cook it. (The food to be cooked is usually steamed or simmered first.) The smoking ingredient of choice in Chinese cooking is tea leaves; black are most popular, although green tea leaves are also used. Other spices and seasonings that may be added to the smoking mix include star anise, and brown or white sugar.

Deep-fried Chicken

Serves 2–4

This tastes delicious dipped in Quick and Easy Sweet-and-Sour Sauce (page 24) or Sweet-and-Sour Worcestershire Sauce (page 23).

2 boneless, skinless chicken breasts
2 teaspoons Chinese rice wine or dry sherry
½ green onion, cut into 1-inch pieces
2 teaspoons soy sauce
2 thin slices ginger
1½ cups oil for frying

1. Cut the chicken into 1-inch cubes. Add the rice wine, green onion, soy sauce, and ginger. Marinate the chicken for 30 minutes.
2. Add oil to a preheated wok or skillet. When oil is hot, add the chicken cubes. Fry until they are browned and evenly cooked (about 4–5 minutes). Remove with a slotted spoon and drain on paper towels.

Deep-fried Breaded Chicken

Serves 2–4

This is an elegant appetizer when served with Hot Mustard Dip (page 20) and garnished with sprigs of cilantro.

2 boneless, skinless chicken breasts
2 teaspoons Chinese rice wine
½ green onion, cut into 1-inch pieces
2 teaspoons soy sauce
2 thin slices ginger
6 tablespoons breadcrumbs
½ teaspoon Szechwan peppercorns, roasted and ground
1 egg, lightly beaten
1½ cups oil for frying

1. Cut the chicken into 1-inch cubes. Add the rice wine, green onion, soy sauce, and ginger. Marinate the chicken for 30 minutes.
2. Process the breadcrumbs and add the peppercorns.
3. Add oil to a preheated wok or skillet. When oil is heating, dip the chicken in the egg and dredge in the breadcrumbs.
4. When oil is hot, add the chicken and fry until it is evenly cooked (about 4–5 minutes). Remove and drain on paper towels.

Mu Shu Chicken

½ pound boneless, skinless chicken legs or thighs
1 tablespoon soy sauce
2½ teaspoons sugar, divided
2 teaspoons cornstarch
4 water chestnuts, fresh if possible
2 green onions
½ cup water
1 tablespoon dark soy sauce
1 tablespoon hoisin sauce
¼ teaspoon sesame oil
2 eggs
¼ teaspoon salt
3–4 tablespoons oil for stir-frying
1 slice ginger, minced

Serves 4–6

While Mu Shu Pork is a popular restaurant dish, the basic recipe can be adjusted to use with chicken, beef, and even vegetables.

1. Cut the chicken into thin slices. Add the soy sauce, 2 teaspoons sugar, and cornstarch, adding the cornstarch last. Marinate the chicken for 30 minutes.
2. If using fresh water chestnuts, peel and cut in half. If using canned, rinse with warm water to remove any "tinny" taste, drain well, and cut in half. Cut the green onions into 1-inch pieces on the diagonal.
3. Combine the water, dark soy sauce, hoisin sauce, ½ teaspoon sugar, and sesame oil, and set aside.
4. Lightly beat the eggs and stir in ¼ teaspoon salt. Add 1 tablespoon oil to a preheated wok or skillet. When oil is hot, turn up the heat and scramble the eggs. Scramble quickly and remove from the wok.
5. Add 2 more tablespoons oil to the wok. When oil is hot, add the chicken and stir-fry until it changes color and is nearly cooked through. Remove from the wok and set aside.
6. Add more oil if needed. Add the ginger and green onions and stir-fry until aromatic. Add the water chestnuts. Make a well in the middle of the wok, add the sauce and bring to a boil. Add the chicken and scrambled egg. Mix through and serve hot.

Sesame Chicken

Serves 4–6

The secret to this popular restaurant dish lies in the sauce—adjust the sweetness level by increasing or decreasing the ratio of vinegar to sugar.

3 whole boneless chicken breasts
2 tablespoons soy sauce
1 tablespoon Chinese rice wine or dry sherry
⅛ teaspoon sesame oil
2 tablespoons flour
¼ teaspoon baking powder
¼ teaspoon baking soda
2 tablespoons water
6 tablespoons cornstarch, divided
1 teaspoon vegetable oil
½ cup water
1 cup chicken stock or broth
2 tablespoons dark soy sauce
½ cup vinegar
2 teaspoons chili sauce with garlic
1 large clove garlic, minced
1 teaspoon rice vinegar
¾ cup sugar
2 tablespoons sesame seeds
4–6 cups oil for deep-frying

1. Cut the chicken into cubes. Mix in the soy sauce, rice wine, sesame oil, flour, baking powder, baking soda, water, 2 tablespoons cornstarch, and vegetable oil. Marinate the chicken for 30 minutes.
2. In a medium bowl, combine ½ cup water, chicken stock, dark soy sauce, vinegar, chili sauce with garlic, garlic clove, rice vinegar, sugar, and 4 tablespoons cornstarch. Set aside.
3. Heat oil in wok to 350°F. Add the marinated chicken and deep-fry until golden brown. Remove from the wok with a slotted spoon and drain on paper towels.
4. Raise the oil temperature in the wok to 400°F. Deep-fry the chicken a second time, until it turns golden brown. Remove and drain.
5. Give the sauce a quick stir. Bring to a boil in a medium-sized saucepan. Pour over the deep-fried chicken. Garnish with the sesame seeds.

Double Deep-frying

Deep-frying meat twice is another technique Chinese restaurant chefs have in their cooking repertoire. Besides adding a crispier coating, the second frying seals in the meat's juices. Replacing egg in the batter with vegetable oil helps increase the crispiness.

Spicy Braised Chicken Wings

12 chicken wings
¼ cup chicken broth
½ cup plain yogurt
1 tablespoon Chinese rice wine or dry sherry
1 tablespoon soy sauce
1 teaspoon honey
1 tablespoon curry paste
4 cups oil for deep-frying

1. Chop the chicken wings into pieces. In a large saucepan, blanch the chicken wing pieces in boiling water for 2 minutes. Drain.
2. Combine the chicken broth, yogurt, rice wine, soy sauce, honey, and curry paste. Set aside.
3. Heat oil for deep-frying. When the oil reaches 350°F, carefully slide the chicken wing pieces into the wok. Deep-fry until they turn light brown. Remove with a slotted spoon and drain on paper towels.
4. Bring the sauce to a boil in a skillet or wok. Add the chicken pieces, cover, and simmer for 10–15 minutes, or until the chicken is cooked through.

Serves 4–6

Madras, a hot curry paste made with turmeric, chili, cumin, and coriander, works well in this recipe.

Sweet-and-Sour Chicken Wings

5 chicken wings
Sweet-and-Sour Sauce with Ketchup (page 24)

1. Cut the wing tip off the wings. Blanch the wings in boiling water for 2 minutes and drain.
2. Brush the chicken wings with the Sweet-and-Sour Sauce with Ketchup, making sure both sides are covered. Reserve any leftover sauce. Marinate the chicken wings for 1 hour.
3. Preheat the oven to 400°F. Place the wings on a baking sheet. Brush the chicken with half the leftover sauce and bake the chicken wings for 30 minutes. Turn over and brush with the remainder of the leftover sauce and bake for another 30 minutes. Remove from the stove and cool.

Serves 5

Unused wing tips are perfect for making soup stock. Serve the sweet-and-sour wings with watercress soup for an interesting combination of flavors.

Oyster Sauce Chicken Wings

Serves 6–8

To make an appealing appetizer, serve the wings cold, with a few sprigs of cilantro for a garnish.

16 chicken wings
⅓ cup soy sauce
1 tablespoon dark soy sauce
3 tablespoons oyster sauce
1 tablespoon Chinese rice wine or dry sherry
2 teaspoons sugar
2 tablespoons water
2 teaspoons sesame oil
3 garlic cloves, minced

1. Rinse the chicken wings and pat dry. Combine the soy sauce, dark soy sauce, oyster sauce, rice wine, sugar, water, and sesame oil. Place the sauce in a plastic bag. Add the chicken, shaking the bag lightly to make sure the sauce coats all the chicken. Seal the bag and place in the refrigerator. Marinate the chicken for 2–3 hours, turning the bag occasionally.
2. Preheat the oven to 350°F.
3. Remove the chicken wings from the bag, reserving the sauce. Place the wings on a baking sheet sprayed with cooking spray. Pour ½ the sauce over. Add the minced garlic. Bake the wings for 20 minutes. Add the remaining half of the sauce and cook for another 15 minutes, or until the wings are cooked.

How to Reduce Splattering During Deep-frying

Make sure the food to be deep-fried is at room temperature. If deep-frying foods are coated in a sauce or batter, use a slotted spoon to drain off any excess before adding the food to the wok.

Stuffed Chicken Wings

10 chicken wings
2 Chinese dried mushrooms
½ 8-ounce can bamboo shoots, drained
½ cup ground pork
½ tablespoon soy sauce
½ tablespoon Chinese rice wine or dry sherry
¼ teaspoon sesame oil
½ teaspoon sugar
Salt and pepper to taste

1. Wash the chicken wings and pat dry. Cut through the middle section and discard the drummette. Take a paring knife and, starting with the end of the midsection that was attached to the drummette, carefully scrape the meat away from the 2 bones in the middle section, taking care not to cut the skin. When the meat is scraped away, pull and remove the 2 bones in the midsection. This will give you a pouch to stuff.
2. Soak the dried mushrooms in hot water for at least 20 minutes to soften. Give the mushrooms a gentle squeeze to remove any excess water. Cut into thin slices. Julienne the bamboo shoots.
3. Place the pork in a medium bowl. Use your hands to mix the soy sauce, rice wine, sesame oil, sugar, and salt and pepper in with the pork.
4. Take a small ball of pork and place inside the chicken skin. Add 2 slices of bamboo and 2 slices of sliced mushrooms. Continue with the remainder of the chicken wings.
5. Steam the chicken wings on a heatproof plate on a bamboo steamer in the wok for about 20 minutes, or until the pork is cooked through.

Serves 10

Serve this appetizer on a bed of lettuce leaves garnished with cilantro, with a dipping sauce.

Drunken Chicken Wings

Serves 4–6

A dry white wine such as a Riesling works best in this recipe. Serve cold.

8–10 chicken wings
¼ teaspoon salt
Pepper to taste
1 green onion, chopped
2 slices ginger
6 cups dry white wine to cover

1. In a large pot, bring 8 cups of water to a boil. While waiting for the water to boil, chop the chicken wings through the middle so that you have a drummette and the midsection. Chop off and discard the wing tips.
2. Cook the chicken wings in the boiling water for 5 minutes.
3. Add the salt, pepper, green onion, and ginger. Cover and simmer the chicken for 45 minutes. Cool.
4. Place the chicken wings in a sealed container and cover with the wine. Refrigerate for at least 12 hours before serving.

Out of Chicken Wings?

You can also make this dish using a whole chicken. Increase the amount of seasonings if desired. When ready to serve, place the whole chicken on a platter and garnish with sprigs of cilantro or Green Onion Brushes (page 75). Carve up the chicken in front of guests.

Turkey with Water Chestnuts

1½ pounds turkey breast
2 tablespoons hoisin sauce
2 tablesoons soy sauce
3 tablespoons water
3 teaspoons brown sugar
3 tablespoons oil for stir-frying
2 garlic cloves, minced
2 slices ginger, minced
1 can water chestnuts, rinsed
¼ teaspoon salt

1. Rinse the turkey. Remove the skin and the breastbone. Chop into 1½-inch cubes.
2. Combine the hoisin sauce, soy sauce, water, and brown sugar in a bowl and set aside.
3. Add oil to a preheated wok or skillet. When the oil is hot, add the garlic and ginger and stir-fry briefly until aromatic. Add the turkey and stir-fry in batches on medium to medium-high heat for about 4–5 minutes, until the meat is tender. Remove from the wok and set aside.
4. Add 1 tablespoon oil. When oil is hot, add the water chestnuts to the wok and stir-fry for about 1 minute. Add the salt and stir-fry until they turn light brown. Push the water chestnuts up to the sides of the wok. Add the sauce in the middle of the wok and bring to a boil. Add the turkey cubes and stir-fry for another couple of minutes, until all the ingredients are mixed together.

Serves 4

For extra flavor, add ¼ teaspoon of chili paste to the sauce. Serve with a spicy dish such as Cold Szechwan Sesame Noodles (page 101).

Peking Duck

Serves 4

A featured dish at many Beijing restaurants, the trick to preparing Peking duck is to make sure the duck is completely dry before roasting.

1 5-pound duck
8 cups water
3 tablespoons honey
1½ tablespoons rice vinegar
1 tablespoon Chinese rice wine or dry sherry

1. Thaw the duck and remove the inner organs. Rinse through with cold water, and pat dry.
2. Take a long piece of string and tie a knot at the end of each of the duck's legs to form a loop. (This will make it easy to hang the duck from a hook or nail.)
3. Bring the water to a boil in a large pot or a wok. Stir in the honey, rice vinegar, and rice wine. Turn down the heat and simmer the sauce, covered, for about 20 minutes, stirring occasionally.
4. Ladle the honey and water mixture over the skin of the duck several times, making sure the skin is completely coated. Dry the duck by hanging in a cool place for at least 4 hours, keeping a pan underneath to catch any drippings.
5. While the duck is drying, preheat the oven to 375°F. Fill the bottom of a roasting pan with water (this prevents the fat from splattering when you remove the duck from the oven). Place the duck on the roasting pan, breast side up. Roast for 30 minutes, turn over and roast for 30 minutes on the other side, and then turn and roast a final 10 minutes on the breast side, or until the duck is cooked. Cool and carve into thin slices. Serve on Mandarin Pancakes (page 270) brushed with hoisin sauce.

Stir-fried Duck with Pineapple

1 pound duck breast
1 tablespoon hoisin sauce
1 teaspoon Chinese rice wine or dry sherry
⅔ cup pineapple juice
2½ tablespoons black rice vinegar
1 teaspoon sugar
½ cup pineapple chunks
2 tablespoons oil for stir-frying
1 tablespoon minced ginger

Serves 2–4

For a balanced meal, serve with Stir-fried Baby Bok Choy (page 243) on a bed of wild rice.

1. Cut the duck breast meat into thin slices approximately 2 inches in length. Marinate the duck in the hoisin sauce and rice wine for 30 minutes.
2. In a small saucepan, bring the pineapple juice, black rice vinegar, and sugar to a boil. Stir in the pineapple chunks. Keep warm on low heat.
3. Add oil to a preheated wok or skillet. When oil is hot, add the ginger. Stir-fry briefly until aromatic. Add the duck and stir-fry for 2–3 minutes.
4. Add the pineapple juice mixture. Heat through and serve.

Clay Pot Cooking

Used since ancient times, clay pot cooking features prominently in Shanghai cuisine. One advantage of clay pot cooking is that the food can be transported straight from stove to dinner table, with the clay pot doing double duty as cooking vessel and serving dish. In contrast to terra cotta pots, clay pots are unglazed on the inside, which is why they are also called sand pots. The main danger with clay pot dishes is unintentional cracking—be sure to follow the manufacturer's instructions very carefully.

Chapter 9

Tofu and Eggs

Deep-fried Tofu

Serves 4–6

Deep-fried tofu cubes make a great substitute for croutons in salads. Use when you want a handy source of protein without the tofu texture.

1 block firm tofu
¼ cup cornstarch
4–5 cups oil for deep-frying

1. Drain the tofu and cut into cubes. Coat with the cornstarch.
2. Add oil to a preheated wok and heat to 350°F. When oil is hot, add the tofu squares and deep-fry until they turn golden. Drain on paper towels.

How to Drain Tofu

Cut the tofu into smaller pieces. To drain, place the tofu on a paper towel on a plate. Cover with paper towels and place a weight on top of the tofu, such as a bowl or a book. Drain for 20 minutes. If possible, the easiest method for draining tofu is to position the plate so that it is tilting over the sink, allowing the water to flow out naturally.

Tofu Shake

Yields 2¾ cups

This tasty and nutritious shake makes an ideal breakfast or afternoon snack. For extra flavor, add seasonal berries.

1 banana, sliced
1 cup canned mandarin oranges with juice
1 cup soft or silken tofu
2 tablespoons honey
1 teaspoon cinnamon

Process all the ingredients in a food processor or blender. Chill and serve.

Slow Fried Tofu

1 block firm tofu
4–5 cups oil for deep-frying

1. Drain the tofu and cut into cubes.
2. Add oil to a preheated wok and heat to 350°F. When oil is hot, add the tofu.
3. Deep-fry until the cubes turn a golden brown. (This will take about 10 minutes.) Drain the deep-fried tofu on paper towels.

Serves 4–6

Although it takes longer to cook, tofu retains more of its texture when it is deep-fried without a starch coating.

Soft and Firm Tofu

Soft tofu is also known as silken tofu. It is used mainly in desserts—its soft texture doesn't hold up well when fried. Soft tofu contains less protein than firm tofu but has a creamy texture that makes it perfect for shakes and puddings.

Thicker and denser than soft tofu, firm tofu can hold its shape in soups and stir-fried and deep-fried dishes. It can even be used in recipes normally requiring the extra-firm texture of pressed tofu when it is pressed and drained for 2 hours or more. Firm tofu should always be drained for at least 20 minutes before using.

Fermented Bean Curd with Spinach

Serves 4

Don't like spinach? Try substituting amaranth, also known as Chinese spinach. The red and green leaves contain even more nutrients.

5 cups spinach leaves
4 cubes fermented bean curd with chilies
A pinch of five-spice powder (less than 1/8 teaspoon)
2 tablespoons oil for stir-frying
2 garlic cloves, minced
1/2 teaspoon sugar

1. Blanch the spinach by plunging the leaves briefly into boiling water. Drain thoroughly.
2. Mash the fermented tofu cubes and mix in the five-spice powder.
3. Add oil to a preheated wok or skillet. When the oil is hot, add the garlic and stir-fry briefly until aromatic. Add the spinach and stir-fry for 1–2 minutes. Add the sugar. Add the mashed bean curd in the middle of the wok and mix with the spinach. Cook through and serve hot.

Fermented Bean Curd

These small cubes of bean curd preserved in rice and spicy seasonings have a pungent aroma reminiscent of strong cheese. Sold in glass jars in Asian markets, fermented bean curd marries well with other savory foods such as garlic and salted black beans. Usually 1 or 2 cubes is all that is needed.

Stewed Tofu

1 pound beef
4 dried mushrooms
8 ounces pressed tofu
1 cup light soy sauce
¼ cup dark soy sauce
¼ cup Chinese rice wine or dry sherry
4 teaspoons white sugar
¼ cup brown sugar
2 tablespoons oil for stir-frying
2 slices ginger
2 garlic cloves, minced
2 cups water
1 star anise

Serves 4–6

Experiment with adding favorite spices to come up with your own version of red-cooked tofu.

1. Cut the beef into thin slices. Soak the dried mushrooms in hot water for at least 20 minutes to soften. Gently squeeze to remove any excess water and slice.
2. Cut the tofu into ½-inch cubes. Combine the light soy sauce, dark soy sauce, rice wine, white sugar, and brown sugar, and set aside.
3. Add oil to a preheated wok or skillet. When oil is hot, add the ginger slices and garlic and stir-fry briefly until aromatic. Add the beef and cook until browned. Before the beef has finished cooking, add the tofu cubes and fry briefly.
4. Add the sauce and 2 cups water. Add the star anise. Bring to a boil, then turn down the heat and simmer. After 1 hour, add the dried mushrooms. Simmer for another 30 minutes, or until the liquid is reduced. If desired, remove the star anise before serving.

Bean Curd with Bean Sauce and Noodles

Serves 4

Slow Fried Tofu (page 191) works well in this recipe. You can substitute other fresh noodles for the Peking noodles.

8 ounces fresh Peking-style noodles
1 12-ounce block firm tofu
3 large stalks bok choy
2 green onions
⅓ cup dark soy sauce
2 tablespoons black bean sauce
2 teaspoons Chinese rice wine or dry sherry
2 teaspoons black rice vinegar
2 teaspoons sugar
¼ teaspoon salt
¼ teaspoon chili paste with garlic
1 teaspoon Hot Chili Oil (page 25)
¼ teaspoon sesame oil
½ cup water
2 tablespoons oil for stir-frying
2 slices ginger, minced
2 garlic cloves, minced
¼ of a red onion, chopped

1. Cook the noodles in boiling water until they are tender. Drain thoroughly. Drain the tofu and cut into cubes.
2. Parboil the bok choy by plunging briefly into boiling water and draining thoroughly. Separate the stalks and leaves. Cut the green onions on the diagonal into 1-inch slices.
3. Combine the dark soy sauce, black bean sauce, rice wine, black rice vinegar, sugar, salt, chili paste with garlic, Hot Chili Oil, sesame oil, and water. Set aside.
4. Add oil to a preheated wok or skillet. When oil is hot, add the ginger, garlic, and green onions. Stir-fry briefly until aromatic. Add the red onion and stir-fry briefly. Push up to the sides and add the bok choy stalks. Add the leaves and stir-fry until the bok choy is a bright green and the onion tender. If desired, season with ¼ teaspoon salt and ¼ teaspoon sugar.
5. Add the sauce in the middle of the wok and bring to a boil. Add the tofu. Simmer for a few minutes to allow the tofu to absorb the sauce. Add the noodles. Mix everything through and serve hot.

Tofu Stuffed with Shrimp

½ pound firm tofu
2 ounces cooked shrimp, peeled and deveined
⅛ teaspoon salt
Pepper to taste
¼ teaspoon cornstarch
½ cup chicken broth
½ teaspoon Chinese rice wine or dry sherry
¼ cup water
2 tablespoons oyster sauce
2 tablespoons oil for stir-frying
1 green onion, cut into 1-inch pieces

Serves 4

This nutritious dish is packed with protein. Serve with a salad for a complete meal.

1. Drain the tofu. Wash the shrimp and pat dry with paper towels. Marinate the shrimp in the salt, pepper, and cornstarch for 15 minutes.
2. Holding the cleaver parallel to the cutting board, cut the tofu in half lengthwise. Cut each half into 2 triangles, then cut each triangle into 2 more triangles. You should now have 8 triangles.
3. Cut a slit lengthwise on one side of the tofu. Stuff ¼–½ teaspoon of the shrimp into the slit.
4. Add oil to a preheated wok or skillet. When oil is hot, add the tofu. Brown the tofu for about 3–4 minutes, turning it over at least once and making sure it doesn't stick to the bottom of the wok. If you have leftover shrimp, add it during the last minute of cooking.
5. Add the chicken broth, rice wine, water, and oyster sauce to the middle of the wok. Bring to a boil. Turn down the heat, cover, and simmer for 5–6 minutes. Stir in the green onion. Serve hot.

Why Drain Tofu?

Think of a block of tofu as a large white sponge. Just as you'd want to drain excess water out of a sponge prior to use, draining the tofu enhances its ability to absorb the flavors of the food it is cooked with.

Pressed Bean Curd with Preserved Szechwan Vegetable

Serves 2–4

Find preserved Szechwan vegetable a little too salty? Try soaking it in warm water for 15 minutes prior to stir-frying, or substitute blanched spinach leaves.

7 ounces (2 blocks) pressed bean curd
¼ cup preserved Szechwan vegetable
½ cup chicken stock or broth
1 teaspoon Chinese rice wine or dry sherry
½ teaspoon sugar
½ teaspoon soy sauce
4–5 cups oil for frying

1. Heat at least 4 cups oil in a preheated wok to 350°F. While waiting for the oil to heat, cut the pressed bean curd into 1-inch cubes. Chop the Szechwan vegetable into cubes. Combine the chicken stock and rice wine and set aside.
2. When oil is hot, add the bean curd cubes, and deep-fry until they turn light brown. Remove from the wok with a slotted spoon and set aside.
3. Remove all but 2 tablespoons oil from the wok. Add the preserved Szechwan vegetable. Stir-fry for 1–2 minutes, then push up to the side of the wok. Add the chicken broth mixture in the middle of the wok and bring to a boil. Mix in the sugar and the soy sauce. Add the pressed bean curd. Mix everything together, simmer for a few minutes, and serve hot.

For Salt Lovers

Who said vegetables are bland? Preserved Szechwan vegetable is famous for its salty taste. The round green vegetable with the reddish trim is one of the ingredients that gives Szechwan cuisine its distinctive flavor. Preserved Szechwan vegetable is sold in cans in Asian markets. Stored in a covered jar after opening, it should last for several months. Pickled first in salt and then in chili paste, it can be a bit overpowering, so use sparingly at first.

Twice Cooked Tofu

½ pound firm tofu
2 tablespoons hoisin sauce
2 tablespoons water
½ teaspoon sugar
1 teaspoon ground Toasted Szechwan Peppercorns (see sidebar on page 93)
1 tablespoon cornstarch
3 cups oil for deep-frying

Serves 4

These tofu cubes make a flavorful addition to stir-fries, cooked noodles, and salad. Cooked Szechwan peppercorns give them an intriguing aroma reminiscent of cinnamon.

1. Preheat oven to 325°F.
2. Drain tofu and cut into ½-inch cubes. Place the tofu cubes on a baking dish.
3. Combine the hoisin sauce, water, and sugar in a small bowl. Spread half the mixture over the tofu cubes. Sprinkle with the Toasted Szechwan Peppercorns. Bake for 15 minutes. Spread the remaining sauce over the tofu and bake for another 15 minutes or until the tofu is browned and cooked.
4. Add oil to a preheated wok and heat to 350°F. While oil is heating, coat the tofu cubes in the cornstarch.
5. When oil is hot, carefully add the tofu cubes into the wok. Deep-fry until browned (this will take 1–2 minutes). Remove and drain on paper towels.

Mapo Dofu (Pockmarked Tofu)

Serves 4

Out of Szechwan peppercorns? Sprinkle the tofu with a bit of freshly ground black pepper.

¾ pound firm tofu
½ pound ground pork
3 tablespoons soy sauce, divided
1½ teaspoons sugar, divided
1½ teaspoons cornstarch
2 stalks bok choy with leaves
1 green onion, chopped
⅔ cup chicken broth
⅓ cup water
1 teaspoon Chinese rice wine or dry sherry
½ teaspoon sesame oil
2 tablespoons oil for stir-frying
2 slices ginger, minced
2 garlic cloves, minced
¼ teaspoon chili paste
2 teaspoons cornstarch
4 teaspoons water
1 teaspoon ground Toasted Szechwan Peppercorns (see sidebar on page 93)

1. Drain the tofu and cut into ½-inch cubes.
2. Place ground pork in a medium bowl. Add 1 tablespoon soy sauce, ½ teaspoon sugar, and cornstarch, adding the cornstarch last. Marinate the pork for 30 minutes.
3. Wash the bok choy and drain thoroughly. Separate the stalks and leaves. Cut into 1-inch pieces. Chop the green onion into 1-inch pieces on the diagonal.
4. Combine the chicken broth, water, 2 tablespoons soy sauce, 1 teaspoon sugar, rice wine, and sesame oil. Set aside.
5. Add oil to a preheated wok or skillet. When oil is hot, add the ginger, garlic, green onion, and chili paste, and stir-fry until aromatic. Add the ground pork. Cook until it changes color, then push up to the side and add the bok choy. Stir-fry until the bok choy turns bright green and tender.
6. Add the sauce to the middle of the wok and bring to a boil. Give the cornstarch-and-water mixture a quick stir and add to the sauce, stirring quickly to thicken. Turn down the heat slightly and add the tofu. Sprinkle the Toasted Szechwan Peppercorns over the tofu. Mix everything through and cook for five more minutes. Serve hot.

Braised Tofu with Three Vegetables

4 dried mushrooms
¼ cup reserved mushroom soaking liquid
⅔ cup fresh mushrooms
½ cup chicken broth
1½ tablespoons oyster sauce
1 teaspoon Chinese rice wine or dry sherry
2 tablespoons oil for stir-frying
1 garlic clove, minced
1 cup baby carrots, halved
2 teaspoons cornstarch mixed with 4 teaspoons water
¾ pound pressed tofu, cut into ½-inch cubes

Serves 2–4

This recipe can easily be doubled to serve as a main dish for 4 people.

1. Soak the dried mushrooms in hot water for at least 20 minutes. Reserve ¼ cup of the soaking liquid. Slice the dried and fresh mushrooms.
2. Combine the reserved mushroom liquid, chicken broth, oyster sauce, and rice wine. Set aside.
3. Add oil to a preheated wok or skillet. When oil is hot, add the garlic and stir-fry briefly until aromatic. Add the carrots. Stir-fry for 1 minute, then add the mushrooms and stir-fry.
4. Add the sauce and bring to a boil. Give the cornstarch-and-water mixture a stir and add to the sauce, stirring quickly to thicken.
5. Add the tofu cubes. Mix everything together, turn down the heat, and simmer for 5–6 minutes. Serve hot.

Pressed Tofu

With most of the moisture removed, pressed tofu is one of the few types of bean curd that doesn't require draining or soaking before cooking. Its firm texture means it holds its shape, making it an excellent choice for braising and grilling. For a different flavor, try boiling pressed tofu in your favorite tea with sugar.

Pork Filled Tofu Triangles

Serves 8

For variety, try adding fresh shrimp marinated in rice wine to the pork stuffing mixture.

½ pound firm tofu
¼ pound ground pork
⅛ teaspoon salt
Pepper to taste
½ teaspoon Chinese rice wine or dry sherry
½ cup chicken broth
¼ cup water
2 tablespoons oyster sauce
2 tablespoons oil for stir-frying
1 green onion, cut into 1-inch pieces

1. Drain the tofu. Place the ground pork in a medium bowl. Add the salt, pepper, and rice wine. Marinate the pork for 15 minutes.
2. Holding the cleaver parallel to the cutting board, cut the tofu in half lengthwise. Cut each half into 2 triangles, then cut each triangle into 2 more triangles. You should now have 8 triangles.
3. Cut a slit lengthwise along one of the edges of each tofu triangle. Stuff a heaping ¼ teaspoon of the ground pork into the slit.
4. Add oil to a preheated wok or skillet. When oil is hot, add the tofu. If you have leftover ground pork, add it also. Brown the tofu for about 3–4 minutes, turning it over at least once and making sure it doesn't stick to the bottom of the wok.
5. Add the chicken broth, water, and oyster sauce to the middle of the wok. Bring to a boil. Turn the heat down, cover, and simmer for 5–6 minutes. Stir in the green onion. Serve hot.

Tofu Pudding

⅔ pound (1⅓ cups) soft tofu
8 Chinese dates
1 large banana, sliced
2 tablespoons honey
½ teaspoon powdered ginger

1. Drain the tofu. Soak the Chinese dates in water for 30 minutes or until softened. Cut in half, removing the pit.
2. Process half of the block of tofu in a blender or food processor until smooth. Add the other half and process. Add the banana, honey, dates, and powdered ginger. Process until smooth.
3. Pour into small bowls and chill for 1 hour.

Serves 4

Out of Chinese dates? Try substituting pitted prunes. This pudding makes a great evening snack, as Chinese dates are rumored to help cure insomnia.

Tea Eggs

6 hard-boiled eggs, cooled
½ cup brewed black tea
1 dried tangerine peel
1 cinnamon stick
3½ cups water

1. Tap each egg very gently with the back of a spoon, until tiny lines form. Try not to actually crack the eggs.
2. Add eggs, black tea, tangerine peel, and cinnamon stick to 3½ cups water and bring to a boil. Simmer, covered, for 2 hours. Turn off the heat, and let the eggs sit in the liquid for a few more hours before serving.
3. To serve, remove the shell and cut into quarters.

Serves 6

This snack puts a new spin on plain hard-boiled eggs. Watch for the "fault" lines traveling down the cooked egg.

Cracked Egg

Don't worry if you crack the egg—the effect of the marbled lines crisscrossing the cooked egg should still be visible.

Egg Foo Yung with Shrimp

Serves 4

This is a great dish for a weekend brunch or days when you want to make something special.

½ cup mung bean sprouts
4 snow peas
¼ red bell pepper
2–4 tablespoons oil
1 oyster mushroom cap, thinly sliced
1–2 button mushrooms, thinly sliced
6 eggs
¼ teaspoon salt
⅛ teaspoon pepper
1 tablespoon oyster sauce
½ teaspoon sugar
1 green onion, cut into 1-inch pieces
6 ounces cooked shrimp, peeled and deveined

1. Blanch the bean sprouts and snow peas by plunging them briefly into boiling water and quickly removing. Drain well.
2. Remove the seeds from the red pepper and cut into thin slices about 1 inch long. Chop the snow peas.
3. Add ½ tablespoon oil to a preheated wok or skillet. When oil is hot, sauté the oyster mushroom slices briefly, just until they collapse. (You can sauté the button mushrooms as well or leave them raw.) Remove from the wok and set aside.
4. Lightly beat the eggs. Stir in the salt, pepper, oyster sauce, and sugar. Mix in the vegetables and the cooked shrimp.
5. Add 2 tablespoons oil to a preheated wok or skillet. When the oil is hot, add a quarter of the egg mixture. Cook until the bottom is cooked, then turn over and cook the other side. Continue with the remainder of the egg mixture, adding more oil if necessary, making 4 omelets. Enjoy as is, or serve with Egg Foo Yung Hoisin Sauce (page 206).

Egg Foo Yung Without the Sauce

Although they taste fine on their own, egg foo yung dishes are normally meant to be accompanied by a savory sauce. If not serving a sauce, consider adding small amounts of powerful seasonings such as chili paste or hoisin sauce to the egg mixture.

Veggie Egg Foo Yung

½ red bell pepper
1 cup mung bean sprouts
6 eggs
¼ teaspoon salt
⅛ teaspoon pepper
1 teaspoon Chinese rice wine or dry sherry
½ teaspoon sugar
4 mushrooms, thinly sliced
1 green onion, thinly sliced
1 cube fermented bean curd, mashed
2–4 tablespoons oil

Serves 4

In this Chinese version of an omelet, the fillings are mixed with the egg prior to cooking, not added in the pan.

1. Remove the seeds from the red pepper and cut into chunks. Blanch the bean sprouts by plunging them briefly into boiling water, and drain.
2. Lightly beat the eggs. Stir in the salt, pepper, rice wine, and sugar. Add the vegetables and mashed bean curd. Mix well.
3. Add 2 tablespoons oil to a preheated wok or skillet. When the oil is hot, add a quarter of the egg mixture. Cook until the bottom is cooked, then turn the omelet over and cook the other side. Continue with the remainder of the mixture, making 4 omelets. Serve with an egg foo yung sauce or soy sauce.

Raw or Cooked?

Lightly cooking vegetables by blanching or sautéing prior to combining with the egg mixture helps coax out their natural flavors. However, if you prefer a crisper texture and higher nutrient content, feel free to skip this step. Another option is to top the egg foo yung with an assortment of raw veggies such as bean sprouts and red and green bell peppers.

Egg Foo Yung with Pork

Serves 6

Barbecued or roast pork works well in this recipe. Be sure to remove any bones before adding the pork to the egg mixture.

¼ red bell pepper
⅔ cup mung bean sprouts
1 stalk celery
1 cup cooked pork, cut into small pieces
4–6 tablespoons oil for stir-frying
½ teaspoon salt, divided
6 eggs
⅛ teaspoon pepper
1 teaspoon Chinese rice wine or dry sherry
4 button mushroom caps, thinly sliced

1. Remove the seeds from the red pepper and cut into thin slices about 1 inch long. Blanch the bean sprouts by plunging briefly into boiling water. Blanch the celery by plunging into the boiling water and boiling for 2–3 minutes. Drain the blanched vegetables thoroughly. Cut the celery into thin slices on the diagonal.
2. Add 2 teaspoons oil to a preheated wok or skillet. When the oil is hot, add the celery and stir-fry on medium high heat. Add ¼ teaspoon salt. Remove the cooked celery from the wok.
3. Lightly beat the eggs. Stir in the pepper, ¼ teaspoon salt, and the rice wine. Add the pork and vegetables, mixing well.
4. Add 2 tablespoons oil to a preheated wok or skillet. When the oil is hot, add one-sixth of the egg mixture. Cook until the bottom is cooked, then turn over and cook the other side. Continue with the remainder of the egg mixture, making 6 omelets. Add more oil while cooking as necessary. Serve with an egg foo yung sauce or soy sauce.

Egg Foo Yung with Chinese Sausage

¼ red bell pepper
½ cup bean sprouts
3 Chinese sausages, cut into small pieces
4–6 tablespoons oil for stir-frying
1 cabbage leaf, shredded
½ teaspoon salt, divided
6 eggs
⅛ teaspoon pepper
1 teaspoon Chinese rice wine or dry sherry
4 button mushroom caps, thinly sliced

Serves 6

This Chinese version of eggs and sausages uses Chinese sausage, which is leaner and contains less fat than many pork sausages.

1. Remove the seeds from the red pepper and cut into thin slices about 1 inch long. Blanch the bean sprouts by plunging briefly into boiling water. Drain thoroughly.
2. Add 2 tablespoons oil to a preheated wok or skillet. When the oil is hot, add the cabbage and stir-fry on medium-high heat. Add ¼ teaspoon salt. Remove from the wok.
3. Lightly beat the eggs. Stir in the pepper, ¼ teaspoon salt, and the rice wine. Add the sausage and vegetables, mixing well.
4. Add 2 tablespoons oil to a preheated wok or skillet. When the oil is hot, add ⅙ of the egg mixture. Cook until the bottom is cooked, then turn over and cook the other side. Continue with the remainder of the egg mixture, making 6 omelets. Add more oil while cooking as necessary. Serve with an egg foo yung sauce or soy sauce.

Egg Foo Yung Hoisin Sauce

Yields ⅓ cup

This savory combination of oyster and hoisin sauce makes a nice accompaniment to Egg Foo Yung with Shrimp (page 202).

1 tablespoon oyster sauce
2 teaspoons hoisin sauce
1 teaspoon Chinese rice wine or dry sherry
2 tablespoons water
1 teaspoon cornstarch mixed with 4 teaspoons water

Bring the oyster sauce, hoisin sauce, rice wine, and water to a boil. Add the cornstarch-and-water mixture and stir vigorously to thicken. Serve with egg foo yung.

Egg Foo Yung Sauce with Beef Broth

Yields ½ cup

This robust sauce goes well with omelet dishes containing meat, such as Egg Foo Yung with Pork (page 204).

½ cup beef broth
1 teaspoon sugar
¼ teaspoon sesame oil
1 tablespoon cornstarch mixed with 4 tablespoons water

1. Bring the beef broth, sugar, and sesame oil to a boil.
2. Add the cornstarch-and-water mixture, stirring vigorously. Serve with egg foo yung.

Egg Foo Yung Chicken Sauce

½ cup chicken broth or stock
1 tablespoon soy sauce
1 tablespoon Chinese rice wine or dry sherry
¼ teaspoon sesame oil
A pinch of freshly ground black pepper

Combine all the ingredients and bring to a boil. Serve with egg foo yung.

Yields ½ cup

For a thicker sauce, add 1 teaspoon cornstarch mixed with 4 teaspoons water. Pour the sauce over the egg foo yung or serve separately.

Basic Scrambled Eggs

4 large eggs, lightly beaten
¼ cup chicken broth or stock
½ teaspoon Chinese rice wine or dry sherry
Up to ⅛ teaspoon salt
Pepper to taste
1½ green onions, thinly sliced on the diagonal
2 tablespoons oil for frying

1. Take the beaten eggs and stir in the chicken broth, rice wine, salt, pepper, and green onions.
2. Add the oil to a preheated wok or heavy skillet and turn the heat on high. When oil is hot, add the egg mixture. Scramble gently until the eggs are almost cooked but still moist. Remove from the heat and let sit for a minute before serving.

Serves 3–4

Long cooking chopsticks are perfect for lightly beating the eggs and scrambling them during cooking.

Scrambled Eggs with Sausage

Serves 4

For extra flavor, feel free to add 2 tablespoons of chopped red onion to this dish.

4 large eggs, lightly beaten
1/4 cup beef broth
Salt and pepper to taste
1/2 teaspoon sugar
1 green onion, thinly sliced on the diagonal
2 tablespoons oil for stir-frying
2 Chinese sausages, cut into small pieces

1. Take the beaten eggs and stir in the beef broth, salt, pepper, sugar, and green onion.
2. Add 1 tablespoon oil to a preheated wok or skillet. When the oil is hot, add the sausages. Stir-fry until they are cooked and drain on paper towels.
3. Add 1 tablespoon oil and turn the heat on high. When oil is hot, add the egg mixture. Scramble gently for about 30 seconds, then add the sausages. Continue scrambling until the eggs are almost cooked but still moist. Remove from the heat and let sit for a minute before serving.

Red Eggs and Ginger

The Chinese celebrate a baby's one-month birthday by holding a Red Egg and Ginger Party. Like any birthday party, guests bring gifts for the baby. Meanwhile, the proud parents hand out dyed red eggs. In Chinese culture, red symbolizes happiness, while eggs are a symbol of fertility.

Scrambled Eggs with Shrimp

4 ounces shrimp, peeled and deveined
4 large eggs, lightly beaten
¼ cup chicken broth or stock
Up to ⅛ teaspoon salt
Pepper to taste
½ teaspoon Chinese rice wine or dry sherry
1 teaspoon oyster sauce
1 green onion, thinly sliced on the diagonal
2 tablespoons oil for frying

Serves 4

If you wish, marinate the shrimp in rice wine or dry sherry and a bit of cornstarch before stir-frying.

1. Wash the shrimp and pat dry. Take beaten eggs and stir in the chicken broth, salt, pepper, rice wine, oyster sauce, and green onion.
2. Add 1 tablespoon oil to a preheated wok or skillet. When the oil is hot, add the shrimp. Stir-fry briefly, until they turn pink. Remove and drain.
3. Add 1 tablespoon oil and turn the heat on high. When oil is hot, add the egg mixture. Scramble gently for about 1 minute, then add the shrimp. Continue scrambling until the eggs are almost cooked but still moist. Remove from the heat and let sit for a minute before serving.

Thousand-Year-Old Eggs

Of course, they're not really 1,000 years old. A better name for the dark, strongly flavored eggs found in Asian markets is preserved eggs. Duck eggs are preserved in a mixture of pine ash, clay or mud, and salt for about 100 days. Refrigerated, thousand-year-old eggs will last for months, but they do need to be rinsed thoroughly before eating.

Chapter 10
Fish and Other Seafood

Shrimply Delicious Pork Balls

Yields 12–14 balls

This dish can be prepared up to the deep-frying stage and frozen until ready to use. Thaw before deep-frying.

3½ ounces fresh shrimp, shells on
¾ pound ground pork
¾ teaspoon grated ginger
2 teaspoons finely minced green onion
2 teaspoons finely chopped water chestnut
1¼ teaspoons Chinese rice wine or dry sherry
⅛ teaspoon salt
Pepper to taste
1 egg
1 teaspoon cornstarch
4–6 cups oil for deep-frying

1. Remove the shells from the shrimp and devein. Mince the shrimp into a fine paste.
2. Add the ground pork to the shrimp. Mix in the ginger, green onion, water chestnut, rice wine, salt, pepper, egg, and cornstarch.
3. Heat oil in a preheated wok to at least 350°F. While oil is heating, shape the shrimp and pork mixture into round balls approximately the size of golf balls.
4. When oil is ready, deep-fry the shrimp-and-pork balls, a few at a time, until they are golden brown. (Make sure the pork is cooked but don't overcook.) Remove from the wok with a slotted spoon and drain on paper towels.

Butter Prawns

2 cups fresh tiger prawns
½ teaspoon Chinese rice wine or dry sherry
¼ teaspoon salt
1 teaspoon cornstarch
½ cup chicken broth
1 tablespoon plus 1 teaspoon oyster sauce
½ teaspoon sugar
2 tablespoons oil for stir-frying
1 tablespoon butter
1 small garlic clove, minced
½ teaspoon chili sauce with garlic

Serves 4–6

Butter prawns taste delicious served with steamed rice, stir-fried noodles, or on toasted French bread.

1. Shell and devein the prawns. Rinse in warm water and pat dry with paper towels. Marinate the prawns in the rice wine, salt, and cornstarch for 15 minutes.
2. Combine the chicken broth, oyster sauce, and sugar, and set aside.
3. Add oil to a preheated wok or skillet. When oil is hot, add the prawns and stir-fry briefly, until they turn pink. Remove and drain on paper towels.
4. Add the butter, garlic, and chili sauce with garlic. Stir-fry briefly, then add the prawns. Stir-fry for about a minute, mixing the prawns in with the butter, then add the sauce. Bring the sauce to a boil. Mix the sauce with the prawns and serve hot.

How to Devein a Prawn

Deveining a prawn or shrimp removes the gray, threadlike intestinal track running along its back. To devein, peel the prawn or shrimp. Take a sharp knife and cut a slit down the back. Remove the vein.

Spicy Fish Fry

Serves 2–4

Young ginger, which has a light color and is quite tender, works well in this dish.

½ pound fish fillets
½ cup chicken broth
1 teaspoon brown sugar
1 teaspoon black rice vinegar
1 green onion
3 tablespoons oil for stir-frying
½ tablespoon minced ginger
¼ teaspoon chili paste
1 cup fresh mushrooms, sliced

1. Wash the fish fillets and pat dry. Cut into slices approximately 2 inches by ½ inch.
2. Combine the chicken broth, brown sugar, and black rice vinegar. Set aside. Cut the green onion into 1-inch slices on the diagonal.
3. Add 2 tablespoons oil to a preheated wok or skillet. When oil is hot, add the fish pieces. Stir-fry until browned. Remove from the wok and drain on paper towels.
4. Add 1 tablespoon oil to the wok. Add the ginger and chili paste and stir-fry until aromatic. Add the mushrooms. Stir-fry until tender, then push up to the sides of the wok. Add the sauce in the middle of the wok and bring to a boil. Add the fish and stir in the green onion. Mix through and serve hot.

Fish Tales

Fish plays an important role in Chinese celebrations. It is common to serve a whole fish on special occasions, as it symbolizes wealth and abundance. If entertaining, the head is pointed toward the guest of honor.

Stir-fried Fish Fillets

½ pound fish fillets
1 teaspoon Chinese rice wine or dry sherry
1 tablespoon soy sauce
2 green onions, divided
2 tablespoons oil for stir-frying
½ cup chicken broth
2 tablespoons oyster sauce
2 teaspoons brown sugar
¼ teaspoon sesame oil
½ tablespoon minced ginger

Serves 2–4

Cod fillets work well in this dish. Serve with rice and stir-fried vegetables for a healthy, protein-packed meal.

1. Wash the fish fillets and pat dry with paper towels. Marinate in the rice wine, soy sauce, and 1 sliced green onion for 30 minutes.
2. Combine the chicken broth, oyster sauce, brown sugar, and sesame oil. Set aside. Cut the remaining green onion into 1-inch pieces.
3. Add oil to a preheated wok or skillet. When oil is hot, add the ginger. Stir-fry briefly until aromatic. Add the fish fillets and cook until they are browned on both sides (2–3 minutes on each side).
4. Add the sauce in the middle of the wok and bring to a boil. Stir in the green onion. Reduce the heat, cover, and simmer for about 10 minutes. Serve hot.

Lumpy Brown Sugar

One of the less attractive features of brown sugar is its tendency to form lumps. This happens when the sugar loses moisture and hardens. There are several ways to remove lumps. First, if the sugar is being used in a hot sauce, simply melt it to remove the lumps before adding to the sauce. Stir constantly while the sugar is melting in the saucepan. If the recipe calls for dry sugar, use a strainer to squeeze out the lumps. Several techniques exist for adding the moisture back into the sugar, but these normally take several days.

Honey Walnut Shrimp

Yields 2 cups

The sweet flavor of coconut milk nicely balances the tart lemon in this popular restaurant dish.

½ cup chopped walnut pieces
¼ cup sugar
½ pound shrimp
1 egg, lightly beaten
4 tablespoons cornstarch
1½ tablespoons honey
3 tablespoons mayonnaise
3¾ teaspoons freshly squeezed lemon juice
3 tablespoons coconut milk
3 cups oil for deep-frying

1. Earlier in the day, boil the walnut pieces for 5 minutes. Drain well. Spread the sugar on a piece of wax paper. Roll the walnut pieces in the sugar and allow to dry.
2. Peel and devein the shrimp. Wash and pat dry with paper towels.
3. Heat oil to 375°F. While waiting for oil to heat, mix the egg with the cornstarch to form a batter. Dip the shrimp in the egg batter. Deep-fry the shrimp until they turn golden brown. Remove from the wok with a slotted spoon and drain on paper towels. Cool.
4. Combine the honey, mayonnaise, lemon juice, and coconut milk. Mix in with the shrimp. Serve on a platter with the sugared walnuts arranged around the shrimp.

Prawns versus Shrimp

If you think a prawn and a shrimp look nearly identical, you're right. One type of prawn is merely an oversized shrimp. (The word prawn is also given to another type of crustacean related to the lobster.) Prawns can be substituted for shrimp in most recipes—just be sure to adjust for differences in volume where necessary.

Kung Pao Shrimp

1 pound shrimp, peeled and deveined
½ cup chicken broth
2 tablespoons Chinese rice wine or dry sherry
2 teaspoons soy sauce
2½–3 tablespoons oil for stir-frying
2 slices ginger, minced
¼ teaspoon chili paste
½ cup peanuts

Serves 4

This simple dish makes an excellent appetizer as well as main course. Like Kung Pao Chicken, it can also be made with cashews instead of peanuts.

1. Wash the shrimp and pat dry with paper towels. Combine the chicken broth, rice wine, and soy sauce, and set aside.
2. Add 1½ tablespoons oil to a preheated wok or skillet. When oil is hot, add the shrimp. Stir-fry very briefly, just until they change color. Remove and set aside.
3. Add 1 tablespoon oil to the wok. When oil is hot, add the ginger and chili paste. Stir-fry briefly until aromatic. Add the peanuts. Stir-fry for about 1 minute until they turn golden but are not burnt.
4. Push the peanuts up to the side of the wok. Add the sauce to the middle of the wok and bring to a boil. Add the shrimp back into the wok. Mix everything together and serve hot.

Storing Ginger

Ginger will keep for several days when stored in a paper bag that is kept in the vegetable crisper section of the refrigerator. For longer storage, place the ginger in a sealed container, fill with Chinese rice wine or a good pale, dry sherry, and store in the refrigerator. As the ginger flavor fades, you will have the flavor of the sherry to compensate.

Shrimp Paste

Yields 1½ cups

Shrimp paste can be made ahead of time and refrigerated in a sealed container. Use within a few days.

½ pound (8 ounces) shrimp, peeled and deveined
1 tablespoon plus 1 teaspoon vegetable shortening
½ teaspoon grated ginger
2 teaspoons minced green onion
2 teaspoons finely minced water chestnut
½ teaspoon Chinese rice wine or dry sherry
⅛ teaspoon salt
Pepper to taste
1 medium egg
1 tablespoon plus 1 teaspoon cornstarch

1. Rinse the shrimp in warm water and pat dry with paper towels. Purée the shrimp and the vegetable shortening in a food processor or blender. Add the ginger, green onion, water chestnut, rice wine, salt, and pepper. Purée.
2. Lightly beat the egg. Mix in the shrimp and vegetable mixture. Add the cornstarch, using your hands to mix it in. The shrimp paste is now ready.

Traditional Shrimp Toast

Yields about 50 toasted squares

The total number of appetizers will depend on how thickly you spread the shrimp paste on the bread.

12–15 slices of white bread, crusts removed
Shrimp Paste
4–6 cups oil for deep-frying

1. Add oil to a preheated wok and heat to 350°F. While oil is heating, cut each slice of bread into 4 triangles. Spread up to ½ teaspoon of shrimp paste on each bread piece.
2. When oil is hot, carefully add the bread into the wok. Cook for 2 minutes on one side, then turn over and cook for 2 minutes on the other side. Remove and drain on paper towels. Serve immediately.

Quick and Easy Shrimp Toast

7 ounces shrimp
½ teaspoon grated ginger
2 teaspoons finely minced green onion
2 teaspoons finely chopped water chestnut
½ teaspoon Chinese rice wine or dry sherry
⅛ teaspoon salt
Pepper to taste
1 egg
1 teaspoon cornstarch
8 slices bread
¼ cup water
4–6 cups oil for deep-frying

Serves 4

This recipe makes a quick and easy lunch or snack. For a more formal dish, try Traditional Shrimp Toast (page 218) or Crispy Fried Shrimp Toast (page 220).

1. Remove the shells from the shrimp and devein. Mince the shrimp into a fine paste.
2. Mix in the ginger, green onion, water chestnut, rice wine, salt, pepper, egg, and cornstarch.
3. Add the oil to a preheated wok and heat to at least 350°F. While oil is heating, break each slice of bread into 4 equal squares. Dip briefly into the water, remove, and use your fingers to squeeze out excess water.
4. Spread a heaping teaspoon of the shrimp mixture onto each square of bread. When oil is hot, slide a few of the squares into the hot oil. Fry one side until it turns brown (about 1 minute), then turn over and brown the other side. Remove from the wok with a slotted spoon and drain on paper towels. Continue with the remainder of the bread squares.

Crispy Fried Shrimp Toast

Yields 25 appetizers

This recipe can also be made with prawns. For added flavor, serve with a bowl of dipping sauce such as Speedy Sweet Chili Sauce (page 28).

¾ cup flour
1 teaspoon baking powder
½ teaspoon sugar
¼ teaspoon salt
2 tablespoons vegetable oil
¾ cup water
6 slices white bread, crusts removed
Shrimp Paste (page 218)
4–6 cups oil for deep-frying

1. Sift together the flour and baking powder. Stir in the sugar, salt, and vegetable oil. Slowly stir in the water, adding more or less as needed to make a batter.
2. Add oil to a preheated wok and heat to 360°F. While oil is heating, cut each slice of bread into 4 triangles. Spread ½ teaspoon of shrimp paste on each side of the triangle.
3. When ready to cook, use your fingers to coat the bread with the batter. Carefully add the bread into the wok, a few slices at a time. Cook on one side for 2 minutes, then turn over and cook the other side for 2 minutes or until the batter has turned golden brown. Remove and drain on paper towels.

Quick and Easy Shrimp Paste

To make shrimp paste, finely mince the shrimp, then hold the cleaver parallel to the cutting board and use it to drag the shrimp along the board.

Butterfly Prawns

10 large tiger prawns
1 large egg
½ teaspoon Szechwan peppercorns, roasted and ground
5 tablespoons breadcrumbs
3–4 cups oil for deep-frying

1. Remove the shells from the prawns, but leave the tails intact. Rinse the prawns in warm water. Pat dry with paper towels.
2. Lightly beat the egg. In a separate bowl, mix the Szechwan peppercorns with the breadcrumbs.
3. Add oil to a preheated wok and heat to at least 350°F. To prepare prawns for deep-frying, grab by the tail and dip into the beaten egg, then coat with the breadcrumbs.
4. When oil is hot, deep-fry the prawns until they turn golden brown (about 1 minute). Remove and drain on paper towels. Serve warm.

Yields 10 prawns

This dish tastes delicious with stir-fried spinach or Chinese greens. For added flavor, serve with a dipping sauce.

Fried Prawn Crackers

1 package prawn crackers
4–6 cups oil for deep-frying

Heat oil to 350°F, and deep-fry the crackers. They will puff up within seconds. Remove immediately and drain on paper towels.

Serves 6

These delicate crackers make a tasty appetizer or snack. Be sure to remove them from the hot oil as soon as they puff up.

Sweet-and-Sour Shrimp

Serves 2–4

The delicate sweet flavor of pineapple goes well with shrimp. Serve with Basic Scented Rice (page 82).

20 large fresh shrimp, peeled and deveined
½ green bell pepper
½ red bell pepper
⅓ cup rice vinegar
¼ cup brown sugar
2 tablespoons ketchup
1 tablespoon soy sauce
½ cup water
2 teaspoons cornstarch mixed with 4 teaspoons water
½ cup pineapple chunks
2 tablespoons oil for stir-frying

1. Rinse the shrimp in warm water and pat dry with paper towels. Wash the peppers, remove the seeds, and cut into cubes.
2. In a small saucepan, combine the rice vinegar, brown sugar, ketchup, soy sauce, and water, and bring to a boil.
3. Stir in the cornstarch-and-water mixture, stirring vigorously to thicken. Add the pineapple and peppers. Turn the heat to low and keep the sauce warm while stir-frying the shrimp.
4. Add oil to a preheated wok or skillet. When oil is hot, add the shrimp. Stir-fry briefly until they are cooked. Remove from the wok.
5. Pour the sauce over the shrimp and serve hot.

Daily Rice Bowl

Rice is so important in southern China that the phrase for eating includes the word "rice." And instead of saying hello, people greet each other by asking, "Have you eaten yet?"

Lobster Cantonese

1 teaspoon fermented black beans
1 clove garlic, minced
¾ cup chicken broth
2 tablespoons Chinese rice wine or dry sherry, divided
1 tablespoon soy sauce
2 tablespoons oil for stir-frying
¼ pound ground pork
3 slices ginger, minced
1 green onion, thinly sliced
1 tablespoon cornstarch mixed with 4 tablespoons water
2 lobster tails, cut into ½-inch pieces
1 teaspoon sugar
1 egg, lightly beaten

Serves 2

The secret to preparing this popular Cantonese dish is not to overcook the lobster tails.

1. Soak the beans in warm water and rinse. Mash, chop finely, and mix with the garlic clove.
2. Combine the chicken broth, 1 tablespoon rice wine, and soy sauce. Set aside.
3. Add oil to a preheated wok or skillet. When oil is hot, add the garlic and black bean mixture. Stir-fry briefly until aromatic. Add the pork and stir-fry for several minutes, until cooked through.
4. Push the ingredients up to the side of the wok. Add the ginger and green onion in the middle. Stir-fry briefly. Add the sauce and bring to a boil. Give the cornstarch-and-water mixture a quick stir and add, stirring quickly to thicken.
5. Add the lobster, the sugar, and 1 tablespoon rice wine. Stir-fry for about 2 minutes, then stream in the egg. Mix together and serve.

Preparing Fermented Black Beans

Soak the beans until they are softened. Mash the beans by flattening them under the blade of a knife or cleaver, and then mince or chop as called for in the recipe.

Pepper-Salt Shrimp or Prawns

Serves 2–4

This quick and easy dish makes an excellent party appetizer. Serve garnished with lemon wedges.

1 pound fresh shrimp or prawns, peeled and deveined
2 egg whites
¼ cup cornstarch
2 tablespoons Szechwan Salt and Pepper Mix (page 22)
1–2 cups oil for deep-frying

1. Wash and pat dry the shrimp or prawns with paper towels.
2. Heat oil in a preheated wok to 375°F. While oil is heating, mix the egg whites with cornstarch to form a smooth batter.
3. Lightly coat the shrimp with the Szechwan Salt and Pepper Mix. Dip into the batter. Place a few shrimp at a time into the wok. Deep-fry until they turn golden brown (about 3 minutes). Remove and drain on paper towels.

Deep-fried Fish

Serves 2–4

Serve the deep-fried fish fillets immediately, or cook further by braising in a flavorful sauce.

½ pound fish fillets
1 egg white
2 teaspoons soy sauce
1 tablespoon cornstarch
4 cups oil for deep-frying

1. Wash fish and pat dry. Cut into bite-sized squares. Add the egg white, soy sauce, and cornstarch, adding the cornstarch last. Marinate the fish for 30 minutes.
2. Heat oil in a preheated wok to 375°F. When oil is hot, add the fish. Fry until golden brown. Remove and drain on paper towels.

Hot and Sour Prawns

2 cups fresh tiger prawns
½ teaspoon Chinese rice wine or dry sherry
¼ teaspoon salt
1 teaspoon cornstarch
½ cup water
2 tablespoons black rice vinegar
½–1 teaspoon Hot Chili Oil (page 25)
1½ teaspoons Worcestershire sauce
2 teaspoons cornstarch mixed with 4 teaspoons water
2 tablespoons oil for stir-frying

Serves 4–6

This hot dish is a great way to enliven plain stir-fried or boiled noodles or steamed rice.

1. Shell and devein the prawns. Rinse in warm water and pat dry with paper towels. Marinate the prawns in the rice wine, salt, and cornstarch for 15 minutes.
2. In a small saucepan, bring the water, black rice vinegar, Hot Chili Oil, and Worcestershire sauce to a boil. Add the cornstarch-and-water mixture, stirring quickly to thicken. Turn the heat to low and keep warm.
3. Add oil to a preheated wok or skillet. When oil is hot, add the prawns and stir-fry briefly, until they turn pink. Push up to the side and add the sauce in the middle of the wok. Mix the prawns with the sauce. Serve hot.

Yin and Yang Harmony

The philosophy of yin and yang permeates every aspect of Chinese culture, including the kitchens of its cooks. Yin and yang represent all the forces in the universe. Things that are feminine, cold, dark, or submissive are said to be yin in nature, while masculinity, heat, light, and dominance are yang forces. Chinese physicians frequently treat illness as an imbalance between yin and yang in the body. For example, since heartburn is thought to come from consuming too many spicy yang foods, a physician might prescribe a soup featuring yin ingredients like walnuts as a tonic.

Sweet-and-Sour Fish

Serves 4–6

Ginger makes a frequent appearance in seafood dishes because it helps to mask fishy odors.

1 pound fish fillets
2 teaspoons Chinese rice wine or dry sherry
2 tablespoons soy sauce
½ cup rice vinegar
½ cup brown sugar
½ cup water
3 tablespoons tomato paste
3–4 tablespoons oil for stir-frying
2 slices ginger, minced
1 cup mushrooms, thinly sliced
1 stalk celery, thinly sliced on the diagonal
⅓ cup canned bamboo shoots, shredded
1 teaspoon cornstarch
4 teaspoons water
1 green onion, thinly sliced on the diagonal

1. Wash fish fillets and pat dry. Cut into pieces approximately 2 inches by ½ inch. Marinate in the rice wine and soy sauce for 30 minutes.
2. Combine the rice vinegar, brown sugar, water, and tomato paste. Set aside.
3. Add 2 tablespoons oil to a preheated wok or skillet. When oil is hot, add the fish and stir-fry until it is nicely browned all over. Remove and drain on paper towels.
4. Add 1 tablespoon oil to the wok. Add the ginger and stir-fry briefly until aromatic. Add the mushrooms. Stir-fry for a minute, then add the celery and the bamboo shoots. Stir-fry until tender, adding salt or sugar to season if desired.
5. Push the vegetables up to the side of the wok and add the sauce in the middle. Bring to a boil. Mix the cornstarch and water, and add to the wok, stirring quickly to thicken. Add the fish and stir in the green onion. Cook for a few more minutes and serve hot.

Prawns with Mangetout (Snow Peas)

20 fresh prawns
1 teaspoon sugar
1 teaspoon cornstarch
1 cup (about 25) snow peas
½ cup mung bean sprouts
2 tablespoons oil for stir-frying
1 slice ginger, finely chopped
1½ teaspoons Chinese rice wine or dry sherry

Serves 2–4

Serve on a bed of steamed rice mixed with green onion, garnished with slices of orange.

1. Shell and devein the prawns. Rinse in warm water and pat dry with paper towels. Marinate in the sugar and cornstarch for 15 minutes.
2. Wash and string the snow peas. Blanch the snow peas and bean sprouts by plunging briefly into boiling water. Drain thoroughly.
3. Add oil to a preheated wok or skillet. When oil is hot, add the ginger and stir-fry briefly until aromatic. Add the prawns and stir-fry briefly until they turn a pinkish-red color.
4. Add the snow peas to the wok. Stir-fry briefly, then add the bean sprouts. Splash with the 1½ teaspoons rice wine. Serve hot.

Mung Bean Sprouts

While raw mung bean sprouts are a popular salad topping in the West, the Chinese prefer their sprouts cooked. Mung bean sprouts feature prominently in stir-fries and appetizers. When choosing mung bean sprouts, look for ones that are plump and don't have any brown coloring. If using within a few days, store the sprouts with a few drops of water in a plastic bag in the refrigerator. They can also be frozen for use later in stir-fries, although the texture won't be as crisp.

Spicy Shrimp with Hot Shanghai Noodles

Serves 4

Adding the hot bean sauce after the noodles helps reduce its strength. Use sparingly at first, and add more to taste if desired.

10 ounces cooked shrimp
¼ teaspoon five-spice powder
½ teaspoon cornstarch
2 stalks bok choy
4 tablespoons oil for stir-frying
2 leaves cabbage, shredded
1 teaspoon soy sauce
2 garlic cloves, finely chopped
2 slices ginger, finely chopped
¾ pound fresh Shanghai noodles
1 tablespoon hot bean sauce, or to taste

1. Rinse the shrimp in warm water and pat dry. Marinate the shrimp in the five-spice powder and cornstarch for at least 15 minutes.
2. Wash the bok choy and drain thoroughly. Separate the stalks and leaves. Cut across the leaves and cut the stalks into 1-inch pieces on the diagonal.
3. Add 2 tablespoons oil to a preheated wok or skillet. When oil is hot, add the shrimp and stir-fry briefly until it changes color. Push the shrimp up to the side and add the bok choy stalks and cabbage. Stir-fry briefly, then add the bok choy leaves. Add 1 teaspoon soy sauce, and stir-fry until the vegetables turn a bright color and are tender. Remove from the wok and set aside.
4. Add 2 tablespoons oil to the wok or skillet. When oil is hot, add the garlic and ginger. Stir-fry briefly until aromatic. Add the noodles. Stir-fry briefly, then mix in the hot bean sauce. If necessary, add 2 tablespoons water. Add the shrimp and vegetables. Mix everything through and serve hot.

Sweet-and-Sour Fish with Lychees

1 pound fish fillets
2 egg whites
4 teaspoons soy sauce
2 tablespoons cornstarch
1 cup lychees, drained
½ cup rice vinegar
½ cup brown sugar
½ cup water
3 tablespoons tomato paste
1 tablespoon minced ginger
1 green onion, thinly sliced
1 teaspoon cornstarch mixed with 4 teaspoons water
4 cups oil for frying

Serves 4–6

The Chinese consider the heart-shaped lychee to be a symbol of romance. Its sweet flavor goes very well with a sweet-and-sour sauce.

1. Wash the fish and pat dry with paper towels. Cut into thin slices.
2. Add the egg whites, soy sauce, and cornstarch, adding the cornstarch last. Marinate the fish for 30 minutes. Cut the lychees in half if desired.
3. Bring the rice vinegar, brown sugar, water, and tomato paste to boil in a small saucepan. Stir in the lychees. Keep warm.
4. Heat oil in a preheated wok to 375°F. When oil is hot, add the fish. Deep-fry until golden brown. Remove and drain on paper towels.
5. Remove all but 2 tablespoons oil from the wok. Add the ginger and stir-fry briefly until aromatic. Add the green onion. Add the sauce and bring to a boil. Give the cornstarch-and-water mixture a quick stir. Add, stirring to thicken. Reduce the heat. Add the fish. Mix through and serve hot.

Lychee Lore

Native to southern China, lychees hold a special place in Chinese food culture. Successions of Emperors prized the small, heart-shaped fruit for its sweet flavor. An exiled Chinese poet is reputed to have consoled himself by consuming 300 lychees daily. Nutritionally, lychees are low in calories and a good source of vitamin C. Fresh lychees come into season during the summer months; they are available canned in syrup year-round. Both are sold in Asian markets.

Shrimp with Lobster Sauce

Serves 4

For a fancier presentation, butterfly the shrimp by removing the shell but leaving the tail intact. Prepare the sauce separately and pour over the shrimp.

½ pound medium shrimp
1 teaspoon fermented black beans
1 clove garlic, minced
¾ cup chicken broth
2 tablespoons Chinese rice wine or dry sherry, divided
1 tablespoon soy sauce
¼ pound ground pork
4 tablespoons oil for stir-frying
1 tablespoon cornstarch
4 tablespoons water
1 teaspoon sugar
1 egg, lightly beaten

1. Shell and devein shrimp.
2. Add 2 tablespoons oil to a preheated wok or skillet. When oil is hot, add the shrimp. Stir-fry until they turn pink and are nearly cooked. Remove from the wok and drain on paper towels.
3. To prepare the lobster sauce: Soak the fermented black beans in warm water and rinse. Mash, chop finely, and mix with the garlic clove. Combine the chicken broth, 1 tablespoon rice wine, and soy sauce. Set aside.
4. Add 1–2 tablespoons oil. When oil is hot, add the garlic and black bean mixture. Stir-fry briefly until aromatic. Add the pork and stir-fry for several minutes, until cooked through.
5. Push the ingredients up to the side of the wok. Add the sauce and bring to a boil. Mix cornstarch and water and add to the wok, stirring quickly to thicken.
6. Mix in the sugar, and 1 tablespoon rice wine. Stream in the egg. Add the shrimp. Mix together and serve hot.

Shrimp with Lobster Sauce

The name of this dish can be confusing, since it doesn't contain any lobster. It derives its name from the dried black beans that lend a savory flavor to the sauce. Fermented black beans are also a key ingredient in Lobster Cantonese (page 223).

Quick and Easy Salt and Pepper Squid

1 pound cleaned squid
2 teaspoons Szechwan Salt and Pepper Mix (page 22)
¼ cup cornstarch
2 tablespoons soy sauce
1 tablespoon Chinese rice wine or dry sherry
1 teaspoon sugar
½ teaspoon sesame oil
½ teaspoon Hot Chili Oil (page 25)
1 clove garlic, minced
2 slices ginger, minced
2–3 cups oil for frying

Serves 4

The trick to this dish is not to overcook the seafood. When cooked too long, squid turns rubbery.

1. Cut the cleaned squid into 1-inch pieces.
2. In a bowl, mix the Szechwan Salt and Pepper Mix in with the cornstarch. In a separate bowl, combine the soy sauce, rice wine, sugar, sesame oil, and Hot Chili Oil. Set aside.
3. Add oil to a preheated wok or skillet. While oil is heating, dip the squid pieces in the Szechwan Salt and Pepper and cornstarch mixture.
4. When oil is hot, add the squid pieces, a few at a time. Deep-fry for about 2 minutes, until they change color. Remove and drain on paper towels.
5. Remove all but 2 tablespoons oil from the wok. Add the ginger and garlic, and stir-fry briefly until aromatic. Add the sauce in the middle of the wok and bring to a boil. Add the squid and cook very briefly. Mix through and serve hot.

CHAPTER 11

Chinese Vegetables

Stir-fried Water Chestnuts and Bamboo Shoots

Serves 4

Use this basic recipe anytime you want to stir-fry vegetables. The only thing that will change is the stir-frying time for different types of vegetables.

2 tablespoons oil for stir-frying
1 teaspoon minced ginger
1 8-ounce can bamboo shoots, rinsed and drained
¼ teaspoon salt
1 can water chestnuts, rinsed and drained
½ cup chicken broth
1 tablespoon soy sauce
1 teaspoon sugar
1 green onion, cut into 1½-inch pieces

1. Cut the water chestnuts in half.
2. Add the oil to a preheated wok or skillet. When the oil is hot, add the ginger. Stir-fry briefly until aromatic. Add the bamboo shoots. Stir-fry for 1–2 minutes, and add the salt. Mix in and add the water chestnuts. Stir-fry for 1–2 more minutes, and then add the chicken broth, soy sauce, and sugar.
3. Bring the broth to a boil, and then turn down the heat and simmer for a few more minutes, until everything is nicely cooked through. Stir in the green onion and serve.

Stir-frying in Order

Stir-fry vegetables according to density, adding the thickest vegetables to the wok first, so that they cook longest. If you're uncertain about the correct order, just stir-fry all the vegetables separately and add back into the wok during the final stages of cooking.

Snow Pea Stir-fry

2 cups snow peas
1½ tablespoons oil for stir-frying
¾ teaspoon sugar
1½ tablespoons Chinese rice wine or dry sherry

1. Wash and string the snow peas. In a frying pan or preheated wok, add the oil.
2. When oil is hot, begin stir-frying the snow peas. Add the sugar and rice wine.
3. Stir-fry until the snow peas turn a bright green and are hot.

Serves 4

Serve as a side dish with Lemony Chicken Stir-fry (page 161), or use where snow peas are called for in recipes.

Parsnips with Creamy Sauce

1 tablespoon cornstarch
6 tablespoons water, divided
1½ tablespoons oil for stir-frying
3 parsnips, sliced on the diagonal
1 teaspoon brown sugar
⅛ teaspoon salt, or to taste
½ cup milk

1. In a small bowl, mix the cornstarch with 2 tablespoons water.
2. Add oil to a preheated wok or skillet. When oil is hot, add the parsnips. Stir-fry for about 1 minute. Add 4 tablespoons water, brown sugar, and salt. Cover and cook on medium heat for about another 5 minutes.
3. Give the cornstarch-and-water mixture a quick stir and add it to the milk. Push the parsnips up the side of the wok and add the cornstarch and milk mixture in the middle. Turn up the heat and stir rapidly to thicken.

Serves 3–4

While milk isn't normally used in Chinese cooking, it is found in this variation on a popular northern Chinese dish.

Glazed Carrots

Serves 4

Brown sugar enhances the carrot's natural sweetness making this a great accompaniment to dishes made with oyster sauce.

2 tablespoons oil for stir-frying
4 large carrots, julienned
4 teaspoons soy sauce
½ teaspoon brown sugar
½ cup chicken broth or water

1. Add oil to a preheated wok or frying pan. When oil is hot, add the carrots. Stir-fry for 2–3 minutes. Add the soy sauce.
2. Add the brown sugar and broth. Turn the heat down to medium-low and simmer, covered for about 5 or 6 minutes, until the carrots are tender.

Stir-fried Spinach

Serves 4

This dish is easy to prepare and can be served hot or cold. It makes a nice accompaniment to Sweet-and-Sour Shrimp (page 222).

18 spinach leaves
1 tablespoon oil for stir-frying
¼ teaspoon sugar
¼ teaspoon salt

1. Wash the spinach leaves. Blanch the spinach in boiling water briefly, just until the leaves begin to wilt. Drain well.
2. Add oil to a preheated wok or skillet. When the oil is hot, add the spinach. Add the sugar and salt and stir-fry briefly, for less than a minute. Serve hot.

Stir-fried Bok Choy

1 bok choy
2 tablespoons oil for stir-frying
¼ teaspoon salt
1½ tablespoons water

1. Separate each stalk and leaves. Cut the stalks diagonally into 1-inch pieces. Cut the leaves crosswise into 1-inch pieces.
2. Add the oil to a preheated wok or skillet. When oil is hot, add the bok choy stalks. Stir-fry for about 1 minute and then add the leaves. Add salt, sprinkle the water over, and cover and cook on medium heat, until the bok choy is tender but still firm and not mushy.

Serves 2–4

Serve on the side, or use to enliven a basic meat dish such as Basic Chicken Stir-fry (page 154).

Better Bok Choy

For best results, always separate bok choy stalks from the leaves prior to stir-frying, as the thick stalks take longer to cook.

Stir-fried Bean Sprouts

1 tablespoon oil for stir-frying
1 cup mung bean sprouts, rinsed and drained
1 tablespoon red rice vinegar
½ teaspoon sugar
¼ teaspoon salt

1. Add the oil to a frying pan or preheated wok. When the oil is hot, add the bean sprouts and stir-fry rapidly for less than a minute.
2. Add the rice vinegar, sugar, and salt. Stir-fry for another few seconds and serve hot.

Serves 4

Tart red rice vinegar contrasts nicely with sweet mung bean sprouts in this quick and easy stir-fry.

Spruced Up Sprouts

Silver sprouts are bean sprouts that have been trimmed at the ends, or "topped and tailed." It gives the sprouts a nicer appearance, but unless you're entertaining it isn't really worth the extra effort.

Sweet-and-Sour Chinese Greens

Serves 4

Both bok choy and napa cabbage can be found in the produce section of most supermarkets.

½ pound bok choy
½ pound napa cabbage
2 tablespoons oil for stir-frying
¼ teaspoon salt
2¼ teaspoons sugar, divided
¼ cup water
3 tablespoons black rice vinegar

1. Separate the bok choy stalks and leaves. Cut the stalk diagonally into 1-inch pieces. Cut the leaves crosswise into 1-inch pieces. Cut the cabbage leaves by piling the leaves on top of each other and cutting lengthwise and then crosswise into 1-inch pieces.
2. Add oil to a preheated wok or skillet. When oil is hot, add the bok choy stalks. Stir-fry for a minute, then add the bok choy leaves and the cabbage. Stir-fry for another minute. Add the salt, ¼ teaspoon sugar, and the water. Cover and cook for 2–3 minutes on medium heat, until the vegetables are tender but still firm.
3. Remove the cover and add the black rice vinegar and 2 teaspoons sugar. Mix thoroughly with the bok choy and cabbage.

Substituting Vinegar

To replace the rice vinegar in this recipe with white distilled vinegar, use 3 tablespoons of distilled vinegar to 2 teaspoons of brown sugar. Increase the amount of brown sugar if the vinegar flavor is a little too overpowering.

Steamed Broccoli

1 pound broccoli
2 tablespoons light soy sauce
1 tablespoon rice wine or dry sherry
1 teaspoon minced ginger
1 tablespoon finely chopped green onion, the green part only
1/4 teaspoon sesame oil

1. Wash the broccoli and drain. Break off the flowerets and cut in half. Cut the spears on the diagonal into thin slices. Steam the broccoli until tender.
2. Mix together the other ingredients and pour over the broccoli.

Serves 4

Looking for an alternative to beef and broccoli with oyster sauce? Try this side dish with a beef stir-fry. Experiment with substituting seasonal vegetables.

Mangetout and Bean Sprouts

1 cup mangetout (snow peas)
1 cup mung bean sprouts, rinsed and drained
1 1/2 tablespoons oil for stir-frying
3/4 teaspoon sugar
1 tablespoon Chinese rice wine or dry sherry

1. String the snow peas. Blanch both the vegetables by plunging them briefly into boiling water and quickly removing. Drain well.
2. Add the oil to a preheated wok or skillet. When the oil is hot, begin stir-frying the snow peas. Stir-fry for a minute and add the bean sprouts. Add the sugar and rice wine. Stir-fry until the snow peas turn a bright green and are hot.

Serves 4

Blanching vegetables prior to stir-frying helps them retain their vivid colors and reduces the cooking time.

Mushrooms and Bamboo Shoots

Serves 2

This dish is commonly called "Fried Two Winters," because the Cantonese word for mushrooms and bamboo shoots are similar to the word for winter.

8 dried mushrooms
½ cup reserved mushroom soaking liquid
1 8-ounce can bamboo shoots, rinsed and drained
2 tablespoons dark soy sauce
2 teaspoons sugar
2 tablespoons oil for stir-frying
1 tablespoon cornstarch mixed with 4 tablespoons water

1. Soak the mushrooms in hot water for 20 minutes to soften or reconstitute. Reserve the soaking liquid. Give the reconstituted mushrooms a gentle squeeze to remove excess water and thinly slice.
2. Cut the bamboo shoots in half, so they are approximately 1 inch in length. Mix together the dark soy sauce and sugar and set aside.
3. Add the oil to a preheated wok or heavy skillet. When oil is hot, add the bamboo shoots. Stir-fry for a minute and add the mushrooms.
4. Add the dark soy sauce and sugar, and the reserved mushroom liquid. Turn the heat down to low, cover, and simmer the vegetables for 10 minutes.
5. Give the cornstarch-and-water mixture a quick stir. Turn the heat up and push the vegetables up to the side of the wok. Add the cornstarch/water in the middle, stirring quickly to thicken. Mix through and serve hot.

Don't Discard the Soaking Liquid

The soaking liquid from reconstituted (softened) ingredients like dried mushrooms and wood fungus makes a flavorful substitute for water in recipes. Before using, strain the water to remove any gritty particles. Vegetarians can use the reconstituted liquid in place of chicken broth.

Mushrooms and Cabbage

4 dried mushrooms
1 8-ounce can bamboo shoots, drained, rinsed and drained
2 cabbage leaves
2 tablespoons light soy sauce
1 tablespoon dark soy sauce
3 teaspoons sugar
2 tablespoons oil for stir-frying
6 fresh mushrooms, sliced
½ cup water
1 tablespoon cornstarch
4 tablespoons water

1. Soak the dried mushrooms in hot water for 20 minutes to reconstitute. Reserve the soaking liquid. Give the reconstituted mushrooms a gentle squeeze to remove excess water and thinly slice.
2. Cut the bamboo shoots in half, so they are approximately 1 inch in length. Blanch the cabbage leaves by plunging briefly into boiling water. Drain thoroughly and shred.
3. Mix together the light soy sauce, dark soy sauce, and sugar. Set aside.
4. Add the oil to a preheated wok or heavy skillet. When oil is hot, add the bamboo shoots and stir-fry. Add the mushrooms and stir-fry. Add the cabbage leaves.
5. Add the soy sauce and sugar mixture, and the reserved mushroom liquid. Add the water. Turn the heat down to low, cover, and simmer the vegetables for 10 minutes.
6. Mix cornstarch and water. Turn the heat up and push the vegetables up to the side of the wok. Give the cornstarch/water mixture a quick stir and add in the middle, stirring quickly to thicken. Mix through and serve hot.

Serves 2

The combination of fresh and dried mushrooms gives this dish a more elegant appearance. Feel free to use either napa or other types of cabbage.

Stir-fried Spinach with Roasted Garlic

Serves 4

Roasted garlic lends a sweet flavor. Ideally, the garlic should be removed from the oven and begin cooling just before you start stir-frying.

3 garlic cloves
¼ cup chicken stock
18 fresh spinach leaves
1 tablespoon oil for stir-frying
1 tablespoon soy sauce
½ teaspoon sugar

1. Begin preparing the garlic 1 hour ahead of time. Preheat the oven to 350°F. Peel the garlic and drizzle with the chicken stock. Bake 1 hour or until the cloves are golden. Cool. Press down on cloves to release the garlic (it should come out easily).
2. Wash the spinach and trim the ends. Make sure the spinach is well drained.
3. Add oil to a preheated wok or skillet. When the oil is hot, add the spinach leaves. Stir-fry for about a minute, then add the soy sauce and sugar. Continue stir-frying until the spinach turns a bright green. Serve with the garlic.

Too Much Garlic

Garlic's pungent aroma nicely complements the strong flavor of spinach, but it can overpower more delicate vegetables such as mushrooms. When in doubt, use ginger instead.

Stir-fried Baby Bok Choy

4 bunches baby bok choy (1 bunch per person)
2 tablespoons oil for stir-frying
2 garlic cloves, chopped
1 tablespoon rice vinegar
1 teaspoon sugar
¼ teaspoon salt
1 teaspoon sesame oil

1. Rinse the baby bok choy and drain well.
2. Add oil to a preheated wok or skillet. When oil is hot, add garlic and stir-fry until aromatic. Add the baby bok choy, and stir-fry briefly.
3. Add the rice vinegar, sugar, and salt. Cook for about another minute. Drizzle the sesame oil over and serve.

Serves 4

For best results, wash bok choy and mung bean sprouts earlier in the day so that they have plenty of time to drain before stir-frying.

Pickled Carrots

1½ cups (12 ounces) baby carrots
⅓ cup rice vinegar
⅓ cup sugar
¼ teaspoon salt
2 cups water

1. Wash the baby carrots. Place them in a glass jar. In a medium saucepan, bring the remaining 4 ingredients to a boil, stirring to dissolve the sugar.
2. Pour the liquid over the carrots, seal the jar, and refrigerate for at least 2 days.

Yields 1½ cups

Pickled vegetables are very popular in Cantonese cuisine; look for them on the menu the next time you dine at a Cantonese restaurant.

Broccoli with Oyster Sauce

Serves 4

Broccoli and savory oyster sauce make a perfect combination. Serve with stir-fried chicken and rice.

1 pound broccoli
2 tablespoons oil for stir-frying
3 teaspoons oyster sauce
2 teaspoons sugar
¼ cup water
1 teaspoon cornstarch
4 teaspoons water

1. Break off the broccoli flowerets and cut in half. Cut the spears on the diagonal into thin slices.
2. Add oil to a skillet or a preheated wok. When oil is hot, add the broccoli, adding the spears first and then the flowerets.
3. Add the oyster sauce, sugar, and ¼ cup water. Cover and cook about 3 minutes, or until the broccoli turns a brilliant green.
4. Mix the cornstarch and water. Uncover the wok, make a well in the middle, and add the cornstarch/water mixture, stirring quickly to thicken. Mix through.

Colorless Vegetables

Covering and cooking firm green vegetables in a bit of water will help make them more tender. Do not lift the wok lid to check on covered green vegetables more than once during cooking. If you do, the vegetable will turn yellow.

Braised Ridged Gourd with Mushrooms

1 ridged gourd (also called angled luffa)
3 tablespoons oil for stir-frying
1 clove garlic, minced
5 mushrooms, sliced
¼ teaspoon salt
¼ cup chicken broth
2 tablespoons Chinese rice wine or dry sherry
2 teaspoons soy sauce
1 teaspoon brown sugar
1 teaspoon cornstarch
4 teaspoons water

Serves 4

Like tofu, this gourd acts like a sponge, soaking up the flavors of the food it is cooked with.

1. Peel the gourd, leaving a few strips of green if desired to add a bit of color. Cut diagonally into thin slices.
2. Add oil to a preheated wok or skillet. When the oil is hot, add the garlic clove. When the garlic is aromatic, add the ridged gourd, and stir-fry for about a minute. Add the mushrooms and the salt.
3. Add the chicken broth and stir-fry for another minute. Add the rice wine, soy sauce, and brown sugar.
4. Mix the cornstarch and water and add to the middle of the wok, stirring quickly to thicken. Mix through.

Too Much Cornstarch

If the mixture of cornstarch and water in a recipe produces a soggier sauce than you would like, try reducing the amount of cornstarch while keeping the ratio of cornstarch to water constant. For example, instead of 1 tablespoon of cornstarch mixed with 4 tablespoons of water, use ½ tablespoon cornstarch and 2 tablespoons water.

Braised Chinese Broccoli (Gai Lan) in Oyster Sauce

Serves 4

Chinese broccoli or gai lan has an attractive appearance and an earthy flavor—plus, it's rich in vitamins A and C.

½ pound Chinese broccoli (gai lan)
1 tablespoon plus 1 teaspoon oyster sauce
2 teaspoons soy sauce
½ teaspoon sugar
¼ cup water
2 tablespoons oil for stir-frying
2 slices ginger
1 teaspoon tapioca starch
4 teaspoons water

1. Blanch the gai lan by plunging briefly into boiling water, until the stalks turn a bright green. Drain thoroughly. Separate the stalks and leaves. Cut the leaves across, and cut the stalks thinly on the diagonal.
2. Combine the oyster sauce, soy sauce, sugar, and water. Set aside.
3. Add oil to a preheated wok or skillet. When oil is hot, add the ginger slices. Stir-fry briefly until aromatic. Add the gai lan stalks. Stir-fry for a minute, then add the leaves. Stir-fry until the leaves turn a bright green. Add the oyster sauce mixture. Turn down the heat and cook, covered, for 4–5 minutes.
4. Mix the tapioca starch and water and add to the middle of the wok, stirring to thicken. Mix with the gai lan and serve hot.

Revamping Recipes

Want to adjust a recipe to suit your family's tastes? The easiest method is simply to double a recipe (it helps to have a second wok or frying pan ready to handle the extra volume). Often, the proportion of meat to vegetables in a Chinese recipe can be a little low for Western tastes. To add more meat, simply increase the amount of marinade, and stir-fry or deep-fry the meat in batches. Be prepared to increase the amount of sauce as well. Again, a second wok or frying pan may be needed when the meat is brought together with the vegetables and sauce in the final stages of cooking.

Stir-fried Young Bamboo Shoots

4 pieces (1 cup) peeled young bamboo shoots
1 green onion
1½ tablespoons oil for stir-frying
1 tablespoon soy sauce
1 teaspoon Chinese rice wine or dry sherry
1 teaspoon rice vinegar

Serves 4

Blanching fresh young bamboo shoots lessens their acidic flavor. Serve with a sweet dish such as Sweet-and-Sour Spareribs (page 138).

1. Blanch the bamboo shoots in boiling water for at least 5 minutes. Drain thoroughly and chop into 1-inch pieces. Cut the green onion on the diagonal into 1-inch slices.
2. Add oil to a preheated wok or skillet. When oil is hot, add the bamboo shoots. Stir-fry for about 2 minutes, then add the soy sauce, rice wine, and rice vinegar. Stir in the green onion. Simmer for 5 more minutes. Chill.

Vegetable Nomenclature

Don't let the use of common Cantonese names prevent you from sampling the colorful profusion of vegetables found in Asian markets. Anything with "choi" or "choy" in the name is a type of cabbage, while "gwa" or "gua" refers to a melon. If you're still confused, just ask; the clerks will be happy to help!

Ridged Gourd with Red Pepper

Serves 4

Sweet red pepper contrasts nicely with the gourd. Serve with chicken for a balanced meal.

1 ridged gourd
1 red bell pepper
2 tablespoons oil for stir-frying
1 slice ginger
½ cup chicken broth
2 tablespoons Chinese rice wine or dry sherry
1 tablespoon soy sauce
1 teaspoon sugar

1. Peel the gourd, leaving a few strips of green if desired to add a bit of color. Cut diagonally into thin slices. Cut the pepper in half, remove the seeds, and cut into thin strips.
2. Add oil to a preheated wok or skillet. When the oil is hot, add the ginger slice and stir-fry until aromatic. Add the ridged gourd, and stir-fry for about a minute. Add the red pepper and stir-fry until it is bright red.
3. Add the chicken broth and bring back to a boil. Add the rice wine, soy sauce, and sugar. Serve hot.

Southern Stir-fry

Because it resembles okra in taste and texture, ridged gourd is sometimes called Chinese okra. Ridged gourd makes an interesting substitute for okra in dishes of the American south, while okra can replace ridged gourd (also known as silk squash) in stir-fries.

Stuffed Red Peppers

1 red bell pepper
1 cup ground pork
1 tablespoon brown bean sauce
2 tablespoons soy sauce, divided
½ teaspoon sugar
1 teaspoon Chinese rice wine or dry sherry
1 green onion, minced
1 clove garlic, chopped

Serves 1

The Chinese version of miso, brown bean sauce is made with soybeans and spicy seasonings such as chili and garlic.

1. Preheat the oven to 300°F.
2. Wash the red pepper; cut off the top and set it aside. Remove the seeds.
3. In a medium-sized bowl, use your hands to mix the ground pork with the brown bean sauce, 1 tablespoon soy sauce, sugar, and rice wine. Add the green onion and chopped garlic.
4. Stuff the red pepper with the ground pork mixture. Add 1 tablespoon soy sauce on top and replace the lid. Place in a heatproof dish in the oven, and bake until the pork is cooked through, about 45–55 minutes.

Picking Peppers

While Szechwan cooks favor fiery chili peppers, bell peppers also make a frequent appearance in Chinese dishes. Like their hotter cousin, sweet bell peppers are a New World fruit, discovered by Christopher Columbus during his trips to the Americas. The intrepid explorer took them back to his homeland, where they eventually spread throughout Europe and Asia. The round shape of bell peppers makes them perfect for stuffing. Be sure to remove all seeds and membranes before filling.

Vegetable Chop Suey

Serves 4

Don't have any bok choy on hand? You can use broccoli instead of bok choy and green beans instead of snow peas.

½ cup water chestnuts
1 green bell pepper
1 red bell pepper
1 bunch bok choy
½ pound snow peas
4 tablespoons oil for stir-frying
¼ teaspoon salt
1½ tablespoons water
½ teaspoon minced ginger
½ teaspoon minced garlic
½ red onion, chopped
1 cup fresh mushrooms
1 teaspoon sugar
1 carrot, thinly sliced on the diagonal
½ cup mung bean sprouts, rinsed and drained
1 tablespoon cornstarch
4 tablespoons water
2 tablespoons oyster sauce

1. Clean the mushrooms with a damp towel and slice. If using fresh water chestnuts, wash and peel. If using canned, rinse in warm water and slice.
2. Cut the green and red bell peppers in half, remove the seeds, and cut into thin strips. For the bok choy, separate each stalk and leaves. Cut the stalk diagonally and cut the leaves across. Wash and string the snow peas.
3. Add 2 tablespoons oil to a preheated wok or frying pan. When oil is ready, add the bok choy stalks. Cook for about 1 minute, then add the leaves. Add the salt, and sprinkle with water. Cover and cook on medium heat until the bok choy is tender but still firm. Remove and set aside.
4. Wipe out the wok with a paper towel and add 2 tablespoons of oil. When oil is ready, add the ginger and garlic and stir-fry until aromatic. Add the red onion and stir-fry. Remove from the wok and set aside. Add the green and red peppers and the snow peas. Stir-fry for about a minute, then add the mushrooms and 1 teaspoon of sugar and continue stir-frying. Remove from the wok and set aside. Add the water chestnuts and carrot. Stir-fry for a minute, then add the bean sprouts.
5. Mix cornstarch and water, then stir in the oyster sauce. Add the removed vegetables back into the wok and mix. Make a well in the center and gradually add the cornstarch/oyster sauce mixture, stirring to thicken. Bring to a boil, remove from the heat, and serve hot.

Stir-fried Potatoes

1 pound potatoes
3 tablespoons chicken broth
1½ tablespoons Chinese rice wine or dry sherry
1½ teaspoons sugar
1½ teaspoons cornstarch mixed with 2 tablespoons water
2 tablespoons oil for stir-frying
1 slice ginger
¼ teaspoon salt

1. Wash the potatoes, peel, and julienne. Bring a large pot of water to a boil and boil the potatoes until they are cooked but still a bit firm (about 15 minutes). Drain well.
2. Add the chicken broth, rice wine, and sugar to the cornstarch-and-water mixture, stirring. Set aside.
3. Add oil to a preheated wok or a frying pan. When oil is hot, add the slice of ginger and stir-fry until it is aromatic. Add the potatoes, stir-frying in batches if necessary. Add the salt. Continue stir-frying until the potatoes are tender, about 4–5 minutes. Taste and add more salt if desired.
4. Stir the broth mixture. Make a well in the middle of the wok by pushing the potatoes up to the side. Add the broth mixture in the middle, stirring vigorously to thicken. Mix with the potatoes.

Serves 4

This Chinese dish proves that you don't need to douse a potato with sour cream and chives to add flavor.

Three Vegetable Stir-fry

Serves 4

The combination of shiitake mushrooms, snow peas, and baby corn provides an interesting contrast in color and texture. Serve with a more highly seasoned dish.

4 ounces snow peas
1½ tablespoons oil for stir-frying
1 can baby corn, rinsed and drained
6 shiitake mushrooms, sliced
1 tablespoon dark soy sauce
½ teaspoon sugar
½ teaspoon salt

1. Wash and string the snow peas.
2. Add oil to a preheated wok or frying pan. Add the baby corn and stir-fry briefly, then add the snow peas. Stir-fry until the snow peas turn a bright green. Push them up to the side and stir-fry the mushrooms. Add the dark soy sauce, sugar, and salt. Mix through.

Lucky Recipes

The Chinese love to create vegetable and dessert recipes with 3, 5, or 8 main ingredients, as these are considered to be lucky numbers. The number 8 is particularly auspicious, symbolizing sudden prosperity and good fortune. The next time you're dining at a Chinese restaurant, look for recipes with these numbers in their name.

Peppers with Potato Stuffing

4 green bell peppers
2 tablespoons chicken broth
2 tablespoons soy sauce
1 teaspoon sugar
4 tablespoons water
¼ teaspoon chili paste
Stir-fried Potatoes (page 251)

1. Preheat oven to 300°F.
2. Wash the green peppers. Cut off the tops and save. Remove the seeds. In a medium bowl, mix together the chicken broth, soy sauce, sugar, water, and chili paste. Add the stir-fried potatoes and toss.
3. Stuff each pepper with the potato mixture and drizzle a bit of the sauce over the top. If any sauce is remaining, add that into each pepper. Place the stuffed peppers in a 9" × 9" baking dish. Bake for 45 minutes or until peppers are tender.

Serves 4

Potato and peppers make a great combination. Substitute red peppers for added color and an intriguing mix of spicy and sweet.

Spicy Eggplant Stir-fry

1 eggplant
3 tablespoons oil for stir-frying
2 tablespoons red rice vinegar
½ teaspoon brown sugar
2 tablespoons soy sauce
1 tablespoon chopped garlic
½ teaspoon chili paste
¼ teaspoon sesame oil

1. Wash the eggplant, cut off the ends, and slice diagonally into 1-inch pieces.
2. Add oil to a preheated wok or skillet. When the oil is hot, add the eggplant slices, stir-frying in batches if necessary. Stir-fry for about 2–3 minutes.
3. Add the red rice vinegar, brown sugar, soy sauce, garlic, and chili paste, and mix through. Drizzle the sesame oil over and give a final stir.

Serves 4

This dish can be made with truncheon-shaped Chinese eggplant or the thicker eggplant commonly available in local supermarkets.

Sweet-and-Sour Celery

Serves 4–6

Blanching the celery before stir-frying gives it a brilliant green color. For an intriguing mix of flavors, serve with a savory dish.

4 stalks celery
2 tablespoons oil for stir-frying
¼ teaspoon salt
3 tablespoons rice vinegar
2 tablespoons sugar
¼ teaspoon cinnamon

1. Bring a large pot of water to a boil. Wash the celery and cut into 1-inch slices on the diagonal. Blanch by plunging into boiling water and boiling for 2–3 minutes.
2. Add oil to a preheated wok or skillet. When the oil is hot, begin stir-frying the celery. Add the salt.
3. Stir in the rice vinegar, sugar, and cinnamon. Remove the celery from the wok and pour any remaining sauce over.

Cutting Green Vegetables

Unless the instructions state differently, cut green vegetables like celery, bok choy spears, and green onions on the diagonal. This gives maximum heat exposure and ensures even cooking.

Bitter Melon Stir-fry

2 bitter melons
1 teaspoon salt
2 tablespoons oil for stir-frying
1 clove garlic, chopped
2 tablespoons hoisin sauce
4 tablespoons water
1 tablespoon Chinese rice wine or dry sherry
½ teaspoon brown sugar

1. Wash the bitter melons, cut in half, and remove the seeds inside the pods. Slice thinly on the diagonal.
2. To degorge the bitter melons, place the slices in a bowl and toss with salt. Leave for 15 minutes and place on paper towels to drain out excess water.
3. Bring a large pot of water to a boil. Boil the bitter melons for 3 minutes. Drain well.
4. Add oil to a preheated wok or skillet. Add the garlic and stir-fry briefly until aromatic. Add the bitter melon and stir-fry for 2–3 minutes. Add the hoisin sauce, water, rice wine, and brown sugar. Mix through and serve hot.

Serves 4–6

Even with degorging, bitter melon has an acrid, almost chalky taste. Feel free to substitute another gourd such as angled luffa.

A Remarkable Melon

Bitter melon is one of those foods that people either love or hate. Native to China, it works best with pungent ingredients such as chilies and black bean sauce that can hold their own against its strong flavor. To reduce the bitterness, try degorging or steaming.

Szechwan Eggplant with Black Rice Vinegar

Serves 4

In order not to waste any oil, strain the oil from stir-frying the eggplant so that it can be used again.

5 tablespoons oil for stir-frying
2 Chinese eggplants, chopped into tiny pieces
2 teaspoons soy sauce
½ teaspoon black rice vinegar
½ teaspoon sugar
1 teaspoon dark soy sauce
¼ teaspoon salt
1 tablespoon chopped ginger
1 garlic clove, chopped
1 teaspoon hot bean sauce
¼ cup chicken stock or broth
¼ teaspoon sesame oil
2 green onions, chopped into thirds

1. Mix together the soy sauce, black rice vinegar, sugar, dark soy sauce, and salt. Set aside.
2. Add 4 tablespoons oil to a preheated wok or skillet. When oil is hot, add the eggplant. Stir-fry about 5 minutes, until the eggplant is soft. Gently press the eggplant with a spatula to remove any excess oil. Remove from the wok.
3. Remove the oil from the wok, and wipe the wok clean with a paper towel. Add 1 tablespoon of oil back into the wok. When the oil is hot, add the ginger, garlic, and hot bean sauce and stir-fry briefly. Add the sauce and the chicken stock. Bring to a boil. Add the eggplant back to the wok, and stir-fry until the sauce is nearly gone.
4. Add the sesame oil and green onions. Give the dish a final stir.

Steamed Carrots with Oyster Sauce

2 cups baby carrots
2 tablespoons oyster sauce
¼ cup water
1 teaspoon Chinese rice wine or dry sherry
1½ tablespoons oil for stir-frying
2 teaspoons minced ginger
½ teaspoon sugar

Serves 4

Oyster sauce is frequently married to broccoli in restaurant dishes, but there are numerous other possibilities—like baby carrots.

1. Steam the carrots until tender. Drain well.
2. Mix together the oyster sauce, water, and rice wine. Set aside.
3. Add oil to a preheated wok or skillet. When oil is ready, add the ginger and stir-fry until it is aromatic.
4. Add the steamed baby carrots. Stir-fry for about 1 minute, until the carrots turn a bright orange color. Add the oyster sauce mixture, and the sugar. Bring the sauce to a boil and stir-fry for another minute, mixing the sauce thoroughly with the vegetables.

Substituting Vegetables

When it comes to making substitutions, the names of Chinese vegetables can be misleading. Although bok choy and choy sum are both types of cabbage, choy sum's delicate pale green leaves bear little resemblance to hardy bok choy. When you need to make a substitution, pay attention to the vegetable's texture and color.

Stuffed Eggplant

Serves 4

Large western eggplant works best in this dish. Freeze any leftover ground pork to use in dishes such as Lion's Head Meatball Stew (page 135).

4 eggplants
2 eggs, lightly beaten
2 tablespoons soy sauce
1/4 teaspoon white pepper
2 tablespoons Chinese rice wine or dry sherry
2 pounds ground pork

1. Preheat the oven to 350°F.
2. Wash the eggplants. Cut in half lengthwise and scoop out as much of the middle as possible without splitting the eggplant. Discard the pulp.
3. Mix the beaten egg, soy sauce, white pepper, and rice wine in with the pork, using your hands. Marinate the pork for 15 minutes.
4. Take a quarter of the pork mixture and stuff it into each eggplant. If possible, cover with the top half of the eggplant.
5. Place the stuffed eggplants in a baking dish. Bake at 350°F for 30 minutes or until the eggplants are cooked.

Braised Baby Bok Choy

Serves 4

Also called Shanghai bok choy, baby bok choy has a sweeter flavor and is more tender than regular bok choy.

4 bunches baby bok choy
1/2 cup chicken stock or broth
1/2 cup water
1 teaspoon sugar
1 1/2 teaspoons rice vinegar
2 tablespoons oil for stir-frying
2 garlic cloves, finely chopped
1/2 teaspoon sesame oil

1. Wash and drain the baby bok choy. Cut off the roots and separate the stalks and leaves.
2. Combine the chicken stock, water, sugar, and rice vinegar.
3. Add oil to a preheated wok or skillet. When oil is ready, add the garlic. Stir-fry until aromatic.
4. Add the bok choy stalks and stir-fry until they turn a bright green. While stir-frying the stalks, add the leaves.
5. Add the chicken broth mixture. Turn down the heat and simmer, covered, for 5 minutes. Turn off the heat and drizzle with the sesame oil.

Mu Shu Vegetables

2 bok choy stalks
½ red bell pepper
¼ cup water
¼ cup chicken broth
1 tablespoon dark soy sauce
1 teaspoon sugar
2 eggs, lightly beaten
¼ teaspoon salt
3 tablespoons oil for stir-frying
4 fresh mushrooms, sliced
½ teaspoon sesame oil

Serves 4

The combination of eggs and vegetables makes this a nutritious, quick, and easy meal for busy weekdays.

1. Separate the bok choy stalks and leaves. Cut the stalks diagonally into 1-inch pieces. Cut the leaves crosswise into 1-inch pieces. Remove the seeds from the pepper and cut into thin strips.
2. Combine the water, chicken broth, dark soy sauce, and sugar. Set aside.
3. Stir ¼ teaspoon salt in to the eggs. Add 1 tablespoon oil to a preheated wok or skillet. When oil is hot, scramble the eggs. Remove from the wok and set aside.
4. Clean out the wok and add 2 tablespoons oil. When oil is hot, add the bok choy stalks. Stir-fry for about 1 minute, then add the mushrooms and red pepper. Stir-fry briefly and add the bok choy leaves. Add the sauce in the middle of the wok. Bring to a boil. Stir in the scrambled egg. Drizzle the sesame oil over. Mix through and serve hot.

Wrap It Up!

Meat and vegetables cooked in the mu shu style make a great filling for tortilla wraps. To make, adjust the above recipe by draining out some of the sauce so that the filling isn't too wet. Lay the wrap in front of you and add ½ cup of filling to the bottom. Fold over the right side of the wrap. Fold the bottom of the wrap over the food, and continue rolling up the wrap. For added variety, try the flavored wraps, such as spinach, pesto, or garlic.

CHAPTER 12

Desserts and Snacks

Almond Cookies

Yields 30–35 cookies

Delicately flavored with a hint of almond, these cookies make a satisfying light afternoon snack or finale to a dim sum brunch.

2 cups flour
1/2 teaspoon baking powder
1/2 teaspoon baking soda
1/2 cup margarine or butter, as preferred
1/2 cup shortening
3/4 cup white sugar
2 eggs
2 teaspoons almond extract
1/4 pound whole, blanched almonds (1 for each cookie)
1 egg, lightly beaten

1. Preheat oven to 325°F.
2. In a large bowl, sift the flour, baking powder, and baking soda. In a medium bowl, use an electric mixer to beat the butter or margarine, shortening, and sugar. Add the eggs and almond extract and beat until well blended. Add to the flour mixture, stirring.
3. Knead the dough into a roll or log. If you find 1 long roll too difficult to work with, split the dough into 2 equal pieces.
4. Cut the dough into 30–35 pieces. (If desired, lightly score the dough before cutting to get an idea of the correct size.) Roll each piece into a ball and place on a lightly greased cookie tray, approximately 2 inches apart. Place an almond in the center of each cookie and press down lightly.
5. Brush each cookie lightly with beaten egg before baking. Bake at 325°F for 15 minutes or until golden brown. Cool and store in a sealed container.

Fortune Cookie Origins

Although a Chinese restaurant meal wouldn't seem complete without them, the fortune cookie is an American creation. Restaurant chefs in both Los Angeles and San Francisco lay claim to having invented the popular baked cookie containing a special message. Today, fortune cookies are catching on in China as well.

Egg Custard Tarts

2 cups flour
¾ teaspoon salt
⅔ cup lard
½ teaspoon vanilla extract
3 tablespoons hot water
2 large eggs
½ cup evaporated milk
½ cup milk
¼ cup sugar

Yields 18 tarts

Egg tarts are a popular dim sum treat. Make sure that the tart pans are well greased so that the pastry does not stick.

1. Preheat oven to 300°F.
2. To make the dough: In a large bowl, sift together the flour and salt. Cut in the lard, and then use your fingers to mix in. When it is mealy and has the consistency of breadcrumbs, add the vanilla extract and hot water and mix together to form a dough. Add another tablespoon of water if necessary. Cut the dough into thirds.
3. On a lightly floured surface, roll each piece of dough out until it is ⅛ inch thick. Cut 6 circles that are each 3 inches in diameter, so that you have a total of 18 circles.
4. Place the circles into greased tart pans or muffin tins, carefully shaping the sides so that they reach the rim.
5. To make the egg custard filling: Lightly beat the eggs, and stir in the evaporated milk, milk, and sugar. Add up to 2 tablespoons of the custard into each tart shell, so that it nicely fills the shell but does not overflow.
6. Bake at 300°F for about 25 minutes or until the custard is cooked through and a knife stuck in the middle comes out clean.

Almond Fruit Gelatin

Serves 4–6

Colorful fresh fruits like strawberries or peaches make a nice contrast to the almond gelatin in this elegant, easy-to-make dessert.

1½ packages Knox unflavored gelatin
1 cup cold water
3 tablespoons sugar
1 cup boiling water
1 cup evaporated milk
2 teaspoons almond extract
1 cup fresh fruit slices

1. Pour the gelatin over the cold water and wait about 3 minutes for it to soften.
2. In a separate bowl, add the sugar to the boiling water, stirring to dissolve. Add the evaporated milk to the sugar and water mixture. Wait a few minutes for the mixture to cool slightly and stir in the almond extract.
3. Add the evaporated milk mixture to the gelatin and water. Stir well and pour into a shallow pan or a serving mold. Chill until firm.
4. Cut into diamond shapes and place on a serving tray. Garnish with the fresh fruit slices.

Aromatic Almonds

Cooks have been exploiting almond's rich flavor since biblical times. In China of days past, peddlers traveled from door to door selling almond tea, a sweet concoction made with almonds ground into a paste. Today, almonds are featured in desserts and some restaurant dishes.

Mango Pudding

2 cups canned mango pieces
½ cup boiling water
2 packages Knox unflavored gelatin
¾ cup sugar
1 cup evaporated milk
1 cup syrup from the canned mango

1. In a food processor, purée the mango pieces. Reserve the syrup and set aside.
2. In a large bowl, pour the boiling water over the gelatin and stir for about 2 minutes until it is dissolved.
3. In a medium saucepan, bring the sugar, evaporated milk, and mango syrup to a boil, stirring. Remove from the heat and add the puréed mango. Add to the bowl of gelatin, stirring.
4. Pour the mixture into a dish or individual serving bowls. Chill until set.

Serves 6

The delicate flavor of Mango Pudding sets it apart from thicker, heavier puddings. Traditionally, agar-agar would have been used in place of gelatin crystals.

Almond Float

Almond Fruit Gelatin (page 264)
2 cups water
½ cup brown sugar
1 teaspoon almond extract
Canned pineapple and mandarin orange slices

1. To make the syrup: In a medium saucepan, add 2 cups of water and ½ cup brown sugar. Heat to boiling, stirring to dissolve the sugar. When the sugar is dissolved, cool. Add 1 teaspoon almond extract and chill.
2. When ready to serve, cut the almond gelatin into ½-inch cubes and place in a large serving bowl. Cover with the chilled sugar water. Add mandarin and pineapple slices along with as much of the canned syrup as desired. Add enough so that the almond gelatin "floats" in the liquid.

Serves 6

For a more tropical flavor, substitute canned lychees and jackfruit for the mandarin orange and pineapple slices.

Poached Asian Pears

Serves 4

Served warm, this mildly spiced treat is very soothing if you have a cough or a sore throat.

1½ cups cranberry juice
3 cups water
2 slices ginger
¾ tablespoon pumpkin spice
4 Asian pears, cored and halved

1. In a large pot, add the cranberry juice, water, and ginger slices. Add the pumpkin pie spice, placing in a cheesecloth bag if desired. Bring to a boil.
2. Add the pears. Simmer, turning occasionally, until they are tender and can be pierced easily with a fork (depending on the firmness of the pear, this can take 30–35 minutes). Serve warm.

Poached Pears with Lemon

Serves 4

For an extra treat, add a dollop of plain yogurt or vanilla ice cream before serving.

3 cups water
1½ cups cranberry juice
¾ cup sugar
1 cinnamon stick
1 teaspoon freshly squeezed lemon juice
4 Asian pears, cored and halved

1. In a large pot, bring all the ingredients except the pears to a boil.
2. Add the pears. Simmer, turning occasionally until they are tender and can be easily pierced with a fork. Remove the pears with a slotted spoon and place in individual serving dishes.
3. Continue to simmer the syrup until it thickens and lightly coats the back of a spoon. Pour the sauce over the pears. Serve warm or chilled.

Steamed Apples

4 apples
4 tablespoons honey
1 teaspoon cinnamon
1½ tablespoons raisins

1. Slice off the top of each apple and set aside to serve as the lid. Core the apples.
2. Mix together the honey, cinnamon, and raisins. Spoon a quarter of the mixture into each apple and replace the lids.
3. Steam the apples until they are soft but not mushy. Serve warm.

Serves 4

This is a perfect treat for cold winter days, providing a healthy alternative to snack foods.

Steamed Fruit

When steaming fruit, it's important to remove the fruit from the pot immediately, so that it doesn't continue cooking in the hot liquid and become mushy.

Sweet Baked Pineapple and Banana

1 cup canned pineapple chunks
2 tablespoons margarine or butter, softened
⅓ cup brown sugar
2 tablespoons reserved pineapple juice
1 teaspoon Chinese rice wine or dry sherry
3 bananas, cut in half lengthwise
2 tablespoons untoasted sesame seeds

1. Preheat oven to 350°F.
2. Drain the can of pineapple chunks, reserving 2 tablespoons juice.
3. In a medium bowl, cream the butter and brown sugar. Stir in the pineapple juice and rice wine.
4. Lay out the bananas and pineapple chunks on a glass baking dish. Spread the brown sugar mixture over. Bake for about 10 minutes, until the bananas are tender but not mushy (the pineapple will retain its texture). Sprinkle with sesame seeds.

Serves 4

Children love this sweet treat. For an added touch, serve with a tropical fruit–flavored ice cream.

Sweetened Walnuts

Yields about ½ cup

Watch the oil temperature in the wok—if it gets too high, the walnuts will turn black before the sugar has a chance to melt.

½ cup chopped walnut pieces
¼ cup sugar
3 cups oil for deep-frying

1. Blanch the walnut pieces in boiling water for 5 minutes to remove their bitter flavor.
2. Spread the sugar out on a piece of waxed paper. Roll the walnuts in the sugar. Spread out on a tray and leave overnight to dry.
3. Heat oil to 275°F. When oil is hot, add the walnuts. Deep-fry until they turn golden brown. Remove and drain. Cool and store in a sealed container.

Steamed Fruit with a Surprise

Serves 4

The world's first sweetener, honey has been used in China since ancient times. When sugarcane was introduced, the Chinese originally called it "stone honey."

4 pears
2 tablespoons honey
4 Chinese honey dates

1. Slice off the top of each pear and set aside. Core the pear from the top, being careful not to go through to the bottom.
2. Spoon ½ tablespoon honey into each pear. Add a Chinese honey date. Replace the lid. Steam until tender and serve hot.

Guilt-free Indulging

This healthy dessert lets you indulge and fight off illness at the same time. According to traditional Chinese medicine, pears lower cholesterol and reduce high blood pressure, while honey dates build up the blood.

Walnut Cookies

2 teaspoons baking powder
3 cups flour
¾ cup lard
½ cup finely chopped walnuts
2 teaspoons vanilla extract
1¼ cups white sugar
3 eggs
1 egg, lightly beaten

1. Preheat oven to 325°F.
2. In a large bowl, sift the baking powder into the flour. Cut the lard into the flour and mix with your fingers until it forms the texture of tiny balls.
3. Add the walnuts, vanilla extract, sugar, and 3 eggs. Mix into the dough to form a paste.
4. Take a piece of dough and form into a round ball the size of a large golf ball. Place the ball in the palm of one hand and press down with the palm of the other hand to form a flat circle about 2 inches in diameter. Continue with the remainder of the dough.
5. Place the dough circles on a greased baking tray. Brush lightly with the beaten egg. Bake at 325°F for about 20–25 minutes, or until a toothpick stuck in the center comes out clean. Cool and store in a sealed container.

Yields 28–30 cookies

These sweet cookies are a popular feature in Chinese bakeries. Food coloring is sometimes used to give them a yellow color.

Chinese Bakery

Need a little inspiration before you're ready to get out the rolling pin and start mixing and measuring? Try visiting a Chinese bakery. Classic treats like Mango Pudding and Sesame Seed Balls share space with sticky rice dumplings, foot-long doughnuts, and buns filled with everything from pineapple and taro to red bean paste. All reflect the Chinese belief that no one flavor should upstage any other. Indulge, and you'll leave feeling pleasantly satisfied but without a case of "sugar hangover."

Mandarin Pancakes

Yields 9 pancakes

Add water slowly until you are sure how much is needed. Everything from altitude to the age of the flour can affect the amount required.

2 cups all-purpose flour
¾–1 cup boiling water
¼ cup sesame oil

1. Place the flour in a large bowl. Add the boiling water and quickly stir with a wooden spoon.
2. As soon as you can withstand the heat, knead the warm dough on a lightly floured surface until it is smooth. Cover with a damp cloth and let stand for 30 minutes.
3. Cut the dough in half. Roll each half into a 9-inch cylinder. Using a tape measure, lightly score and cut the dough into 1-inch pieces. You will have 18 pieces at this point.
4. Shape each piece into a ball and then flatten into a circle between the palms of your hands. Brush the top of each piece with sesame oil, and then place the pieces on top of each other, oiled sides together.
5. Using a lightly floured rolling pin, roll the pieces into a 5½–6-inch circle. (Don't worry if the edges overlap.) Continue with the rest of the dough.
6. Heat a dry pan on low-medium heat. When the pan is hot, add one of the paired pancakes and cook on each side for 2 minutes or until brown bubbles appear (the second side will cook more quickly). Remove from the pan and pull the pancakes apart while they are still hot. Place on a plate and cover with a damp cloth while cooking the remainder.

Pancakes for Dinner

Besides making a tasty snack, mandarin pancakes are served with the northern dishes mu shu pork and Peking duck. In the case of mu shu pork, the pork is wrapped in the pancakes, which are brushed with hoisin sauce. To be completely authentic, the sauce should be brushed on with Green Onion Brushes (page 75).

Sweet Red Bean Paste

½ cup dried red beans
1½ cups water
¼ cup sugar (or to taste)
1¼ tablespoons oil

1. Rinse the beans and soak overnight in water to cover, adding more water if necessary. Drain.
2. In a medium saucepan bring 1½ cups of water to a boil. Add the beans and simmer for at least 2 hours or until they are tender. Drain.
3. Place the beans and the sugar in a blender and process until smooth. Heat the oil in a preheated wok or saucepan. Add the processed bean paste and stir-fry until it is dry. Store in a sealed container in the refrigerator. The bean paste will last for approximately 1 week.

Yields 1–1½ cups

Use with Sesame Seed Balls (page 273) and Fried Pancakes with Red Bean Paste, or as a filling for steamed buns.

Fried Pancakes with Red Bean Paste

Mandarin Pancakes (page 270)
1 can red bean paste
Oil for stir-frying

When the Mandarin Pancakes have cooled, add approximately 1 tablespoon of red bean paste to each pancake and spread it out evenly. Roll up the pancake and stir-fry until golden. Serve warm.

Yields 9 pancakes

For an added treat, dust the mandarin pancakes with sugar or icing sugar after frying.

Pineapple and Ginger "Ice Cream"

Serves 6–8

This simple treat tastes best with fresh pineapple. Serve as a light dessert in place of fruit.

1 cup sugar
½ cup water
2 cups diced fresh pineapple
1 teaspoon peeled, grated ginger
3 cups milk

1. Bring the sugar and water to a boil, stirring. Add the diced pineapple and ginger. Simmer, uncovered, for 10 minutes.
2. Strain the syrup to remove the ginger and pineapple. Add the milk to the syrup. Freeze. Chill the pineapple.
3. When the ice cream is partially frozen, stir the chilled pineapple back in. Continue freezing. Thaw slightly before serving.

Grass Jelly Dessert

Serves 4

The flavor of this darkish green gelatin can be a little overpowering, but it works well when balanced with sweet, syrupy fruits like canned lychees.

1 can grass jelly
1 can lychees
1 small can mandarin orange sections

1. Remove the grass jelly from the can, slice, and cut into cubes.
2. Place the grass jelly cubes in a large bowl. Add the lychees and mandarin orange sections, and pour the syrup from the canned fruits over.

Grass Jelly Drink

A popular Southeast Asian drink consists of grass jelly cubes mixed with rock sugar. But, however you enjoy your grass jelly, it's important to neutralize its strong flavor with sugar, leaving you free to enjoy the slippery texture.

Sesame Seed Balls

¾ cup packed brown sugar
1 cup boiling water
2⅓ cups glutinous rice flour
1 cup sweet red bean paste
¼ cup white sesame seeds
6 cups oil for deep-frying

Yields 22–24 balls

Glutinous rice flour, also known as sweet rice flour, is used mainly for desserts and dim sum snacks. It is sold in bags in Asian markets.

1. Add the brown sugar to the boiling water, stirring to dissolve. Cool.
2. Place the glutinous rice flour in a large bowl, making a well in the middle. Give the sugar/water mix a quick stir and slowly pour into the well, stirring to mix with the flour. Continue stirring until well mixed. You should have a sticky, caramel-colored dough at this point.
3. Rub your hands in a bit of the rice flour so that the dough doesn't stick to them. Take a heaping tablespoon of dough and shape into a ball roughly the size of a golf ball.
4. Flatten the ball with the palm of your hand, then use your thumb to make an indentation in the middle. Take no more than 1 teaspoon of red bean paste, and use your hand to shape the paste into a circle. Place the paste in the indentation in the dough. Fold the dough over the paste and roll back into a ball. Continue with the remainder of the dough.
5. Sprinkle the sesame seeds on a sheet of waxed paper. Roll the balls in the seeds.
6. In a wok or large pot, heat 6 cups of oil to between 330–350°F. Deep-fry the sesame seed balls a few at a time, carefully pushing them against the sides of the wok when they float to the top. The sesame balls are cooked when they expand to approximately 3 times their size and turn golden brown. Drain on paper towels. Serve warm.

Bowties for Kids

Yields 2 bowties per egg roll wrapper

Children love this sweet dessert, and they can help prepare this easy version made with egg roll wrappers.

1 package egg roll wrappers
1 cup brown sugar
¼ cup white sugar
2 tablespoons honey
½ cup water
Oil for deep-frying

1. Cut each wrapper vertically into 4 equal pieces. Cut a ¾-inch slit in the middle of each piece.
2. Lay one piece on top of the other and make a knot like a bow tie: Fold the top and thread the 2 pieces through the slit. Turn over, fold the bottom and thread through the other way. Spread out the folded ends slightly to make sure the entire surface is deep-fried.
3. Heat 1½ inches of oil in a heavy skillet. Deep-fry a few of the bowties at a time until they are golden brown, turning over once. Remove from the pan with a slotted spoon and drain on paper towels.
4. When all the bowties are deep-fried, bring the brown sugar, white sugar, honey, and water to boil in a medium-sized saucepan. Boil for 5 minutes, stirring constantly over low heat. Dip each of the bowties into the boiling syrup, drain, and set aside to harden. Serve cold.

Bowties for Adults

1 package egg roll wrappers
¼ cup powdered sugar
Oil for deep-frying

1. Cut each wrapper vertically into 4 equal pieces. Cut a ¾-inch slit in the middle of each piece.
2. Lay one piece on top of the other and make a knot like a bow tie: Fold the top and thread the 2 pieces through the slit. Turn over, fold the bottom and thread through the other way. Spread out the folded ends slightly to make sure the entire surface is deep-fried.
3. Heat 1½ inches of oil in a heavy skillet. Deep-fry a few of the bowties at a time until they are golden brown, turning over once. Remove from the pan with a slotted spoon and drain on paper towels.
4. Cool the bowties and dust lightly with powdered sugar. Serve cold. Store in an airtight container.

Yields 2 bowties for every wrapper

The trick to making these is to ensure the entire surface is lightly dusted with powdered sugar.

Marinated Cashews

½ cup honey
¼ cup sugar
1 tablespoon orange juice
1 tablespoon Grand Marnier
1 cup unsalted cashews

1. Combine the honey, sugar, orange juice, and Grand Marnier in a medium-sized bowl. Stir in the cashews. Place in a medium-sized saucepan and bring to a boil.
2. Boil for 2 or 3 minutes. Remove from the heat and pour onto a baking sheet. Separate the nuts with a slotted spoon. Leave for at least 2 hours to allow the cashews to soak up the sugar and dry. Store in a sealed container.

Yields about 1 cup

Glazed nuts are a popular Chinese snack food, similar to Italian candied chestnuts.

Spicy Roasted Peanuts

Yields 2 cups

Spicy Roasted Peanuts are popular during the Chinese New Year season because peanuts symbolize longevity in Chinese culture.

1¼ teaspoons salt
¼ cup hot water
¼ teaspoon five-spice powder
2 cups unblanched peanuts

1. Preheat the oven to 300°F.
2. Add the salt to the hot water, stirring to dissolve. Repeat with the five-spice powder.
3. In a medium-sized bowl, add the flavored water to the peanuts, stirring well to mix.
4. Spread the peanuts out on a roasting pan. Pour any leftover liquid over the peanuts. Roast at 300°F for about 45 minutes or until the peanuts are a rich golden brown. Stir every 15 minutes to make sure they cook evenly. Cool and store in a sealed container.

Five-Flavor Taste Sensation

Five-spice powder contains all five flavors—sweet, sour, salty, pungent, and bitter. Its unique taste is achieved through blending popular baking spices cinnamon, fennel, and cloves with the more exotic star anise and Szechwan peppercorns.

Quick and Easy Fried Melon

2 pounds winter melon
7 tablespoons flour
½ cup flaked coconut
4 cups oil for deep-frying

Serves 6

Deep-frying brings out the melon's natural sweetness. Watermelon can be substituted for the Chinese winter melon.

1. Peel and remove the seeds from the winter melon. Cut into bite-sized pieces. Lightly dust the melon with the flour.
2. In a preheated wok or skillet, heat 4 cups of oil to 250°F. Slide the winter melon into the wok, a few pieces at a time. Deep-fry until light brown, being sure to keep the oil temperature around 250°F.
3. Remove from the wok. Dust with the coconut and serve immediately.

Winter Melon—Not Just for Soup

What can you say about a vegetable that looks like a green pumpkin, has a sweet flavor similar to watermelon, but is actually a type of squash? Winter melon is famous for making a banquet soup, but you can enjoy it anytime. Stir-fried, winter melon adds flavor to stews, curries, and even sandwiches. As this recipe shows, it can also be deep-fried.

Candied Ginger

Yields ¾ cup

The combination of ginger's sharp bite and sweet sugar is incomparable. Enjoy alone, or use to enliven salads and desserts such as Szechwan Peppered Fruit (page 279).

6 ounces fresh ginger
1½ cups water
1¾ cups sugar

1. Soak the ginger overnight and drain. Peel the ginger, removing any knobs, and cut into chunks.
2. Fill a large saucepan with water and bring to a boil. Add the ginger and simmer for about 1½ hours. Drain. Repeat again, simmering until the ginger is tender and can be easily pierced with a fork. Drain well.
3. Bring 1½ cups water combined with 1½ cups sugar to a boil, stirring. When the sugar and water have formed a thick syrup, reduce the heat and add the ginger. Simmer until the water is nearly absorbed and the hardened sugar coats the ginger. Remove and roll the ginger in the remaining ¼ cup of sugar. Cool and store in an air-tight container.

Versatile Ginger

Queen Elizabeth may have invented the gingerbread man, but Chinese cooks have been putting ginger's subtle flavor to use since ancient times. Fresh ginger is featured in soups, salads, stews, and stir-fries; it is also used to flavor oil and remove fishy odors. And nothing beats a comforting cup of ginger tea when you're feeling run-down.

Szechwan Peppered Fruit

2 tablespoons Szechwan peppercorns or pink peppercorns
1 can Asian jackfruit
1 can pineapple slices (reserve the juice)
3 tablespoons honey
1–2 teaspoons margarine or butter
A few slices Candied Ginger (page 278), optional

Serves 4

This foolproof dessert combines sweet honey with fiery Szechwan peppercorns. Feel free to experiment with other canned fruits like lychees.

1. Rub the Szechwan peppercorns onto the jackfruit and pineapple slices.
2. In a saucepan, add the honey and heat, stirring. Add ½ cup of the reserved pineapple juice. Turn down the heat to low.
3. Add the margarine to a skillet and heat on low. If using the candied ginger, add to the frying pan and make sure it is heated through. Remove and set aside. Add the pineapple and jackfruit to the pan. Heat, shaking and turning over the slices to make sure the Szechwan peppercorns are heated through and become aromatic. Turn the heat down to low and add the candied ginger back into the pan.
4. Bring the honey and pineapple juice to a boil and give a final stir. Pour over the fruit. Serve immediately.

Tropical Temptations

Tropical fruits live up to their exotic names. Durian is famous for its unique combination of foul odor and heavenly taste, while a single jackfruit can weigh up to 100 pounds. While fresh Asian fruit is subject to seasonal availability, canned versions can be found in Asian markets.

Glazed Bananas

Serves 5

Don't worry if the results don't look too professional the first few times you make this dish—it will still taste great!

Banana Fritters (page 282)
2 tablespoons oil
5 tablespoons sugar
2 tablespoons sesame seeds
Bowl of ice water

1. Prepare Banana Fritters recipe, deep-frying the bananas a second time.
2. Heat oil in a skillet. Add the sugar, stirring constantly, until it dissolves and turns a light brown. Immediately add the deep-fried banana slices to the pan, sprinkle with the sesame seeds, and toss to coat with the caramelized sugar. Remove and plunge, one piece at a time, into the bowl of ice water so that the caramelized sugar hardens.

Almond-Flavored Egg Cake

Serves 6

This treat can serve as a snack or light breakfast. A heartier version, made with seafood or ground pork, is served as a main dish.

1/4 cup milk
1 tablespoon sugar
1/4 teaspoon almond extract
3 eggs, lightly beaten

1. In a small saucepan, scald the milk. Mix 3 tablespoons of the milk with the sugar, stirring. (You can discard the leftover milk.) Add the almond extract to the milk and sugar mixture, and add the mixture to the beaten egg.
2. Pour the egg mixture into a pie plate, and steam in a wok on medium to medium-high heat until a toothpick comes out clean.

Cooking Tips

For best results, it's important not to let too much air into the egg mixture. Lightly beat the eggs so that, if possible, no air bubbles form. Scalding the milk makes for a shorter cooking time.

New Year's Sticky Cake

6 Chinese dates
3 cups glutinous rice flour
1 cup boiling water
1¼ cups brown sugar
2 tablespoons milk or as required
1 egg
1 tablespoon vegetable oil
1 tablespoon sesame seeds

Serves 6–8

Sticky Cake is one of many foods symbolizing good luck that play a large role in Chinese New Year celebrations.

1. Soak the Chinese dates in hot water for at least 30 minutes to soften. Cut in half and remove the pits.
2. Place the glutinous rice flour in a large bowl. In a separate bowl, mix the boiling water and the sugar.
3. Make a well in the middle of the glutinous rice flour and stir in the sugar-and-water mixture. Add the milk and the egg. Stir until the batter is well mixed.
4. Prepare the wok for steaming. Grease a cake pan with the vegetable oil and pour the cake batter into the pan. Decorate with the dates and sesame seeds.
5. Set the cake pan on a bamboo steamer and place in the wok. Steam the cake for 50 minutes, or until the edges move away from the cake pan. Cool. To serve, cut the cake into wedges.

Chinese Dates

Also known as jujubes, these tiny red berries with the crinkly skin have been enjoyed in China since ancient times. Their delicate sweetness makes them a valuable addition to desserts and soups; they can also be enjoyed alone as a snack. Soak in water to soften before using.

Banana Fritters

Serves 5

Deep-frying the banana enhances its natural sweetness. For heightened flavor, deep-fry a second time at 325°F for about a minute.

½ cup flour
1 egg, beaten
2 tablespoons sesame oil
3 tablespoons water
5 bananas, cut into 1½-inch pieces
Flour for dusting
4 cups oil for deep frying

1. Stir the flour into the egg. Add the sesame oil and water and stir until a smooth batter is formed, adding a bit more water if necessary.
2. Lightly dust the banana pieces with the flour. Dip the banana pieces into the batter and cover, using your fingers.
3. Heat the oil to 350°F. Carefully slide the banana pieces into the hot oil, a few pieces at a time, and briefly deep-fry until they are golden. Remove and drain on paper towels.

Sweet Orange Tea

Serves 4

This sweet soup takes the place of a sorbet at Chinese banquets. It also make a refreshing dessert soup.

4 medium oranges
4 cups water
⅓ cup brown sugar
⅓ cup white sugar
1 tablespoon cornstarch

1. Cut the oranges in half. Use a sharp knife to scoop out the pulp over a large bowl to catch the juice.
2. In a large saucepan, add the water, sugars, and cornstarch. Bring to a boil, stirring constantly.
3. Add the orange pulp and juice to the water-and-sugar mixture, stirring.
4. Serve hot or cold.

Introduction to Thai Cooking

The key flavoring agents found in a Thai kitchen include coconut, lime, chili, garlic, ginger, cilantro, and dried fish (to make fish sauce). These ingredients are as basic as salt and pepper are to a Western kitchen. All of these foodstuffs are indigenous to the Asian continent with one notable exception: chilies, which the Portuguese introduced to Asia in the sixteenth century after "discovering" them in the New World. This is perhaps one of the most profound influences on Thai cuisine, as modern Thai cooking is almost impossible to imagine without the heat of chilies. However, the Portuguese are not the only people to have significantly influenced Thai cuisine as we know it today. The Chinese introduced the concept of stir-frying, the Indians brought curry, and the Indonesians introduced numerous spices.

Thai cuisine reflects the country's ample waterborne resources. Both saltwater and freshwater fish are eaten in abundance. Fish sauce is as common as ketchup and is used as a condiment, a salt substitute, and a general flavoring agent. Shrimp paste is used as we use anchovy paste, and dried fish are eaten as snacks.

The cuisine also reflects Thailand's tropical climate with an almost endless supply of exotic fruits that are eaten in salads, savory dishes, desserts, and by themselves. But by far the most important foodstuff in Thailand is rice. It is farmed everywhere and comes in endless varieties suitable for every growing condition from mountaintops to floodplains. It is Thailand's number one export.

Rice is so important in Thai culture that the word for rice is the same as the word for food. It is eaten with every meal and made into endless forms, from gruel to beverages to puffed cakes and desserts. Rice is believed to have a soul, called Mae Posop, or "The Rice Mother." She is born from rice, becomes pregnant when the rice flowers, and gives birth to rice. Rice farmers pay homage to Mae Posop, offering her food and shelter throughout the year.

Rice is a type of grass, the grain of which can only be extracted by milling or pounding. Thai people take great pride in the quality of their rice, and the whiter and more perfumed the better. For this reason, Jasmine rice is the long-grained variety preferred above all others.

Meat, although readily consumed, is not the centerpiece of a Thai meal, but instead is looked upon as a special treat. Theravada Buddhism, which forbids the killing of animals but not the eating of meat, is practiced by 95 percent of the population of Thailand. To make meat more palatable to the Buddhist psyche, meat is almost always shredded or cut into very small pieces. Rarely will you find a steak or chop served.

Dinner in Thailand is not served in courses, but rather soups, starters, rice, noodles, side dishes, and main courses are all served together to allow the cook to enjoy his or her guests. Only dessert is served separately. Condiments such as dried chilies, chili paste, chopped peanuts, fish sauce, and soy sauce are usual additions to the Thai table, just as salt and pepper are in the West. Fresh fruits are the typical end to a Thai meal. Desserts as we know them are usually served only at the end of a fancy banquet.

What You'll Need

Knife Types and Their Uses

PARING KNIFE—a short-bladed knife (usually 2 to 4 inches) used to trim fruits and vegetables

CHEF'S KNIFE—a medium-bladed knife used for chopping, slicing, and mincing

SLICING KNIFE—a long-bladed knife, either smooth-edged or serrated used for slicing meats or breads

Other useful knives include: boning, utility, cleaver, and fillet.

Specialty Utensils

Thai cooking really doesn't require a kitchen-full of fancy gadgets: Most often you will use standard mixing bowls and measuring cups, pots and pans, wooden and slotted spoons, and knives. But there are a few items that will make your Thai cooking easier and more enjoyable. So if you are in the mood to splurge, here's the wish list:

WOK—a high-sided, sloping, small-bottomed pan–the quintessential Asian utensil

RICE COOKER—an electric gizmo that takes the guessing out of rice

FOOD PROCESSOR—the workhorse of the kitchen when it comes to mixing, chopping, puréeing, and shredding

BLENDER—great for making sauces and purées

CHINOIS—a sieve perfect for straining stocks, sauces, and purées

HAND BLENDER—great for making sauces and purées right in the pot

COLANDER—perfect for straining noodles

MORTAR and PESTLE—a stone bowl and club used to crush spices and herbs

MANDOLINE—an extremely sharp utensil used for precise paper-thin cutting

Using a Blender with Hot Ingredients
Hot (as in temperature, not spiciness) ingredients in a blender can expand causing its lid to blow off. Instead of the lid, use a kitchen towel as a cover.

Basic Food Substitutions

There are three very common ingredients in Thai cooking that can be rather difficult to find in the United States. Luckily they have very inexpensive and common substitutions. In this book I have always used brown sugar in place of palm sugar, ginger in place of galangal, and vegetable oil in place of peanut oil. Substitutions for some common Thai ingredients are found in the following chart.

THAI INGREDIENT	SUBSTITUTION
Fish sauce	Soy sauce
Cilantro	Parsley
Kaffir lime leaves	Lime peel
Lemongrass	Lemon peel
Rice vinegar	Dry sherry or white vinegar
Long beans	Green beans
Thai eggplant	Green peas
Shallots	Small onions
Homemade curry paste	Store-bought curry paste

CHAPTER 13

Thai Curry Pastes, Marinades, and Other Concoctions

Green Curry Paste—1

Yields 1 cup

Curry pastes are the basis for many Thai recipes. Adding a tablespoon or so to a cup of coconut milk forms a poaching liquid for anything you want to cook—vegetables, meats, fish, or noodles.

10 green serrano chilies
3 shallots, coarsely chopped
5 cloves garlic
1 (1½-inch) piece gingerroot, peeled and chopped
1 stalk lemongrass, tough outer leaves removed, inner tender portion chopped
2 teaspoons grated lime zest
½ teaspoon shrimp paste
2 teaspoons ground coriander
2 teaspoons ground nutmeg
1 teaspoon ground cumin
1 teaspoon black pepper
½ teaspoon ground cloves
1 teaspoon salt
½ cup chopped cilantro
¼ cup vegetable oil

Place the first 6 ingredients in a food processor and process until well mixed. Add the remaining ingredients, except the vegetable oil, and process until smooth. Slowly add the oil until a thick paste is formed. May be refrigerated up to 4 weeks.

Curry Paste

Curry pastes are the foundation of most Thai preparations and are essentially concentrated flavoring agents meant to add complexity and depth. They are usually relatively moist concoctions of chili peppers, lime, and various herbs. Typically, curry pastes are mixed with either broth or coconut milk to create a sauce or cooking liquid.

Thai curries are famous throughout the world. But the Western term curry powder isn't indicative of a spice at all. Instead, it's a varying mixture of ingredients such as cumin, turmeric, garlic, paprika, ginger, clove, coriander, etc. If you find a store-bought variety that you like, stick with it. Each brand can taste completely different.

Green Curry Paste—2

3 tablespoons coriander seeds, toasted
2 teaspoons cumin seeds, toasted
2–4 green jalapeño chilies, seeded and chopped
2 green bell peppers, seeded and chopped
1 medium onion, chopped
3 cloves garlic, chopped
1 teaspoon shrimp paste
4 tablespoons chopped cilantro
2 teaspoons chopped lemongrass
1 (1-inch) piece ginger, peeled and chopped
4 tablespoons Tamarind Concentrate (see recipe on page 304)
3 teaspoons water
2 tablespoons vegetable oil
1 teaspoon salt

Yields approx. 1 cup

Green pastes tend to be a bit more pungent than their red cousins simply because chilies sweeten somewhat as they ripen and become red.

1. Place all the ingredients in a food processor and blend until smooth. Transfer to a small saucepan and bring to a simmer over medium-low heat. Reduce heat to low and cook, stirring frequently, for 5 minutes.
2. Stir in 1 cup of water and bring the mixture to a boil. Reduce heat, cover, and simmer for 30 minutes.

Storing Pastes

Making homemade curry pastes can be a bit time-consuming. Luckily, they store very well. They can be refrigerated in an airtight container for a month or frozen for up to a year. To freeze, place the paste in an ice cube tray. After they are frozen, remove the cubes from the tray and store them in freezer bags.

Red Curry Paste—1

Yields approx. ½ cup

You can substitute 1 fresh jalapeño pepper for every 2 red serrano chilies.

3 tablespoons coriander seeds, toasted
2 teaspoons cumin seeds, toasted
6–8 red serrano chilies, seeded and chopped
1 medium onion, chopped
2 garlic cloves, chopped
1 stalk lemongrass, outer leaves removed and discarded, inner core finely chopped
1 (½-inch) piece ginger, finely chopped
3 kaffir lime leaves or the peel of 1 lime, chopped
2 teaspoons paprika
4 tablespoons water
2 tablespoons Tamarind Concentrate (see recipe on page 304)
3 tablespoons vegetable oil
1 teaspoon salt

1. Place all the ingredients in a food processor and blend until very smooth.
2. Transfer to a small saucepan and bring to a simmer over medium-low heat. Reduce heat to low and cook, stirring frequently, for 5 minutes.
3. Stir in 1 cup of water and bring the mixture to a boil. Reduce heat, cover, and simmer 30 minutes.

Red Curry Paste—2

3 large dried red California chilies, seeded and chopped
5 dried Thai bird or similar chilies, seeded and chopped
2 stalks lemongrass, tough outer leaves removed and discarded, inner core finely minced
1 (2-inch) piece ginger, peeled and finely minced
2 cloves garlic, minced
1 small onion, chopped
2 tablespoons ground turmeric

Yields approx. 1 cup

Curry pastes that feature dried chilies tend to have a smoky, complex nuance, whereas those made mostly from fresh chilies have a cleaner, crisper taste.

1. Place the chilies in a bowl and cover them with hot water. Let stand for at least 30 minutes. Drain the chilies, reserving 1 cup of the soaking liquid.
2. Place all the ingredients and 2–3 tablespoons of the soaking liquid in a food processor. Process to form a thick, smooth paste. Add additional liquid if necessary.

Red Curry Paste Applications

While green curry paste is usually used for specific purposes, red curry paste is often treated as a "general purpose" paste that can be added to almost any Thai recipe. Whenever you see a recipe call for "common" or "plain" curry paste, it is almost always referring to the red. And if not, you'll be safe using it!

Southern (or Massaman) Curry Paste

Yields approx. 1 cup

Massaman is the Thai word for "Muslim." The sweet spices featured in this paste were brought to the Thai peninsula from the West by the Muslims.

6–8 large dried red chilies (often called California chilies), soaked in hot water for 5 minutes and drained
2 tablespoons coriander seeds, toasted
2 teaspoons cumin seeds, toasted
½ teaspoon cardamom seeds, toasted
2 whole cloves
¼ teaspoon whole black peppercorns
¼ teaspoon ground cinnamon
1 teaspoon shrimp paste (optional)
1 stalk lemongrass, tough outer leaves removed and discarded, inner core finely chopped
1 (1-inch) piece ginger, peeled and minced
1 teaspoon salt
1 teaspoon lime peel
2 teaspoons brown sugar
2 tablespoons vegetable oil
3 tablespoons Tamarind Concentrate (see recipe on page 18)
3 tablespoons water

1. Place all ingredients in a food processor and blend until smooth.
2. Transfer to a small saucepan and bring to a simmer over medium-low heat. Reduce heat to low and cook, stirring frequently, for 5 minutes.
3. Stir in 1 cup of water and bring the mixture to a boil. Reduce heat, cover, and simmer 30 minutes.

The Chili Infusion

Chilies are not indigenous to Asia. They arrived in Thailand from South America with the Portuguese traders and missionaries. Today, the Thai people eat more chilies on the average per person than any other country in the world.

Northern (or Jungle) Curry Paste

2 tablespoons vegetable oil
12 serrano chilies, seeded and chopped
6–8 Thai bird chilies, seeded and chopped
1 tablespoon shrimp paste
1 stalk lemongrass, tough outer leaves removed and discarded, inner core minced
1 (3-inch) piece ginger, peeled and chopped
4 shallots, chopped
1 cup chopped basil
½ cup chopped mint
¼ cup chopped chives
¼ cup chopped arugula

Yields approx. 2 cups

This curry has the look of a pesto. In fact, you can use it in a similar manner, tossing a tablespoon or so to taste with hot pasta.

1. In a medium-sized sauté pan, heat the oil on medium. Add the chilies, shrimp paste, lemongrass, ginger, and shallots, and sauté until the shallots begin to turn translucent and the mixture is very fragrant.
2. Transfer the mixture to a food processor and process until smooth, adding 1 or 2 tablespoons of water to help with the grinding.
3. Add the remaining ingredients and more water if necessary and continue to process until coarsely blended.

Arugula

Arugula is a specialty green with a peppery, somewhat bitter taste. Although we Westerners associate it with Italian cuisine, it was originally cultivated in Western Asia. If you can't find it (check in the herb section), you can substitute spinach in this recipe, although with a slightly less flavorful result.

Chili Tamarind Paste

Yields approx. 3 cups

This paste is a study of contrasts. The searingly hot Thai chilies are balanced by the sweetness of the tamarind and brown sugar and the saltiness of the dried shrimp and fish sauce.

½ cup dried shrimp
1¾ cups vegetable oil, divided
⅓ cup garlic
1 cup sliced shallots
12 small Thai chilies or 6 serrano chilies
3 tablespoons Tamarind Concentrate (see recipe on page 304)
3 tablespoons brown sugar
1 tablespoon fish sauce

1. Place the dried shrimp in a small bowl. Cover the shrimp with water, stir briefly, and drain; set aside.
2. Pour 1½ cups of the vegetable oil in a medium-sized saucepan. Bring the oil to approximately 360 degrees over medium-high heat.
3. Add the garlic and fry until golden brown. Using a slotted spoon, transfer the garlic to a bowl lined with paper towels.
4. Add the shallots to the saucepan and fry for 2 to 3 minutes; transfer the shallots to the bowl with the garlic.
5. Fry the reserved shrimp in the saucepan for 2 minutes; transfer to the bowl.
6. Fry the chilies until they become brittle, about 30 seconds; transfer them to the bowl. (Allow oil to cool to room temperature before discarding.)
7. Combine the fried ingredients, the remaining oil, and the tamarind in a food processor; process to form a smooth paste.
8. Place the paste in a small saucepan over medium heat. Add the sugar and fish sauce, and cook, stirring occasionally, for about 5 minutes.
9. Allow the paste to return to room temperature before placing in an airtight container.

Yellow Bean Sauce

2 tablespoons vegetable oil
1 medium to large onion, minced
2 serrano chilies, seeded and chopped
1 (½-inch) piece ginger, peeled and chopped
1 teaspoon ground coriander
4 tablespoons fermented yellow beans (fermented soy beans)
2 tablespoons lime juice
2 tablespoons water

Yields approx. 1 cup

This bean sauce is often used in Thai recipes to add depth, not only of flavor but also of texture.

1. In a medium-sized sauté pan, heat the oil over medium heat. Add the onion and chilies, and sauté until the onion becomes translucent. Stir in the ginger and coriander, and continue to cook for 30 seconds.
2. Add the beans, lime juice, and water, and simmer over low heat for 10 minutes.
3. Transfer the mixture to a blender and process until smooth.

Minty Tamarind Paste

1 bunch mint leaves
1 bunch cilantro leaves
¼ cup peanuts
½ cup Tamarind Concentrate (see recipe on page 304)
4–5 Thai bird peppers or 2 serrano chilies, seeded and chopped

Yields approx. 2 cups

This is a perfect way to use a lot of those extra herbs growing in your garden—to make a curry paste bursting with the tastes of summer.

Place all the ingredients in a food processor and blend to form a paste.

Black Bean Paste

Yields approx. ½ cup

Fermented soybeans remind me of garbanzo beans. When they are cooked and ground they have a somewhat mealy texture and the fermentation process yields a slightly sharp, vinegary taste.

2 tablespoons vegetable oil
1 medium to large onion, minced
2 jalapeños, seeded and chopped
2 cloves garlic, chopped
3 green onions, trimmed and sliced
4 tablespoons canned black beans or black soy beans
1 teaspoon brown sugar
1 tablespoon fish sauce
2 teaspoons lime juice

1. In a medium-sized sauté pan, heat the oil over medium-high heat. Add the onions, jalapeños, garlic, and green onions, and sauté until the onion becomes translucent.
2. Using a slotted spoon, transfer the sautéed vegetables to a food processor or blender (set aside the oil in the sauté pan). Add the remaining ingredients and process briefly to create a not-too-smooth paste.
3. Reheat the reserved oil in the sauté pan. Transfer the paste to the pan and heat for 5 minutes, stirring constantly. If the paste seems too thick, add a bit of water.

Marinating Safely

When you marinate foods, you should always do it in the refrigerator to reduce the possibility of bacteria growth unless otherwise directed in a recipe.

Thai Marinade—1

2 tablespoons fish sauce
¼ cup fresh lime juice
½ cup sesame oil
1 large stalk lemongrass, crushed
¼ teaspoon hot pepper flakes
2 tablespoons chopped peanuts
3 cloves garlic, minced
¼ cup chopped cilantro
1 tablespoon brown sugar

Combine the fish sauce and lime juice in a small bowl. Slowly whisk in the sesame oil, then stir in remaining ingredients.

Yields approx. 1 cup

This marinade contains the classic ingredients of Thai cuisine: fish sauce, lime juice, peanuts, chili peppers, and lemongrass. It works well with chicken, pork, or beef.

Thai Marinade—2

3 tablespoons fish sauce
1 tablespoon sweet soy sauce
½ cup rice wine
¼ cup peanut oil
¼ cup chopped basil leaves
¼ cup chopped mint leaves
3 cloves garlic, minced
1 tablespoon chopped gingerroot
1 small onion, chopped
2 tablespoons chopped lemongrass

Combine the fish sauce, sweet soy sauce, and the rice wine in a small bowl. Slowly whisk in the peanut oil, then stir in remaining ingredients.

Yields approx. 1½ cups

The basil and mint in this recipe are more traditional, but you can substitute almost any slightly spicy herb. Try parsley or arugula, or, for a milder version, baby spinach works well, too.

Thai Marinade—3

Yields approx. 2 cups

This marinade is infused with the flavors of India. In addition to the lemongrass, lime juice, and fish sauce, curry paste and coconut milk add to the complexity of the flavors.

1 (12-ounce) can coconut milk
½ cup Red Curry Paste (see pages 290 and 291)
1 stalk lemongrass, roughly chopped
6 kaffir lime leaves, finely sliced
1 teaspoon fresh gingerroot, chopped
¼ cup chopped cilantro leaves
¼ cup lime juice
2 tablespoons fish sauce
1 tablespoon sweet soy sauce

1. Combine the coconut milk, curry paste, lemongrass, and kaffir leaves in a small saucepan; bring to a simmer over medium heat.
2. Reduce heat and continue to simmer for 15 minutes.
3. Remove from heat and allow to cool to room temperature.
4. Stir in all the remaining ingredients.

Asian Marinade—1

Yields approx. 1¼ cups

This recipe uses ingredients more common to other Asian countries, yet still has Thai overtones. Soy sauce, which is more characteristic of China and Japan, smooths out the bite of the fish sauce.

¼ cup fish sauce
¼ cup soy sauce (preferably low-sodium)
½ cup freshly squeezed lime juice
2 tablespoons crunchy peanut butter
1 tablespoon light brown sugar
1 tablespoon curry powder
1 teaspoon minced garlic
Crushed dried red pepper

Combine all the ingredients in a blender or food processor and blend until smooth.

Asian Marinade—2

½ cup lime juice
¼ cup soy sauce
2 tablespoons hoisin sauce
1 tablespoon honey
⅓ cup vegetable oil
2 tablespoons sesame oil
¼ teaspoon ground anise
1 teaspoon Chinese 5-spice powder
1 tablespoon freshly grated gingerroot
3 cloves garlic, minced
3 tablespoons chopped cilantro
¼ cup chopped green onion

Combine the lime juice, soy sauce, hoisin sauce, and honey, and blend well. Slowly whisk in the vegetable and sesame oils. Add the remaining ingredients and mix thoroughly.

Yields approx. 1¼ cups

This recipe has a definite Chinese influence, featuring soy sauce, hoisin sauce, 5-spice powder, and sesame oil.

Tamarind Marinade

1½ cups Tamarind Concentrate (see recipe on page 304)
4 pieces lime peel (approximately ½-inch by 2-inches)
¼ cup fresh lime juice
1 tablespoon soy sauce
¼ cup vegetable oil
1 shallot, chopped
2 garlic cloves, minced
1 tablespoon diced fresh gingerroot
1 tablespoon brown sugar
¼ cup toasted, unsweetened coconut
½ cup chopped cilantro leaves

1. Combine the tamarind and lime peel in a small saucepan and bring to a simmer; cook for 5 minutes.
2. Remove from heat and cool to room temperature. Stir in the remaining ingredients.

Yields approx. 2 cups

This slightly sweet marinade works well with chicken or shellfish. Let some of the coconut and cilantro stick to your food while cooking.

Coconut Marinade

Yields approx. ½ cup

This wonderful marinade is ideal for shellfish such as scallops and prawns. The acidity of the lime is perfectly balanced with the sweetness of the coconut, sugar, and curry.

3 tablespoons rice wine vinegar
2 tablespoons shredded, unsweetened coconut
1 tablespoon minced fresh ginger
3 tablespoons lime juice
1 tablespoon grated lime zest
¼–½ teaspoon red chili pepper flakes
2 teaspoons sugar
⅛ teaspoon curry powder

1. Warm the vinegar over low heat. Add the coconut and ginger to soften.
2. Remove from heat and stir in the remaining ingredients.

Malaysian Marinade

Yields approx. 1 cup

Muslim traders brought with them the sweet spices of the West as they ventured into what is now Singapore and Indonesia. Try this fragrant marinade with any poultry.

2 tablespoons honey
3 tablespoons lime juice
1 teaspoon grated lime zest
¼ cup soy sauce
¼ cup vegetable oil
2 tablespoons grated gingerroot
1 green onion, trimmed and thinly sliced
½ teaspoon ground cumin
½ teaspoon coriander
¼ cup chopped cilantro

1. Combine the honey, lime juice, lime zest, and soy sauce in a small bowl.
2. Slowly whisk in the oil.
3. Stir in the remaining ingredients.

Thai Vinegar Marinade

4 cloves garlic, minced
6 dried red chilies, seeded and crumbled
3 tablespoons chopped green onion
1 tablespoon fresh grated gingerroot
2–3 tablespoons vegetable oil
3½ cups rice wine vinegar
1 tablespoon sugar
¼ cup chopped lemongrass

Yields approx. 3 cups

The rice wine in this marinade packs a terrific flavor surprise. Try it with beef or pork.

1. Place the garlic, chilies, green onions, and ginger in a food processor or blender and process to form a paste.
2. Heat the oil in a wok or frying pan, add the paste, and stir-fry for 4 to 5 minutes. Remove from heat and allow the mixture to cool to room temperature.
3. In a small saucepan, bring the vinegar to a boil. Add the sugar and the lemongrass; reduce heat and simmer for 20 minutes.
4. Stir in the reserved paste.

The Elements of a Marinade

Most marinades will include three specific elements: an acid, such as a citrus juice or vinegar, acts as a softening agent; an oil, which adds flavor and moisture; and the spices, which impart aroma and flavor to your dish.

Lemongrass Marinade

Yields approx. $1\frac{1}{3}$ cups

What is more Thai than lemongrass? If you are a lemongrass fan, this marinade is for you. I think it works well with poultry, beef, and pork, especially if you plan to grill.

1 cup extra-virgin olive oil
2 stalks lemongrass, trimmed and smashed
2 cloves garlic, minced
1/4 tablespoon soy sauce
1 tablespoon fish sauce
2 tablespoons lime juice
1 jalapeño chili pepper, seeded and chopped
2 tablespoons chopped cilantro

1. Pour the olive oil into a pan and heat until warm. Add the lemongrass and garlic, and cook for 1 minute. Remove from heat and let cool to room temperature.
2. Stir in the remaining ingredients.

Toasted Coconut

Toasted coconut is a nice item to have on hand—and not only as an ingredient for Thai recipes. Try sprinkling some over the top of a frosted cake or over a fruit salad, or stir some into your favorite tuna salad. Place 1 cup of dried, unsweetened coconut flakes in a heavy skillet over low heat, stirring frequently for 8 to 10 minutes, until golden brown.

Shredded Fresh Coconut

1 heavy coconut, with liquid

1. Preheat the oven to 400 degrees.
2. Pierce the eye of the coconut with a metal skewer or screwdriver and drain the coconut water (reserve it for later use if you like).
3. Bake the coconut for 15 minutes, then remove and let cool.
4. When the coconut is cool enough to handle, use a hammer to break the shell. Using the tip of a knife, carefully pull the flesh from the shell. Remove any remaining brown membrane with a vegetable peeler.
5. Shred the coconut using a 4-sided grater. Fresh coconut will keep in the refrigerator for up to 1 week.

Yields approx. 1 cup

This is a good activity for anger management. Take out your aggressions on a coconut—it's amazing how satisfying it can be!

Lemon Chili Vinegar

1 quart white wine vinegar
Peel of 4 limes
8–10 serrano chilies

1. Combine all the ingredients in a medium-sized saucepan and bring to a simmer over medium heat.
2. Reduce heat and simmer for 10 minutes.
3. Cool to room temperature, then strain.

Yields approx. 1 quart

Try using this tasty vinegar as a substitute for white vinegar—use it to make salad dressing, in mayonnaise, or to liven up soup.

Chili Vinegar

Yields approx. ½ cup

Because vinegars are acids, they have quite a long shelf life, almost an indefinite one. Store your infused vinegars in a well-sealed jar in the refrigerator. Just be warned that the flavors will intensify as they sit!

½ cup white vinegar
2 teaspoons fish sauce
3 serrano chilies, seeded and finely sliced

Place all of the ingredients in a bowl. Let sit at least 20 minutes to allow the flavors to develop.

Tamarind Concentrate

Makes approx. 1 cup

Another Thai flavoring staple, Tamarind Concentrate is a necessity for a well-stocked Thai kitchen. Although homemade is always best, tamarind concentrate (or paste) is available in Asian specialty markets.

2 ounces seedless tamarind pulp (sold in Asian markets)
1 cup warm water

1. Place the tamarind pulp and water in a small bowl for 20 minutes or until the pulp is soft.
2. Break the pulp apart with the back of a spoon and stir to combine.
3. Pour the mixture through a fine-mesh sieve, pushing the soft pulp through the strainer. Discard any fibrous pulp remaining in the strainer.

Thai Grilling Rub

4 teaspoons salt
1 teaspoon ground ginger
1 teaspoon dried lime peel
1 teaspoon freshly ground black pepper

1. Combine all the ingredients and mix thoroughly. Store in an airtight container.
2. To use, rinse the meat of your choice under cool water and pat dry; sprinkle the meat with the spice mixture (to taste) and rub it in along with some olive oil, then grill or broil to your liking.

Spice Rubs

There is a virtually infinite number of spice rub combos and variations. One helpful hint for creating your own spice rub: Check out some of the seasonings used in your favorite sauces, then mix together roughly equal parts of these ingredients to use as a rub for the meat, poultry, fish, or vegetable that was also involved in that recipe. You should also feel free to experiment!

Yields approx. 7 teaspoons

I love spice rubs. They may be the easiest way to add flavor quickly to anything you put on the grill (or under the broiler). This rub is ideal for pork or chicken.

CHAPTER 14

Dipping Sauces, Salsas, and Vinaigrettes

Peanut Dipping Sauce—1

Yields approx. 2 cups

Many people's first contact with Thai cooking is with skewered, grilled meat (usually chicken, beef, or shrimp), called "satays." These terrific appetizers are dipped in peanut sauce.

2/3 cup crunchy peanut butter
1 1/2 cups coconut milk
1/4 cup lemon juice
2 tablespoons soy sauce
2 tablespoons brown sugar
1 teaspoon grated gingerroot
4 cloves garlic, pressed
3–4 dashes (or to taste) Tabasco
1/4 cup chicken or vegetable stock
1/4 cup heavy cream

1. Combine the peanut butter, coconut milk, lemon juice, soy sauce, brown sugar, ginger, garlic, and Tabasco in a small saucepan over medium heat. Cook, stirring constantly, until the sauce has the consistency of heavy cream, about 15 minutes.
2. Transfer the mixture to a blender and purée briefly.
3. Add the stock and cream, and blend until smooth.

Allergy Alert

There are a fair number of people who are allergic to peanuts. Before inviting guests over for a Thai dinner, you should ask–just in case.

Peanut Dipping Sauce—2

⅔ cup crunchy peanut butter
1½ cups unsweetened canned coconut milk
¼ cup fresh lime juice
2 tablespoons soy sauce
2 tablespoons brown sugar
1 teaspoon grated gingerroot
2 teaspoons minced garlic
Ground cayenne or crushed red pepper flakes to taste
¼ cup low-sodium beef broth
¼ cup half-and-half or heavy cream

1. In a medium-sized saucepan, combine the peanut butter, coconut milk, lime juice, soy sauce, brown sugar, ginger, garlic, and cayenne.
2. Stirring constantly, cook over medium heat until the sauce thickens, about 15 minutes.
3. Remove the sauce from the heat and add the beef broth and cream. Using a hand mixer, blend until smooth. Heat briefly just prior to serving.

Yields approx. 2 cups

This peanut sauce can be used as a dip for any type of meat, but, because it is made with beef broth, it goes best with beef, lamb, or chicken.

Peanut Dipping Sauce—3

3 shallots
1 cup canned coconut milk
½ cup smooth peanut butter
2 teaspoons light brown sugar
1 teaspoon Tabasco
1 tablespoon fish sauce
2 teaspoons soy sauce
1 teaspoon fresh lemon juice
2 tablespoons fresh lime juice

1. Roast the shallots in an oven preheated to 325 degrees for about 5 minutes or until soft. Let them cool to roughly room temperature.
2. Place all ingredients in a blender or food processor and blend until smooth.

Yields approx. 2 cups

This quick peanut sauce is a delicious dip for fish, shrimp, or chicken satays. It can also be used as a base for a variety of Thai dishes—or simply toss it with rice noodles for a quick snack.

Minty Dipping Sauce

Yields approx. 1/3 cup

Don't be afraid to substitute items in this recipe. For example, you can use basil instead of the mint, jalapeño instead of the serrano, lemon instead of lime, and soy instead of fish sauce.

1/4 cup chopped mint leaves
1 serrano chili, seeded and diced
2 cloves garlic, minced
1 tablespoon grated lime zest
1/4 cup lime juice
2 tablespoons fish sauce

Place all the ingredients in a blender and process until smooth. Serve with a variety of grilled, skewered meats and raw or blanched vegetables.

Quick Hot Dipping Sauce

Yields approx. 1/2 cup

This sauce is an ideal dip for any type of meat. I always have a jar of chili-garlic sauce in the pantry. You can find it in almost any grocery store these days, either in the Asian department or in specialty foods.

1 heaping tablespoon prepared chili-garlic sauce
1/2 cup white vinegar

Combine the 2 ingredients and serve.

Sweet-and-Sour Dipping Sauce

½ cup white vinegar
1 cup sugar
½ teaspoon salt
1 heaping tablespoon prepared chili-garlic sauce

1. Combine the vinegar, sugar, and salt in a small saucepan over medium-high heat; bring to a boil, reduce to a simmer, and cook for 8 to 10 minutes, stirring occasionally.
2. Stir in the chili sauce and remove from heat. Let cool to room temperature before serving.

Yields approx. 1½ cups

You can vary the sweet and sour of this recipe by playing with the amount of sugar and/or chili sauce. Or you can substitute different brands or types of chili sauce—even Cajun or Jamaican!

Thai-Style Plum Dipping Sauce

⅔ cup plum preserves
⅔ cup white vinegar
⅔ cup water
2 tablespoons honey
Tabasco to taste

1. Place all the ingredients except the Tabasco in a food processor or blender, and process until smooth.
2. Transfer the mixture to a small saucepan and bring to a boil over medium heat; reduce heat and simmer until thick, about 12 to 15 minutes.
3. Allow to cool to room temperature, then stir in the Tabasco.

Yields approx. 2 cups

Traditionally used in Chinese cooking—think Moo Shu—plum sauce has a sweet-and-sour taste that is a perfect complement to poultry.

5-Minute Dipping Sauce

Yields approx. 4 tablespoons

This simple sauce is delicious as a dip for rice balls. I particularly like the pungency of the fresh ginger.

1 teaspoon sugar
1 tablespoon lime juice
1 tablespoon fish sauce
1 teaspoon minced fresh ginger
½ teaspoon dried red pepper flakes

In a small bowl, dissolve the sugar in 1 tablespoon of water. Stir in the remaining ingredients; adjust seasonings if necessary. Serve at room temperature.

Mango-Pineapple Salsa

Yields approx. 4 cups

A salsa is a condiment usually composed of roughly chopped fresh ingredients that are meant to enliven whatever they are served with. This salsa is perfect served with grilled shrimp, chicken, or fish.

1 cup mango pieces
1 cup diced pineapple
1 cup seeded and chopped tomato
½ cup diced red onion
¼ cup snipped chives
3 tablespoons chopped cilantro
1 serrano chili, seeded and chopped
2 tablespoons lime juice
2 tablespoons vegetable oil
Salt and pepper to taste

Combine all the ingredients in a small bowl. Cover and refrigerate for at least 2 hours before serving.

Mango-Cucumber Salsa

1 firm, ripe mango, peeled, seeded, and cut into ¼-inch dice
1 medium cucumber, seeded and cut into ¼-inch dice
¼ cup sliced green onion
¼ cup orange juice
2 teaspoons lime juice
1 teaspoon vegetable oil
Salt and pepper to taste

Combine all the ingredients in a small bowl.

Yields approx. 2 cups

This salsa can be served alongside grilled fish or used as a small salad.

Banana, Tamarind, and Mint Salsa

4 ripe bananas, peeled and finely diced
¼ cup Tamarind Concentrate (see recipe on page 304)
1 roasted red jalapeño, seeded and chopped
1 tablespoon chopped fresh mint
1 teaspoon brown sugar
1 tablespoon lime juice

Gently fold all the ingredients together.

Yields approx. 2 cups

This unique salsa goes perfectly with roasted or grilled poultry or game.

Spicy Thai Dressing

Yields approx. 1/3 cup

Try brushing this dressing over the top of meats or poultry as they grill to add a nice zing.

2 tablespoons soy sauce
1 tablespoon plus 1 teaspoon rice wine vinegar
1 tablespoon sesame oil
3 tablespoons water
1 teaspoon sugar
2 cloves garlic
1 teaspoon grated gingerroot
1 fresh red cayenne pepper or 2 Thai peppers, stemmed, seeded, and cut into pieces

Place all the ingredients in a blender and process until smooth.

Peanut Pesto

Yields approx. 2 cups

Serve this pesto tossed with pasta or as a unique spread for veggie or chicken sandwiches. Use it as you would any pesto.

1 cup unsalted roasted peanuts
1/2 cup soy sauce
1/4 cup honey
1/3 cup water
2–3 cloves garlic, minced
1/2 cup sesame oil
1/4 teaspoon (or to taste) red pepper flakes

Place the peanuts in a food processor fitted with a metal blade; process until fine. While continuing to blend, add the remaining ingredients one at a time through the feed tube until well blended.

Jalapeño-Lime Vinaigrette

1 jalapeño, seeded and chopped
1/3 cup lime juice
1 tablespoon sugar
Salt and pepper to taste
1 cup vegetable or canola oil

Place the jalapeño, lime juice, sugar, and salt and pepper in a food processor; blend for 1 minute. While continuing to blend, slowly add the oil; blend for 30 seconds or until well emulsified.

Yields approx. 1 1/3 cups

Serve over grilled fish or vegetables or a fresh salad.

Ginger-Lemongrass Vinaigrette

1 quart rice wine vinegar
2 stalks lemongrass, outer leaves removed and discarded, inner core slightly mashed
1/4 cup grated fresh gingerroot

Combine all the ingredients in a nonreactive pot and simmer over low heat for 30 minutes. Remove from heat and let stand overnight. Strain before serving.

Yields approx. 1 quart

This vinaigrette is fantastic as a dressing for salad or as a marinade for crudités.

Mint-Cilantro "Chutney"

Yields approx. 2 cups

I like to spoon some of this chutney on a plate and top it with roasted cauliflower. The cauliflower acts as a sponge, soaking up every last drop.

⅓ cup unsalted peanuts, toasted
¾ cup packed mint leaves
¾ cup packed cilantro
3 tablespoons sour cream
2 teaspoons honey
½ teaspoon minced honey
Salt and pepper to taste

Place the peanuts in a food processor and finely grind. Add the remaining ingredients to the processor and blend until well combined.

What's a Chutney?

A chutney is a traditional accompaniment to Indian foods. It is a coarse relish or condiment usually made from tropical fruits, ginger, and herbs. Chutneys usually have notes of spicy, sweet, and sour, and can be used as a dipping sauce, a bread spread, or as a glaze.

Chapter 15

Appetizers

Rice Paper Rolls

Serves 2–4

This healthy appetizer is the perfect finger food and is a great introduction to Thai cuisine: There are no scary ingredients, it isn't tongue-numbingly hot, and yet it is definitely not Western in style or flavor.

1 cup thin rice noodles
8–10 medium to large cooked shrimp, cut in half
4 (8" × 10") sheets of rice paper
1 cup grated carrot
2 scallions, thinly sliced
1 small cucumber, shredded
20 mint leaves
1 small bunch cilantro

1. Soak the rice noodles in very hot water until they are soft, usually 10 to 20 minutes; drain. You can leave the noodles whole, or cut them into 2-inch pieces if you prefer.
2. Place a clean kitchen towel on a work surface with a bowl of hot water nearby. Put a sheet of the rice paper in the hot water for approximately 20 seconds, just until soft; lay it out flat on the towel.
3. In the middle of the rice paper, place 2 to 3 pieces of shrimp and ¼ of the noodles, carrots, scallions, and cucumbers. Top with mint and cilantro.
4. Quickly roll up the rice paper, keeping it fairly tight; then roll up the whole thing in plastic wrap, making sure to keep it tight. Refrigerate until ready to serve.
5. To serve, trim the ends off the rolls. Cut the remaining roll into pieces and remove the plastic wrap. Serve with your favorite dipping sauce.

Crab Spring Rolls

1 pound crabmeat, picked over to remove any shells, and shredded
1 tablespoon mayonnaise
¼–½ teaspoon grated lime peel
15 spring roll or egg roll wrappers
2 egg yolks, lightly beaten
Canola oil for deep frying
15 small, tender Boston lettuce leaves
Mint leaves
Parsley leaves

1. In a small bowl, mix the crabmeat with the mayonnaise and lime peel.
2. Place 1 tablespoon of the crabmeat mixture in the center of 1 spring roll wrapper. Fold a pointed end of the wrapper over the crabmeat, then fold the opposite point over the top of the folded point. Brush a bit of the egg yolk over the top of the exposed wrapper, then fold the bottom point over the crabmeat and roll to form a tight packet; set aside. Repeat with the remaining crabmeat and wrappers.
3. Heat the oil to 365 degrees in a skillet or deep fryer. Deep-fry the rolls 3 to 4 at a time for 2 minutes or so, until they are a golden brown; drain on paper towels.
4. To serve, wrap each spring roll in a wrapper with a single piece of lettuce, and a sprinkling of mint and parsley. Serve with your favorite dipping sauce.

Yields 15 rolls

Don't let the deep-frying steer you away from these light, crunchy rolls. The key to keeping the fat to a minimum is using clean, hot cooking oil and immediately transferring the rolls to papers towels.

Pork, Carrot, and Celery Spring Rolls

Yields 20 rolls

Thai recipes often call for ground meat. Make sure to use low-fat meat so that when you combine it with other ingredients, it remains crumbly and doesn't add excess moisture or fat to your dish.

2 tablespoons vegetable oil
1 teaspoon minced garlic
1 cup minced or ground pork
2 cups grated carrots
2 cups chopped celery
1/4 cup fish sauce
2 tablespoons sugar
1/4 teaspoon white pepper
1 cup bean sprouts
20 spring roll wrappers
2 egg yolks, beaten
Vegetable oil for deep frying

1. In a large skillet, heat the 2 tablespoons of vegetable oil over medium-high heat. Add the garlic and pork, and sauté until the pork is cooked through.
2. Add the carrots, celery, fish sauce, sugar, and white pepper. Increase heat to high and cook for 1 minute.
3. Drain any liquid from the pan and allow the mixture to cool to room temperature, then stir in the bean sprouts.
4. On a clean, dry work surface, place the egg roll wrapper with an end pointing toward you, forming a diamond. Place approximately 2 tablespoons of the filling on the lower portion of the wrapper. Fold up the corner nearest you and roll once, then fold in the sides. Brush the remaining point with the egg yolk and finish rolling to seal. Repeat with the remaining wrappers and filling.
5. Heat 2 to 3 inches of oil to 350 degrees. Deep-fry the spring rolls until golden brown; remove immediately to drain on paper towels.
6. Serve with sweet-and-sour sauce.

Omelet "Egg Rolls"

For the filling:

1 teaspoon vegetable oil
½ pound ground pork or chicken
2 green onions, trimmed and thinly sliced
1 cup shredded Chinese cabbage
½ teaspoon sugar
1 tablespoon fish sauce
1 tablespoon minced cilantro

For the omelets:

8 eggs
6 tablespoons water
1 tablespoon soy or fish sauce
1 teaspoon vegetable oil
Bibb lettuce
Soy sauce, fish sauce, and/or hot sauce
Garnish of your choice

Yields 16–20 pieces

Using omelets in place of the usual egg roll wrapper is a fun twist on a classic favorite. These rolls use traditional filling ingredients and dipping sauces.

1. To make the filling: In a medium-sized skillet, warm the vegetable oil over medium heat. Add the ground meat and sauté until it is no longer pink. Add the green onions and cabbage and cook until soft. Add the sugar, fish sauce, and cilantro; cook for 1 more minute. Set the filling aside, keeping it warm.
2. To make the omelets: Combine the eggs, water, and soy sauce in a medium-sized bowl. Place an omelet pan over medium heat for 1 minute. Add approximately ¼ teaspoon of vegetable oil, swirling it to coat the pan evenly. Pour approximately ¼ of the egg mixture into the pan, then let it rest for approximately 30 seconds. When the bottom is firm, flip the omelet and cook until done. Remove to a plate and cover with foil to keep warm. Repeat to make 3 more omelets.
3. To fill the "egg rolls," place 1 omelet in the center of a plate. Place ¼ of the filling slightly off-center and then roll up. Trim the ends and cut the rolls into bite-sized pieces.
4. To serve, use Bibb lettuce leaves to pick up the rolls. Dip in additional soy sauce, fish sauce, hot sauce, or other favorite dipping sauce, and add the garnish of your choice.

Basil and Shrimp Wedges

Serves 4–6 as an appetizer or 2 as a brunch item

When is basil not just plain old basil? When it's Horapa, Ga-prow, or Manglug. Don't be afraid to experiment with different basils. They all taste great!

1½ teaspoons vegetable oil, divided
½ pound cooked salad shrimp
1 green onion, trimmed and thinly sliced
½ cup julienned basil
1 teaspoon fish sauce
4 eggs
2 tablespoons water
Salt and pepper to taste

1. Place 1 teaspoon of the vegetable oil in a sauté pan over medium heat. Add the shrimp and green onion, and sauté until the shrimp are warmed through, approximately 2 minutes. Add the basil and fish sauce and cook for 1 more minute. Set aside.
2. In a large bowl, whisk together the eggs, water, and salt and pepper, then stir in the shrimp mixture.
3. Place the remaining ½ teaspoon of vegetable oil in an omelet pan over medium heat. Add the egg mixture and cook until the omelet begins to brown. Flip over the omelet and continue to cook until set.
4. To serve, slide the omelet onto a serving plate and cut it into wedges. Serve it with your favorite Thai dipping sauce.

Crispy Mussel Pancakes

1 cup shelled mussels (about 1 pound before shelling)
½ cup tapioca flour
¼ cup all-purpose flour
¼ teaspoon salt
1 teaspoon baking powder
¾ cup water
2 cups bean sprouts
2 tablespoons chopped cilantro, plus extra for garnish
Salt and ground pepper to taste

Serves 2–4

I know these sound weird, but you have to trust me on this. They're great! The slightly herbed pancakes make a perfect foil for the subtle taste of the mussels.

1. To prepare the mussels, rinse them quickly under cold running water. Debeard the mussels by pulling out the brown membrane that is sometimes still attached. Discard any mussels that are already open. Fill a large skillet with ½ to 1 inch of water. Bring the water to a boil, then add the mussels, cover, and let steam about 4 minutes or until the mussels have opened, shaking the pan every so often. Drain the mussels through a colander. Let cool to room temperature and then use a small fork to pull the meat from the shell; set aside on paper towels.
2. In a medium-sized mixing bowl, stir together the flours, the salt, and the baking powder. Whisk in the water to form a thin batter.
3. Preheat the oven to 200 degrees. In a large, heavy-bottomed skillet, heat the vegetable oil over medium-high heat. Pour half of the batter into the skillet and top with half of the mussels. Cook until the batter has set and turned golden, about 2 minutes. Carefully flip the pancake over and continue cooking until golden. Remove the pancake to a baking sheet lined with some foil and place it in the oven to keep warm. Repeat to make a second pancake with the remaining batter and mussels.
4. Add 1 teaspoon of vegetable oil to the skillet if it is dry, and increase the heat to high. Add the bean sprouts, sprinkle with salt and ground pepper to taste, and stir-fry quickly just to heat through, about 30 seconds.
5. To serve, place each pancake in the center of a plate. Top with the bean sprouts, some cilantro, and a grind of fresh pepper. Serve with a sweet-and-sour sauce of your choice.

Chicken, Shrimp, and Beef Satay

Makes 4–6 chicken skewers or 6–8 shrimp or beef skewers

Satays are served hot but are almost as delicious at room temperature, and they go great with a cold beer. Don't forget to have a lot of peanut sauce!

Chicken

1 recipe Thai Marinade (see recipes in Chapter 13)
3 whole boneless, skinless chicken breasts, cut into long strips about ½-inch wide
1 recipe Peanut Dipping Sauce (see recipes in Chapter 14)

1. Thread the chicken strips onto presoaked bamboo skewers or onto metal skewers. Place the skewers in a flat pan and cover with marinade. Marinate the chicken in the refrigerator overnight.
2. Cook the skewers on the grill or under the broiler, basting and turning them until they are cooked through, about 6 to 8 minutes.
3. Serve with the peanut sauce for dipping.

Shrimp

1 recipe Thai Marinade
24 large shrimp, shelled and deveined
1 recipe Peanut Dipping Sauce

1. Thread the shrimp onto presoaked bamboo skewers or onto metal skewers (about 3 shrimp per skewer). Place the skewers in a flat pan and cover with marinade. Marinate the shrimp for at least 15 minutes, but no longer than 1 hour.
2. Cook the skewers on the grill or under the broiler, basting and turning them often until just opaque, about 3 to 4 minutes.
3. Serve with the peanut sauce for dipping.

(recipe continues on the next page)

Chicken, Shrimp, and Beef Satay

(continued)

Beef

1 recipe Thai Marinade
1–1½ pounds sirloin steak, fat and sinew removed, cut into ½-inch-wide strips
1 recipe Peanut Dipping Sauce

1. Thread the beef strips onto presoaked bamboo skewers or onto metal skewers. Place the skewers in a flat pan and cover with marinade. Marinate the beef in the refrigerator overnight.
2. Cook the skewers on the grill or under the broiler, basting and turning them often until done to your liking, about 6 to 8 minutes for medium.
3. Serve with the peanut sauce for dipping.

The Origin of Satay

Satay was first introduced to Thailand by Arab traders from the Middle East.

Shrimp Toast

Yields 32 pieces

The pork in this recipe not only adds a bit of extra flavor, but also helps to bind the ingredients together. You could also use ground chicken or turkey if you don't want the pork.

8 slices of white bread, left to sit out overnight, crusts removed
½ pound shrimp, cleaned, deveined, and coarsely chopped
¼ pound ground pork
1 tablespoon chopped cilantro
2 cloves garlic, minced
⅛ teaspoon cayenne
¼ teaspoon salt
1 egg, beaten
2 teaspoons soy sauce
2 tablespoons sesame seeds
2 teaspoons vegetable oil, divided
32 slices cucumber

1. In a small bowl, combine the shrimp and pork; set aside.
2. In another small bowl, combine the cilantro, garlic, cayenne, and salt. Pour the spice mixture over the shrimp and pork, and combine.
3. Stir in the beaten egg and soy sauce; mix well. Divide the mixture into 8 parts.
4. Smoothly spread a thin layer of the mixture on each slice of bread and sprinkle with sesame seeds.
5. Heat ¼ teaspoon vegetable oil in nonstick skillet. When it is very hot, place 1 piece of bread, meat side down, in the oil. Cook until golden in color, then remove to a paper towel, blotting any excess oil. Repeat for all of the bread sides.
6. Cut each slice of bread into quarters and top each quarter with a cucumber slice.

Pork Toast Triangles

¼ pound of large shrimp, peeled and deveined
1 tablespoon dried shrimp
1 tablespoon chopped cilantro
2 cloves garlic, peeled
1 pound ground pork (the leaner the better)
1 egg
1 tablespoon fish sauce
6 slices day-old bread, crusts trimmed off
Vegetable oil for frying

1. Fill a medium-sized saucepan with water and bring it to a boil. Reduce the heat, add the shrimp, and simmer until the shrimp are opaque. Drain the shrimp and let cool to room temperature. Coarsely chop and set aside.
2. Place the dried shrimp, cilantro, and the garlic in a food processor and blend until a smooth paste is formed. Add the reserved shrimp and ground pork; process again. Add the egg and fish sauce and process once more.
3. Spread the mixture evenly over each slice of bread. Cut the bread into 4 equal slices, either from corner to corner forming triangles or from top to bottom forming squares.
4. Add approximately ½ inch of vegetable oil to a large skillet. Bring the oil to approximately 375 degrees over medium-high heat. Place 4 to 5 toasts in the oil, filling side down. Make sure that the toasts are not crowded in the oil or they will not brown evenly. After the filling side is nicely browned, use a slotted spoon or metal strainer to flip the toasts. Watch the toasts carefully, as the bottoms will brown quickly. Remove the toasts to a stack of paper towels to drain. Carefully pat the tops of the toasts with paper towels to remove any oil.
5. Serve the toasts with sweet-and-sour or plum sauce.

Yields 24 pieces

Similar in concept to the Shrimp Toast, this recipe features pork and uses the shrimp as the primary accent flavor, resulting in a milder overall taste.

Mee Krob

Serves 4–6

This dish has a royal background, but is now an everyday Thai staple. Mee krob is usually served either as an appetizer or as a noodle salad, but I like to eat it as a snack.

⅓ cup honey
⅓ cup rice or white vinegar
5 tablespoons sugar
2–3 drops red food coloring
1 tablespoon Tamarind Concentrate (see recipe on page 304)
Vegetable oil for deep-frying
2 eggs, beaten
½ pound thin rice stick noodles, broken into handfuls
½ cup dried shrimp
1 cup bean sprouts
10 small lime wedges

1. Combine the honey, vinegar, sugar, food coloring, and tamarind in a medium-sized saucepan. Bring the mixture to a boil over medium heat, stirring occasionally. Reduce heat and simmer for 2 to 3 minutes or until the mixture begins to thicken; remove from heat and set aside.
2. Bring about 3 inches of vegetable oil to 360 degrees in a deep fryer or skillet. Drop a single layer of the rice stick noodles into the hot oil, making sure to leave enough room for them to cook evenly. Turn the noodles with a slotted spoon as soon as they begin to puff up. As soon as the noodles are golden, remove them to paper towels to drain. Repeat until all of the noodles are cooked.
3. Add the dried shrimp to the oil and cook for 45 seconds or so. Remove to paper towels.
4. Pour out all but a thin coat of the oil from the skillet. Add the beaten eggs and stir-fry them quickly, shirring them into long strips. As soon as they are cooked, remove them to paper towels.
5. Bring the sauce back to a boil. Stir in the shrimp and continue to boil for 2 minutes.
6. Place about ⅓ of the noodles on a serving platter and spoon about ⅓ of the sauce over the top; gently toss to coat the noodles evenly being careful not to crush the noodles. Repeat until all of the noodles are coated in sauce.
7. To serve, mound the noodles, place the egg strips over them, and top with the bean sprouts. Pass the lime wedges.

Son-in-Law Eggs

¼ cup vegetable oil
10 hard-boiled eggs, cooled and peeled
2 shallots, thinly sliced
⅓ cup light brown sugar
3 tablespoons fish sauce
⅓ cup Tamarind Concentrate (see recipe on page 304)
¼ cup chopped cilantro
Dried hot chili flakes to taste

Yields 20

A version of deviled eggs with all of the characteristic Thai flavors—sweet, sour, salty, and spicy—these eggs make a delightful addition to a picnic basket, a summer barbecue, or as a quick snack.

1. Heat the vegetable oil in a skillet over medium heat. Place the whole eggs in the skillet and fry until golden brown. Remove the eggs to paper towels and set aside. (If your skillet can't hold all of the eggs comfortably, do this in batches.)
2. Add the shallots to the skillet and sauté until just beginning to brown. Remove the shallots from the oil with a slotted spoon and set aside.
3. Put the brown sugar, fish sauce, and tamarind in the skillet. Stir to combine and bring to a simmer. Cook the mixture, stirring constantly, until the sauce thickens, about 5 minutes; remove from heat.
4. Cut the eggs in half vertically and place them face-up on a rimmed serving dish. Spread the shallots over the eggs and then drizzle the eggs with the sauce. Garnish with cilantro and chili pepper flakes.

The Secret to Making Perfect Hard-Boiled Eggs

The perfect hard-boiled egg has a delicate white and a fully cooked yolk, without even a hint of the unattractive gray shadow that affects an improperly cooked egg. The perfect hard-boiled egg is also easy to peel. To achieve this, put the eggs in enough cold water to cover them by 1 inch and boil for 1 minute only. Then remove from heat, cover, and let them sit for 15 minutes. Then, transfer the eggs to a bath of ice water for 15 to 20 minutes. They should then peel easily.

Salt-Cured Eggs

Yields 1 dozen eggs

Salt-cured eggs are delicious as is—just peel and eat. I used them for Easter eggs this year, much to the delight of my husband, who is a real hard-boiled egg fan. They were beautiful and tasted great.

6 cups water
1½ cups salt
1 dozen eggs

1. Combine the water and the salt in a large saucepan and bring to a boil over high heat. Remove from heat and let cool to room temperature.
2. Carefully place the eggs in a container. Pour the salt water over the eggs and seal the container tightly. Place the container in the refrigerator and let the eggs cure for at least 1 month.
3. To serve, hard-boil the eggs, let cool to room temperature, then peel, slice, and enjoy.

3-Flavor Rice Sticks

Serves 4–6

These crunchy sticks are irresistible: I challenge you to eat just a handful! Don't be shy about experimenting with other spice blends or flavoring agents.

1 pound rice sticks, broken into 3-inch segments
Vegetable oil for frying
Salt to taste
Curry powder to taste
Cayenne pepper to taste

1. Pour 2 to 3 inches of vegetable oil into a large skillet and heat to 350 degrees. Fry the rice sticks in batches (making sure not to overcrowd the pan), turning them quickly as they puff up. After they stop crackling in the oil, transfer the puffed sticks to paper towels to drain.
2. While the rice sticks are still hot, sprinkle salt on 1 batch; sprinkle a second batch with curry powder; and a third batch with cayenne pepper to taste.

Thai Fries

2 medium-sized sweet potatoes
4 green plantains
1 pound taro root
1 cup rice flour
1 cup sticky rice flour
Water
1 teaspoon black pepper
1 teaspoon salt
2 tablespoons sugar
3 tablespoons black sesame seeds
1 14-ounce bag shredded sweetened coconut

Serves 4–8

A great finger food super for casual get-togethers, these fried vegetables sometimes never leave the kitchen because sneaky fingers grab them right off the paper towels! They are that good!

1. Peel the root vegetables and cut them into flat ⅓-inch-thick strips about 3 inches long and 1 inch wide.
2. Combine the flours in a large mixing bowl and stir in ½ cup of water. Continue adding water ¼ cup at a time until a mixture resembling pancake batter is formed. Stir in remaining ingredients.
3. Fill a medium-sized saucepan a third to a half full with vegetable oil. Heat the oil over high heat until very hot, but not smoking.
4. Add some of the vegetables to the batter, coating them well. Using a slotted spoon or Asian strainer, place the vegetables in the hot oil. (Be careful here: The oil may spatter.) Fry the vegetables, turning them occasionally, until golden brown. Transfer the fried vegetables to a stack of paper towels to drain, then serve immediately.

Spicy Coconut Bundles

Serves 4

These fun, "make it yourself" bundles are one of my favorite snacks. They are packed full of flavor and texture—so much so that it's probably not a bad idea to make a double recipe!

1 cup shredded fresh coconut
⅔ cup brown sugar
⅓ cup shrimp paste
½ cup diced red onion
½ cup chopped lime segments
½ cup chopped peanuts
½ cup dried shrimp
1–2 jalapeños, seeded and sliced
20–25 medium-sized spinach leaves, washed and patted dry

1. Place the coconut in a medium-sized sauté pan and cook over medium heat until browned, about 20 minutes; set aside to cool.
2. In a small saucepan, melt the brown sugar over medium heat, stirring constantly. Mix in the shrimp paste until well combined. Set the sauce aside.
3. Place the coconut, onion, lime pieces, peanuts, dried shrimp, and jalapeños in a medium-sized serving bowl; gently toss to combine.
4. To serve, place 4 to 5 spinach leaves (depending on the size of the leaves) on each serving plate. Top each leaf with approximately 1 tablespoon of the coconut mixture and drizzle a bit of sauce over the coconut.
5. To eat, roll up the spinach leaf around the coconut mixture and pop the whole bundle in your mouth. Pass additional sauce separately.

Curried Fish Cakes

¼ cup chopped shallots
¼ cup chopped garlic
¼ cup chopped lemongrass, inner portion only
1 tablespoon chopped ginger
½ teaspoon peppercorns
1 teaspoon grated lime peel
1 tablespoon shrimp paste
5–10 dried chilies, seeded, soaked, and shredded
½ tablespoon salt
1 pound boneless whitefish steak, minced
1 egg, beaten
½ pound French beans, trimmed and finely chopped
Vegetable oil for frying

Yields 15–20 small cakes

One of my favorite dishes growing up was my mother's salmon cakes. Here is a Thai version. Whitefish is used so that the lemongrass and ginger aren't overpowered by the fish.

1. Place the shallots, garlic, lemongrass, ginger, peppercorns, lime peel, shrimp paste, chilies, and salt in a food processor or blender and process to form a smooth paste.
2. Add the fish to the food processor and pulse until well combined with the spice paste. Add the beaten egg and combine once more. Transfer the fish mixture to a large mixing bowl and stir in the green beans.
3. Using approximately 1 tablespoon of fish mixture, form a flat, round cake; repeat until all of the mixture is used.
4. Heat approximately ⅛ to ¼ inch of vegetable oil to 350 degrees over medium-high heat in a skillet or deep fryer; fry the fish cakes until golden.
5. Serve with your favorite dipping sauce.

Spicy Scallops

Serves 4

These scallops are simple to make but are sure to impress even your most fussy guests. They are also tasty over pasta as a main course. Make sure to use the freshest scallops you can find.

1 teaspoon vegetable oil
1 clove garlic, minced
1 jalapeño, seeded and minced
1 (½-inch) piece of ginger, peeled and minced
⅛ teaspoon ground coriander
2 tablespoons soy sauce
2 tablespoons water
8 large scallops, cleaned

1. In a pan large enough to hold all of the scallops, heat the oil over medium heat. Add the garlic, jalapeño, and ginger, and stir-fry for about 1 minute.
2. Add the coriander, soy sauce, and water, stirring to combine; simmer for 2 to 3 minutes. Strain the liquid through a fine-mesh sieve. Allow the pan to cool slightly.
3. Add the scallops to the pan and spoon the reserved liquid over the top of them. Return the pan to the stove, increasing the heat to medium-high. Cover the pan and let the scallops steam for about 2 to 3 minutes, or until done to your liking. Serve immediately.

Cleaning Out Whole Scallops

If you buy scallops whole, there is an easy way to clean out the meat! Simply put the scallops on ice for about 10 minutes, which will cause them to open up. Then, using a sturdy tablespoon, slide the spoon in-between the open shell and twist open. Then use the spoon to scoop out the meat—that's it!

Spicy Ground Pork in Basil Leaves

Juice of 1–2 limes
½ pound ground pork
3 tablespoons fish sauce
1 shallot, thinly sliced
¼ tablespoon (or to taste) ground dried chili pepper
5 sprigs cilantro, chopped
1 tablespoon toasted rice powder (available in Asian specialty stores)
Lettuce and/or large basil leaves

1. Squeeze the juice of half of a lime over the ground pork and let marinate for a few minutes.
2. Heat a large skillet on high. Add a couple of tablespoons of water and then immediately add the pork; stir-fry until the pork is cooked through. (Don't worry if the pork sticks at first—it will eventually loosen.)
3. Pour off any fat that has accumulated in the pan and then put the pork in a large mixing bowl. Add the remaining lime juice (to taste), fish sauce, shallot, ground chili pepper, cilantro, and toasted rice; stir to combine thoroughly.
4. To serve, place the mixture in a serving bowl and let guests use the lettuce and basil leaves to scoop out the mixture.

Serves 4

I remember the first time I went to an Ethiopian restaurant and was encouraged to eat using flatbread instead of utensils. This Thai dish is eaten using basil and lettuce leaves as utensils.

Skewered Thai Pork

Serves 2–3

This recipe is similar to satay, but the coconut milk in this dish infuses it with a certain tropical nuance, and it is rarely served with peanut sauce. Although, if peanut sauce is your thing, don't let me stop you.

2 tablespoons sugar
1 teaspoon salt
3 cloves garlic, minced
1 tablespoon fish sauce
1 tablespoon coconut milk
1 pound pork, thinly sliced into long strips
20–30 bamboo skewers, soaked in water for 1 hour

1. In a medium-sized bowl, combine the sugar, salt, garlic, fish sauce, and coconut milk.
2. Toss the pork strips in the mixture to coat thoroughly. Cover the bowl and marinate for at least 30 minutes, but preferably overnight in the refrigerator.
3. Thread the pork strips onto the bamboo skewers.
4. Grill the skewers for about 3 to 5 minutes per side.
5. Serve with your favorite sauce or as is.

Using Bamboo Skewers

When using bamboo skewers for grilling, always be sure to soak them in water for at least an hour (to prevent them from catching on fire or charring badly). Another way to reduce charring of the skewers is to make sure as much of the skewer is covered by food as possible—leave only 1/4–1/2 inch of space at the end.

Fried Won Tons

1 clove garlic, minced
2 tablespoons minced cilantro
1 tablespoon soy sauce
½ cup chopped white mushrooms
Pinch white pepper
½ pound ground pork
25 won ton skins
Vegetable oil for frying

1. In a medium-sized mixing bowl, thoroughly combine the garlic, cilantro, soy sauce, mushrooms, white pepper, and ground pork.
2. To make the won tons, place approximately ½ teaspoon of the filling in the middle of a won ton skin. Fold the won ton from corner to corner, forming a triangle. Press the edges together to seal closed. Repeat with the remaining skins and filling.
3. Add about 2 to 3 inches of vegetable oil to a deep fryer or wok. Heat the oil on medium until it reaches about 350 degrees. Carefully add the won tons, 2 or 3 at a time. Fry until they are golden brown, turning them constantly. Transfer the cooked won tons to drain on paper towels as they are done.
4. Serve the won tons with either sweet-and-sour sauce or the sauce of your choice.

Yields approx. 25 won tons

Although won tons and spring rolls often have similar fillings, their wrappers set them apart. Spring rolls use rice flour wrappers; won ton wrappers are made with wheat flour.

Fried Tofu with Dipping Sauces

Serves 2–4

Although this recipe calls for frying, it is one of the healthiest dishes you can eat. Tofu, which is made from soybeans, is one of the best foods on the planet—low fat, high protein, no dairy, and no sodium.

1 package of tofu, cut into bite-sized cubes
Vegetable oil for frying
Dipping sauces of your choice

1. Add about 2 to 3 inches of vegetable oil to a deep fryer or wok. Heat the oil on medium until it reaches about 350 degrees. Carefully add some of the tofu pieces, making sure not to overcrowd them; fry until golden brown, turning constantly. Transfer the fried tofu to paper towels to drain as each batch is cooked.
2. Serve the tofu with a choice of dipping sauces, such as Sweet-and-Sour, Peanut, and Minty Dipping Sauce (see recipes in Chapter 14).

Cold Sesame Noodles

Serves 2–4

I first made this tasty, inexpensive dish back when I was in college, My roommates and I would make huge bowlfulls of sesame noodles and chase it down with a cold beer.

1 pound angel hair pasta
2 tablespoons sesame oil
1/4 cup creamy peanut butter or tahini
2 tablespoons rice vinegar
1 tablespoon grated ginger
1/4–1/2 teaspoon dried red pepper flakes
1–2 green onions, trimmed and thinly sliced (optional)

1. Cook the pasta according to package directions. Rinse under cold water, then set aside.
2. Vigorously whisk together the remaining ingredients; pour over pasta, tossing to coat.
3. Garnish with green onion if desired.

Chinese-Style Dumplings

¼ cup sticky rice flour
1 cup rice flour
½ cup water
¼ cup tapioca flour
1 teaspoon vegetable oil
2 cups chives, cut into ½-inch lengths
1 tablespoon soy sauce

Yields 15–20 dumplings

If you prefer your dumplings pan-fried, follow steps 1 through 6, then fry them in a sauté pan with a bit of vegetable oil over medium-high heat until browned to your liking.

1. In a medium-sized saucepan, stir together the sticky rice flour, the rice flour, and the water. Turn the heat to medium and cook, stirring constantly until the mixture has the consistency of glue. (If the mixture becomes too sticky, reduce the heat to low.) Remove the batter from the heat and quickly stir in the tapioca flour. Set aside to cool to room temperature.
2. Meanwhile, add the vegetable oil to a skillet large enough to easily hold the chives, and heat on high. Add the chives and the soy sauce. Stir-fry the chives just until they wilt. Be careful not to let the chives cook too much. Remove from heat and set aside.
3. Once the dough has reached room temperature, check its consistency. If it is too sticky to work with, add a bit more tapioca flour.
4. To make the dumplings, roll the batter into balls 1 inch in diameter. Using your fingers, flatten each ball into a disk about 4 inches across. Spoon about 1 tablespoon of the chives into the middle of each disk. Fold the disk in half and pinch the edges together to form a half-moon-shaped packet.
5. Place the dumplings in a prepared steamer for 5 to 8 minutes or until the dough is cooked. Serve with a spicy dipping sauce of your choice.

CHAPTER 16
Soups

Tom Yum

Serves 4–6

You can substitute chicken for the shrimp in this dish. Cut up 1 boneless, skinless chicken breast into bite-sized pieces, add the pieces during step 2, and poach for about 8 minutes before proceeding.

4–5 cups water
3 shallots, finely chopped
2 stalks lemongrass, bruised and cut into 1-inch-long segments
2 tablespoons fish sauce
2 tablespoons minced fresh ginger
20 medium-sized shrimp, shelled but with tails left on
1 can straw mushrooms, drained
2–3 teaspoons sliced kaffir lime leaves or lime zest
3 tablespoons lime juice
2–3 Thai chili peppers, seeded and minced

1. Pour the water into a medium-sized soup pot. Add the shallots, lemongrass, fish sauce, and ginger. Bring to a boil, reduce heat, and simmer for 3 minutes.
2. Add the shrimp and mushrooms, and cook until the shrimp turn pink. Stir in the lime zest, lime juice, and chili peppers.
3. Cover and remove from the heat. Let the soup steep for 5 to 10 minutes before serving.

Tom Yum Soup for Life

A joint study by Thailand's Kasetsart University and Japan's Kyoto and Kinki Universities has found that the ingredients in Tom Yum soup are 100 times more effective in inhibiting cancerous tumor growth than other foods. No wonder it's Thailand's bestselling soup!

Tom Ka Kai

2 cups chicken broth
1 teaspoon sliced kaffir lime leaves
1 (2-inch) piece of lemongrass, bruised
1 (1-inch) piece ginger, sliced thinly
4 tablespoons fish sauce
2 tablespoons lime juice
1 boneless, skinless chicken breast, cut into bite-sized pieces
5 ounces coconut milk
2–4 Thai chilies (to taste), slightly crushed

Serves 4–6

This soup can be served as is or ladled over mounds of rice in individual serving bowls. I love it with some cooked noodles thrown in.

1. In a medium-sized soup pot, heat the broth on medium. Add the lime leaves, lemongrass, ginger, fish sauce, and lime juice.
2. Bring the mixture to a boil, add the chicken and coconut milk, and bring to a boil again.
3. Reduce the heat, add the chilies, and cover; let simmer until the chicken is cooked through, about 3 to 5 minutes.
4. Remove the chilies and the lemongrass stalk with a slotted spoon before serving.

Handling Lemongrass

Lemongrass is a very popular ingredient in Thai and other Asian recipes. It can usually be found fresh in most well-stocked supermarkets and can be stored in the fridge for about 3 weeks or frozen for up to 6 months. Many recipes call for lemongrass to be "bruised." This helps add more flavor to your recipe. If you like the strong flavor, feel free to bruise lemongrass even when not called for in a recipe.

Chicken Soup with Lemongrass

Serves 4–6

This soup is an explosion of flavors—spicy from the curry paste and ginger, sweet from the coconut milk, and sour from the lime leaves. The mushrooms and the chicken let these vibrant flavors shine.

1 tablespoon vegetable oil
1 medium onion, minced
1 clove garlic, minced
1 stalk lemongrass, trimmed, bruised, and cut into 2 to 3 pieces
2 teaspoons prepared Red Curry Paste (see recipes in Chapter 13) or curry powder
1 (1-inch) piece ginger, cut into 6 pieces
3 lime leaves (fresh or dried)
4 cups chicken broth
1 (14-ounce) can unsweetened coconut milk
¾ pound boneless, skinless chicken breast, trimmed and cut into bite-sized pieces
2 cups wild or domestic mushrooms, cut into bite-sized pieces (if necessary)
Juice of 2 limes
2 tablespoons fish sauce
Salt and pepper to taste

1. In a medium-sized saucepan, combine the oil, onion, and garlic. Cook over medium heat for 1 minute. Add the lemongrass, curry paste, ginger, and lime leaves.
2. Cook, stirring, for 3 minutes, then add the broth. Bring to a boil, reduce heat to medium, and continue to cook for 10 more minutes.
3. Add the coconut milk, the chicken pieces, and the mushrooms. Continue to cook for 5 minutes or until the chicken is done.
4. Stir in the lime juice and fish sauce. Season to taste with salt and pepper.
5. Remove the lemongrass, lime leaves, and ginger pieces before serving.

Asian Chicken Noodle Soup

2 tablespoons vegetable oil
½ cup chopped onion
2 tablespoons chopped ginger
3 cloves garlic, minced
1 cup chopped cilantro
2 cups chicken broth
5 cups water, divided
2 star anise
1 carrot, peeled and julienned
3 ounces snow peas, trimmed
1 medium-sized sweet red pepper, seeded and julienned
2 whole boneless, skinless chicken breasts, cut into long strips
4 ounces, cellophane noodles, soaked in boiling water for 5 minutes and drained
2 tablespoons fish sauce
Peanuts, coarsely chopped
Lemon or lime wedges

Serves 4 to 6

No matter where you are, there's something comforting about chicken noodle soup. This soup is definitely Thai—together, the ginger, anise, and fish sauce create a delightful broth.

1. In a large saucepan, heat the oil on high. Add the onion and sauté until translucent. Add the ginger, garlic, and cilantro, and sauté for 1 more minute. Stir in the broth and 2 cups of the water. Add the star anise. Bring to a boil, reduce heat, and cover; simmer for 20 to 30 minutes.
2. In another saucepan, bring the remaining water to a boil. Add the vegetables and blanch for 1 minute or until tender-crisp. Drain and run very cold water over the vegetables to stop the cooking process; set aside.
3. Strain the broth into a clean soup pot and bring to a boil. Add the chicken strips and reduce heat. Poach the chicken over low heat until opaque, approximately 10 minutes. Add the cellophane noodles and reserved vegetables, and continue to simmer for 2 more minutes. Season to taste with fish sauce.
4. To serve, ladle the soup into warm bowls. Sprinkle with peanuts and garnish with lime wedge.

Lemony Chicken Soup

Serves 4–6

This soup is sure to make you pucker! The lemon and the chilies brighten the broth of this easy-to-make and oh-so-flavorful soup. If you like lemon, this soup is for you.

½ cup lemon slices, including peel
3 tablespoons fish sauce
1½ teaspoons fresh hot chili pepper, seeded and chopped
2 green onions, thinly sliced
1½ teaspoons sugar
1½ cups coconut milk
2 cups chicken broth
3 teaspoons lemongrass, peeled and chopped
1 cup straw mushrooms
1 tablespoon minced fresh ginger
1 whole boneless, skinless chicken breast, poached and shredded

1. Combine the lemon slices, fish sauce, chili pepper, green onion, and sugar in a small glass bowl; set aside.
2. Combine the coconut milk, chicken broth, lemongrass, mushrooms, and ginger in a saucepan. Bring to a boil, reduce heat, and simmer for 20 to 25 minutes. Add the chicken and lemon mixture; heat through.
3. To serve, ladle into warmed bowls.

Spicy Seafood Soup

1 tablespoon vegetable oil
1 pound medium-sized raw shrimp, peeled and deveined, shells reserved
2 quarts fish or chicken stock
1 quart water
3 stalks lemongrass, peeled and chopped
Zest of 1 lime, grated
6–8 kaffir lime leaves
10 (1/8-inch-thick) slices fresh ginger
2 fresh serrano chilies, seeded and chopped
24 fresh mussels, cleaned
2 tablespoons lime juice
2 tablespoons fish sauce
3 tablespoons chopped fresh cilantro
Red pepper flakes to taste
1/4 cup sliced green onions
Salt

Serves 4–6

This soup is a Thai version of the French classic bouillabaisse—although frankly I would bet that the Thai version has been around longer than the French one. Either way, it's a great way to serve seafood.

1. Heat the vegetable oil in a large saucepan. Add the shrimp shells and sauté until they turn bright pink. Add the stock, water, lemongrass, lime zest, lime leaves, ginger, and serrano chilies. Bring to a boil, reduce heat, and simmer for 30 minutes. Strain the broth into a clean soup pot.
2. Bring the broth to a boil. Add the mussels, cover, and cook until the shells open, about 2 minutes. Use a slotted spoon to remove the mussels, discarding any that have not opened. Remove the top shell of each mussel and discard. Set aside the mussels on the half shell.
3. Add the shrimp to the boiling broth and cook until they are opaque, about 2 minutes. Reduce heat to low.
4. Add the mussels to the pot. Stir in the lime juice, fish sauce, cilantro, red pepper flakes, and green onions. Simmer for 1 to 2 minutes. Season to taste with salt.
5. Serve immediately.

Pumpkin Soup

Serves 4

This hearty soup makes a great dinner when served with a light salad and some crusty bread. I'm sure it will become one of your favorites.

For the broth:

2 tablespoons butter
1 small pumpkin, peeled, seeded, and cut into small chunks
1 medium-sized leek, sliced
1½ stalks celery, sliced
1 small banana, sliced
1 red chili pepper, cut in half and seeded
3 stalks lemongrass, peeled and thinly sliced
1 clove of garlic, halved
1 tablespoon finely chopped ginger
3¼ cups vegetable broth
⅓ cup half-and-half
⅓ cup coconut milk
1 tablespoon Green Curry Paste (see recipes in Chapter 13)
Salt and pepper to taste

For the chicken and vegetables:

2 tablespoons butter
1 whole boneless, skinless chicken breast, trimmed and cut into strips
2 teaspoons finely chopped ginger
2 kaffir lime leaves, cut into strips
2 teaspoons prepared Green Curry Paste (see recipes in Chapter 13)
1 tablespoon vegetable oil
1 small Japanese eggplant, cut into 4 pieces
2 red chili peppers, cut in half and seeded (optional)
¾ cup cooked rice
Thai basil

(recipe continues on the next page)

Pumpkin Soup
(continued)

To prepare the broth:

1. In a large pot, melt the butter over medium heat. Add the pumpkin, leeks, celery, bananas, chili pepper, lemongrass, garlic, and ginger; sweat for 5 minutes.
2. Add the vegetable broth and heat until warm.
3. Add the half-and-half, coconut milk, and curry paste; simmer for 15 to 20 minutes.
4. Remove the chili pepper halves. Transfer the broth mixture to a blender or food processor and purée until smooth. Strain if desired, and season to taste with salt and pepper. Pour the mixture into a clean pot and keep warm.

To prepare the chicken and vegetables:

5. Melt the butter in a heavy-bottomed sauté pan over medium heat. Add the chicken strips, ginger, lime leaves, and curry paste. Sauté until the chicken is cooked, but not browned. Add the chicken mixture to the broth.
6. In another sauté pan, heat the vegetable oil. Add the eggplant and sauté until just warmed through.
7. To serve, divide the rice among 4 soup bowls. Spoon the broth over the rice. Top with a piece of eggplant, a chili pepper half (if desired), and some basil.

Thai-Spiced Beef Soup with Rice Noodles

Serves 4–6

I like using leftover pot roast for the beef because I prefer the more tender texture, but any cooked beef will do. And frankly, you could leave out the meat entirely and still have a really great dish.

8 cups beef broth
1 whole star anise, crushed
1 (2-inch) cinnamon stick
2 (¼-inch) pieces peeled gingerroot
8 ounces rice noodles, soaked in hot water for 10 minutes, strained and rinsed in cold water
1 stalk lemongrass, tough outer leaves removed, inner core crushed and minced
¾ cup leftover beef roast, chopped or shredded
¼ cup fish sauce
1 tablespoon prepared chili-garlic sauce
2½ tablespoons lime juice
3–4 teaspoons (or to taste) salt
Freshly ground black pepper to taste

1. In a medium-sized saucepan, simmer the beef broth, star anise, cinnamon stick, and ginger over low heat for 30 to 40 minutes.
2. Strain the stock and return to the saucepan.
3. Add the noodles, lemongrass, shredded beef, fish sauce, chili sauce, and garlic. Bring the soup to a boil over medium heat. Reduce heat and simmer for 5 minutes. Stir in the lime juice, salt, and pepper.

Vegetarian Lemongrass Soup

8 cups low-sodium vegetable broth
1 teaspoon (or to taste) crushed red peppers
4–6 stalks lemongrass, bruised
4 tablespoons soy sauce
Juice of ½ lime or to taste
1 can straw mushrooms, drained
1 cup snow peas, trimmed
½ cup coarsely shredded carrots
½ cup sliced celery
1 red serrano chili, seeded and thinly sliced

Serves 4–6

The original recipe for this Lemongrass Soup calls for chicken broth and fish sauce, but I regularly use vegetable broth and soy sauce instead, and still enjoy this soup very much.

1. Bring the broth to a simmer in a large saucepan. Add the crushed red peppers, lemongrass, soy sauce, and lime juice. Simmer for 10 minutes.
2. Add the remaining ingredients. Continue to simmer until the vegetables are just done, about 2 to 3 minutes. Remove the lemongrass stalks before serving.

Vegetarian Thai Food

If you're a vegetarian, or just trying to cut back on your meat consumption, then Thai food is for you! Most Thai dishes start with rice or noodles with vegetables—meat and sauce are placed on top. Meat is rarely the main focus of the meal, and the flavors of the dish mostly come from the spices and vegetables. Generally, you can substitute tofu in any recipe that includes meat.

Chilled Mango Soup

Serves 2–4

I know it sounds like a dessert soup, but it's not. Mangoes and papayas are regularly used in both savory and sweet dishes throughout Asia, and this chilled soup is a great example. It is a perfect summer dish.

2 large mangoes, peeled, pitted, and chopped
1½ cups chilled chicken or vegetable broth
1 cup plain yogurt
1 teaspoon sugar (optional)
1 tablespoon dry sherry
Salt and white pepper to taste

Place all of the ingredients in a blender or food processor and process until smooth. Adjust seasonings. This soup may be served immediately or refrigerated until needed. If you do refrigerate the soup, let it sit at room temperature for 10 minutes or so before serving to take some of the chill off.

CHAPTER 17

Salads

Fiery Beef Salad

Serves 2–4

This entrée salad is one of my favorites—somehow hearty and light at the same time. If the weather doesn't permit grilling, the steak can be broiled instead—and it will still be good.

For the dressing:

¼ cup basil leaves
2 tablespoons chopped serrano chilies
2 cloves garlic
2 tablespoons brown sugar
2 tablespoons fish sauce
¼ teaspoon black pepper
¼ cup lemon juice

For the salad:

1 pound beef steak
Salt and pepper to taste
1 stalk lemongrass, outer leaves removed and discarded, inner stalk finely sliced
1 small red onion, finely sliced
1 small cucumber, finely sliced
1 tomato, finely sliced
½ cup mint leaves
Bibb or romaine lettuce leaves

1. Combine all of the dressing ingredients in a blender and process until well incorporated; set aside.
2. Season the steak with salt and pepper. Over a hot fire, grill to medium-rare (or to your liking). Transfer the steak to a platter, cover with foil, and let rest for 5 to 10 minutes before carving.
3. Slice the beef across the grain into thin slices.
4. Place the beef slices, any juices from the platter, and the remaining salad ingredients, except the lettuce, in a large mixing bowl. Add the dressing and toss to coat.
5. To serve, place lettuce leaves on individual plates and mound the beef mixture on top of the lettuce.

Spicy Rice Salad

For the dressing:

1/2 cup rice vinegar
1/2 cup fish sauce
1/4 cup sesame oil
1/4 cup hot chili oil
1/4 cup lime juice

For the salad:

2 cups long-grained rice (preferably Jasmine)
4–6 green onions, trimmed and thinly sliced
2 carrots, peeled and diced
1 sweet red pepper, seeded and diced
1 serrano chili pepper, seeded and minced
1/4–1/2 cup chopped mint
1/4–1/2 cup chopped cilantro
1 pound cooked shrimp
1/3 cup chopped unsalted peanuts
Lime wedges

Yields approx. 8 cups

This salad is equally delicious with shredded chicken or turkey instead of the shrimp. Or if you would prefer a vegetarian salad, simply omit the shrimp! I like to have this confetti-like salad for a light lunch.

1. Whisk together all of the dressing ingredients; set aside.
2. Cook the rice according to the package directions. Fluff the rice, then transfer it to a large mixing bowl. Allow the rice to cool slightly.
3. Pour approximately 1/3 of the dressing over the rice and fluff to coat. Continue to fluff the rice every so often until it is completely cooled.
4. Add the green onions, carrots, red pepper, serrano chili pepper, mint, cilantro, and shrimp to the rice. Toss with the remaining dressing to taste.
5. To serve, place on individual plates and garnish with peanuts and lime wedges.

Vinegar Distinctions

Rice wine vinegar has a less sharp flavor than distilled white vinegar and matches particularly well with sesame oil.

Spicy Shrimp Salad

Serves 2–4

The cooked shrimp add great color and texture to this salad, but it's equally tasty if you substitute cooked mussels or scallops. Why not try combining all of them?

For the dressing:

3 tablespoons sugar
4 tablespoons fish sauce
⅓ cup lime juice
2 tablespoons prepared chili sauce

For the salad:

¾ pound cooked shrimp
¼ cup chopped mint
1 small red onion, thinly sliced
2 green onions, trimmed and thinly sliced
2 cucumbers, peeled and thinly sliced
Bibb lettuce leaves

1. In a small bowl, combine all the dressing ingredients. Stir until the sugar dissolves completely.
2. In a large bowl, combine all of the salad ingredients except the lettuce. Pour the dressing over and toss to coat.
3. To serve, place the lettuce leaves on individual plates. Mound a portion of the shrimp salad on top of the leaves. Serve immediately.

Peeling Tomatoes

The trick to peeling tomatoes is to quickly blanch them in boiling water before removing the skin. Bring a pan of water to boil, then throw in the tomato for 15 to 30 seconds. Using a slotted spoon, remove the tomato from the water and run it under cold water until it is cool enough to handle. Using the tip of a knife, pull up a small piece of skin, then simply pull the skin off the flesh.

Shrimp and Noodle Salad

8 ounces rice noodles
1 stalk lemongrass, finely minced (inner core only)
1 cup citrus fruit (oranges, grapefruit, tangerines, etc.) peeled, sectioned, and chopped
⅓ cup chopped peanuts, plus extra for garnish
1 medium tomato, peeled, seeded, and chopped
3 green onions, sliced
⅓ cup chopped mint leaves
⅓ cup chopped cilantro, plus extra for garnish
½–1 teaspoon dried red pepper flakes
1 clove garlic, minced
1 tablespoon brown sugar
¾ cup lime juice (approximately 4–5 limes)
2 tablespoons fish sauce
24 medium shrimp, peeled and deveined
1 tablespoon vegetable oil
Salt and ground pepper to taste

Serves 6

I like the noodle and fruit mixture in this recipe so much, I even eat it without the shrimp. Or, you can top the noodles with anything you like—grilled scallops, grilled chicken, or grilled pork tenderloin.

1. Soak the rice noodles in hot water for 10 to 20 minutes or until soft. While the noodles are soaking, bring a large pot of water to boil.
2. Meanwhile, in a large bowl, mix together the lemongrass, citrus, peanuts, tomato, scallions, mint, and cilantro.
3. In a small bowl, combine the red pepper flakes, garlic, sugar, lime juice, and fish sauce. (Adjust seasoning to your taste.)
4. Drain the noodles from their soaking liquid and add them to the boiling water. When the water returns to a boil, drain them again and rinse thoroughly with cold water. Allow the noodles to drain thoroughly.
5. Add the noodles and the dressing to the citrus mixture and toss to combine. Set aside.
6. Brush the shrimp with the vegetable oil and season with salt and pepper. Grill or sauté for approximately 2 minutes per side or until done to your liking.
7. To serve, mound the noodles in the center of a serving platter. Place the grilled shrimp on top and garnish with peanuts and cilantro.

Thailand Seafood Salad

Serves 4–6

The different textures and flavors of the seafood in this recipe complement one another well. Still, don't hesitate to try other crustaceans in this recipe, such as bay scallops or lobster.

½ pound squid rings, poached in salted water for 30 seconds
½ pound salad shrimp
1 (6-ounce) can chopped clams, drained
2 medium cucumbers, peeled, halved, seeded, and very thinly sliced
1 stalk celery, cleaned and thinly sliced
1 small onion, finely chopped
1 stalk lemongrass, outer leaves removed, inner core minced
1 small serrano chili, seeded and finely chopped
2 tablespoons chopped mint
1 clove garlic, minced
1 green onion, trimmed and thinly sliced
¼ cup fish sauce
Sugar to taste
Bibb lettuce leaves

1. In a large mixing bowl, gently combine the squid, shrimp, clams, cucumber, and celery; set aside.
2. In a small mixing bowl, stir together the onion, lemongrass, serrano chili, mint, garlic, green onion, and fish sauce. Add sugar to taste.
3. Pour the dressing over the seafood mixture, tossing to coat. Cover and let sit for at least 30 minutes before serving.
4. To serve, place lettuce leaves in the center of 4 to 6 plates. Mound the seafood salad on top of the lettuce leaves.

Asian Noodle and Vegetable Salad

8 ounces dried rice noodles, cooked al dente and rinsed under cold water
2 teaspoons vegetable oil
1 teaspoon sesame oil
1 teaspoon soy sauce
¼ pound snow peas, trimmed and cut on the diagonal
1 small red bell pepper, cored, seeded, and cut into thin strips
1 medium carrot, peeled and thinly sliced on the diagonal
1 recipe Spicy Thai Dressing (see recipe on page 314)
10 basil leaves, shredded (preferably Thai or lemon)
4 green onions, thinly sliced
1 cup bean sprouts
1 lime, cut into 6–8 wedges
½ cup toasted peanuts, chopped

Serves 4–6

The riot of colors and the intense flavors of the lime, peanuts, and dressing in this salad will have you so impressed, you'll forget you were ever an omnivore.

1. In a large bowl, toss the noodles with the oils and the soy sauce.
2. Blanch the snow peas in boiling water for 30 seconds and then rinse them under cold water.
3. Add the snow peas, bell pepper, and the carrot to the noodles and toss.
4. Drizzle the Spicy Thai Dressing over the noodle mixture to taste, add the basil, half of the green onions, and half of the bean sprouts, and toss well.
5. To serve, place the noodle salad on a chilled serving platter. Scatter the remaining green onions, remaining bean sprouts, and the peanuts over the top. Squeeze the juice of 2 lime wedges over the whole dish, and use the remaining wedges as garnish. Serve immediately.

Grilled Calamari Salad

Serves 2–4

When I was a kid I thought that calamari was disgusting, but now I'm a huge fan. This recipe features calamari grilled with a light vinaigrette that I'm sure will please even the most conservative eaters.

For the dressing:

1 tablespoon fish sauce
⅓ cup water
1 stalk lemongrass, inner core finely chopped
3 kaffir lime leaves, chopped or 1 tablespoon lime zest
1 small onion, thinly sliced
5 teaspoons lime juice
1–5 red chili peppers, seeded and chopped (the more you use, the spicier it'll be!)

For the salad:

1 pound calamari, cleaned
15–20 mint leaves, chopped
6–8 sprigs cilantro, chopped
1 green onion, thinly sliced
Baby greens (optional)

1. Combine all the dressing ingredients in a small bowl; set aside.
2. Prepare a grill or broiler. Place the calamari on a broiler pan or in a grill basket and cook over high heat until tender, about 3 minutes per side. Let cool to room temperature.
3. Place the grilled calamari in a mixing bowl. Stir the dressing and pour it over the calamari.
4. If serving immediately, add the mint, cilantro, and green onions. Alternatively, allow the calamari to marinate for up to 1 hour before serving, and then add the additional ingredients.
5. To serve: Use individual cups or bowls to help capture some of the wonderful dressing. Alternatively, mound the calamari mixture over a bed of baby greens and spoon additional dressing over the top.

What Is Calamari?

Calamari is squid! Sometimes you will see the smallest ones sold whole. Otherwise it comes in pearly white pieces that you slice into bite-sized morsels. Calamari has a sweet, mild flavor and only becomes chewy when overcooked.

Thai Dinner Salad

For the dressing:

2 tablespoons fish sauce
1 tablespoon lemon juice
1 clove garlic, minced
2 teaspoons sugar
1 tablespoon water
¾ teaspoon rice wine vinegar
Pinch of red pepper flakes

For the salad:

1 small head of romaine or Bibb lettuce, torn into bite-sized pieces
2 small carrots, grated
1 cucumber, peeled, seeded, and diced
¼ cup chopped cilantro
¼ cup chopped mint leaves
Chopped unsalted peanuts (optional)

Serves 2–4

This salad gets its Thai character from the mint and cilantro in the salad and the fish sauce, rice wine vinegar, and red pepper flakes in the dressing. It's not fancy, but it's a great start to any meal.

1. In a small bowl, stir together all of the salad dressing ingredients; set aside.
2. In a large bowl, toss together all of the salad ingredients. Add dressing to taste and toss until well coated. Sprinkle chopped peanuts over the top of each salad, if desired.

Thai Salads

Thai salads are often light, flavorful, and work fantastically to get you ready for the main meal. Many of the all-vegetable salads are too light to be a meal of their own, but by simply adding some sautéed chicken, shrimp, or tofu to any salad, you've got yourself a nice lunch!

Sweet-and-Sour Cucumber Salad

Serves 2–4

This is a terrific summer salad to bring on a picnic. It's great served alongside grilled chicken, chops, even burgers!

5 tablespoons sugar
1 teaspoon salt
1 cup boiling water
½ cup rice or white vinegar
2 medium cucumbers, seeded and sliced
1 small red onion, sliced
2 Thai chilies, seeded and minced

1. In a small bowl, combine the sugar, salt, and boiling water. Stir to thoroughly dissolve sugar and salt. Add the vinegar and allow the vinaigrette to cool to room temperature.
2. Place the cucumbers, onion slices, and the chili peppers in a medium-sized bowl. Pour the dressing over the vegetables. Cover and let marinate in the refrigerator at least until cold, preferably overnight.

Seeding Cucumbers

Seeding a cucumber is simple! Cut the cucumber in half lengthwise. Using a small spoon, scoop out the soft inner flesh and seeds in one quick swoop. That's it!

Cucumber Salad with Lemongrass

½ cup white vinegar
1 Thai chili, very finely minced
1 garlic clove, very finely minced
2 stalks lemongrass
3 cups thinly sliced cucumber
1 cup bean sprouts
1 cup cubed tart apple (such as Granny Smith)
½ cup shredded carrot
¼ cup minced mint
¼ cup minced parsley
1 tablespoon fish sauce
1 tablespoon vegetable oil

Serves 6–8

I think the Thai have figured out more ways to use cucumber than anyone else on the planet, and each one seems better than the last. The cucumber and apple in this salad yield a great contrast of flavors.

1. In a small saucepan, combine the vinegar, chili, and garlic. Bring the mixture to a boil. Cover the pan, remove it from the heat, and let cool.
2. Trim and finely chop 1 lemongrass stalk. Place it in a small saucepan with ½ cup of water, cover, and bring to a boil. Turn off heat and let cool.
3. Trim the remaining lemongrass stalk, peel off the tough outer layers, and finely mince the white portion of the tender stalk within. Reserve approximately 1 tablespoon.
4. Combine the cucumber, bean sprouts, apple, carrot, mint, and parsley in a large mixing bowl. In a small bowl combine the fish sauce, oil, minced lemongrass, the vinegar mixture, and the lemongrass water.
5. Toss the vegetables with the lemongrass vinaigrette to taste.

Preserving Fresh-Cut Apples

To keep the apple pieces from turning brown before you use them, put them in a small container of cool water to which you have added a couple of drops of lemon or lime juice. The citric acid prevents the apple from discoloring.

Papaya Salad

Serves 4–6

This recipe calls for salting the papaya in order to extract some of its liquid. This is the same method used to prepare eggplant slices for the grill or for use in an Eggplant Parmesan.

1 medium papaya, peeled and julienned, or cut into small pieces
½–1 teaspoon salt
3 jalapeño peppers, seeded and thinly sliced
4–6 cloves of garlic, chopped coarsely
½ cup long beans (green beans), cut into 1-inch pieces
2 teaspoons fish sauce
4 tablespoons Tamarind Concentrate (see recipe on page 304)
2 tomatoes, thinly sliced
Sticky rice, cooked according to package directions

1. Place the papaya on a sheet pan and sprinkle it with salt. Let the papaya stand for 30 minutes. Pour off any juice and then squeeze the fruit with your hands to extract as much fluid as possible. Place the pulp of the papaya in a large food processor.
2. Add the chilies and pulse briefly to combine. Add the remaining ingredients except the tomato and pulse again until mixed.
3. Transfer the papaya mixture to a serving bowl and garnish with tomato slices. Serve with sticky rice.

Zesty Melon Salad

6 cups assorted melon cubes
2 cucumbers, peeled, halved, seeded, and sliced
6–8 tablespoons lime juice
Zest of 1 lime
¼ cup honey
1 serrano chili, seeded and minced (for a hotter salad, leave the seeds in)
¼ teaspoon salt

1. In a large mixing bowl, combine the melon and the cucumber.
2. Mix the remaining ingredients together in a small bowl. Pour over the fruit and toss well to coat.
3. Serve immediately, or if you like a zestier flavor, let the salad sit for up to 2 hours to allow the chili flavor to develop.

Serves 4–6

A lively looking and tasting salad, it's a sure winner at a picnic. Using a hollowed out watermelon as a serving dish makes an impressive, yet easy and inexpensive, serving dish.

Crunchy Coconut-Flavored Salad

1 cup julienned jicama
1 medium cucumber, peeled, seeded, and julienned
2–3 tablespoons chopped fresh basil
1 recipe Coconut Marinade (see recipe on page 300)

Place the jicama, cucumber, and basil in a large bowl. Pour the marinade over the vegetables and let rest in the refrigerator for at least 2 hours before serving.

Jicama

Jicama is indigenous to the Americas and looks like a big brown, rather unappetizing, root. But beneath the ugly skin is a light, crunchy vegetable with a slightly sweet taste reminiscent of apple.

Serves 2–3

The cucumber and the jicama offer very different crunches—one rather juicy and one rather snappy—in this appealing salad. The basil adds just enough bite to balance the sweetness of the coconut marinade.

Thailand Bamboo Shoots

Serves 4

Bamboo is a great plant. Humans throughout the world have used it as a food, a building material, and in hats, just to name a few uses. Here we use it as a simple salad ingredient.

1 20-ounce can of bamboo shoots, shredded, liquid reserved
Juice of ½ lime
1 teaspoon ground dried chili pepper
2 green onions, sliced
1 teaspoon fish sauce
2 tablespoons finely crushed peanuts, divided
Sticky rice, cooked according to package directions

1. Place the shredded bamboo shoots and approximately ¼ cup (half) of the reserved bamboo liquid in a medium-sized saucepan. Bring the contents of the pan to a boil, reduce heat, and let simmer until tender, about 5 minutes. Remove from heat.
2. Stir in the lime juice, chili pepper, green onions, fish sauce, and 1 tablespoon of the peanuts.
3. Serve with sticky rice, sprinkled with the remaining peanuts.

CHAPTER 18
Meat Dishes

Green Curry Beef

Serves 4–6

This quick and easy curry is a great introduction to Thai cuisine. It contains most of the key Thai ingredients—coconut milk, fish sauce, chilies, and basil. Serve with lots of steamed Jasmine rice.

2 cans coconut milk, thick cream separated from the milk
1/4 cup (or to taste) Green Curry Paste (see recipes in Chapter 13)
1 1/2 pounds sirloin, cut into thin strips
1/4 cup brown sugar
1/4 cup fish sauce
1 pound eggplant (Japanese, Thai, or a combination), cut into 1/4-inch slices
6 serrano chilies, stemmed, seeded, and cut in half lengthwise
1 cup basil

1. Place the thick cream from the coconut milk and the curry paste in a large soup pot and stir to combine. Place over medium-high heat and bring to a boil. Reduce heat and simmer for 2 to 3 minutes.
2. Add the beef and the coconut milk, stirring to combine. Return the mixture to a simmer.
3. Add the sugar and the fish sauce, stirring until the sugar dissolves, about 2 minutes.
4. Add the eggplant and simmer for 1 to 2 minutes.
5. Add the serrano chilies and cook 1 minute more.
6. Remove from heat and stir in the basil.

Hot Stuff

Let your guests know that the chilies are hot and are not to be eaten by the faint of heart. They add plenty of heat and flavor just being on the plate!

Curried Beef and Potato Stew

2–3 tablespoons vegetable oil
1½ pounds beef stew meat, cut into bite-sized cubes
1 large onion, chopped
1 large russet potato, peeled and cut into bite-sized cubes
2 (14-ounce) cans coconut milk
½–¾ cup prepared Massaman Curry Paste (see recipe on page 292)
½ cup brown sugar
7 tablespoons fish sauce
¼ cup Tamarind Concentrate (see recipe on page 304)
1 cup chopped fresh pineapple
Jasmine rice, cooked according to package directions
½ cup unsalted roasted peanuts, chopped

Serves 4

Who doesn't like beef stew on a cold winter evening? This one isn't quite like Mom used to make (unless your mother is Thai), but it's still satisfying and comforting with tender chunks of beef and silky potatoes.

1. Heat the oil in a large soup pot over medium-high heat. When the oil is hot, brown the meat on all sides. Add the onion and cook until translucent, about 2 to 3 minutes.
2. Add enough water to just cover the meat and onions. Bring to a boil, reduce heat, cover, and simmer for 30 to 60 minutes.
3. Add the potatoes and continue to simmer for 15 more minutes. (The potatoes will not be quite cooked through at this point.)
4. Strain the solids from the broth, reserving both.
5. In another soup pot, combine the coconut milk with the curry paste until well blended. Bring the contents to a simmer over medium-high heat and cook for 2 to 3 minutes.
6. Add the reserved meat and potato mixture, the sugar, fish sauce, and tamarind, stirring until the sugar dissolves. Add some of the reserved broth to thin the sauce to desired consistency.
7. Stir in the pineapple and continue to simmer until the potatoes are cooked through.
8. To serve, place some Jasmine rice in the middle of individual serving plates and spoon the stew over the top. Garnish with the chopped peanuts.

Red Beef Curry

Serves 4

This curry is slightly milder than the green version. The primary flavor difference comes from the bell peppers, which are not as common in Thai recipes as the more intense varieties of peppers.

1 tablespoon vegetable oil
2 tablespoons Red Curry Paste (see recipes in Chapter 13)
½ cup plus 2 tablespoons coconut milk
1 pound lean beef, cut into thin strips
2 tablespoons (roughly) ground peanuts
1–3 tablespoons (to taste) fish sauce
Sugar to taste
1 green or red sweet pepper, seeded and cubed
¼ cup chopped basil
Rice, cooked according to package directions

1. Heat the oil in a large sauté pan over low heat. Add the curry paste and cook, stirring constantly, until fragrant, about 1 minute.
2. Stir in the ½ cup of coconut milk and bring the mixture to a simmer. Add the beef strips and poach for 5 minutes.
3. Add the peanuts and continue to poach for an additional 5 minutes.
4. Add the fish sauce and sugar to taste; continue to cook until the mixture is almost dry, then add the sweet pepper and basil and cook for 5 more minutes.
5. Serve with rice.

Chili Varieties

The most typical fresh chilies used in Thai cuisine include jalapeños, serranos, Thai bird, and Scotch bonnet. The jalapeño is the mildest of the bunch, adding more flavor than actual heat. Serranos are a bit more searing.

Hot and Sour Beef

1 tablespoon lime juice
1 tablespoon fish sauce
1 tablespoon dark, sweet soy sauce
3 tablespoons chopped onion
1 teaspoon honey
1 teaspoon dried chili powder
1 green onion, trimmed and thinly sliced
1 teaspoon chopped cilantro
1½ pound sirloin steak
Salt and pepper to taste

Serves 1–2

This flavorful dish couldn't be any easier. It's great to serve when you are introducing your guests to Thai flavors, because they can add as little or as much of the sauce as they prefer.

1. Make the sauce by thoroughly combining the first 8 ingredients; set aside.
2. Season the steak with salt and pepper, then grill or broil it to your preferred doneness. Remove the steak from the grill, cover with foil, and let rest for 5 to 10 minutes.
3. Thinly slice the steak, cutting across the grain.
4. Arrange the pieces on a serving platter or on 1 or 2 dinner plates. Spoon the sauce over the top. Serve with rice and a side vegetable.

Adjusting Flavors

Don't be afraid to adjust the amount of curry paste you put in a recipe. If you want the end product to be a bit more flavorful, add a bit more; if you are looking for a more delicate taste, reduce the amount a bit

Grilled Ginger Beef

Serves 6

This may be my favorite recipe in this book. Its complex, aromatic overtones will make your taste buds beg for more. It's well worth the effort.

8 cups low-salt beef broth
2 stalks lemongrass
5 cloves garlic
1 (3-inch) piece ginger, cut in half
1 onion, cut in half
1 cinnamon stick
2 dried red chili peppers
1 (2-inch) piece of ginger, minced
1 small package of rice noodles
1 pound green vegetables
2 tablespoons (or to taste) soy sauce
6 (6-ounce) strip steaks
Salt and pepper to taste
6 scallions, minced

1. Place the beef broth, lemongrass, and garlic in a large pot; bring to a boil.
2. In the meantime, place the ginger and onion halves, cut-side down, in a dry skillet over high heat and cook until black. Add the onion and ginger to the broth mixture.
3. Place the cinnamon and dried chili peppers in the dry skillet and toast over medium heat for 1 minute; add to the broth mixture.
4. Reduce the heat and simmer the broth for 1 to 2 hours. Cool, strain, and refrigerate overnight.
5. Before you are ready to eat, remove the broth from the refrigerator and skim off any fat that may have accumulated. Bring the broth to a simmer and add the minced ginger.
6. Soak the rice noodles in hot water for 10 to 20 minutes or until soft; drain.
7. Blanch the vegetables for about a minute. Using a slotted spoon, remove them from the boiling water and shock them in cold water.
8. Season the broth to taste with the soy sauce. Season the steaks with salt and pepper and grill or broil to your liking.
9. To serve, slice the steaks into thin strips (cutting across the grain) and place them in 6 large bowls. Add a portion of noodles and vegetables to the bowls and ladle the broth over the top.

Thai Beef with Rice Noodles

3/4 pound sirloin, trimmed of all fat, rinsed and patted dry
1/2 pound dried rice noodles
1/4 cup soy sauce
2 tablespoons fish sauce
2 tablespoons dark brown sugar
Freshly ground black pepper
5 tablespoons vegetable oil, divided
2 tablespoons minced garlic
1 pound greens (such as spinach or bok choy), cleaned and cut into 1/2-inch strips
2 eggs, beaten
Crushed dried red pepper flakes to taste
Rice vinegar to taste

Serves 2–4

I like to use a bag of organic baby spinach leaves for the greens in this recipe because they are prewashed and small enough that you can skip the process of cutting them into strips.

1. Slice the meat into 2-inch-long, 1/2-inch-wide strips.
2. Cover the noodles with warm water for 5 minutes, then drain.
3. In a small bowl, combine the soy sauce, fish sauce, brown sugar, and black pepper; set aside.
4. Heat a wok or heavy skillet over high heat. Add approximately 2 tablespoons of the vegetable oil. When the oil is hot, but not smoking, add the garlic. After stirring for 5 seconds, add the greens and stir-fry for approximately 2 minutes; set aside.
5. Add 2 more tablespoons of oil to the wok. Add the beef and stir-fry until browned on all sides, about 2 minutes; set aside.
6. Heat 1 tablespoon of oil in the wok and add the noodles. Toss until warmed through, approximately 2 minutes; set aside.
7. Heat the oil remaining in the wok. Add the eggs and cook, without stirring until they are set, about 30 seconds. Break up the eggs slightly and stir in the reserved noodles, beef, and greens, and the red pepper flakes. Stir the reserved soy mixture, then add it to the wok. Toss to coat and heat through. Serve immediately with rice vinegar to sprinkle over the top.

Minty Stir-Fried Beef

Serves 4–6

If the mint in this recipe is too pungent for your tastes, you can easily substitute cilantro, but I suggest being adventuresome and giving this a try. The beef in this recipe also makes great fajitas!

7–14 (to taste) serrano chilies, seeded and coarsely chopped
1/4 cup chopped garlic
1/4 cup chopped yellow or white onion
1/4 cup vegetable oil
1 pound flank steak, sliced across the grain into thin strips
3 tablespoons fish sauce
1 tablespoon sugar
1/2–3/4 cup water
1/2 cup chopped mint leaves

1. Using a mortar and pestle or a food processor, grind together the chilies, garlic, and onion.
2. Heat the oil over medium-high heat in a wok or large skillet. Add the ground chili mixture to the oil and stir-fry for 1 to 2 minutes.
3. Add the beef and stir-fry until it just begins to brown.
4. Add the remaining ingredients, adjusting the amount of water depending on how thick you want the sauce.
5. Serve with plenty of Jasmine rice.

Peeling Garlic

To peel garlic, place the clove on a cutting board and smash it with the back or side of a knife, which will split the skin.

Chilied Beef

3 serrano chilies, stems removed and sliced
¼ cup white vinegar
1 pound flank steak
1 large red onion, sliced
4 scallions, trimmed and thinly sliced
Juice of 1 large lime
2 tablespoons fish sauce
1 teaspoon dried red pepper flakes
Bibb or romaine lettuce leaves

Serves 4–6

This one is a zinger! Between the serranos and the dried pepper flakes, it really packs a punch. Luckily the lime juice helps to quench the fire, as does a cold beer or even a margarita!

1. Place the sliced chilies in a small bowl with the vinegar; let stand for at least 15 minutes.
2. Grill or broil the flank steak to your desired doneness. Remove from the grill, cover with foil, and let stand 10 minutes. Thinly slice the streak across the grain.
3. Place the beef slices in a large bowl. Add the red onion, scallions, lime juice, and red pepper flakes; toss all of the ingredients together. Cover the dish, place in the refrigerator, and let marinate for at least 1 hour.
4. Before serving, let the beef return to room temperature. Mound the beef on top of lettuce leaves and serve with white rice. Pass the serrano/vinegar sauce separately.

Grill Safety

Be careful around a grill. Do not add lighter fluid to a fire or hot coals. Keep your grill clean of excess grease to guard against fires. Don't forget to turn off the gas after you are finished cooking. Don't throw water on a fire to douse a flame. Instead, move the food away from the fire and let the fire burn itself out.

Pork and Eggplant Stir-Fry

Serves 2–4

If you love garlic, this is the dish for you! This pungent dish could be the official dish of Gilroy, California—the self-proclaimed garlic capital of the world.

3 tablespoons vegetable oil
5–10 cloves garlic, mashed
½ pound ground pork
½ teaspoon freshly ground pepper
1 tablespoon fish sauce
1 tablespoon Yellow Bean Sauce (see recipe on page 295)
1 pound Japanese eggplant, cut into ¼-inch slices
¼ cup chicken stock
2 tablespoons (or to taste) sugar

1. Heat the oil in a wok or large skillet over medium-high heat. When the oil is hot, add the garlic and stir-fry until fragrant, about 30 seconds.
2. Add the pork and continue to stir-fry until the pork loses its color, about 1 minute.
3. Add the pepper, fish sauce, bean sauce, and eggplant; cook for 1 minute.
4. Add the chicken stock. Continue to stir-fry for 2 minutes.
5. Stir in the sugar to taste and cook until the eggplant is cooked through, about 2 more minutes.

Meat Grades

Meats are graded prime, choice, and select. For dishes that cook quickly, like stir-fries, choose prime or choice. For slow-cooked dishes, like a braise, select meat will be just fine.

Pork with Garlic and Crushed Black Pepper

10–20 garlic cloves, mashed
2–2½ teaspoons black peppercorns, coarsely ground
4 tablespoons vegetable oil
1 pork tenderloin, trimmed of all fat and cut into medallions about ¼-inch thick
¼ cup sweet black soy sauce
2 tablespoons brown sugar
2 tablespoons fish sauce

Serves 2

Be sure to use the freshest, highest quality pepper you can find. I like the rich Tellicherry peppercorns from India. Also, make sure it is freshly ground in order to achieve its maximum flavor potential.

1. Place the garlic and the black pepper in a small food processor and process briefly to form a coarse paste; set aside.
2. Heat the oil in a wok or large skillet over medium-high heat. When the oil is hot, add the garlic-pepper paste and stir-fry until the garlic turns gold.
3. Raise the heat to high and add the pork medallions; stir-fry for 30 seconds.
4. Add the soy sauce and brown sugar, stirring until the sugar is dissolved.
5. Add the fish sauce and continue to cook until the pork is cooked through, about another 1 to 2 minutes.

Slicing Meat Paper Thin

To make thinly slicing meat easier, wrap the meat in plastic wrap and place it in the freezer until it's very cold, but not frozen. Always use the sharpest knife possible.

Bangkok-Style Roasted Pork Tenderloin

Serves 4

When I'm in a hurry, but still want a satisfying meal, this is it. While the tenderloins are roasting, I prepare a salad, some vegetables, and some rice or cous cous. The whole dinner is ready in less than 30 minutes!

1 teaspoon salt
1/4 teaspoon ground ginger
1/4 teaspoon ground cardamom
1/4–1/2 teaspoon freshly ground black pepper
2 (1-pound) pork tenderloins, trimmed
Olive oil
1/2 cup chicken, pork, or vegetable stock, or water

1. Place rack on bottom third of the oven, then preheat the oven to 500 degrees.
2. Combine the spices in a small bowl.
3. Rub each of the tenderloins with half of the spice mixture and a bit of olive oil. Place the tenderloins in a roasting pan and cook for 10 minutes.
4. Turn the tenderloins over and roast for 10 more minutes or until done to your liking.
5. Transfer the pork to a serving platter, cover with foil, and let rest.
6. Pour off any fat that has accumulated in the roasting pan. Place the pan on the stovetop over high heat and add the stock (or water). Bring to a boil, scraping the bottom of the pan to loosen any cooked-on bits. Season with salt and pepper to taste.
7. To serve, slice the tenderloins into thin slices. Pour a bit of the sauce on top, passing more separately at the table.

Chiang Mai Beef

3¼ cups water
2 cups uncooked long-grained rice
1 pound lean ground beef
3–4 tablespoons soy sauce
1 tablespoon vegetable oil
1 tablespoon chopped garlic
1 tablespoon small dried chilies
2 green onions, trimmed and sliced
Fish sauce

1. In a large saucepan, bring the water to a boil, then stir in the rice. Cover, reduce heat to low, and cook until the water is absorbed, about 20 minutes.
2. Put the cooked rice in a large mixing bowl and let cool to room temperature.
3. Add the ground beef and soy sauce to the rice, mixing thoroughly. (I find using my hands works best.)
4. Divide the rice-beef mixture into 8 to 12 equal portions, depending on the size you prefer, and form them into loose balls. Wrap each ball in foil, making sure to seal them well.
5. Steam the rice balls for 25 to 30 minutes or until cooked through.
6. While the rice is steaming, heat the vegetable oil in a small skillet. Add the garlic and the dried chilies and sauté until the garlic is golden. Transfer the garlic and the chilies to a paper towel to drain.
7. To serve, remove the rice packets from the foil, slightly smash them, and put on serving plates. Pass the garlic-chili mixture, the green onions, and the fish sauce separately to be used as condiments at the table.

Serves 4–6

Chiang Mai is the principal city in Northern Thailand, known for its mountain scenery, fertile valleys, and handicrafts. This is one of the main starting points for tourists interested in jungle treks and elephant rides.

Barbecued Pork on Rice

Serves 2–3

This is not a typical barbecue. Nevertheless, I think you will find yourself asking for more once you've tried this Asian version of what we Americans think of as an indigenous cuisine.

1 pork tenderloin, trimmed of excess fat
2 tablespoons sugar
2 tablespoons soy sauce
1 teaspoon Chinese 5-spice powder
1 hard-boiled egg, peeled
2 tablespoons flour
1½ cups water
2 tablespoons rice vinegar
1 tablespoon sesame seeds, toasted
Jasmine rice, cooked according to package directions
1 cucumber, thinly sliced
1 green onion, trimmed and thinly sliced

1. Slice the tenderloin into medallions approximately ¼-inch thick. Place the medallions in a mixing bowl.
2. Combine the sugar, soy sauce, and 5-spice powder in a small bowl.
3. Pour the soy mixture over pork strips and toss the strips until thoroughly coated. Let marinate at least 30 minutes, but preferably overnight.
4. Preheat the oven to 350 degrees. Place the pork pieces in a single layer on a baking sheet lined with foil. Reserve any leftover marinade.
5. Bake the pork for approximately 1 hour. The pork with be firm and rather dry, but not burned. It will also have a reddish color.
6. Place the reserved marinade in a small saucepan and heat to boiling. Turn off the heat and add the peeled egg, rolling it in the sauce to color it. Remove the egg and set it aside. When cool enough to handle, slice it into thin pieces.
7. Combine the flour and water, and add it to the marinade. Bring to a boil to thicken, then remove from heat.
8. Add the vinegar and the sesame seeds. Adjust seasoning by adding additional sugar and/or soy sauce.
9. To serve, place some Jasmine rice in the center of each plate. Fan a few pieces of the pork around 1 side of the rice. Fan some cucumber slices and sliced hard-boiled egg around the other side. Spoon some of the sauce over the pork and sprinkle with the green onion slices.

Lemongrass Pork

½ cup brown sugar
½ cup fish sauce
½ cup dark soy sauce
½ cup chopped lemongrass stalks (inner white portion only)
¼ cup whiskey
¼ cup chopped shallots
¼ cup minced garlic
¼ cup coconut milk
3 tablespoons sesame oil
1 teaspoon cayenne pepper
1 pound lean pork, cut into bite-sized pieces

Serves 2

You don't run across many Asian recipes that call for liquor. The whiskey complements the lemongrass in this dish incredibly well, while adding a complexity that only a fermented beverage can.

1. In a medium-sized saucepan, combine the brown sugar, fish sauce, soy sauce, lemongrass, whiskey, shallots, and garlic. Over medium heat, bring to a boil and cook until the mixture is reduced by half. Remove the marinade from the heat and allow it to cool to room temperature. Stir in the coconut milk, sesame oil, and cayenne pepper.
2. Place the pork and the marinade in a large Ziplock bag. Marinate the pork in the refrigerator for at least 3 hours, or overnight.
3. Drain the meat, reserving the marinade. Thread the meat onto metal skewers (or soaked bamboo skewers), and grill or broil to your liking.
4. Place the reserved marinade in a small saucepan and bring it to a boil over medium-high heat. Reduce the heat and simmer the marinade for 2 to 3 minutes. Use the marinade as a dipping sauce for the pork.

Pork and Spinach Curry

Serves 1–2

Some meat departments actually offer meats precut into strips, which dramatically reduces prep time. If pork strips are not available, try this recipe with beef, chicken, or turkey.

1 cup coconut milk, divided
1 tablespoon Red Curry Paste (see recipes in Chapter 13)
½ cup lean pork strips
2 cups water
½ lime
3–4 kaffir lime leaves, crumbled
4 tablespoons fish sauce
2 tablespoons sugar
½ pound baby spinach
Rice, cooked according to package directions

1. In a medium-sized saucepan, heat ½ cup of the coconut milk and the curry paste over medium-low heat, stirring to combine thoroughly. Cook for 5 minutes, stirring constantly, so that the sauce does not burn.
2. Add the pork cubes, the remaining coconut milk, and the water. Return the mixture to a simmer and let cook for 5 minutes. Squeeze the juice of the lime half into the curry. Add the lime half.
3. Stir in the kaffir lime leaves, fish sauce, and sugar. Continue simmering for 5 to 10 more minutes or until the pork is cooked through. Remove the lime half.
4. Add the baby spinach and cook for 1 minute.
5. Serve over rice.

Spinach

Spinach is an amazingly healthy leaf vegetable. Spinach is low in calories, and is a good source of vitamin C, vitamin A, and minerals, especially iron.

Thai-Style Beef with Broccoli

3 tablespoons vegetable oil
1 medium shallot, chopped
1 teaspoon chili powder
2 tablespoons brown sugar
2 tablespoons fish sauce
2 tablespoons sweet soy sauce
1 tablespoon preserved soy beans (optional)
1 pound lean beef, cut into bite-sized pieces
2 cups water
½ of a 7–8-ounce package of rice sticks
1 cup broccoli pieces
Lime wedges (optional)
Hot sauce (optional)

Serves 2–4

I enjoy traditional Chinese-style beef with broccoli, but I like the spiciness of this Thai version better. To make this a vegetarian dish, I omit the beef and use 3 cups of broccoli instead of only 1.

1. Heat the vegetable oil in a wok over medium-high heat. Add the shallot and stir-fry until it begins to soften. Add the chili powder and continue to stir-fry until well combined.
2. Add the brown sugar, fish sauce, soy sauce, and soy beans; stir-fry for 30 seconds.
3. Add the beef and continue to stir-fry until the beef is almost done, approximately 2 minutes.
4. Stir in the water and bring it to a boil. Add the rice sticks, stirring until they start to cook. Reduce the heat to medium, cover, and let cook for 30 seconds. Stir and reduce the heat to medium-low, cover, and let cook for 3 minutes.
5. Add the broccoli pieces, cover, and cook for 1 minute. Remove the wok from the heat and adjust seasoning to taste.
6. Serve with wedges of lime and hot sauce passed separately at the table.

Pork with Tomatoes and Sticky Rice

Serves 2

This intriguing dish comes from Northern Thailand, where sticky rice is eaten with just about everything. The dried chilies give it a smokiness that I particularly enjoy.

7 small dried chilies
½ teaspoon salt
½ teaspoon shrimp paste
2 tablespoons chopped shallot
1 tablespoon chopped garlic
1 tablespoon vegetable oil
½ pound coarsely chopped lean pork
20 cherry tomatoes, quartered
1 tablespoon fish sauce
1 teaspoon brown sugar
Sticky rice, cooked according to package directions

1. Trim the chilies of their stems and shake out the seeds. Cut them into small pieces, cover them with warm water, and let them soak for 20 minutes to soften; drain.
2. Using a food processor or mortar and pestle, grind (or process) the chilies and salt together until a thick paste is formed. Add the shrimp paste, shallot, and garlic. Process until well combined; set aside.
3. Heat a wok or heavy-bottomed skillet over low heat. Add the vegetable oil and heat for 1 minute. Add the chili purée and cook for approximately 3 minutes or until the color of the paste deepens.
4. Increase the heat to medium and add the pork; stir-fry for 1 minute. Add the tomatoes and continue to cook for 3 to 4 minutes, stirring frequently.
5. Stir in the fish sauce and brown sugar; simmer for 2 minutes. Adjust seasoning to taste.
6. Serve this beef dish with sticky rice either warm or at room temperature.

Cinnamon Stewed Beef

1½ quarts water
2 tablespoons sugar
2 whole star anise
5 tablespoons soy sauce
1 clove garlic, smashed
2 tablespoons sweet soy sauce
1 (2-inch) piece of cinnamon stick
5 sprigs cilantro
1 celery stalk, sliced
1 pound beef sirloin, trimmed of all fat and cut into 1-inch cubes
1 bay leaf

1. Place the water in a large soup pot and bring to a boil. Reduce heat to low and add the remaining ingredients.
2. Simmer, adding more water if necessary, for at least 2 hours or until the beef is completely tender. If possible, let the stewed beef sit in the refrigerator overnight.
3. To serve, place noodles or rice in the bottom of 4 soup bowls. Add pieces of beef and then ladle broth over. Sprinkle with chopped cilantro or sliced green onions if you like. Pass a vinegar-chili sauce of your choice as a dip for the beef.

Serves 4

Cinnamon is not a spice we Westerners typically use in savory dishes, but it is great at balancing spice or salt.

CHAPTER 19

Chicken Dishes

Siamese Roast Chicken

Serves 2–4

The longer you let the bird take on the flavor nuances of the spice rub, the more aromatic your roast chicken will be. So if you can plan ahead, do so. It will be well worth the wait.

2 stalks lemongrass, thinly sliced (tender inner core only)
1 medium onion, chopped
1 clove garlic, minced
1 teaspoon (or to taste) dried red pepper flakes
1 tablespoon fish sauce
1 whole roasting chicken
Salt and pepper to taste
Vegetable oil

1. To prepare the marinade, place the lemongrass, onion, garlic, red pepper, and fish sauce in a food processor. Process until a thick paste is formed. Refrigerate for at least 30 minutes, overnight if possible.
2. Spread the marinade throughout the chicken cavity and then sprinkle the cavity with salt and pepper. Rub the outside of the bird with a bit of vegetable oil (or butter if you prefer) and season with salt and pepper. Place the bird in a roasting pan, and cover it with plastic wrap. Refrigerate for a few hours to marinate, if possible. Remove the chicken from the refrigerator approximately 30 minutes before roasting.
3. Preheat the oven to 500 degrees. Remove the plastic wrap and place the bird in the oven, legs first, and roast for 50 to 60 minutes or until the juices run clear.

Using Pan Drippings

Pan drippings from any roasted poultry or meat make a great "sauce" for pouring over potatoes or noodles. After you have removed the roast from the pan, pour off any fat. Place the roasting pan on a burner over medium-high heat. Add approximately ½ cup of liquid—water, stock, wine—and bring to a boil. Scrape up the browned bits off the bottom of the roaster. Cook until the liquid is reduced by about half. Remove from heat and check seasonings; adjust if necessary.

Tamarind Stir-Fried Chicken with Mushrooms

2 tablespoons vegetable oil
1–2 whole boneless, skinless chicken breasts, cut into bite-sized cubes
Salt and freshly ground black pepper
1 teaspoon sugar
4 ounces domestic mushrooms, sliced
½ cup sliced onions
1 clove garlic, minced
2 tablespoons Tamarind Concentrate (see recipe on page 304)
2 tablespoons water
1 cup bean sprouts
1 small jalapeño, seeded and minced
¼ cup chopped basil

Serves 1–2

This recipe calls for domestic mushrooms and it's great as is. But don't hesitate to experiment—try portobellos, creminis, shitakes, or morels. Just cut them into bite-sized pieces and go for it!

1. Heat the vegetable oil in a large sauté pan or wok over high heat. Season the chicken with the salt, pepper, and sugar.
2. Add the chicken to the pan and stir-fry for 2 minutes. Add the mushrooms, onions, and garlic; continue to cook for an additional 2 to 3 minutes. Add the tamarind and water; stir.
3. Add the remaining ingredients. Adjust seasonings to taste and serve.

Chili-Fried Chicken

Serves 4–6

Like the colonel's version, this fried chicken is good hot, at room temperature, or cold.

3 tablespoons Tamarind Concentrate (see recipe on page 304)
Pinch of turmeric
½ teaspoon ground coriander
1½ teaspoons salt, divided
½ teaspoon white pepper
3 pounds chicken pieces, rinsed and patted dry
2 tablespoons vegetable oil
8 large red chilies, seeded and chopped
2 small onions, thinly sliced
Vegetable oil for deep-frying

1. In a small bowl combine the tamarind, turmeric, coriander, 1 teaspoon of the salt, and the pepper.
2. Place the chicken pieces in a large Ziplock bag. Pour the tamarind mixture over the chicken, seal the bag, and marinate at least 2 hours or overnight in the refrigerator.
3. In a small sauté pan, heat 2 tablespoons of vegetable oil over medium heat. Add the red chilies, onions, and the remaining salt; sauté for 5 minutes. Set aside to cool slightly.
4. Transfer the chili mixture to a food processor and pulse briefly to form a coarse sauce.
5. Drain the chicken and discard the marinade. Deep-fry the chicken pieces in hot oil until the skin is golden and the bones are crispy. Remove the cooked chicken to paper towels to drain.
6. Place the cooked chicken in a large mixing bowl. Pour the chili sauce over the chicken and toss until each piece is evenly coated.

Thai-Style Green Curry Chicken

1/4 cup vegetable oil
3 whole boneless, skinless chicken breasts, cut into bite-sized pieces
1/4 cup Green Curry Paste (see recipes in Chapter 13)
2 cups coconut milk
3 tablespoons fish sauce
1/4 cup (or to taste) chopped cilantro leaves
Steamed white rice

Serves 4–6

Vegetables can easily be added to this dish if you like: Stir in snow peas 5 minutes before the curry is done cooking and a handful of baby spinach leaves just at the last moment.

1. Heat 2 tablespoons of vegetable oil in a large sauté pan or wok over medium heat. Add the chicken and sauté until lightly browned on all sizes. Remove the chicken and set aside.
2. Add the remaining vegetable oil to the sauté pan. Stir in the curry paste and cook for 2 to 3 minutes. Add the coconut milk and continue to cook for 5 minutes. Add the reserved chicken and fish sauce. Reduce heat and simmer until chicken is tender, 15 to 20 minutes. Stir in the cilantro.
3. Serve with steamed white rice.

Reducing Chili Fire

Roasting chilies is another way to tone down their heat, as is soaking them in ice water for an hour.

Ginger Chicken

Serves 2

Ginger is one of the most well-known of all of the Asian flavoring agents. Its bright, clean, slightly sweet, slightly hot flavor is found in everything from savory stir-fries like this one to desserts to beverages.

2 tablespoons fish sauce
2 tablespoons dark soy sauce
2 tablespoons oyster sauce
3 tablespoons vegetable oil
1 tablespoon chopped garlic
1 whole boneless, skinless chicken breast, cut into bite-sized pieces
1 cup sliced domestic mushrooms
3 tablespoons grated ginger
Pinch of sugar
3 tablespoons chopped onion
2–3 habanero or bird's eye chilis
Jasmine rice, cooked according to package directions
3 green onions, trimmed and cut into 1-inch pieces
Cilantro

1. In a small bowl combine the fish, soy, and oyster sauces; set aside.
2. Heat the oil in a large wok until very hot. Add the garlic and chicken, and stir-fry just until the chicken begins to change color.
3. Add the reserved sauce and cook until it begins to simmer, stirring constantly.
4. Add the mushrooms, ginger, sugar, onion, and chilies; simmer until the chicken is cooked through, about 8 minutes.
5. To serve, ladle the chicken over Jasmine rice and top with green onion and cilantro.

Poultry Protection

Be careful with raw poultry. It often contains bacteria that can cause food-borne illness. Keep it refrigerated at all times, even when thawing it, in a leak-proof container. Thoroughly clean all utensils and cutting boards. Sanitize them in a dishwasher or with a bleach solution. Thoroughly wash your hands with hot water and soap after handling raw poultry.

Red Chili Chicken

1 tablespoon vegetable oil
1–3 tablespoons Red Curry Paste (see recipes in Chapter 13)
½ cup coconut milk
1 whole boneless, skinless chicken breast, cut into bite-sized pieces
2 kaffir lime leaves or 2 (2-inch-long, ½-inch wide) pieces of lime zest
1 tablespoon basil leaves
2 tablespoons fish sauce
1 tablespoon brown sugar
4 ounces Thai eggplant (green peas can be substituted)

Serves 2

This relatively mild curry is a perfect example of basic Thai cooking—simple ingredients and simple cooking methods leading to a flavor-packed result. No wonder Thai cooking is becoming so popular!

1. In a large skillet or wok, heat the oil over medium-high heat. Stir in the curry paste and cook until fragrant, about 1 minute.
2. Reduce the heat to medium-low and add the coconut milk. Stirring constantly, cook until a thin film of oil develops on the surface.
3. Add all of the remaining ingredients except the eggplant. Bring to a boil, reduce heat, and simmer until the chicken begins to turn opaque, about 5 minutes.
4. Add the eggplant and continue to cook until the chicken is done to your liking, about 3 minutes more.

Is a Thai Eggplant the Same as a Japanese Eggplant?

No. A Japanese eggplant is long and narrow, almost the shape and size of a large banana, but with a deep purple color. They have a mild flavor and a smooth texture. Thai eggplants, on the other hand, are green and shaped like small cherries. They have a firmer bite than the Japanese variety and can be very difficult to find. Green peas make a fine substitute.

Basil Chicken

Serves 4

The basil is just barely cooked so that it retains its lively character and color, so make sure to find absolutely fresh leaves for this recipe—nothing limp or beginning to brown. Don't use stems either.

2 tablespoons fish sauce
1½ tablespoons soy sauce
1 tablespoon water
1½ teaspoons sugar
2 whole boneless, skinless chicken breasts, cut into 1-inch cubes
2 tablespoons vegetable oil
1 large onion, cut into thin slices
3 Thai chilies, seeded and thinly sliced
3 cloves garlic, minced
1½ cups chopped basil leaves, divided

1. In a medium-sized bowl, combine the fish sauce, the soy sauce, water, and sugar. Add the chicken cubes and stir to coat. Let marinate for 10 minutes.
2. In a large skillet or wok, heat oil over medium-high heat. Add the onion and stir-fry for 2 to 3 minutes. Add the chilies and garlic and continue to cook for an additional 30 seconds.
3. Using a slotted spoon, remove the chicken from the marinade and add it to the skillet (reserve the marinade.) Stir-fry until almost cooked through, about 3 minutes.
4. Add the reserved marinade and cook for an additional 30 seconds. Remove the skillet from the heat and stir in 1 cup of the basil.
5. Garnish with the remaining basil, and serve with rice.

Fragrant Roast Chicken

For the marinade:

½ cup fish sauce
½ cup sweet dark soy sauce
2 tablespoons crushed garlic
2 tablespoons freshly grated gingerroot
1 tablespoon freshly ground black pepper

For the stuffing:

½ cup freshly grated ginger
½ cup fresh grated galangal
½ cup sliced bruised lemongrass stalks
½ cup chopped cilantro
½ cup chopped mushrooms
1 roasting chicken, cleaned and patted dry

Serves 2–4

The stuffing in this recipe is certainly edible, but is really used for the flavor it will give to the chicken.

1. Combine all of the marinade ingredients in a plastic bag large enough to hold the whole chicken. Add the chicken, making sure to coat the whole bird with the marinade. Place the chicken in the refrigerator and leave overnight.
2. Remove the chicken from the plastic bag, reserving the marinade.
3. Place all of the stuffing ingredients in a large mixing bowl. Stir in the reserved marinade.
4. Stuff the bird's cavity and place it breast side up in a roasting pan. Place the roasting pan in a preheated 400 degree oven and roast for 50 to 60 minutes, or until the juices run clear.

Picking Lemongrass

To choose fresh lemongrass, look for stalks that are firm, full, and pale green. The color indicates freshness. Bend the stalk slightly and smell it. It should be very fragrant.

Sweet-and-Sour Chicken

Serves 4

A classic Asian dish that we have all tried at one time or another. The green and red peppers complement the sweetness of the pineapple. The chili sauce offsets the plum sauce.

2 tablespoons soy sauce
2 cloves garlic, minced
1 (1-inch) piece of ginger, peeled and minced
1–2 tablespoons prepared chili sauce
1 pound boneless, skinless chicken breasts, cut into 1-inch cubes
1 tablespoon vegetable oil
1 small onion, thinly sliced
1 green and 1 red bell pepper, seeded and cut into 1-inch pieces
8 ounces canned pineapple pieces, drained
4–6 tablespoons prepared Plum Sauce (see recipe on page 311)
Jasmine rice, cooked according to package directions

1. In a small bowl, combine the soy sauce, garlic, ginger, and chili sauce. Add the chicken pieces, stirring to coat. Set aside to marinate for at least 20 minutes.
2. Heat the oil in a wok or large skillet over medium heat. Add the onion and sauté until translucent, about 3 minutes.
3. Add the chicken mixture and continue to cook for another 3 to 5 minutes.
4. Add the bell peppers, the pineapple, and plum sauce. Cook for an additional 5 minutes or until the chicken is cooked through.
5. Serve over lots of fluffy Jasmine rice.

Thai Cashew Chicken

3 tablespoons vegetable oil
5–10 dried Thai chilies
5–10 cloves garlic, mashed
1 large whole boneless, skinless chicken breast, cut into thin strips
4 green onions, trimmed and cut into 1-inch lengths
1 small onion, thinly sliced
2–3 teaspoons Chili Tamarind Paste (see recipe on page 294)
¼ cup chicken broth
1 tablespoon oyster sauce
1 tablespoon fish sauce
2 tablespoons sugar
¾ cup whole cashews

Serves 2–4

This is a rather pungent curry. To tone it down, reduce the number of chilies and garlic, and warn guests not to eat the dried chilies.

1. In a wok or large skillet, heat the oil over medium-high heat until hot.
2. Add the chilies and stir-fry briefly until they darken in color. Transfer the chilies to a paper towel to drain; set aside.
3. Add the garlic to the wok and stir-fry until just beginning to turn golden.
4. Raise the heat to high and add the chicken. Cook, stirring constantly, for approximately 1 minute.
5. Add the green onions and onion slices and cook for 30 seconds.
6. Add the Chili Tamarind Paste, broth, oyster sauce, fish sauce, and sugar. Continue to stir-fry for 30 more seconds.
7. Add the reserved chilies and the cashews; stir-fry for 1 more minute or until the chicken is cooked through and the onions are tender.

Chili Nutrition

Fresh chilies are rich in vitamins A, C, and E. Red chilies (i.e., ripe) have the most nutritional value. Cooking chilies lessens their vitamin levels and drying them destroys most of their vitamins.

Lemongrass Chicken Skewers

Serves 4

These skewers are based on a recipe from award-winning chef Jean-Georges Vongerichten, whose Thai cuisine has won praise worldwide. He has a line of tasty sauces and marinades that is available in stores.

5 stalks lemongrass, trimmed
12 large cubes chicken breast meat, a little over 1 ounce each
Black pepper
2 tablespoons vegetable oil, divided
Pinch of dried red pepper flakes
Juice of 1 lime
2 teaspoons fish sauce
Pinch of sugar
Sea salt to taste

1. Remove 2 inches from the thick end of each stalk of lemongrass; set aside. Bruise 4 of the lemongrass stalks with the back of a knife. Remove the tough outer layer of the fifth stalk, exposing the tender core; mince.
2. Skewer 3 cubes of chicken on each lemongrass stalk. Sprinkle the skewers with the minced lemongrass and black pepper, and drizzle with 1 tablespoon of oil. Cover with plastic wrap and refrigerate for 12 to 24 hours.
3. Chop all of the reserved lemongrass stalk ends. Place in a small saucepan and cover with water. Bring to a boil, cover, and let reduce until approximately 2 tablespoons of liquid is left; strain. Return the liquid to the saucepan and further reduce to 1 tablespoon.
4. Combine the lemongrass liquid with the red pepper flakes, lime juice, fish sauce, sugar, and remaining tablespoon of oil; set aside.
5. Prepare a grill to high heat. Grill the chicken skewers for approximately 2 to 3 minutes per side, or until done to your liking.
6. To serve, spoon a little of the lemongrass sauce over the top of each skewer and sprinkle with sea salt.

Brandied Chicken

1 whole roasting chicken, rinsed and trimmed of excess fat
¼ cup vegetable oil
6 tablespoons soy sauce
2 tablespoons black soy sauce
1 teaspoon salt
8 cloves garlic, minced
2 shots brandy
1 (1-inch) piece ginger, sliced

Serves 4–6

Be careful when you are lowering the bird into the scalding water. Instead of using a utensil, I actually grab the legs in my hands and carefully lower the chicken into the water.

1. Fill a pot large enough to hold the whole chicken approximately ⅓ full of water. Bring the water to a boil over high heat. Reduce the heat to medium and carefully add the chicken to the pot. Adjust the heat so that the water is just simmering.
2. Poach the whole chicken for 20 to 30 minutes or until cooked through. Carefully remove the chicken from the pot, making sure to drain the hot water from the cavity of the bird. Set the chicken aside to cool.
3. Remove the skin from the bird and discard. Remove the meat from the chicken and cut it into 1-inch pieces; set aside. (This portion of the recipe can be done 1 or 2 days in advance.)
4. Add the oil to a large skillet or wok and heat on medium. Add the soy sauces, salt, and garlic. Stir-fry until the garlic begins to soften, about 30 seconds to 1 minute.
5. Add the chicken pieces, stirring to coat. Stir in the brandy and the ginger.
6. Cover the skillet or wok, reduce the heat to low, and simmer 5 to 10 more minutes.

Thai Glazed Chicken

Serves 2–4

The marinade for this dish looks rather like watered-down milk, but don't let the blah appearance fool you: It's delicious. Unlike many Thai marinades, this one is not terribly spicy.

1 whole chicken, cut in half (ask your butcher to do this for you)
1 teaspoon salt
4 cloves garlic, chopped
1 teaspoon white pepper
1 tablespoon minced cilantro
2 tablespoons rice wine
2 tablespoons coconut milk
1 tablespoon fish sauce
1 teaspoon chopped ginger
2 tablespoons soy sauce

1. Rinse the chicken under cold water, then pat dry. Trim off any excess fat or skin. Place the chicken halves in large Ziplock bags.
2. Stir the remaining ingredients together in a small bowl until well combined.
3. Pour the marinade into the Ziplock bags, seal closed, and turn until the chicken is evenly coated with the marinade. Let the chicken marinate for 30 minutes to 1 hour in the refrigerator.
4. Preheat the oven to 350 degrees.
5. Remove the chicken from the bags and place them breast side up in a roasting pan large enough to hold them comfortably. (Discard the remaining marinade.)
6. Roast the chicken for 45 minutes.
7. Turn on the broiler and broil for approximately 10 minutes or until done.

Chicken with Black Pepper and Garlic

1 tablespoon whole black peppercorns
5 cloves garlic, cut in half
2 pounds boneless, skinless chicken breasts, cut into strips
1/3 cup fish sauce
3 tablespoons vegetable oil
1 teaspoon sugar

Serves 4–6

Serve the chicken with mounds of Jasmine rice. Garnish plates with slices of cucumber and tomato.

1. Using either a mortar and pestle or a food processor, combine the black peppercorns with the garlic.
2. Place the chicken strips in a large mixing bowl. Add the garlic-pepper mixture and the fish sauce, and stir to combine.
3. Cover the bowl, place in the refrigerator, and let marinate for 20 to 30 minutes.
4. Heat the vegetable oil over medium heat in a wok or skillet. When it is hot, add the chicken mixture and stir-fry until cooked through, about 3 to 5 minutes.
5. Stir in the sugar. Add additional sugar or fish sauce to taste.

The Glory of the Mortar (and Pestle)

The grinding action of a mortar and pestle releases the oils and flavor essence of the substances being mashed. Unlike a food processor, a mortar will mash ingredients together completely and fully, creating a much more intense and flavorful combination. However, using a mortar and pestle can sometimes be very tiresome. If you enjoy cooking, using a mortar and pestle will probably be something you'll love—both the process and the results!

Jungle Chicken

Serves 2–3

Like the tiger, this dish can be a bit ferocious and can pack quite a bite! So beware!

2–4 serrano chilies, stems and seeds removed
1 stalk lemongrass, inner portion roughly chopped
2 (2-inch-long, ½-inch wide) strips of lime peel
2 tablespoons vegetable oil
½ cup coconut milk
1 whole boneless, skinless chicken breast, cut into thin strips
2–4 tablespoons fish sauce
10–15 basil leaves

1. Place the chilies, lemongrass, and lime peel into a food processor and process until ground.
2. Heat the oil over medium-high heat in a wok or large skillet. Add the chili mixture and sauté for 1 to 2 minutes.
3. Stir in the coconut milk and cook for 2 minutes.
4. Add the chicken and cook until the chicken is cooked through, about 5 minutes.
5. Reduce heat to low and add the fish sauce and basil leaves to taste.
6. Serve with plenty of Jasmine rice.

CHAPTER 20

Fish and Seafood Dishes

Snapper Baked with Fish Sauce and Garlic

Serves 2

I love this flavorful yet oh-so-simple dish. The recipe calls for leaving the fish whole, but if you have a hard time eating fish that still has the head intact, by all means have your fish-monger remove it.

2 whole small red snappers, cleaned but left whole
¼ cup fish sauce
1 tablespoon sesame oil
2 cloves garlic, minced

1. With a sharp knife, make 3 deep diagonal slits on each side of the fish. Place the fish in an ovenproof baking dish.
2. Combine the fish sauce, sesame oil, and garlic in a small bowl. Spoon the mixture over the fish, making sure it goes into the slits. Let the fish sit at room temperature for 30 minutes.
3. Bake the fish in a 425-degree oven for 30 minutes or until the skin is crisp.

How to Find the Freshest Seafood

The best source for great fish is a great fishmonger, someone who will steer you to the best fish he or she has. If you are on your own, follow your nose. Fresh fish should NOT smell fishy. Instead it should smell clean, and if an ocean fish, like the sea. If there is any fishy smell at all, don't buy it. Other things to look for: Feel the skin; it should be slippery and moist. Press the fish; it should feel firm. Look at the eyes; they should be plump and clear.

Lime-Ginger Fillets

4 tablespoons unsalted butter, at room temperature
2 teaspoons lime zest
½ teaspoon ground ginger
½ teaspoon salt
4 fish fillets, such as whitefish, perch, or pike
Salt and freshly ground black pepper

Serves 2–4

These delicate fillets cook in a jiffy, so make sure to pay attention while they are under the broiler. Overcooking fish dries it out and causes it to lose its flaky texture.

1. Preheat the broiler.
2. In a small bowl, thoroughly combine the butter, lime zest, ginger, and ½ teaspoon salt.
3. Lightly season the fillets with salt and pepper and place on a baking sheet.
4. Broil for 4 minutes. Brush each fillet with some of the lime-ginger butter and continue to broil for 1 minute or until the fish is done to your liking.

Storing Fish

How to store fresh fish: The best way to store fresh fish is not to store it at all, but rather use it the day you purchase it. If that's not an option, lay the fish on a bed of ice and then cover it. Make sure that the ice has somewhere to drain so that the fish doesn't end up sitting in water, which will cause it to turn mushy.

Baked Redfish with Lime Vinaigrette

Serves 2

It's hard to go wrong flavoring something with garlic and lime. This easy-to-make baked fish is no exception. I like to serve this with a flavored rice dish (dill works well) and a nice summery salad.

2 (6-ounce) redfish fillets, rinsed and patted dry (skate, sole, or flounder also work well)
1 clove garlic, minced
2 tablespoons lime juice
2 teaspoons soy or fish sauce
½ teaspoon sugar
¼ teaspoon salt
2 tablespoons vegetable oil

1. Place the fillets in a shallow baking dish.
2. In a small bowl, combine the garlic, lime juice, soy sauce, sugar, and salt, then whisk in the oil.
3. Pour the vinaigrette over the fish and bake in a 450-degree oven for 6 to 7 minutes or until done to your liking.

Eco-Friendly Fish Choices

Many types of fish are on their way to extinction due to overfishing. But here are a few, according to the Audubon Society, that are still plentiful—Alaska salmon, mahi-mahi, striped bass, Pacific halibut, catfish, farmed tilapia, farmed scallops, pole-caught tuna, and rainbow trout.

Broiled Salmon with 5-Spice Lime Butter

Vegetable oil
2 (6-ounce) salmon fillets, rinsed and patted dry
1 tablespoon unsalted butter
1/4–1/2 teaspoon Chinese 5-spice powder
2 teaspoons lime juice

Serves 2

I'm a salmon fan. I like it poached, grilled, broiled, and smoked—any way really. No matter what variety you buy, they all seem to share that slightly sweet flavor that I haven't found in any other fish.

1. Using paper towels, wipe a thin coat of vegetable oil over a broiler pan.
2. Preheat the broiler on high, with the rack set on the upper third of the oven.
3. Melt the butter over low heat in a small saucepan. Stir in the 5-spice powder and lime juice; keep warm.
4. Place the salmon on the broiler pan, skin side up. Broil for 2 to 4 minutes or until the skin is crispy. Turn the salmon over and broil 2 minutes more or until done to your liking.
5. Transfer the salmon to 2 plates and spoon the butter sauce over the top.

Fatty Fish

Fatty fish are good for you! Fish such as tuna, salmon, and mackerel have high levels of Omega-3, a fatty acid shown to help prevent blood clots. Omega-3 has also been linked to lowering triglycerides and cholesterol.

Roasted Southeast Asian Fish

Serves 4

A great light meal is created when you let the fish in this recipe cool to room temperature and place it on a bed of greens that have been tossed in Thai Vinaigrette (see recipes in Chapter 14).

¼ cup chopped green onion
3 cloves garlic
4 thin slices of gingerroot
4 small fresh red chilies, seeded, 2 left whole and 2 julienned
Zest of 1 lime
1 teaspoon salt
4 (8-ounce) fish fillets (salmon or mackerel are good choices)
4 (12-inch-square) pieces of aluminum foil
12 fresh cilantro sprigs
8 thin lime slices, cut in half

1. In a food processor, combine the green onions, garlic, gingerroot, the 2 seeded whole chilies, the lime zest, and salt.
2. Preheat the oven to 450 degrees.
3. Rinse the fish under cold water and pat dry. Place each fillet in the center of a piece of foil. Rub generously with the green onion paste. Top with the cilantro leaves, lime slices, and julienned chilies. Wrap the fish in the foil.
4. Place the fish on a baking sheet and roast for approximately 10 minutes per inch of thickness.
5. To serve, place unopened packets on each plate. Let guests unwrap.

Roasting Meat

Roasting or grilling meats, poultry, and fish in aluminum foil is a terrific way to seal in juices and flavor. It makes additional fat unnecessary, and—maybe best of all—it makes cleanup a breeze. Give it a try and you may never go back!

Steamed Red Snapper

1 whole red snapper (about 2 pounds), cleaned, but left whole
Vegetable oil
1 recipe of sauce, such as Minty Dipping Sauce (see page 310), Sweet-and-Sour Dipping Sauce (see page 311), or Mango-Pineapple Salsa (see page 312)

1. Quickly rinse the fish under cold water. Pat dry with paper towels. With a sharp knife, deeply score the fish 3 to 4 times on each side.
2. Fill the base of a tiered steamer 1/3 full of water. Bring the water to a boil.
3. In the meantime, lightly coat the steamer rack with vegetable oil. Place the fish on the rack.
4. Place the rack over the boiling water, cover, and let steam for 10 to 12 minutes, until the flesh of the fish is opaque when pierced with a knife.
5. Serve the sauce on the side.

Serves 4

This is a great dinner party dish. Its vibrant color makes a dramatic presentation. Place the whole fish on a serving platter and garnish with lime slices, whole chilies, and coconut wedges. Pass the sauce separately.

Red Snapper

Red snapper is one of the most cherished of fish. Its moist, white flesh has a delicate, sweet flavor. It can readily be found fresh or frozen, and can be served broiled, baked, steamed, poached, fried, or grilled. If not available, rock cod, white sea bass, and calico bass are popular substitutions.

Marinated Steamed Fish

Serves 4

This fish gets its flavoring from the unique marinade, which is more of a paste than a traditional liquid. The finished fish is packed with flavor, but if you like, a squeeze of lemon or lime juice certainly won't hurt.

1 whole lean flatfish (such as redfish, flounder, or bass), cleaned
1 large mushroom, thinly sliced
2 tablespoons grated ginger
1 tablespoon sliced jalapeño pepper
2 green onions, finely sliced
3 tablespoons fish sauce
1 tablespoon soy sauce
1 tablespoon shrimp paste
1 teaspoon Tabasco
Vegetable oil

1. Quickly rinse the fish under cold water. Pat dry with paper towels. With a sharp knife, deeply score the fish 3 to 4 times on each side.
2. Stir together all of the remaining ingredients except the vegetable oil.
3. Place the fish in a large plastic bag. Pour the marinade over the fish and seal. Let the fish marinate for about 1 hour in the refrigerator.
4. Fill the base of a tiered steamer ⅓ full of water. Bring the water to a boil.
5. In the meantime, lightly coat the rack with vegetable oil. Place the fish on the rack.
6. Place the rack over the boiling water, cover, and let steam for 15 to 20 minutes, until the flesh of the fish is opaque when pierced with a knife.

Don't Over-Marinate

If your fish marinade has an acid in it (such as lemon or lime juice), don't marinate it for more than an hour or the marinade will begin "to cook" your fish. (Unless, of course, you are making cerviche.)

Quick Asian-Grilled Fish

1 whole fish, such as sea bass or mackerel, cleaned
4 tablespoons chopped cilantro
3 tablespoons chopped garlic, divided
1 teaspoon freshly ground black pepper
3 tablespoons lime juice
1 tablespoon sliced jalapeño chili peppers
2 teaspoons brown sugar

Serves 4–6

Alternatively, this fish can be cooked on a baking sheet in a 450-degree oven for approximately 10 to 12 minutes. Serve it with a variety of Thai-inspired salads—one featuring rice, one featuring veggies, and one with fruit.

1. Quickly rinse the fish under cold water. Pat dry with paper towels. Set the fish on a large sheet of aluminum foil.
2. Place the cilantro, 2 tablespoons of the garlic, and the black pepper in a food processor and process to form a thick paste.
3. Rub the paste all over the fish, both inside and out. Tightly wrap the fish in the foil.
4. To make the sauce, place the remaining garlic, the lime juice, jalapeños, and brown sugar in a food processor and pulse until combined.
5. Place the fish on a prepared grill and cook for 5 to 6 minutes per side or until the flesh is opaque when pierced with the tip of a knife.
6. Serve the fish with the sauce.

Thai Manners

Cleaning your plate in Thailand makes you a bad dinner guest. It makes your host appear not to be generous.

Seafood Stir-Fry

Serves 2–4

When I'm in the seafood section of the grocery store and everything looks great, I start thinking about this simple stir-fry. I buy a little of everything that strikes my fancy, go home, and have a seafood feast.

3 tablespoons vegetable oil
3 teaspoons garlic, chopped
2 shallots, chopped
1 stalk lemongrass, bruised
¼ cup chopped basil
1 can bamboo shoots, rinsed and drained
3 tablespoons fish sauce
Pinch of brown sugar
1 pound fresh shrimp, scallops, or other seafood, cleaned
Rice, cooked according to package directions

1. Heat the oil in a skillet or wok over high heat. Add the garlic, shallots, lemongrass, and basil, and sauté for 1 to 2 minutes.
2. Reduce heat, add the remaining ingredients, and stir-fry until the seafood is done to your liking, approximately 5 minutes.
3. Serve over rice.

Bamboo

Bamboo, a favorite of panda bears, is indigenous to Asia. However, bamboo is farmed in California and actually grows wild in some parts of Arizona!

Curried Mussels

2 tablespoons butter
2 shallots, minced
½ cup sweet white wine, such as Riesling
2 pounds mussels, debearded and rinsed well
½ cup sour cream
1 teaspoon (or to taste) curry powder
1 tablespoon lemon juice

Serves 2–4

Make sure to have empty bowls on the table to hold all of the empty shells. Use appetizer forks if you have them. Their smallish size and reduced number of tines make it easier to get at the mussels.

1. In a pan large enough to hold all of the mussels, melt the butter over medium heat. Add the shallots and sauté until softened and translucent.
2. Add the wine and the mussels and increase the heat to high. Cover and cook, shaking the pan occasionally, until the mussels open, approximately 10 minutes.
3. Remove the mussels from the pan, discarding any mussels that haven't opened. Strain the pan liquid through a strainer and return it to the pan. Bring to a boil, then stir in the sour cream and curry powder.
4. Reduce the heat to medium-low and add the lemon juice. Cook for 2 to 3 minutes. Adjust the seasonings of the sauce if necessary with salt and curry powder.
5. Return the mussels to the broth, coating them. Reheat and serve.

Cleaning Mussels

Don't clean the mussels until just before you cook them. Scrape off any barnacles that are on the shells with a knife or scouring pad. Pull off any strands. (This is called debearding.) Throw out any mussels that are open. Place the mussels in a colander and rinse thoroughly under cool water. Use as soon as possible.

Steamed Mussels with Lemongrass

Serves 2–4

This recipe includes four of the most commonly-used Thai flavoring ingredients—lemongrass, lime peel, ginger, and chilies. If you are a fan of one flavor more than another, don't be afraid to adjust the amounts.

3 cups water
2 stalks lemongrass, outer leaves removed and discarded, inner portion bruised
Peel of 1 lime
5 cloves garlic
3 (1/2-inch) slices unpeeled ginger
2 pounds mussels, cleaned
1 serrano chili
Tabasco to taste

1. Place the water, lemongrass, lime, garlic, and ginger in a pot large enough to hold all of the mussels. Bring to a boil, reduce heat, and let simmer for 5 minutes.
2. Bring the liquid back to a boil and add the mussels; cover and let steam for 5 minutes, shaking the pan every so often.
3. Transfer the mussels to a serving platter, discarding any mussels that have not opened.
4. Add the chili pepper to the broth and simmer for an additional 2 minutes. Strain the broth, then pour over the mussels.
5. Serve the mussels with Tabasco on the side.

Closed Mussels

Do not eat any mussels that have not opened during the cooking process. Throw them away!

Clams with Hot Basil

1 tablespoon vegetable oil
2 small dried red chili peppers, crushed
2 cloves garlic
2 pounds Manila clams, cleaned
4 teaspoons fish sauce
2 teaspoons sugar
1 bunch basil (Thai variety preferred), trimmed and julienned

1. Heat the oil in a large skillet on high. Add the chili peppers, garlic, and clams. Stir the clams until they open, about 4 to 5 minutes. Discard any clams that remain closed.
2. Add the fish sauce and sugar; stir until well combined.
3. Add the basil and stir until it wilts.
4. Serve immediately either as an appetizer or with rice as a main course.

Serves 4–6

Handle the clams in the same manner you do mussels—rinse them, debeard them, and discard any that are open before you cook them.

Stir-Fried Shrimp and Green Beans

1 tablespoon vegetable oil
1 tablespoon Red Curry Paste (see recipes in Chapter 13)
½ cup cleaned shrimp
1½ cups green beans, trimmed and cut into 1-inch lengths
2 teaspoons fish sauce
2 teaspoons sugar

1. Heat the vegetable oil over medium heat. Stir in the curry paste and cook for 1 minute to release the fragrance.
2. Add the shrimp and the green beans at the same time, and stir-fry until the shrimp become opaque. (The green beans will still be quite crispy. If you prefer your beans softer, cook an additional minute.)
3. Add the fish sauce and the sugar; stir to combine.
4. Serve immediately with rice.

Serves 2–3

The green beans are the stars of this simple stir-fry, but the shrimp are the highlight. They give the beans a bit more flavor and the dish more color and protein!

Seared Coconut Scallops

Serves 2

These sweet scallops have just a hint of heat and are so good, they may not make it to the dinner table. They may just disappear right off the paper towels!

1½ cups sweetened, flaked coconut
2 cups boiling water
¼ teaspoon cayenne
½ teaspoon salt
10 medium sea scallops, cleaned, rinsed, and patted dry
Salt and pepper
1 large egg, beaten

1. Preheat the oven to 350 degrees.
2. Place the coconut in a small bowl. Pour the boiling water over the coconut, stir, and then drain through a colander. Pat dry.
3. Spread the coconut on a baking sheet and bake for 10 minutes or until golden.
4. Place the toasted coconut in a small bowl and mix in the cayenne and salt.
5. Season the scallops with salt and pepper.
6. Heat a heavy, nonstick pan over high heat until almost smoking.
7. Dip each scallop in the beaten egg, letting most of the egg drip off, then press the scallops into the coconut mixture.
8. Place the scallops in the pan and sear for 1 to 1½ minutes per side until just done.

Choosing Scallops

The best scallops in the world are called "diver scallops" because they are harvested by-you guessed it-scuba divers! This method, although costly, is environmentally superior to the net method for the same reasons the scallops taste better-the entire environment is not disturbed, shells are not cracked, and only the mature scallops are taken.

Curried Shrimp with Peas

1½ teaspoons Red Curry Paste (see recipes in Chapter 13)
1 tablespoon vegetable oil
1 (14-ounce) can unsweetened coconut milk
4 teaspoons fish sauce
2-3 teaspoons brown sugar
2 pounds large shrimp, peeled and deveined
1 cup packed basil leaves, chopped
1 cup packed cilantro, chopped
1 (10-ounce) package thawed frozen peas
Jasmine rice, cooked according to package directions

1. In a large pot, combine the curry paste, vegetable oil, and ¼ cup of the coconut milk; cook over medium heat for 1 to 2 minutes.
2. Stir in the remaining coconut milk and cook for another 5 minutes.
3. Add the fish sauce and sugar, and cook for 1 minute more.
4. Add the shrimp, basil, and cilantro; reduce heat slightly and cook for 4 to 5 minutes or until the shrimp are almost done.
5. Add the peas and cook 2 minutes more.
6. Serve over Jasmine rice.

Serves 4-6

A beautifully colored curry-pink shrimp in a pink sauce peppered with green peas! The shrimp and the peas have a freshness that perfectly complements the silkiness of the Jasmine rice.

Shrimp Sizes

Shrimp are sized according to how many come in a pound. Medium means that there are about 40 shrimp per pound. Large equals 30, extra-large equals 25, jumbo equals 20, and colossal equals about 15. Salad shrimp are too tiny to count, so they are weighed instead.

Basil Scallops

Serves 2–4

Small, yet flavorful, bay scallops cook quickly, so be ready to serve this stir-fry as soon as the scallops are done to your liking. Overcooking scallops will make them somewhat tough and chewy.

2 tablespoons vegetable oil
3 cloves garlic, chopped
3 kaffir lime leaves, julienned, or the peel of 1 small lime cut into thin strips
½ pound bay scallops, cleaned
1 (14-ounce) can straw mushrooms, drained
¼ cup shredded bamboo shoots
3 tablespoons oyster sauce
15–20 fresh basil leaves

1. In a wok or skillet, heat the oil on high. Add the garlic and lime leaves, and stir-fry until fragrant, about 15 seconds.
2. Add the scallops, mushrooms, bamboo shoots, and oyster sauce; continue to stir-fry for approximately 4 to 5 minutes or until the scallops are done to your liking.
3. Mix in the basil leaves and serve immediately.

Chapter 21

Vegetable Dishes

Thai Vegetable Curry

Serves 4–6

Don't be afraid to experiment. In this recipe you can add just about any veggies you want. Try substituting sweet potatoes for the boiling potatoes and Brussels sprouts for the broccoli.

2 tablespoons vegetable oil
¼ cup Green Curry Paste (see recipes in Chapter 13)
3 cups canned, unsweetened coconut milk
3 tablespoons fish sauce
1 pound small boiling potatoes, quartered (or halved if large)
1 pound Japanese eggplant, cut into 1-inch slices
12 ounces baby carrots
2 cups broccoli florets
3–4 ounces green beans, cut into 1-inch lengths
½ cup fresh minced cilantro

1. In a heavy stew pot, heat the oil. Add the curry paste and cook for 2 to 3 minutes.
2. Add the coconut milk and fish sauce; simmer for 5 minutes.
3. Add the potatoes, eggplant, and carrots, and bring to a boil. Reduce heat and simmer for 10 minutes. Add the broccoli and green beans; continue to simmer until the vegetables are cooked through, about 10 minutes.
4. Just before serving stir in the cilantro.

Soy Sauce?

The Thai will know immediately that you are a foreigner if you ask for soy sauce. It's usually available, but it is not a traditional condiment. Fish sauce is the way to go.

Vegetables Poached in Coconut Milk

1 cup coconut milk
1 shallot, finely chopped
1 tablespoon soy sauce
1 tablespoon brown sugar
1 tablespoon Thai chilies, seeded and finely sliced
1 tablespoon green peppercorns, tied together in a small pouch made from a Handi Wipe
½ teaspoon sliced kaffir lime leaves
½ cup long beans or green beans, broken into 2-inch pieces
½ cup sliced mushrooms
1 cup shredded cabbage
½ cup peas
Rice, cooked according to package directions

Serves 2–4

Each vegetable in this dish is rather mild in flavor and tends to absorb different amounts of the poaching liquid, giving the diner a slightly different flavor sensation with every bite.

1. In a saucepan bring the coconut milk to a gentle simmer over medium heat. Stir in the shallots, soy sauce, brown sugar, chilies, green peppercorn pouch, and lime leaves. Simmer for 1 to 2 minutes until aromatic.
2. Add the green beans, mushrooms, and cabbage, and return to a simmer. Cook for 5 to 10 minutes or until tender.
3. Add the peas and cook 1 more minute. Remove the pouch of peppercorns before serving over rice.

Kaffir Limes

The kaffir lime tree produces fruit and leaves that make great additions to dishes. It imparts a wonderful tropical fruit flavor to any dish.

Southeastern Vegetable Stew

Serves 8

One of the great things about Asian cooking is that you can go wild with substitutions and omissions. Don't like tofu? Leave it out. Is your garden being overrun with Swiss chard? Throw it in. There are no rules.

8 cups vegetable stock
3 tablespoons fish sauce
2 tablespoons dark soy sauce
2 tablespoons brown sugar
4 cups turnip, cut into bite-sized pieces
1 Chinese cabbage, cut into bite-sized pieces
1 Western cabbage, quartered, cored, and cut into bite-sized pieces
1 cup sliced leeks
2 cups sliced celery
4 cups roughly chopped kale
1 can straw mushrooms, drained
5 cakes hard tofu, cut into bite-sized pieces
1 teaspoon vegetable oil
6 tablespoons soybean paste
3 tablespoons chopped garlic
1 tablespoon minced ginger
3 cups bean noodles, soaked, and cut into short lengths
½ cup chopped cilantro
Freshly ground pepper to taste

1. Bring the stock to a boil and add the fish sauce, soy sauce, and brown sugar.
2. Reduce the heat, add the vegetables and tofu, and simmer until the vegetables are almost tender.
3. In a small sauté pan, heat the oil over medium heat. Add the soybean paste and stir-fry until fragrant. Add the garlic and ginger, and stir-fry until the garlic is golden.
4. Add the soybean paste mixture to the soup. Stir in the noodles and cilantro, and simmer 5 more minutes.
5. Season with the pepper and additional fish sauce to taste.

Vegetarian Stir-Fry

1–2 tablespoons vegetable oil
2 cups bite-sized tofu pieces
2 tablespoons minced garlic
2 tablespoons grated ginger
4 tablespoons seeded and sliced Thai chilies
4 tablespoons soy sauce
2 tablespoons dark sweet soy sauce
1 small onion, sliced
¼ cup snow peas
¼ cup thinly sliced celery
¼ cup water chestnuts
¼ cup bite-sized pieces bell pepper
¼ cup sliced mushrooms
¼ cup cauliflower florets
¼ cup broccoli florets
¼ cup asparagus tips
1 tablespoon cornstarch, dissolved in a little water
¼ cup bean sprouts
Rice, cooked according to package directions

Serves 4-6 as a main course

If your vegetable bin ends up looking like mine, with a bit of this and a bit of that, this is the recipe for you. You can follow the ingredient list precisely, or substitute to your heart's desire.

1. Heat 1 tablespoon of oil in a large skillet or wok over medium-high heat. Add the tofu and sauté until golden brown. Transfer the tofu to paper towels to drain.
2. Add additional oil to the skillet if necessary, and stir-fry the garlic, ginger, and chilies to release their fragrance, about 2 to 3 minutes. Stir in the soy sauces and increase the heat to high.
3. Add the reserved tofu and all the vegetables except the bean sprouts; stir-fry for 1 minute.
4. Add the cornstarch mixture and stir-fry for another minute or until the vegetables are just cooked through and the sauce has thickened slightly.
5. Add the bean sprouts, stirring briefly to warm them.
6. Serve over rice.

Thai Pickled Vegetables

Yields approx. 6 cups

These pickled vegetables are great as a side dish, a snack, or on top of a bed of greens. The longer they sit in the marinade, the spicier and more vinegary they will get.

4 cups water
1 cup baby corn
1 cup broccoli florets
1 cup sliced carrots
½ cup bok choy
1 large cucumber, seeded and cut into 3-inch-long, ½-inch wide strips
1 recipe Thai Vinegar Marinade (see recipe on page 301)
½ cup cilantro leaves
2–3 tablespoons toasted sesame seeds

1. Bring the water to a boil in a large pan. Add the vegetables and blanch for 2 to 3 minutes. Strain the vegetables and shock with cool water to stop the cooking process.
2. Place the vegetables in a large bowl and pour the Thai Vinegar Marinade over the top. Let cool to room temperature and then refrigerate for at least 4 hours or up to 2 weeks (yes, weeks).
3. Stir in the cilantro and sesame seeds just before serving.

Asian Grilled Vegetables

2 bell peppers (red, yellow, or green, in any combination), seeded and cut into 2-inch squares
1 zucchini, cut into 1-inch slices
1 summer squash, cut into 1-inch slices
12 whole mushrooms, approximately 1-inch in diameter
12 whole pearl onions or 12 (2-inch) pieces of white onion
1 recipe Asian Marinade (see recipes in Chapter 13)

Serves 6

If you are planning on serving your vegetables from a bowl, don't bother with the skewers. Simply place the vegetables in a pan, marinate them, and then place them in a grill basket to cook.

1. Alternate the vegetables on 6 skewers (soak the skewers in water until soft if using wooden skewers).
2. Place the skewers in a pan large enough to allow them to lay flat. Pour the marinade over the skewers and let sit for approximately 1 hour.
3. Place the skewers in a lightly oiled grill basket and place on a hot grill. Cook approximately 5 minutes on each side or until vegetables are done to your liking.

Grilling Isn't Just for Meats!

Grilling vegetables may be my favorite way to prepare them. Even when I just baste them in a little olive oil and sprinkle them with salt and pepper, grilling gives them this special taste you just can't get any other way. And if you burn them a little bit—who cares—the charring just adds a little more flavor!

Pumpkin with Peppercorns and Garlic

Serves 4–6

Pumpkin? Really? Yes, really. The slightly sweet flavor of the pumpkin handles the strong flavors of the peppercorns and the garlic astonishingly well. I like to serve this as an accompaniment to simple grilled meats.

30 peppercorns
2 cloves garlic
1 tablespoon vegetable oil
2 cups fresh pumpkin pieces, cut into 1-inch cubes
1 cup water
2 tablespoons fish sauce
1 teaspoon sugar

1. Using a mortar and pestle, crush together the peppercorns and the garlic.
2. Add the vegetable oil to a large sauté pan and heat on high. Add the peppercorn-garlic mixture and stir-fry until the garlic just begins to brown.
3. Add the pumpkin pieces, stirring to coat.
4. Add the water and bring the water to a simmer. After the water has been reduced by half, stir in the fish sauce and sugar.
5. Continue to cook until the pumpkin is tender but not mushy.
6. Serve as a side dish.

Thai Pumpkins

In Thailand, the differences between pumpkins and squashes are not very well defined—they basically treat them all the same. The Thai version of a pumpkin is Fug Tong, but almost any fleshy hard squash can be substituted (with different, but delicious, results).

Gingered Green Beans

2 tablespoons vegetable oil
1 stalk lemongrass, minced (inner tender portion only)
1 tablespoon peeled and minced ginger
1–3 (to taste) serrano chilies, seeded and minced
½ cup coconut milk
¼ teaspoon salt
½ pound green beans, trimmed

1. In a medium-sized saucepan, heat the oil on medium-high. Stir in the lemongrass, ginger, and chilies; sauté for 1 to 2 minutes.
2. Stir in the coconut milk and the salt until well combined.
3. Add the green beans, raise the heat to high, and cook for 3 minutes or until the beans are done to your liking.

Serves 2–4

This recipe goes well with grilled steak, especially if the beans have been soaked in an Asian marinade. They also complement seared tuna exceedingly well. Or try tossing them into a salad.

Curried Green Beans

2 tablespoons vegetable oil
2 tablespoons Red Curry Paste (see recipes in Chapter 13)
6 cups chicken or vegetable broth
1 pound green beans, trimmed
Steamed rice

1. In a large saucepan, heat the vegetable oil over medium-high heat.
2. Add the curry paste and stir-fry for 1 minute.
3. Stir in the broth until well combined with the paste. Add the green beans and bring to a low boil. Cook for 15 to 20 minutes to reduce the liquid.
4. Reduce the heat to maintain a hard simmer and continue cooking until the beans are very well done.
5. Serve the beans over steamed rice, ladling the sauce over the top.

Serves 4–6

I usually like my green beans like a really rare steak—just barely heated through. But in this instance, you have to cook the beans almost to a pulp. As the beans break down, they help form the sauce.

Green Beans with Macadamia Nut Sauce

Serves 4–6

The macadamia sauce in this recipe is amazing. I love the complexity of tastes, and the nuts add flavor as well as texture. The sauce is also delicious over some pasta (without the beans).

1 medium onion, chopped
4 whole raw macadamia nuts, chopped
2 cloves garlic, chopped
2 tablespoons vegetable oil
2 tablespoons water
½ teaspoon cayenne pepper
1 teaspoon ground coriander
½ teaspoon ground cumin
1 cup coconut milk
1 bay leaf
½–1 teaspoon salt to taste
1 pound green beans, trimmed

1. Place the onion, macadamia nuts, garlic, vegetable oil, and water in a blender or food processor and process until smooth. Transfer the paste to a small bowl and stir in the cayenne pepper, coriander, and cumin.
2. In a medium-sized saucepan, heat the macadamia nut paste, coconut milk, and bay leaf over medium-high heat. Bring to a simmer, reduce heat, and cook until reduced by half.
3. Stir in the salt. Add the green beans and continue simmering, stirring occasionally, until the beans are done to your liking, about 8 to 10 minutes. Add salt to taste if necessary.

Roasted Asian Cauliflower

1 head cauliflower, broken into florets (cut the florets in half if large)
1 recipe Asian Marinade (see recipes in Chapter 13)

1. Place the cauliflower florets in a large Ziplock bag and pour marinade over them; let rest in the refrigerator for 4 to 6 hours.
2. Preheat the oven to 500 degrees.
3. Place the cauliflower florets in a roasting pan. Roast for approximately 15 minutes or until tender, turning after 7 to 8 minutes.

Serves 6–8

Roasting cauliflower? Yes, another strange idea, but it's actually quite good and it couldn't be much easier.

Spicy Stir-Fried Corn

2 tablespoons vegetable oil
1 stalk lemongrass, minced (tender inner portion only)
2 teaspoons minced garlic
1 tablespoon butter
1 medium onion, minced
4 cups corn kernels (fresh or frozen and thawed are best)
1 cup low-sodium vegetable broth
2 teaspoons lime zest
2 tablespoons fish sauce
Tabasco to taste
2 tablespoons lime juice

1. Place the oil in a large skillet over high heat. Add the lemongrass. As soon as it begins to brown, add the garlic, butter, and onion. Continue to cook on high, letting the ingredients brown somewhat.
2. Add the corn kernels and cook until they brown. Stir in the vegetable stock; stirring constantly, cook the mixture for 2 minutes, scraping the bottom of the pan to loosen any burned-on bits.
3. Stir in the remaining ingredients and cook for 30 more seconds.

Serves 6–8

This corn recipe can be addicting. So be warned! Try serving it with any grilled meat or fish dish.

Grilled Eggplant with an Asian Twist

Serves 4–6

I like cooking with Japanese eggplant because you don't have to go through the process of salting them in order to extract their extra moisture like you do with our larger, more familiar Western ones.

4–8 Japanese eggplants (about 1½ pounds in all)
Olive oil
Salt and pepper to taste
Juice of 1 lemon or lime
1 tablespoon fish sauce
Basil leaves

1. Prepare a grill or broiler. Allow it to achieve high heat.
2. If the eggplants are relatively large, cut in half vertically. Toss them with a little olive oil just to coat, and season with salt and pepper. Place the eggplant either in a vegetable grilling basket or directly on the grill grate or broiler pan. Cook until tender, about 15 to 20 minutes, turning midway through the cooking process.
3. Remove from the heat. Sprinkle with lemon juice and fish sauce.
4. Garnish with basil leaves. Serve either hot or at room temperature.

Japanese Eggplant with Tofu

Serves: 2–4

Both eggplant and tofu are extremely mild by themselves. The zest from this recipe comes from the garlic, serrano chili, and basil—all of which pack quite a punch.

4–6 tablespoons vegetable oil
2–3 cloves garlic, finely chopped
3 cups sliced Japanese eggplant, about ⅛-inch thick
¼ pound extra-firm tofu, cut into small cubes
1–5 (to taste) serrano chili peppers, seeded and minced
10–15 basil leaves
1–3 tablespoons Yellow Bean Sauce (see recipe on page 295)

1. Heat the oil in a large skillet over medium-high heat. Add the garlic and sauté until it turns golden.
2. Add the eggplant and tofu pieces; sauté, stirring constantly, for 5 to 6 minutes or until the eggplant is done to your liking.
3. Carefully stir in the remaining ingredients.
4. Serve immediately to avoid discoloration of the eggplant and basil.

Stir-Fried Black Mushrooms and Asparagus

1 ounce dried Chinese black mushrooms
1 tablespoon vegetable oil
1–2 cloves garlic, minced
3–4 tablespoons oyster sauce
Tabasco (optional)
1 pound asparagus spears, trimmed

1. Place the dried mushrooms in a bowl and cover with hot water. Let soak for 15 minutes. Drain, discard the stems, and slice into strips; set aside.
2. Heat the oil on medium-high in a large skillet. Add the garlic and sauté until golden.
3. Stir in the mushrooms and continue cooking, stirring constantly, for 1 minute.
4. Stir in the oyster sauce and a few drops of Tabasco if desired.
5. Add the asparagus spears. Sauté for 2 to 4 minutes or until the asparagus is done to your liking.

Serves 4–6

The unique sauce in this dish is a far cry from the traditional, super-rich hollandaise sauce or butter and nutmeg traditionally served with asparagus in the West.

Thai-Style Fried Okra

1/3 cup all-purpose flour
1/2 cup tapioca flour
1 teaspoon baking powder
1/2 cup water
1 pound small okra, trimmed
1 cup vegetable oil
1 recipe chili dipping sauce of your choice (see recipes in Chapter 14)

1. In a medium-sized mixing bowl, combine the flours, the baking soda, and water to form a batter. Add the okra pieces.
2. Heat the vegetable oil in a frying pan or wok over high heat. (It should be hot enough that a test piece of batter puffs up immediately.)
3. Add the battered okra, a few at a time, and fry until golden.
4. Using a slotted spoon, remove the okra to paper towels to drain.
5. Serve hot with your favorite chili dipping sauce.

Yields approx. 20

If ever there was a way to eat okra, this is it. The tapioca flour creates a batter that fries up superlight. This dish make a fun appetizer or snack.

Tropical Vegetables

Serves 8–10

Not every ingredient used in Thai cooking is healthy. Coconut, coconut milk, coconut cream, and palm oil are all high in saturated fat. If you are watching your cholesterol, use "lite" coconut milk in this recipe.

1 teaspoon vegetable oil
1 shallot, minced
1 tablespoon sesame seeds
1 tablespoon Red Curry Paste (see recipes in Chapter 13)
½ cup coconut milk
1 tablespoon Tamarind Concentrate (see recipe on page 18)
2 tablespoons brown sugar
1 tablespoon fish sauce
2½ cups green beans, trimmed and cut into 1-inch lengths
1 yellow or red bell pepper, seeded and julienned
2 cups bamboo shoots
2½ cups baby spinach leaves
2 cups bean sprouts

1. To make the sauce, heat the vegetable oil in a small sauté pan on medium-high. Add the minced shallot and fry until golden. Transfer the fried shallot to paper towels to drain.
2. Using a mortar and pestle, crush half of the sesame seeds and half of the fried shallots together; set aside.
3. In a small saucepan, combine the Red Curry Paste and the coconut milk, and bring to a simmer over medium-low heat. Add the tamarind, brown sugar, fish sauce, and the reserved sesame seed–shallot mixture. Reduce heat to low and keep warm.
4. Bring a large saucepan of water to a boil. Add the green beans, the bell pepper pieces, and the bamboo shoots to the water and blanch for 30 seconds to 1 minute or until done to your liking. Using a slotted spoon, remove the vegetables from the water to a colander to drain.
5. Let the water return to boiling and add the spinach leaves and the bean sprouts. Immediately remove them from the water to drain.
6. Toss all of the vegetables together.
7. To serve, place the vegetables in the center of a serving plate. Pour some of the sauce over the vegetables. Pass additional sauce separately.

Thai-Style Bean Sprouts and Snap Peas

2 tablespoons vegetable oil
1 small onion, thinly sliced
1 (1-inch) piece ginger, peeled and minced
Pinch of white pepper
1 tablespoon soy sauce
½ pound sugar snap peas, trimmed
1 pound bean sprouts, rinsed thoroughly and trimmed if necessary
Salt and sugar to taste

1. Heat the vegetable oil over medium-high heat in a large skillet.
2. Add the onion and the ginger and sauté for 1 minute.
3. Stir in the white pepper and the soy sauce.
4. Add the sugar snap peas and cook, stirring constantly, for 1 minute.
5. Add the bean sprouts and cook for 1 more minute while stirring constantly.
6. Add up to ½ teaspoon of salt and a large pinch of sugar to adjust the balance of the sauce. Serve immediately.

Serves 4–6

This recipe lets the peas shine without overpowering their sweet, delicate flavor with anything heavy or overly spicy. The bean sprouts add a nice contrast.

CHAPTER 22

Noodle Dishes

Pad Thai

Serves 2–4

Anyone who has ever eaten in a Thai restaurant has probably had this most famous of Thai noodle dishes. The actual sauce has a rather sweet taste offset by the garlic and peanuts.

8 ounces rice noodles
2 tablespoons vegetable oil
5–6 cloves garlic, finely chopped
2 tablespoons chopped shallots
½ cup cooked salad shrimp
¼ cup fish sauce
¼ cup brown sugar
6–8 teaspoons Tamarind Concentrate (see recipe on page 304)
¼ cup chopped chives
½ cup chopped roasted peanuts
1 medium egg, beaten
1 cup bean sprouts

Garnish:

1 tablespoon lime juice
1 tablespoon Tamarind Concentrate
1 tablespoon fish sauce
½ cup bean sprouts
½ cup chopped chives
½ cup coarsely ground roasted peanuts
1 lime cut into wedges

1. Soak the noodles in water at room temperature for 30 minutes or until soft. Drain and set aside.
2. Heat the vegetable oil in a wok or skillet over medium-high heat. Add the garlic and shallots, and briefly stir-fry until they begin to change color.
3. Add the reserved noodles and all the remaining ingredients except the egg and the bean sprouts, and stir-fry until hot.
4. While constantly stirring, slowly drizzle in the beaten egg.
5. Add the bean sprouts and cook for no more than another 30 seconds.
6. In a small bowl mix together all of the garnish ingredients except the lime wedges.
7. To serve, arrange the Pad Thai on a serving platter. Top with the garnish and surround with lime wedges.

Fire Noodles

15–20 (or to taste) Thai bird chilies, stemmed and seeded
5–10 (or to taste) cloves garlic
1 pound presliced fresh rice noodles (available at Asian grocery stores and on the Internet)
2 tablespoons vegetable oil
2 whole boneless, skinless chicken breasts, cut into bite-sized pieces
2 tablespoons fish sauce
2 tablespoons sweet black soy sauce
1 tablespoon oyster sauce
1 teaspoon white pepper
1½ tablespoons sugar
1 (8-ounce) can bamboo shoots, drained
1½ cups loose-packed basil and/or mint

Serves 4–6

These noodles live up their name—they are not for the faint of heart! The thick, lush noodles somehow have the ability to stand up to the power of the superhot Thai bird chilies and their garlic sidekick.

1. Place the chilies and garlic cloves in a food processor and process until thoroughly mashed together; set aside.
2. Bring a kettle of water to a boil. Place the noodles in a large colander and pour the hot water over them. Carefully unfold and separate the noodles; set aside.
3. Heat the oil in a wok or large skillet over medium-high heat. When it is quite hot, carefully add the reserved chili-garlic mixture and stir-fry for 15 seconds to release the aromas.
4. Raise the heat to high, add the chicken, and stir-fry until it begins to lose its color, about 30 seconds.
5. Stir in the fish sauce, soy sauce, oyster sauce, white pepper, and sugar.
6. Add the noodles and continue to stir-fry for 30 seconds, tossing them with the other ingredients.
7. Add the bamboo shoots and cook for another minute.
8. Turn off the heat and add the basil.

Cooling Down

If you bite into a chili that is just too hot to handle, try sucking on a spoonful of sugar or sucking on a hard candy.

Rice Stick Noodles with Chicken and Vegetables

Serves 2–4

Rice noodles don't really have a Western equivalent. Silky smooth and a bit chewy, these rather flavorless delights absorb the flavors of the other ingredients, becoming one with the dish.

Noodles:

8 ounces rice stick noodles
2 tablespoons vegetable oil
1 tablespoon sweet black soy sauce

Chicken and vegetables:

2 tablespoons vegetable oil
4 cloves garlic, chopped
1 large whole boneless, skinless chicken breast, cut into bite-sized strips
¼ pound broccoli, chopped
1 small onion, finely sliced
1½ cups sliced Japanese eggplant
½ teaspoon Tabasco
2 tablespoons fish sauce
2 tablespoons Yellow Bean Sauce (see recipe on page 295)
3 tablespoons brown sugar
¼ cup chicken broth
1 tablespoon cornstarch mixed with 1 tablespoon water
1 cup bean sprouts
¼–⅓ cup sliced green onions
1 small red bell pepper, seeded and cut into strips

(recipe continues on the next page)

Rice Stick Noodles with Chicken and Vegetables (continued)

Noodles:

1. Soak the noodles in warm water for 15 minutes or until soft; drain.
2. Place a wok over medium-high heat and add the vegetable oil. When the oil is hot, add the noodles and stir-fry vigorously until they are heated through, about 45 seconds to 1 minute.
3. Add the soy sauce and continue to stir-fry for 1 more minute.
4. Place the noodles on a serving platter, covered in foil, in a warm oven until ready to serve.

Chicken and vegetables:

1. Place a wok over medium-high heat and add the vegetable oil. When the oil is hot, add the garlic and stir-fry briefly to release its aroma.
2. Add the chicken and cook until it starts to become opaque.
3. Add the broccoli and stir-fry for 30 seconds.
4. Add the onion and eggplant and stir-fry for 2 minutes.
5. Add the Tabasco, fish sauce, yellow bean sauce, and sugar. Stir-fry for 1 minute.
6. Add the broth, cornstarch mixture, bean sprouts, green onions, and red bell pepper; cook until vegetables are tender-crisp.
7. To serve, ladle the chicken and vegetable mixture over the reserved noodles.

Thai Rice Noodles

Thai rice stick noodles have a transparent appearance, a slightly chewy texture, and almost no flavor, which makes them great for absorbing dressings and sauces. They are also known as rice vermicelli. Cellophane noodles look similar to rice sticks, but are made of mung bean flour. They are also known as bean threads, silver threads, and shining noodles. Before boiling or stir-frying either cellophane or rice stick noodles, they are first soaked in hot water for a few minutes and then cut to the desired length with scissors. Both products can also be fried without soaking, creating a crunchy topping or snack.

Chiang Mai Curried Noodles

Serves 1–2

The combination of red curry paste, yellow curry powder, and gold turmeric produces a lovely orange-tinged sauce in this dish.

½ cup coconut milk
1 tablespoon Red Curry Paste (see recipes in Chapter 13)
1 tablespoon chopped garlic
1 tablespoon curry powder
Pinch of turmeric powder
2 tablespoons fish sauce
Pinch of sugar
1 teaspoon lime juice
¼ pound ground pork
4 ounces rice noodles, soaked in water for 20 to 30 minutes or until soft
Lime wedges, for garnish

1. Heat the coconut milk in a wok or heavy skillet over medium heat. Stir in the curry paste and cook until aromatic and a thin film of oil separates out.
2. Add the garlic and cook for about 30 seconds. Add the remaining ingredients except the pork, noodles, and limes, and cook until the sauce thickens slightly, stirring constantly.
3. Add the pork and continue to stir until the meat is cooked through. Reduce heat and keep the sauce warm.
4. Bring a pan of water to a rolling boil. Place the noodles in a wire basket or strainer and dip the noodles in the water for 10 to 20 seconds. Drain the noodles and transfer to serving plate.
5. Pour the sauce over the noodles. Serve with lime wedges.

Thai Noodle Meals

Ground meat is commonly used in Thai noodle dishes, not only for flavor, but for textural contrast with the noodles.

Pan-Fried Noodles

¾ pound fresh lo mein noodles or angel hair pasta
¼ cup minced chives
2 tablespoons (or to taste) prepared chili-garlic paste
3 tablespoons vegetable oil, divided
Salt to taste

Serves 6–8

People are always amazed when I tell them that the wedge on their plate is noodles! They are crispy on the outside and still noodlelike inside. I like to serve this with anything grilled or roasted.

1. Boil the noodles in a large pot for no more than 2 to 3 minutes. Drain, rinse under cold water, and drain again.
2. Add the chives, chili paste, 1 tablespoon of the oil, and salt to the noodles; toss to coat, and adjust seasonings.
3. In a heavy-bottomed 10-inch skillet, heat the remaining oil over medium-high heat. When it is hot, add the noodle mixture, spreading evenly. Press the noodles into the pan with the back of a spatula. Cook for approximately 2 minutes. Reduce heat and continue to cook until the noodles are nicely browned. Flip the noodles over in 1 piece. Continue cooking until browned, adding additional oil if necessary.
4. To serve, cut the noodles into wedges.

Noodles of Fun

Other Asian noodles include mein, which are Chinese in origin and are similar to Western egg noodles. They are made with wheat flour, water, and egg, and come fresh, dried, or frozen. Japan also has a variety of noodles, including buckwheat Soba, thin wheat Somen, and thicker, rounder Udon, to name a few.

Clear Noodles with Baked Shrimp

Serves 2

Traditionally, this Chinese-inspired dish would be baked in a clay pot, making for a spectacular presentation.

1 7-ounce package rice noodles
2 cloves garlic, chopped
¼ cup chopped cilantro
20–30 black peppercorns
1 tablespoon vegetable oil
1 medium onion, thinly sliced
1 teaspoon sugar
1 tablespoon soy or fish sauce
Sesame oil to taste
6 large shrimp, shell on, rinsed and patted dry

1. Soak the noodles in hot water until soft, about 10 minutes. Drain and set aside.
2. Using a mortar and pestle or a food processor, thoroughly combine the garlic, cilantro, and peppercorns.
3. Add the vegetable oil to a wok or large skillet over low heat. Add the garlic mixture and stir-fry for 1 minute. Add the sliced onion and continue cooking until the onion is tender, then turn off the heat.
4. Add the sugar, soy sauce, and a few drops of sesame oil to the wok; stir to combine. Add the noodles and toss to coat. Pour the noodle mixture into an ovenproof baking dish. Place the whole shrimp on top of the noodles, cover the dish, and bake for 20 minutes in a 400-degree oven. Serve immediately.

Thai Table Setting

A traditional Thai table setting includes only a fork and spoon. The fork is used to push the food onto the spoon, not to place food into the mouth. Only a spoon is used for this.

Sesame Noodles with Veggies

2 tablespoons vegetable oil
2 cloves garlic, minced
2 cups broccoli, cut into bite-sized pieces
1 red bell pepper, seeded and cut into strips
2 tablespoons water
8 ounces egg noodles
4 ounces tofu, cut into bite-sized cubes
1 tablespoon sesame oil
2–3 tablespoons soy sauce
2–3 tablespoons prepared chili sauce
3 tablespoons sesame seeds

1. Heat the oil in a large sauté pan or wok over medium heat. Add the garlic and sauté until golden, approximately 2 minutes.
2. Add the broccoli and red bell pepper, and stir-fry for 2 to 3 minutes. Add the water, cover, and let the vegetables steam until tender, approximately 5 minutes.
3. Bring a large pot of water to boil. Add the noodles and cook until al dente; drain.
4. While the noodles are cooking, add the remaining ingredients to the broccoli mixture. Remove from heat, add the noodles, and toss to combine.

Serves 2–4

Sesame oil is a standard ingredient in most Asian cuisines but is not as common in Thai cooking. However, here it pairs well with the other ingredients to create a subtle perfumed quality.

Panang Mussels and Noodles

Serves 4

The white wine pairs with chicken stock in this dish to form the base of the sauce. The Asian notes come from the Black Bean Paste. If you are a mussel fan, you are sure to think this is a winner.

1 pound Asian egg noodles
2 tablespoons vegetable oil
1 teaspoon Black Bean Paste (see recipe on page 296)
1 medium onion, chopped
6–8 stalks celery, chopped
¼ cup white wine
2 cups chicken broth
1 pound mussels, washed and debearded

1. Bring a large pot of water to a boil over high heat. Add the noodles and cook until al dente. Rinse the noodles under cold water and set aside.
2. Heat the oil in a large sauté pan over medium heat. Add the Black Bean Paste, onion, and celery, and sauté for 5 minutes.
3. Add the wine and chicken broth, and bring to a boil.
4. Add the mussels and reduce heat to low; cover and steam for 5 minutes.
5. To serve, divide the noodles between 4 soup plates. Divide the mussels between the plates (discarding any that have not opened) and pour the broth over the top.

Flowered Lime Noodles

Serves 4

Subtly flavored with lime juice and rose petals, this is not exactly a traditional Thai dish (the Parmesan gives it away), but it's so good I had to include it. If you are a purist, leave the cheese out.

8 ounces angel hair pasta
1 tablespoon salted butter
2–3 tablespoons lime juice
4 ounces grated Parmesan cheese
Rose petals or other organic edible flowers
Lime slices
Black pepper

1. Bring a large pot of water to a boil over high heat. Add pasta and cook according to package instructions; drain.
2. Toss the pasta with butter, lime juice, and parmesan.
3. To serve, top with rose or flower petals and lime slices. Pass black pepper at the table.

Poached Chicken Breast with Peanut Sauce and Noodles

⅔ cup crunchy peanut butter
1½ cups coconut milk
2 tablespoons fish sauce
¼ cup lime juice
2 teaspoons brown sugar
4 cloves garlic, minced
Salt and pepper to taste
¼ cup chicken stock
¼ cup half-and-half
1 pound Chinese egg noodles (mein)
1 tablespoon peanut oil
1 tablespoon sesame oil
6–8 green onions, trimmed and thinly sliced
3 whole boneless, skinless chicken breasts, halved and poached
1 pound snow peas, trimmed and blanched

Serves 6

Using chicken satay as a starting point, this dish is a bit more upscale. It's a great luncheon or brunch item because it's not heavy or overpowering, but still rich in flavor.

1. Combine the peanut butter, coconut milk, fish sauce, lime juice, brown sugar, garlic, salt, and pepper in a small saucepan over low heat. Cook until smooth and thick, stirring frequently.
2. Transfer to a blender and purée.
3. Add the chicken stock and half-and-half, and blend; set aside.
4. Bring a large pot of water to a boil. Add the noodles and cook until al dente. Drain, rinse under cold water, and drain again.
5. Toss the noodles with the peanut and sesame oils.
6. To serve, place some pasta in the middle of each serving plate. Spoon some of the peanut sauce over the pasta. Slice each chicken breast on the diagonal. Transfer 1 sliced breast to the top of each portion of noodles. Spoon some additional peanut sauce over the chicken. Surround the noodles with the snow peas. Garnish with the sliced green onions.

Thai Noodles with Chicken and Pork

Serves 4–6

Hot chili oil adds heat, depth of flavor, and a bit of color. If you use it as a condiment, do so sparingly. It packs a punch and, because it is an oil, quickly permeates whatever it's put on.

For the sauce:

½ cup peanut butter
½ cup soy sauce
1 teaspoon minced garlic
3 tablespoons sesame oil
3 tablespoons honey
1 teaspoon hot chili oil
¼ teaspoon white pepper

For the noodles:

1 pound dry flat Asian noodles
1 tablespoon vegetable oil
1 teaspoon sesame oil
½ teaspoon minced garlic
½ pound boneless, skinless chicken breast, sliced thin
½ pound boneless pork tenderloin, cut into thin strips
1 large yellow onion, diced
6 ounces salad shrimp
6–8 green onions, trimmed, white portions sliced, green portions julienned

1. Place all of the sauce ingredients in a blender and process until smooth; set aside.
2. Bring a large pot of water to boil over high heat. Prepare the noodles according to package directions, drain, and stir in the sauce mixture, reserving ¼ cup; set aside.
3. Heat the oils in a large sauté pan over high heat. Add the garlic and sauté briefly.
4. Add the chicken, pork, and onion, and sauté for 5 to 6 minutes or until the meats are cooked through.
5. Add the white portion of the green onion and the shrimp and sauté for 2 more minutes.
6. Add the green parts of the onions and the remaining sauce, stirring until everything is well coated.
7. To serve, place the noodles on a large platter and top with the meat sauté. Pass additional hot chili oil separately.

Spicy Egg Noodles with Sliced Pork

1 small cabbage, shredded
1 cup bean sprouts
1 package fresh angel hair pasta
½ teaspoon vegetable oil
4 tablespoons minced garlic
2 tablespoons fish sauce
2 tablespoons sugar
4–6 tablespoons rice vinegar
2 teaspoons ground dried red chili pepper (or to taste)
1 small Barbecued Pork Tenderloin (see recipe on page 380), thinly sliced
Freshly ground black pepper to taste
2 scallions, trimmed and thinly sliced
2 teaspoons chopped cilantro

Serves 2 as a main course or 4 as an appetizer.

If you don't have left-over pork, but still want to make a quick version of this dish, slice some store-bought roast chicken over the top.

1. Bring a large pot of water to a boil over high heat. Add the cabbage and blanch about 30 seconds. Using a slotted spoon, remove the cabbage from the boiling water; set aside.
2. Let the water return to boiling. Add the bean sprouts and blanch for 10 seconds. Using a slotted spoon, remove the sprouts from the water; set aside.
3. Return the water to boiling. Add the fresh angel hair pasta and cook according to package directions. Drain the pasta and place it in a large mixing bowl.
4. In a small sauté pan, heat the vegetable oil over medium heat. Add the garlic and sauté until golden. Remove from heat. Stir in the fish sauce, sugar, rice vinegar, and dried chili pepper.
5. Pour the sauce over the pasta and toss to coat.
6. To serve, divide the cabbage and the bean sprouts into 2 to 4 portions and place in the center of serving plates. Divide the noodles into 2 to 4 portions and place over the cabbage and sprouts. Divide the pork slices over the noodles. Grind black pepper to taste over the noodles and top with the sliced scallions and chopped cilantro.

Curried Rice Noodles with Tofu and Egg

Serves 2 as a main course or 4 as an appetizer.

The combination of ingredients in this dish create a curry that is a bit spicy but has definite sweet overtones.

½ teaspoon ground coriander
½ teaspoon ground cumin
1 teaspoon curry powder
1 tablespoon Red Curry Paste (see recipes in Chapter 13)
1 cup coconut milk
2–3 cups water
2 tablespoons minced shallots
2 tablespoons sugar
2 tablespoons fish sauce
½ of a 7-ounce package rice noodles
1 hard-boiled egg, sliced
⅓ cup cubed extra-firm tofu
⅓ cup bean sprouts
1 green onion, trimmed and thinly sliced
2 tablespoons chopped cilantro

1. In a small bowl, thoroughly combine the coriander, cumin, curry powder, and curry paste.
2. Pour the coconut milk into a medium-sized saucepan. Stir in the curry paste mixture and place over medium heat. Bring to a simmer and cook for about 5 minutes or until a thin layer of yellow oil begins to form on the surface of the sauce.
3. Stir in 2 cups of the water, the shallots, sugar, and fish sauce. Return the sauce to a simmer and let cook 30 minutes, stirring occasionally and adding additional water if necessary.
4. Meanwhile, soak the noodles in hot water for 10 minutes or until soft.
5. To serve, mound the noodles into serving bowls. Top the noodles with the sliced egg, tofu, and bean sprouts. Ladle some of the curry sauce over top. Sprinkle with green onion slices and chopped cilantro.

Broccoli Noodles with Garlic and Soy

1 pound broccoli, trimmed into bite-sized florets
16 ounces rice noodles
1–2 tablespoons vegetable oil
2 cloves garlic, minced
2 tablespoons soy sauce
1 tablespoon sweet soy sauce
1 tablespoon sugar
Hot sauce
Fish sauce
Lime wedges

1. Bring a pot of water to boil over high heat. Drop in the broccoli and blanch until tender-crisp or to your liking. Drain and set aside.
2. Soak the rice noodles in hot water until soft, about 10 minutes.
3. In a large sauté pan, heat the vegetable oil on medium. Add the garlic and stir-fry until golden. Add the soy sauces and the sugar, stirring until the sugar has completely dissolved.
4. Add the reserved noodles, tossing until well coated with the sauce. Add the broccoli and toss to coat.
5. Serve immediately with hot sauce, fish sauce, and lime wedges on the side.

Serves 2–4

Try substituting other sturdy green vegetables such as asparagus, quartered Brussels sprouts, or green beans.

CHAPTER 23

Rice Dishes

Basic White Rice

Serves 2–4

If you take only one thing away from this book, it should be how to make great rice from scratch. No parboiled, precooked, or dehydrated rice would ever find its way into a true Thai cook's kitchen.

1 cup long-grain rice (such as Jasmine)

2 cups water

1. Place the rice in a colander and run under cool water.*
2. Place the rice and the water in a medium-sized pot. Stir briefly. Bring to a rolling boil over medium-high heat. Reduce heat to low, cover, and simmer for 18 to 20 minutes.
3. Remove the rice from the heat, keeping it covered, and let it rest for at least 10 minutes.
4. Fluff the rice just before serving.

* Washing rice is completely optional. By rinsing the rice, you remove some of the starch. The end result will be slightly whiter rice, but rice with a little less nutritional value.

Can I Use a Cooking Liquid Other Than Water?

Traditionally, Thai meals call for white rice that has been steamed in water. However, rice is terrific when a low-salt stock such as chicken or vegetable is used in place of the water. Another flavorful liquid substitution is a combination of half water and half coconut milk.

Basic Sticky Rice

1 cup glutinous rice
Water

1. Place the rice in a bowl, completely cover it with water, and let soak overnight. Drain before using.
2. Line a steamer basket or colander with moistened cheesecloth. (This prevents the grains of rice from falling through the holes in the colander.)
3. Spread the rice over the cheesecloth as evenly as you can.
4. Bring a pan of water with a cover to a rolling boil. Place the basket over the boiling water, making sure that the bottom of it does not touch the water. Cover tightly and let steam for 25 minutes.

Serves 2–4

Sticky rice takes a little more practice to master (well, at least it did for me), but this, too, is a staple in the Thai kitchen. Take the time to get it right and don't get upset if it takes you a few tries to get it exactly right.

Sticky Rice Varieties

Sticky rice comes in white, red, and black varieties. If you choose either red or black, you will need to increase the steaming time to at least 1 hour.

Sweet-Spiced Fried Rice

Makes approx. 4 cups

Although sweet spiced, this is still a savory side dish, great alongside grilled meat or fish.

1½ cups long-grained rice (such as Jasmine)
3 tablespoons vegetable oil
½ onion, sliced into rings
1 (1-inch) cinnamon stick
1 bay leaf
3 cloves
½ teaspoon mace
1 tablespoon brown sugar
Salt
2¼ cups water

1. Soak the rice in cold water for 20 minutes.
2. Meanwhile, heat the oil in a medium-sized pot over medium heat. Add the onions and sauté until golden, approximately 10 to 15 minutes.
3. Add the spices and sauté for an additional 2 minutes. Sprinkle the brown sugar over the onion mixture and caramelize for 1 to 2 minutes, stirring constantly. Add the rice and sauté for an additional 3 minutes, stirring constantly.
4. Add the salt and the water to the pot and bring to a boil. Reduce heat, cover, and simmer until the rice is tender, approximately 10 to 15 minutes.
5. Remove the cinnamon stick and cloves before serving.

Rice Nutrition

Rice's nutritional value is dependent on its processing method, not just its variety. Modern polishing methods, which produce gleaming white kernels, remove most of the minerals and vitamins, leaving only carbohydrates. More traditional polishing methods retain vitamins A, B, C, D, and E and protease inhibitors, which are all cancer retardants.

Fried Rice with Pineapple and Shrimp

1 ripe whole pineapple
4 tablespoons vegetable oil
⅓ cup finely chopped onion
2 garlic cloves, finely minced
10 ounces peeled shrimp, deveined and cut into ½-inch pieces
½ teaspoon turmeric
½ teaspoon curry powder
½ teaspoon shrimp paste
2¼ cups day-old, cooked Jasmine or other long-grained rice
Salt to taste
Sugar to taste

Serves 2–4

This dish makes a great presentation and the fruit and spices complements the shrimp perfectly. Make some extra—this dish reheats in a microwave perfectly, as do almost all fried rice dishes.

1. To prepare the pineapple, cut it in half lengthwise, leaving the leaves intact on 1 side. Scoop out the pineapple flesh of both halves, leaving a ½-inch edge on the half with the leaves. Reserve the hollowed-out half to use as a serving bowl. Dice the pineapple fruit and set aside.
2. Preheat the oven to 350 degrees.
3. In a wok or heavy sauté pan, heat the oil on medium. Add the onion and garlic, and sauté until the onion is translucent. Using a slotted spoon, remove the onions and garlic from the wok and set aside.
4. Add the shrimp and sauté approximately 1 minute; remove and set aside.
5. Add the turmeric, curry powder, and shrimp paste to the wok; stir-fry briefly. Add the rice and stir-fry for 2 to 3 minutes. Add the pineapple and continue to cook. Add the reserved shrimp, onions, and garlic. Season to taste with salt and sugar.
6. Mound the fried rice into the pineapple "serving bowl." Place the pineapple on a baking sheet and bake for approximately 10 minutes. Serve immediately.

Vegetarian Fried Rice

Serves 4–6

Yes, this fried rice is vegetarian, but it's certainly not boring. It's chock full of flavorful veggies and gets a flavor boost from both lime juice and brown sugar, ingredients not too common in fried rice.

3 tablespoons vegetable oil, divided
3 cups day-old long-grained rice
½ cup finely diced onion
2 garlic cloves, finely chopped
1 tablespoon finely chopped fresh gingerroot
2 red chili peppers, seeded, veined, and thinly sliced
4 scallions, sliced
7 ounces green beans, trimmed and cut into 1-inch pieces
2 medium carrots, peeled and julienned into 1-inch pieces
2 stalks of celery, sliced
½ cup vegetable stock
9 ounces tomatoes, peeled, seeded, and diced
2 tablespoons vegetarian "oyster" sauce
3 tablespoons soy sauce
½ teaspoon ground turmeric
Salt and freshly ground pepper to taste
Grated zest and juice of ½ of a lime
½ teaspoon brown sugar

1. In a wok or large sauté pan, heat 2 tablespoons of the vegetable oil over medium-high heat. Add the rice and stir-fry for 2 to 3 minutes. Remove the rice from the wok and set aside.
2. Add the remaining tablespoon of oil to the wok. Add the onion, garlic, and ginger; sauté for 1 minute.
3. Add the chilies, scallions, green beans, carrots, and celery; stir-fry for 3 minutes.
4. Add the stock and bring to a boil; reduce heat and simmer for 5 minutes.
5. Add the tomatoes and simmer for an additional 2 minutes.
6. Add the "oyster" and soy sauces and turmeric. Season to taste with salt and pepper.
7. Stir in the lime zest, lime juice, brown sugar, and rice. Mix until combined.

Chicken Fried Rice

1 tablespoon vegetable oil
1 tablespoon minced garlic
1 tablespoon minced ginger
1 medium onion, sliced
½ medium head Chinese cabbage, coarsely chopped
3 cups cooked long-grain white rice
¼ cup fish sauce
¼ cup dry sherry
¼ cup chicken stock
1 cup snow peas, trimmed and cut into bite-sized pieces
1 cup shredded, cooked chicken
2 eggs, beaten

Serves 4–6

Chicken and rice, comfort foods the world over, are combined here in a great tasting entrée. Cabbage and snow peas give the dish a little crunch and the aromatic garlic, ginger, and onion embolden the flavor.

1. In a large skillet or wok, heat the oil over medium-low heat. Add the garlic, ginger, and onion, and stir-fry for 5 minutes or until the onion becomes translucent.
2. Add the cabbage, increase the heat to medium, and stir-fry for 10 minutes.
3. Add the rice and stir-fry for 2 minutes.
4. Combine the fish sauce, sherry, and stock in a small bowl; add to the wok and stir to combine.
5. Add the snow peas and chicken; stir-fry for 2 minutes more.
6. Move the rice to the sides of the wok, forming a hole in the middle. Pour the eggs into the hole and cook for about 1 minute, stirring the eggs with a fork. Fold the cooked eggs into the fried rice.

Serving Rice

In Southeast Asia, baskets are lined with banana leaves or lettuce and used as serving dishes for rice.

Far East Fried Rice

Serves 4–6

This fried rice dish uses fish sauce, rice vinegar, and red pepper flakes to add spark. The recipe does not call for any meat, but if you have any left over by all means use it here!

2 tablespoons fish sauce
1½ tablespoons rice vinegar
2 tablespoons sugar
2½ tablespoons vegetable oil
2 eggs, beaten
1 bunch green onions, trimmed and thinly sliced
2 tablespoons minced garlic
1 teaspoon dried red chili pepper flakes
2 large carrots, peeled and coarsely shredded
2 cups bean sprouts, trimmed if necessary
5 cups day-old long-grain white rice, clumps broken up
¼ cup chopped mint or cilantro leaves
¼ cup roasted peanuts, chopped

1. Combine the fish sauce, rice vinegar, and sugar in a small bowl; set aside.
2. In a wok or large skillet, heat the oil over medium-high heat. Add the eggs and stir-fry until scrambled.
3. Add the green onions, garlic, and pepper flakes and continue to stir-fry for 15 seconds or until fragrant.
4. Add the carrots and bean sprouts; stir-fry until the carrots begin to soften, about 2 minutes.
5. Add the rice and cook for 2 to 3 minutes or until heated through.
6. Stir in the fish sauce mixture and add the fried rice, tossing until evenly coated.
7. To serve, garnish the rice with chopped mint, or cilantro, and chopped peanuts.

Fried Rice with Tomatoes

3 tablespoons vegetable oil
1 whole boneless, skinless chicken breast, cut into bite-sized pieces
1 clove garlic, minced
1 medium onion, slivered
2 eggs
4 cups cooked rice
1 tomato, cut into 8–10 wedges
1 green onion, trimmed and sliced
2 teaspoons soy sauce
1 teaspoon fish sauce
1 teaspoon sugar
1 teaspoon ground white pepper

Serves 2–4

You don't see tomatoes used very often in Thai cooking, so they are definitely a surprise in this fried rice recipe. I like the color and the flavor they add to an otherwise basic dish.

1. In a large skillet or wok, heat the vegetable oil on medium-high. Add the chicken pieces and the garlic, and stir-fry 1 minute.
2. Add the onion and continue to stir-fry for an additional minute.
3. Break in the eggs, mixing well.
4. Stir in all the remaining ingredients; stir-fry for 2 more minutes.
5. Serve immediately.

Storing Cooked Rice

Cooked rice is very susceptible to spoilage. It should not be left at room temperature longer than it needs to be for serving, and should not be stored in the fridge for more than 3 days (in an airtight container). Rice can also be frozen in an airtight container for up to 6 months.

Fried Rice with Chinese Olives

Serves 2–3

Here's another ingredient you probably don't associate with Asian food—olives. Chinese olives are rather small and quite salty. They aren't the easiest thing to find: check a local Asian market.

3 tablespoons vegetable oil
3 cloves garlic, minced
½ cup ground pork or chicken
10 Chinese olives, pitted and chopped
3 cups day-old cooked rice
Fish sauce (optional)
Cucumber slices
Lime wedges
Chopped cilantro
Hot sauce

1. Heat the oil in a wok or large skillet on medium. Add the garlic and stir-fry briefly. Add the pork and olives. Stir-fry until the pork is cooked through and any juices that have accumulated have cooked off.
2. Add the rice, breaking up any clumps, and stir-fry until the rice is hot. Adjust the saltiness with a bit of fish sauce if necessary.
3. Serve accompanied by cucumber slices, lime wedges, chopped cilantro, and hot sauce.

Cilantro

It is a proven fact that some people cannot stand the taste of cilantro—it is like an allergy of the tastebuds! If you or someone you're cooking for falls into this category, fresh parsley makes an acceptable—if not dull—substitute.

Ginger Rice

2 tablespoons vegetable oil
1 (½-inch) piece of gingerroot, peeled and thinly sliced
1 stalk lemongrass, sliced into rings (tender inner portion only)
2–3 green onions, sliced into rings
1 red chili pepper, seeded and minced
1½ cups long-grained rice
Pinch of brown sugar
Pinch of salt
Juice of ½ lime
2¾ cups water

Serves 4–6

It may take a few extra minutes to prep the flavoring agents in this rice side dish, but it's well worth the effort. I like it so much that sometimes I eat the leftovers for lunch without anything else

1. In a medium-sized pot, heat the oil over medium heat. Add the gingerroot, lemongrass, green onions, and chili pepper; sauté for 2 to 3 minutes.
2. Add the rice, brown sugar, salt, and lime juice, and continue to sauté for an additional 2 minutes. Add the water to the pot and bring to a boil.
3. Reduce the heat, cover with a tight-fitting lid, and simmer for 15 to 20 minutes, until the liquid is absorbed.

Do Not Disturb

As a general rule, do not stir simmering rice—as it causes the grains to break, resulting in a gummy end product.

Curried Rice

Serves 4–6

This rice dish shines with the flavors of India. Curry powder, golden raisins, and mango chutney give the rice a slightly sweet, slightly spicy taste that works really well with grilled chicken.

2 tablespoons vegetable oil
½ cup finely chopped onion
1½ cups long-grained rice
1 teaspoon curry powder
2¾ cups vegetable stock
Salt to taste
¼ cup golden raisins (regular raisins can be substituted)
2 teaspoons Mango Chutney *(see recipe on page 560)*

1. In a medium-sized pot, heat the oil over medium heat. Add the onions and sauté for 2 minutes, until the onions are soft but not browned.
2. Add the rice and continue to sauté for an additional 2 minutes. Add the curry powder and sauté for 1 more minute.
3. Pour in the vegetable stock and season with salt. Bring to a boil, then reduce heat and cover. Simmer the rice for 15 to 20 minutes, stirring occasionally.
4. Add the raisins and the chutney. Continue to simmer for an additional 5 minutes or until tender.

Chutney Convenience

Chutneys are one of those few blessings that are almost better in preserved jar form. However, a good jarred chutney can be pricey, and it isn't so hard to make!

Lemon Rice

1 1/3 cups water
Pinch of salt
1 cup basmati rice, soaked in cold water for 30 minutes
1/2 teaspoon turmeric
1 tablespoon vegetable oil
1 green chili pepper, seeded and minced
1/4 cup cashew nuts, soaked in cold water for 5 minutes
1/4 teaspoon mustard seed
8 fresh curry leaves
Juice of 1/2 lemon

Serves 2–4

Fresh curry leaves add a delightful flavor and aroma to this dish. The leaves are edible, but you will be chewing for a long time if you try.

1. In a medium-sized pan, bring the water to a boil. Add the salt, rice, and turmeric; reduce heat, cover, and simmer for 10 minutes. (At the end of the 10 minutes, the rice will have absorbed all of the liquid.) Remove from heat and let cool.
2. In a wok, heat the oil and stir-fry the chili pepper. Add the nuts, mustard seed, and curry leaves; continue to cook for an additional 30 seconds. Stir in the lemon juice. Add the cooled rice to the wok and toss until heated.

Chili Safety

The oils in chilies are very caustic. Wear gloves while you work with them and make sure not to touch your eyes.

Dill Rice

Serves 2–4

I like to add fresh dill to everything, especially when it's growing like a weed in my garden. I throw it in soups, tuna or chicken salad, or use it as a green in a tossed salad.

2 tablespoons vegetable oil
2 green cardamom pods
4 tablespoons chopped fresh dill
1 cup long-grained rice (such as Jasmine)
1 green chili pepper, seeded and minced
Salt
1½ cups water

1. In a medium-sized pot, heat the vegetable oil over medium heat. Add the cardamom pods and sauté for 1 minute. Add the chili and sauté briefly. Stir in the salt and the dill and cook for an additional 2 to 3 minutes. Add the rice and sauté for 3 more minutes.
2. Stir in the water and bring the mixture to a boil. Reduce heat, cover, and simmer for 20 to 25 minutes or until the liquid has been absorbed.
3. Remove the cardamom pods and fluff the rice before serving.

Fragrant White Rice

Serves 6–8

Fresh aromatic herbs and spices flavor this sublime side dish. The rice is cooked in a combination of coconut milk and water, which gives it a richer consistency than if it were only cooked with water.

2 tablespoons vegetable oil
10 fresh curry leaves
1 stalk lemongrass, cut into thin rings (inner tender potion only)
Zest of ½ kaffir lime
2 mace blades
6 cloves
2½ cups Jasmine rice
1¾ cups water
1¼ cups coconut milk
Salt and freshly ground pepper to taste

1. In a medium-large saucepan, heat the oil on medium. Add the curry leaves and sauté until you can begin to smell the aroma. Add the lime zest and the remaining spices and sauté for an additional 2 to 3 minutes, stirring constantly.
2. Add the rice to the pot and stir to combine with the spice mixture. Add the water, coconut milk, and salt and pepper. Bring to a boil; reduce heat, cover, and simmer for 15 to 20 minutes or until the liquids have been absorbed. Adjust seasoning.

Shrimp Rice

5 tablespoons dried shrimp, soaked in cold water for 10 minutes
2 red chili peppers, seeded, veined, and finely minced
1 medium to large onion, finely chopped
2 cloves garlic, finely chopped
5 tablespoons vegetable oil
4 tablespoons fish sauce
1 tablespoon lime juice
Salt to taste
1¾ cups long-grained rice
1 stalk lemongrass, halved and crushed (inner white potion only)
1 quart water

Serves 4–6

This is not shrimp fried rice, but rather shrimp-flavored rice. In fact, there are no fresh shrimp in it at all. The rice gets its shrimp overtones from the combination of dried shrimp and fish sauce.

1. Make a shrimp paste by combining the dried shrimp, chili peppers, onion, and garlic in a blender or food processor and processing until smooth.
2. In a medium-sized saucepan, warm the oil over medium heat. Add the shrimp paste and cook for 3 to 4 minutes, stirring constantly.
3. Add the fish sauce, lime juice, and salt to the paste and stir until well blended; set aside.
4. Pour the rice into a large pot and place the lemongrass on top. Add the water and bring to a boil; reduce heat, cover, and simmer for 15 minutes.
5. Remove the lemongrass stalk and stir in the shrimp paste. Continue cooking for 5 to 10 minutes or until the rice is done.

Flavorful Steamed Rice

Serves 2–4

This rice is prepared in a manner similar to that of glutinous or sticky rice, the result being a slightly softer, but not mushy, long-grained rice. The extra softening allows the flavoring agents to be better absorbed.

¾ cup long-grained rice
2 cloves garlic, minced
1 teaspoon salt
¼ cup chicken or vegetable broth
1 tablespoon minced gingerroot
2 green onions, trimmed and thinly sliced
2 teaspoons lime juice
1 teaspoon fish sauce
½ cup finely chopped cilantro

1. Bring a pot of water to a rolling boil. Add the rice, let the water return to a boil, and cook for 10 minutes. Drain in a sieve, rinse, and set aside. (Leave the rice in the sieve.)
2. Add 1 inch of water to the pot and bring to a boil. Set the sieve over the boiling water, cover it with a clean kitchen towel and a lid, and let steam for about 20 minutes. (Check occasionally, adding more water if necessary.)
3. Mash together the garlic and the salt to form a paste.
4. In a large bowl, combine the garlic paste, broth, gingerroot, green onions, lime juice, and fish sauce.
5. Add the steamed rice and toss until well combined. Let cool to room temperature.
6. Stir the cilantro into the rice.

Fragrant Brown Rice

2 tablespoons vegetable oil
2 garlic cloves, minced
4 green onions, trimmed and thinly sliced
1½ stalks celery, trimmed and thinly sliced
1 medium carrot, peeled and julienned
2 red chili peppers, seeded and minced
1 tablespoon finely chopped gingerroot
1⅔ cups brown rice (white rice can be substituted)
4½–5½ cups vegetable stock
1 kaffir lime leaf or 2 (2-inch-long, ½-inch-wide) pieces of lime zest
1 tablespoon lime juice
Salt and freshly ground pepper to taste

Serves 4–6

Just because this dish is extra healthy, that doesn't mean it doesn't taste terrific. Brown rice is more nutritious than white because the nutrient-rich outer layer is not rubbed off in the polishing process.

1. In a medium to large saucepan, heat the vegetable oil on medium. Add the garlic and green onions, and cook for 2 minutes. Add the celery, carrots, chilies, and ginger, and cook for an additional 2 minutes.
2. Add the rice and stir until well combined. Add half of the vegetable stock, the kaffir lime leaf, lime juice, and salt and pepper. Bring to a boil; reduce heat and simmer, uncovered, for 45 to 50 minutes, adding additional stock as needed.

CHAPTER 24

Desserts

Sweet Sticky Rice

Serves 6

There is not much to this dessert, but it's delicious. I love the somewhat gelatinous quality this rice takes on. The rice is intended to be eaten alongside fresh fruits, but I think it's pretty tasty all by itself.

1½ cups white glutinous rice
1⅓ cups canned coconut milk
½ cup granulated sugar
½ teaspoon salt

1. Place the rice in a bowl and add enough water to completely cover the rice. Soak for at least 4 hours or overnight. Drain.
2. Line a steamer basket with wet cheesecloth. Spread the rice evenly over the cheesecloth. Place the container over rapidly boiling water. Cover and steam until tender, about 25 minutes; set aside.
3. In a medium-sized saucepan, combine the coconut milk, sugar, and salt and heat on medium-high. Stir until the sugar is completely dissolved. Pour over the rice, stir to combine, and let rest for 30 minutes.
4. To serve, place in small bowls or on plates. Garnish with mangoes, papayas, or other tropical fruit.

Tropical Coconut Rice

Serves 6–8

Coconut and rice are the most typical ingredients found in Thai desserts. This one calls for coconut, not only coconut in a semiliquid form but also toasted.

2 cups short-grained rice
2 cups water
1 cup coconut cream
¼ cup toasted coconut (see "Toasted Coconut" on page 302)
½ cup finely chopped tropical fruits of your choice

1. Put the rice, water, and coconut cream in a medium-sized saucepan and mix well. Bring to a boil over medium-high heat. Reduce heat and cover with a tight-fitting lid. Cook for 15 to 20 minutes or until all of the liquid has been absorbed.
2. Let the rice rest off the heat for 5 minutes.
3. Fluff the rice and stir in the toasted coconut and fruit.

Sticky Rice with Coconut Cream Sauce

1 cup coconut cream
4 tablespoons sugar
1 teaspoon salt
4 ripe mangoes, thinly sliced (or other tropical fruits)
3 cups cooked Sweet Sticky Rice (see recipe on page 470)

1. For the sauce, place the coconut cream, sugar, and salt in a small saucepan. Stir to combine and bring to a boil over medium-high heat. Reduce heat and simmer for 5 minutes.
2. To serve, arrange mango slices on each plate. Place a mound of rice next to the fruit. Top the rice with some of the sauce.

Serves 6

Here the coconut is not cooked into the sticky rice, but makes its way into the sauce. Tropical fruit is served alongside.

Peeling, Pitting, and Slicing a Mango

Cut the skin off the mango lengthwise on both sides and peel back the skin. Cut the flesh off the mango pit in long vertical strips. Slice or dice as desired.

Pineapple Rice

Serves 4–6

As you have probably noticed, rice is used in every Thai meal—breakfast, lunch, and dinner.

1 ripe pineapple
¼ cup sugar
Pinch of salt
½ cup short-grained rice
Zest and juice of 1 lemon
2 teaspoons chopped crystallized ginger, divided
3 tablespoons roasted cashew nuts, chopped

1. Cut the pineapple in half lengthwise, leaving the leaves intact on 1 side. Scoop out the pineapple flesh of both halves, leaving a ½-inch edge on the half with the leaves. Dice the pineapple fruit from 1 half and purée the fruit from the other half in a food processor along with the sugar and salt; set aside.
2. Strain the fruit purée through a fine-mesh sieve into a measuring cup. Add enough water to make 1¾ cups. Transfer to a small saucepan and bring to a boil over medium-high heat.
3. Rinse and drain the rice. Stir the rice into the pineapple purée. Stir in the lemon zest, lemon juice, and 1 teaspoon of the ginger. Bring to a boil; reduce heat, cover, and simmer until the liquid has been absorbed, about 20 minutes.
4. Mix the reserved pineapple cubes into the rice.
5. To serve, spoon the rice into the hollowed out pineapple that has the leaves. Garnish with the remaining ginger and the roasted cashews.

Crystallized Ginger

Crystallized ginger is small ginger pieces, usually about ¼-inch dice, that has been simmered in syrup and then dried. The result is a slightly chewy, spicy-sweet candylike condiment. It can be found in specialty grocery stores.

Crispy Crepes with Fresh Fruit

1 package frozen puff pastry sheets, thawed according to package instructions
2 tablespoons confectioner's sugar, divided
2 cups raspberries, blueberries, or other fresh fruit, the best 12 berries reserved for garnish
1 cup heavy cream
¼ cup shredded, unsweetened coconut
1 tablespoon unflavored rum or coconut-flavored rum

Serves 4

If you want to substitute a mixture of tropical fruits for the berries, feel free.

1. Preheat oven to 400 degrees.
2. Place the puff pastry sheet on a work surface and cut into 12 equal-sized pieces. Place the pastry pieces on a baking sheet.
3. Bake the pastry approximately 10 minutes. Remove from the oven and use a sifter to shake a bit of the confectioner's sugar over the puff pastry. Return to the oven and continue baking for approximately 5 minutes or until golden. Place the puff pastry on a wire rack and let cool to room temperature.
4. Place the berries in a food processor and briefly process to form a rough purée.
5. Whip the cream with the remaining confectioner's sugar until thick, but not stiff. Stir in the coconut and the rum.
6. To serve, place 1 piece of puff pastry in the middle of each serving plate, spoon some cream over the pastry, and then top with some purée. Place another pastry on top, garnish with some of the remaining berries, any leftover juice from the purée, and a sprinkle of confectioner's sugar.

Tropical Fruit with Ginger Crème Anglaise

Yields 1½ cups

Here I've taken a standard crème anglaise and infused it with fresh ginger, giving the sauce a slightly piquant flavor. This sauce is equally tasty over gingerbread or sponge cake.

4 (1-inch) pieces peeled gingerroot, slightly mashed
1 cup half-and-half
3 egg yolks
2 tablespoons sugar
A variety of tropical fruits, sliced

1. In a small heavy saucepan over medium-low heat, bring the ginger and the half-and-half to a slight simmer. Do not boil.
2. In the meantime, whisk together the eggs yolks and the sugar.
3. Slowly pour the hot half-and-half into the egg mixture, stirring constantly so that the eggs do not cook.
4. Pour the custard back into the saucepan and cook over medium-low heat, stirring constantly with a wooden spoon for 5 minutes or until slightly thickened.
5. Pour the crème anglaise through a mesh strainer into a clean bowl and let cool to room temperature.
6. Pour over slices of your favorite tropical fruits.

Freezing Ginger

Ginger freezes fantastically. However, you may want to peel it, cut it into 1-inch pieces, and then wrap it tightly before doing so.

Fresh Oranges in Rose Water

8 oranges
3 cups water
1½ cups sugar
4–6 teaspoons rose water

1. Peel and segment the oranges. Place them in a bowl, cover, and set aside in the refrigerator.
2. In a saucepan, bring the water and the sugar to a boil over medium-high heat. Boil gently for 15 to 20 or until the mixture becomes syrupy. Remove from heat and stir in the rose water. Let cool to room temperature and then refrigerate.
3. To serve, place orange segments in individual dessert cups. Pour rose water syrup over the top.

Serves 6–8

This is one of the most refreshing desserts I know. The perfumy syrup can be made ahead and used to top almost any combination of citrus fruits, but don't be locked into just oranges.

Rose Water

Rose water is a subtle flavoring agent made from distilling the oil of rose petals. The oil is then infused into water. It can be found in specialty food shops.

Banana Coconut Soup

Serves 6–8

This is such an incredibly soothing soup. It reminds me of eating warm pudding, only it's a lot better!

4 cups canned coconut milk
4 cups banana slices, plus extra for garnish
2 tablespoons minced gingerroot
1 cinnamon stick
1 tablespoon lemon juice
Salt to taste
(see "Toasted Coconut" on page 302)

1. In a large saucepan, bring the coconut milk to a boil. Add the banana, ginger, cinnamon stick, lemon juice, and a pinch of salt. Reduce heat and simmer for 10 to 15 minutes or until the banana is very soft.
2. Remove the cinnamon stick and allow to cool slightly.
3. Using a handheld blender (or a blender or food processor), purée the soup until smooth.
4. Serve the soup in preheated bowls, garnished with banana slices and coconut.

Thai Dessert Origins

Many of the desserts in this chapter are not of pure Thai origin. Some are derived from traditional Portuguese recipes since they were the first Westerners to reach the area. Soon after, eggs became an important ingredient in Thai desserts along with flour, sugar, fruit, and coconut ingredients which were already used extensively.

Lemongrass Custard

2 stalks fresh lemongrass, finely chopped (tender inner portion only)
2 cups whole milk
6 egg yolks
½ cup sugar

1. Preheat oven to 275 degrees.
2. In a medium-sized saucepan, over medium-high heat, bring the milk and the lemongrass to a boil. Reduce the heat and simmer for 5 minutes. Cover the milk mixture, turn off the heat, and let sit for 10 minutes on the burner.
3. In a mixing bowl, beat the egg yolks with the sugar until thick.
4. Strain the milk mixture through a fine-mesh sieve, then slowly pour it into the egg yolks, whisking constantly.
5. Divide the mixture between 6 small custard cups and place the cups in a high-sided baking or roasting pan. Add warm water to the pan so that it reaches to approximately 1 inch below the top of the custard cups. Cover the pan tightly with foil.
6. Place the pan in the oven and bake for approximately 20 minutes or until the custards are set on the sides but still slightly wobbly in the center.

Serves 6

This is a standard custard that has simply been infused with lemongrass and it is nothing short of divine. It can be served warm or chilled.

Coconut Custard

Serves 6

This coconut custard uses coconut milk in place of whole milk. Melted butter brings the fat content up to where it needs to be in order for the custards to set.

1 (16-ounce) can coconut cream
2/3 cup fine granulated sugar
6 large eggs, lightly beaten
3 tablespoons butter
Fresh tropical fruit (optional)

1. In a large, heavy-bottomed saucepan, stir together the coconut cream and the sugar.
2. Over medium heat, cook and stir the mixture until the sugar is completely dissolved.
3. Reduce the heat to low and stir in the eggs. Cook, stirring occasionally, until the mixture is thick and coats the back of a spoon, about 10 to 12 minutes.
4. Remove the pan from the heat and add the butter. Stir until the butter is completely melted and incorporated.
5. Pour the custard into six 4-ounce custard cups. Place the cups in a baking pan. Pour boiling water into the baking pan until it comes halfway up the sides of the custard cups.
6. Carefully transfer the baking pan to a preheated 325-degree oven. Bake the custards for 30 to 40 minutes until set. (The tip of a knife should come out clean when inserted into the middle of the custard.)
7. Serve warm or at room temperature. Garnish with chopped tropical fruit, if desired.

Steamed Coconut Cakes

5 eggs
4 tablespoons finely granulated sugar
½ cup rice flour
¼ cup all-purpose flour
Pinch of salt
½ cup coconut milk
½ cup grated sweet coconut

1. In a large mixing bowl, beat the eggs and the sugar together until thick and pale in color.
2. Add the rice flours and salt.
3. Beating constantly, slowly pour in the coconut milk. Beat the batter for 3 more minutes.
4. Bring some water to boil in a steamer large enough to hold 10 small ramekins. When the water begins to boil, place the ramekins in the steamer to heat for 2 minutes.
5. Divide the shredded coconut evenly between all of the ramekins and use a spoon to compact it in the bottom of the cups.
6. Pour the batter evenly between the cups. Steam for 10 minutes.
7. Remove the cakes from the cups as soon as they are cool enough to handle.
8. Serve warm or at room temperature.

Yields 10 cakes

The combination of flours gives these cakes a light, almost a soufflélike, quality. The shredded coconut forms a slightly chewy crust. They are quite tasty with warm chocolate sauce drizzled over the top.

Coconut-Pineapple Soufflé for 2

Yields 2

The egg whites provide the lightness and the ladyfingers, the pineapple, and the coconut provide both the flavor and the texture in this wonderful dessert. Serve the soufflés with champagne by candlelight.

Softened butter for the molds
Sugar for the molds
½ cup (½-inch) cubes ladyfingers or sponge cake
2 tablespoons dark rum
2 tablespoons finely chopped fresh pineapple
1 egg yolk
2½ tablespoons grated sweetened coconut
2 egg whites
Lemon juice
2 tablespoons sugar

1. Preheat oven to 400 degrees.
2. Butter 2 ¾- or 1-cup soufflé molds and then sprinkle them with sugar. Refrigerate the molds until ready to use.
3. Place the ladyfinger cubes in a small bowl. Pour the rum over the cubes and let soak for 5 minutes.
4. Squeeze the juice from the pineapple, saving both the pulp and 1 tablespoon of the juice.
5. In a small bowl, beat the egg yolk with the pineapple juice until very thick. Fold in the cake cubes, pineapple pulp, and coconut.
6. In another small bowl, beat the egg whites with a few drops of lemon juice until foamy. Gradually add the 2 tablespoons of sugar, while continuing to beat until the whites are stiff and glossy.
7. Gently fold the pineapple mixture into the egg whites.
8. Spoon the batter into the prepared molds and bake for 8 to 10 minutes or until puffy and lightly browned.

Mango Fool

2 ripe mangoes, peeled and flesh cut from the pits
2 tablespoons lime juice
¼ cup sugar
1 cup heavy cream
1 tablespoon confectioners' sugar
Crystallized ginger (optional)
Mint leaves (optional)

1. Place the mangoes in a food processor with the lime juice and sugar. Purée until smooth.
2. In a large bowl beat the heavy cream with the confectioners' sugar until stiff.
3. Thoroughly fold the mango purée into the heavy cream.
4. Serve in goblets garnished with crystallized ginger or sprigs of mint, if desired.

Serves 4–6

A fool is usually a combination of heavy whipped cream and a fruit purée. The fruit is just barely folded into the cream, leaving slight stripes. This grown-up "pudding" is simple, light, and a true delight

Citrus Fool

½ cup orange, lime, or lemon juice
3 tablespoons sugar
3 tablespoons unsalted butter
1 large egg, beaten
2 (3-inch-long, ½-inch wide) strips of citrus zest, minced
½ cup heavy cream

1. Place the juice in a small saucepan. Over medium-high heat, reduce the liquid by half.
2. Remove the pan from the heat and stir in the sugar and butter. Stir in the egg until well combined.
3. Return the pan to the burner and cook on medium-low heat for 3 to 5 minutes or until bubbles just begin to form.
4. Remove the pan from the heat and stir in the citrus zest. Place the pan in a bowl of ice and stir the mixture until it is cold.
5. In another bowl, whip the cream until stiff. Fold the citrus mixture thoroughly into the cream.

Serves 4

Make sure that you remove the pan from the heat source before you stir in the egg or it will scramble right before your eyes and the recipe will be ruined.

Pineapple-Mango Sherbet

Serves 4–6

You can try different varieties of this same concept. How about Grapefruit-Papaya?

1 large orange, peeled and segmented
2 mangoes, peeled, pitted, and cut into 1-inch cubes
1 cup pineapple pieces
1 tablespoon lime zest
⅓ cup sugar
½ cup plain yogurt
1 teaspoon orange-flavored liqueur (optional)

1. Place the orange segments, mango cubes, and pineapple pieces on a baking sheet lined with waxed paper; place in the freezer for 30 to 45 minutes or until just frozen.
2. Transfer the fruit to a food processor. Add the lime zest and sugar, and process until well combined.
3. With the machine running, add the yogurt and liqueur. Process for an additional 3 minutes or until the mixture is fluffy.
4. Pour the mixture into an 8" × 8" pan, cover with foil, and freeze overnight.
5. To serve, let the sherbet temper at room temperature for 10 to 15 minutes, then scoop into glass dishes.

Sherbet versus Sorbet

Sherbet differs from sorbet in that the latter is dairy-free. In this sherbet the dairy is provided by plain yogurt, which adds creaminess and a bit of bite.

Mango Sauce over Ice Cream

2 mangoes, peeled, pitted, and diced
1 banana, peeled and chopped
⅔ cup (or to taste) sugar
Juice of 2 large limes (or to taste)
1 tablespoon brandy (optional)
Vanilla ice cream

1. In a medium-sized saucepan over low heat, simmer the mangoes, banana, sugar, and lime juice for 30 minutes, stirring frequently.
2. Add the brandy and simmer 5 more minutes.
3. Remove from heat and allow to cool slightly or to room temperature.
4. To serve, scoop ice cream into individual serving bowls. Spoon sauce over top.

Yields 2 cups

This outstanding mango, banana, and lime sauce is great over ice cream, pound cake, or angel food cake. You might even try it spooned over some grilled fish!

Pumpkin Custard

1 small cooking pumpkin
5 eggs
⅓ cup brown sugar
Pinch of salt
1 cup coconut cream

1. With a small sharp knife, carefully cut the top off of the pumpkin.
2. Using a spoon, remove and discard the seeds and most of the soft flesh; set the pumpkin aside.
3. In a medium-sized mixing bowl, whisk the eggs together. Stir in the brown sugar, salt, and coconut cream until well combined.
4. Pour the mixture into the pumpkin.
5. Place the pumpkin in a steamer and let steam for approximately 20 minutes or until the custard is set.

Serves 4

This custard variation uses pumpkin, brown sugar, and coconut cream to create a rich, autumnal dessert. It is steamed right in the pumpkin shell, so not only does it taste delicious, it makes a great presentation, too.

Watermelon Ice

Serves 6–8

An ice is just that—ice. In this case the ice comes mainly from a watermelon, not water. The result is a dessert that looks like pink snow, with a delicate taste that is sure to please on a hot, humid day.

⅓ cup water
½ cup sugar
1 (3-pound) piece of watermelon, rind cut away, seeded, and cut into small chunks (reserve a bit for garnish if desired)
1 tablespoon lime juice
Mint sprigs (optional)

1. Place the water and sugar in a small saucepan and bring to a boil. Remove from heat and allow to cool to room temperature, stirring frequently. Set the pan in a bowl of ice and continue to stir the syrup until cold.
2. Place the watermelon, syrup, and lime juice in a blender and purée until smooth.
3. Pour the purée through a sieve into a 9-inch baking pan. Cover the pan with foil.
4. Freeze the purée for 8 hours or until frozen.
5. To serve, scrape the frozen purée with the tines of a fork. Spoon the scrapings into pretty glass goblets and garnish with a small piece of watermelon or mint sprigs.

Taro Balls Poached in Coconut Milk

2 cups glutinous rice flour
1 cup corn flour
1 cup cooked taro, mashed
4 cups coconut milk
1 cup brown sugar
⅛ teaspoon salt
Fresh tropical fruit (optional)

Serves 6–12

Here we have a dessert that is unfamiliar to most Americans. The balls have a texture unlike anything else I know, but are a little reminiscent of dumplings or a stiff pudding.

1. In a large mixing bowl, combine the rice and the flours.
2. Add the mashed taro and knead to form a soft dough.
3. Roll into small bite-sized balls and set aside.
4. In a medium to large saucepan, heat the coconut milk over low heat.
5. Add the brown sugar and the salt, stirring until dissolved.
6. Bring the mixture to a low boil and add the taro balls.
7. Poach the balls for 5 to 10 minutes or until done to your liking.
8. Serve hot in small glass bowls, garnished with tropical fruit.

What Is Taro?

Taro is a large tropical plant, also known as "the elephant ear." It has very large, broad leaves (hence the name) and a big, thick, starchy root. "Taro" in ingredients lists refers to the root. Taro is very similar to an Irish potato in texture and taste, but is healthier and easier to digest. Taro is a very important crop to many people living in tropical climates.

Bananas Poached in Coconut Milk

Serves 2–3

The sugar in this recipe makes for a really sweet dessert, and the Thai love it. If you would prefer to let the banana flavor stand more on its own, add less sugar.

2–3 small, slightly green bananas
4 cups coconut milk
1 cup sugar
¼ teaspoon salt
Fresh coconut wedges (optional)
Fresh pineapple wedges (optional)

1. Peel the bananas and slice them in half lengthwise.
2. Pour the coconut milk into a pan large enough to hold the bananas laid flat in a single layer. Add the sugar and salt and bring to a boil.
3. Reduce the heat, add the bananas, and simmer until the bananas are just warmed through, about 3 to 5 minutes.
4. Serve the bananas warm on small plates garnished with fresh coconut and pineapple wedges.

Tofu with Sweet Ginger

Yields 3 cups of sauce

Soft tofu has the texture of a very thick yogurt. If you're lactose intolerant, it's the way to go. Plus it's high in protein and low in fat. Even the sugar content in this recipe is relatively low.

3 cups water
1 (2- to 3-inch) piece of ginger, peeled and smashed with the back of a knife
⅓ cup brown sugar
1 12-ounce package soft tofu

1. Place the water, ginger, and brown sugar in a small saucepan. Bring to a boil over high heat. Reduce the heat to a simmer and let the sauce cook for at least 10 minutes. (The longer you let the mixture cook, the spicier it will get.)
2. To serve, spoon some of the tofu into dessert bowls and pour some sauce over the top. (This sauce is equally good over plain yogurt.)

Pumpkin Simmered in Coconut Milk

1 cup water
½ teaspoon salt
⅓ cup brown sugar
2 cups fresh pumpkin meat cut into large julienned pieces (acorn squash is a good substitute)
½ cup coconut milk

1. Put the water and the coconut milk in a medium-sized pan over low heat. Add the salt and half of the sugar; stir until well combined. Adjust the sweetness to your liking by add more water or sugar if necessary.
2. Add the julienned pumpkin to the pan and bring to a boil over medium heat. Reduce to a simmer and cook until soft, about 5 to 10 minutes depending on both the texture of the pumpkin and your own preference.
3. The pumpkin may be served hot, warm, or cold.

Serves 4

The trick to this simple recipe is using a flavorful pumpkin. I've found that pumpkins straight from the patch are the best. They seems to be left on the vine longer, which allows their flavor to develop.

Chapter 25
Drinks and Teas

Ginger Tea

Yields 8 cups

Although not really a tea, this ginger infusion is refreshing no matter what it's called.

8 cups water
1 large branch (approximately 1/3 pound) of ginger, cut into long pieces
1/2–3/4 cup sugar

1. Bring the water to a boil in a large pan. Add the ginger, reduce heat, and simmer for 10 to 20 minutes, depending on how strong you like your tea.
2. Remove the ginger and add the sugar to taste, stirring until it is completely dissolved.
3. Serve hot or over ice.

Lemongrass Tea

Yields 8 cups

Another infusion, this "tea" is light, flavorful, and oh-so Thai. A 50–50 mix of this tea with Ginger Tea is also great!

8 cups water
1 cup lemongrass stalks, chopped
1/4–1/3 cup sugar

1. Bring the water to a boil in a large pan. Add the lemongrass, remove from heat, and let steep for 10 to 20 minutes, depending on how strong you like your tea.
2. Remove the lemongrass and add the sugar to taste, stirring until it is completely dissolved.
3. Serve hot or over ice.

Thai Limeade

1 cup lime juice, lime rinds reserved
8 cups water
⅓–½ cup sugar
Salt to taste (optional)

1. Combine the lime juice and the sugar; set aside.
2. Bring the water to boil in a large pot. Add the lime rinds and remove from heat. Let steep for 10 to 15 minutes. Remove the lime rinds.
3. Add the lime juice mixture to the hot water, stirring to completely dissolve the sugar. Add salt if desired.
4. Serve over ice.

Yields 9 cups

Do you remember Lemon Shakeups from the county fair? This is sort of the Thai version of a shakeup without the shaking!

Iced Sweet Tea

1 tablespoon sugar
1 tablespoon sweetened condensed milk
1–2 tablespoons Thai tea leaves
1 cup hot water
Ice
1 teaspoon milk

1. Put the sugar and sweetened condensed milk into a large glass.
2. Place the tea leaves into a tea ball and place it in the glass.
3. Add the hot water. Let steep until done to your preferred strength.
4. Stir to dissolve the sugar and sweetened condensed milk.
5. Add ice and top with milk.

Yields slightly more than 1 cup.

Thai like their tea milky and super sweet. If you prefer your tea hot, reduce the sugar and sweetened condensed milk by half. And, of course, don't add the ice!

Thai Iced Tea

Yields approx. 8 cups

Similar to the previous recipe but without the condensed milk, this tea is slightly less rich, but certainly no less sweet.

6 cups water
1 cup Thai tea leaves
1 cup sugar
Ice
1–1½ cups half-and-half

1. Bring the water to boil in a medium-sized pot. Remove from heat and add the tea leaves, pushing them into the water until they are completely submerged. Steep approximately 5 minutes or until the liquid is a bright orange.
2. Strain through a fine-mesh sieve or coffee strainer.
3. Stir in the sugar until completely dissolved.
4. Allow the tea to reach room temperature and then refrigerate.
5. To serve, pour the tea over ice cubes, leaving room at the top of the glass to pour in 3 to 4 tablespoons of half-and-half; stir briefly to combine.

Super-Simple Thai Iced Tea

Yields approx. 1 cup

After you have become addicted to tea Thai-style but you are rushing to that morning meeting, here is the brew for you. Add milk or condensed milk if you like.

2 tablespoons sugar
1–2 tablespoons Thai tea leaves
1 cup hot water
Ice

1. Put the sugar into a large glass.
2. Place the tea leaves in a tea ball and place it in the glass.
3. Add the hot water. Let steep until done to your preferred strength.
4. Stir to dissolve the sugar and add ice.

Fresh Coconut Juice

1 young coconut
Ice
Sprig of mint for garnish

1. Using a meat cleaver, make a V-shaped slice on the top of the coconut.
2. Pour the juice over a glass of ice.
3. Garnish with a mint sprig.

Serves 1–2, depending on the size of the coconut.

Exactly what the recipe title says, this recipe calls for whacking open a coconut and drinking the juice. Remember Gilligan's Island?

Thai-Inspired Singapore Sling

2 tablespoons whiskey
1 tablespoon cherry brandy
1 tablespoon orange liqueur
1 tablespoon lime juice
1 teaspoon brown sugar
Dash of bitters
$\frac{1}{4}$–$\frac{1}{3}$ cup pineapple juice
Mint sprig (optional)

1. Place all of the ingredients into a cocktail shaker and shake well to combine.
2. Serve over crushed ice and garnish with a sprig of mint if desired.

Pass on the Wine

Beer is the most popular alcoholic beverage served with Thai food. Three brands are domestically brewed—Singha, Amarit, and Kloster. In each case, the barley is homegrown, but the hops come from Germany.

Yields 1 cocktail

Created in 1915 by a Raffles Hotel bartender, the Singapore Sling was originally meant to be a woman's drink. Nowadays, no trip to Singapore, is complete without sipping this classic at Raffles's famous Long Bar.

Tom's Thai "Martinis"

Yields 3 quarts

This is my brother's favorite cocktail to serve at his pool parties. If desired, you can easily reduce this recipe by using a third of a bottle of each rum, a third of a pineapple, and 1 stalk of lemongrass.

1 whole ripe pineapple
1 bottle dark rum
1 bottle light rum
1 bottle coconut rum
3 stalks lemongrass, trimmed, cut into 3-inch lengths and tied in a bundle

1. Remove the pineapple greens and then quarter the remaining fruit. Place the pineapple quarters and the lemongrass bundle in a container large enough to hold all of the liquor.
2. Pour the rums over the fruit and stir to combine. Cover the container and let infuse for at least 1 week at room temperature.
3. Remove the lemongrass bundle and discard.
4. Remove the pineapple quarters and cut into slices for garnish.
5. To serve, pour some of the rum into a martini shaker filled with ice; shake well. Pour into martini glasses and garnish with a pineapple slice.

What Not to Eat

Lime leaves, lemongrass, and Siamese ginger are all great flavoring agents, but they are really difficult to chew. Don't eat them.

Tropical Fruit Cocktail

1 small mango, papaya, banana, or other tropical fruit, peeled and roughly chopped (reserve a bit for garnish if desired)
4 tablespoons lime or lemon juice
1 teaspoon grated ginger
1 tablespoon brown sugar
1¼ cups orange or grapefruit juice
1¼ cups pineapple juice
⅓–½ cup (or to taste) rum

1. Place the chopped fruit, lime juice, ginger, and sugar in a blender and process until smooth.
2. Add the remaining ingredients to the blender and process until well combined.
3. To serve, pour over crushed ice and decorate with fruit slices of your choice.

Yields 3–4 cups

When you think of fruit cocktail, you probably think of either the canned fruit you ate as a child or some kiddie cocktail. Well, this is neither. It is sophisticated, not too sweet, and very adult thanks to the rum.

Mango Bellini

2 tablespoons puréed mango
1 teaspoon mango schnapps (optional)
½ teaspoon lemon juice
Chilled champagne

Place the mango purée, mango schnapps, and lemon juice in a champagne flute. Fill the flute with champagne and stir.

Yields 1 glass

Similar to the Royal Thai Kir, this Mango Bellini is a bit fruitier. The lemon juice helps to balance the fruit. Whichever cocktail you choose, you can't go wrong with a combination of mango and champagne!

Royal Thai Kir

Yields 1 glass

In Paris, I was introduced to a cocktail that still remains a favorite, a Kir Royal. This is my Thai version, in toast to my wonderful friends in France, who forever changed my outlook on food and wine. Merci!

1–2 teaspoons crème de mango or mango schnapps

Chilled dry champagne

Pour the crème into a champagne flute and fill with champagne.

Wine Choices

Pairing wine with Thai food is not an easy endeavor because of the complexity of flavors that appear in a single dish. Sparkling wine or champagne act to quell a bit of the fire. (As does a cold glass of beer!) Slightly chilled Alsacian-style Rieslings, Pinot Gris, and Pinot Blanc can also do the trick. If you are absolutely set on drinking red, please do. Try a full-flavored, yet fruity, wine such as a Zinfandel. Or if you want a cold glass of red, chill a bottle of Beaujolais. Its low tannins help offset the heat of the chilies.

Chapter 26

Thai-Inspired Cooking

Asian Carrot Sticks

Serves 4–6

Dinner parties at Tim and John's are always special. From Italian Summer Solstice parties to Chinese New Year's celebrations, they always do it up. I adjusted this recipe of theirs to give it a bit of a Thai taste.

1 pound thin carrots, peeled and cut into quarters lengthwise
4 tablespoons water
4 tablespoons olive oil
2 cloves garlic, minced
2 tablespoons rice vinegar
1/8–1/4 teaspoon cayenne pepper
1/2–1 1/2 teaspoons paprika
1/2–1 teaspoon Chinese 5-spice powder
3 tablespoons chopped cilantro
Salt and pepper to taste

1. Place the carrots in a pan large enough to hold them comfortably. Cover the carrots with water and bring to a boil over high heat. Drain the carrots and return them to the pan.
2. Add the 4 tablespoons of water, the olive oil, and the garlic; bring to a boil, reduce to a simmer, and cook until just tender. Drain.
3. In a small bowl, stir together remaining ingredients; pour over the carrots, tossing to coat.
4. Season to taste with salt and pepper.
5. The carrots may be eaten immediately, but develop a richer flavor if allowed to marinate for a few hours.

Spicy Shrimp Dip

5 tablespoons butter
1 tablespoon minced chives
½ teaspoon salt
½ serrano chili, seeded and minced
½ teaspoon grated lemon zest
8 ounces shrimp, cleaned and chopped
Salt and freshly ground black pepper to taste

1. In a medium-sized sauté pan, melt the butter over medium heat. Stir in the chives, salt, chili pepper, and lemon zest; sauté for 2 minutes.
2. Reduce the heat to low and add the shrimp; sauté for 3 minutes or until opaque.
3. Transfer the mixture to a food processor and coarsely purée. Season with salt and pepper.
4. Firmly pack the purée into a small bowl. Cover with plastic wrap, and refrigerate for 4 hours or overnight.
5. To serve, remove the shrimp dip from the refrigerator and allow it to sit for 5 to 10 minutes. Serve the dip with an assortment of crackers and toast points or some favorite veggies.

Yields approx. 1 cup

There is no filler in this dip. It's shrimp, shrimp, and more shrimp. The butter binds it together and the rest of the ingredients give the shrimp a little zip.

Cream of Coconut Crabmeat Dip

Yields approx. 2 cups

In this knockoff of a typical crab dip, the coconut cream is essentially a substitute for mayonnaise. It is a bit sweet, but not overwhelmingly so, and the jalapeño adds a nice contrast to the coconut.

¾ cup cream of coconut
1¼ pounds (10 ounces) crabmeat, picked over to remove shell pieces
¼ teaspoon salt
2 green onions, trimmed and thinly sliced
2 tablespoons chopped cilantro
1 tablespoon lemon or lime juice
1 jalapeño, seeded and minced
Ground white pepper to taste

1. In a small saucepan, combine the cream of coconut, crabmeat, and salt; bring to a simmer over medium-low heat. Simmer for 5 minutes.
2. Stir in the green onions, cilantro, lemon juice, jalapeño, and pepper. Pour into a serving dish and let stand at room temperature until cool.
3. Serve with fresh vegetables and crackers.

Marinated Mushrooms

Makes 25–35 mushrooms

I'm warning you, these marinated mushrooms are addictive. Serve them as part of a Thai antipasto, as a side dish for grilled meats, or as a super snack.

¾ cup olive oil
½ cup water
¼ cup rice wine vinegar
Juice of 1 lime
3 cloves garlic
1 whole serrano or jalapeño pepper
2 stalks lemongrass
3 (½-inch) pieces gingerroot
1½ pounds whole small white mushrooms

1. Place all of the ingredients except the mushrooms in a large pot; bring to a boil, reduce heat, and simmer for 10 to 15 minutes.
2. Add the mushrooms to the pot, stirring to coat.
3. Remove the pot from the heat and let cool to room temperature, about 1 hour.
4. Refrigerate for at least 2 hours, preferably overnight.

Thai-Spiced Guacamole

2 ripe avocados, pitted and chopped
4 teaspoons lime juice
1 large plum tomato, seeded and chopped
1 tablespoon chopped onion
1 small garlic clove, minced
1 teaspoon grated lime zest
1 teaspoon grated gingerroot
1 teaspoon chopped serrano or jalapeño chili
1–2 tablespoons chopped cilantro
Salt and freshly ground black pepper to taste

1. Place the avocado in a medium-sized bowl. Add the lemon juice and coarsely mash.
2. Add the remaining ingredients and gently mix together.
3. Serve within 2 hours.

Yields 2 cups

This recipe is a great example of how lime zest and ginger can give a Mexican favorite a Southeast Asian twist. Try serving the guacamole with some rice chips alongside the tortillas chips.

Thai Mexican Similarities

If you look through a Mexican cookbook, you'll find many typical Mexican ingredients that are also Thai staples—lime juice, chilies, cilantro, garlic, and onion.

Asian-Inspired Chicken and Wild Rice Soup

Serves 6–8

The chewy quality of the rice in this soup complements the crispy pea pods and delicate chicken, and its nutty flavor substitutes for peanuts.

1 tablespoon vegetable oil
2 whole boneless, skinless chicken breasts, trimmed and cut into thin strips
1–2 garlic cloves, minced
2–3 teaspoons minced ginger
2 tablespoons fish sauce
6 cups low-fat, low-salt chicken broth
2 cups cooked wild rice
½ cup sliced green onions
½ pound snow peas, trimmed and diagonally sliced
Salt and freshly ground white pepper

1. In a large soup pot, heat the oil on medium-high. Add the chicken strips and sauté for 2 to 3 minutes.
2. Add the garlic and gingerroot and sauté for another minute.
3. Stir in the fish sauce, broth, and rice. Bring to a boil; reduce heat, cover, and simmer for 10 minutes.
4. Add the green onions and snow peas; simmer to heat through.
5. Adjust seasoning with salt and freshly ground white pepper to taste.

Wild Rice

Wild rice isn't rice at all, but the seed of a native American grass. Processed white rice typically needs less water added than long-grain brown rice or wild rice, which can take up to 6 cups of water per cup of dry rice. Unlike its white and brown counterparts, wild rice is a very heavy and filling dish.

Chicken Salad—1

For the dressing:

¼ cup vegetable oil
2 tablespoons rice wine vinegar
1 tablespoon soy sauce
2 teaspoons grated gingerroot
Pinch of sugar
¼ teaspoon (or to taste) salt

For the salad:

2 cups chopped cooked chicken
4 ounces snow peas, trimmed
3 green onions, trimmed and sliced
1 cup bean sprouts
1 medium head of Chinese cabbage, shredded
1 tablespoon toasted sesame seeds

Serves 4

This light, flavorful chicken salad is great for a summer lunch. Serve it with some slices of mango and papaya, some great bread, and a glass of Vouvray—and you are ready to go.

1. Place the salad dressing ingredients in a small bowl and whisk vigorously to combine.
2. In a medium-sized bowl, combine the chicken, snow peas, green onions, and bean sprouts. Add the dressing and toss to coat.
3. To serve, arrange the cabbage on a serving platter. Mound the chicken salad over the cabbage. Garnish with the sesame seeds.

Chicken Salad—2

Serves 4–6

Unlike many Thai recipes, this one has no chilies or ginger, thus it is relatively mild. But it has many typical Asian characteristics, namely the rice sticks, the peanuts, and the sesame oil.

3 tablespoons hoisin sauce, divided
1 tablespoon soy sauce
1 tablespoon dry sherry
2 whole boneless, skinless chicken breasts
1 tablespoon vegetable oil
4 tablespoons lime juice
1 teaspoon sesame oil
3 tablespoons sesame seeds, toasted
3 tablespoons peanuts, chopped
1/3 cup sliced scallions
1/4 cup chopped cilantro, plus extra for garnish
Peanut oil for frying
1/4 pound rice sticks
Bibb or romaine lettuce leaves

1. Combine 1 tablespoon of the hoisin sauce, the soy sauce, and the sherry in a medium-sized bowl. Add the chicken breasts and marinate for 20 to 30 minutes.
2. Heat the vegetable oil in a large skillet over medium-high heat. Add the chicken breasts, reserving the marinade. Brown the breasts on both sides. Add the reserved marinade to the skillet, cover, and cook over medium-low heat until tender, about 20 minutes.
3. Let the chicken cool to room temperature, then shred it into bite-sized pieces; set aside.
4. In a medium-sized bowl, combine the shredded chicken with the remaining hoisin sauce, the lime juice, sesame oil, sesame seeds, peanuts, scallions, and cilantro. Add the shredded chicken and stir to coat.
5. Add approximately 1 inch of peanut oil to a large skillet and heat on high until the oil is very hot, but not smoking.
6. Add the rice sticks carefully and fry for approximately 6 to 8 seconds or until puffed and golden; turn the rice sticks with tongs and fry for another 6 to 8 seconds. Remove the rice sticks to a stack of paper towels to drain.
7. Toss about 2/3 of the rice sticks with the chicken mixture.
8. To serve, place a mound of salad on a lettuce leaf on the center of each plate. Top with the remaining rice sticks and garnish with additional cilantro.

Chicken Salad—3

1 cup cooked chicken meat
2 cups shredded bok choy
½ cup very thinly sliced celery
1 scallion, thinly sliced
1 teaspoon vegetable oil
1 clove garlic, minced
1 (¼-inch) piece ginger, peeled and minced
¼ cup soy sauce
2 tablespoons rice vinegar
1 tablespoon sugar
¼ teaspoon sesame oil (optional)

1. In a medium-sized bowl, toss together the chicken, bok choy, celery, and scallion.
2. In a small bowl, thoroughly whisk together the remaining ingredients. Pour over the salad and toss well to combine.

Makes 3–4 cups

This salad makes a great packed lunch, because the salad holds up pretty well at room temperature and the dressing doesn't require refrigeration. Keep the salad and dressing in separate containers.

Jicama, Carrot, and Chinese Cabbage Salad

1 teaspoon ground anise
½ cup chopped cilantro
⅓ cup vegetable oil
2 tablespoons lime juice
½ teaspoon prepared chili-garlic sauce
2 pounds jicama, peeled and finely julienned
2 large carrots, peeled and finely julienned
¾ pound Chinese cabbage, thinly shredded
Salt and black pepper to taste

1. Thoroughly combine the ground anise, cilantro, vegetable oil, lime juice, and chili-garlic sauce in a large mixing bowl.
2. Add the vegetables and toss to coat.
3. Season with salt and pepper.

Serves 6–8

This crunchy salad reminds me of coleslaw. All of the vegetables are cut in a fine julienne and then tossed in a dressing. Serve it as a side dish, a salad, or as a topping for sandwiches.

Peanut-Potato Salad

Serves 8–10

The first time you try this potato salad, the peanuts, peanut butter, and mint will jolt your taste buds. But after you get used to it, you'll be hard-pressed to go back to the traditional stuff!

3 pounds peeled boiling potatoes
1 cup salted peanuts, coarsely chopped, divided
1 medium-sized red bell pepper, cored and chopped
2 stalks celery, sliced
4 green onions, trimmed and sliced
¼ cup chopped cilantro
¼ cup chopped mint
¾ cup mayonnaise
¼ cup peanut butter
3 tablespoons rice vinegar
Salt and pepper to taste

1. Bring a large pot of water to a boil over high heat. Add the potatoes and cook until tender. Drain and cool. Cut into ½-inch cubes.
2. In a large bowl, combine the potato cubes, ¾ cup of peanuts, red bell pepper, celery, green onion, cilantro, and mint.
3. In a small bowl, whisk together the mayonnaise, peanut butter, and vinegar. Season to taste with salt and pepper.
4. Pour the dressing over the potato mixture and toss to coat. Refrigerate for at least 1 hour. Garnish with the remaining peanuts before serving.

Thai Potatoes?

Potatoes were originally cultivated by South American native populations, but then spread throughout the world. Potatoes have yet to be infused too deeply into Thai cuisine, with most recipes involving potatoes originating from a taro recipe, or a different potato recipe is given a Thai kick.

Asian Couscous Salad

¾ pound snow peas, trimmed
1 red bell pepper, cored, seeded, and chopped
1 yellow bell pepper, cored, seeded, and chopped
5–7 green onions, trimmed and thinly sliced
1 medium-sized red onion, chopped
1–2 jalapeño chilies, seeded and finely chopped
1 clove garlic, minced
2¾ cups couscous
3½ cups boiling water, divided
1 packed cup basil
1 packed cup mint
1 packed cup cilantro
½ cup vegetable oil
2 tablespoons lemon juice
3 tablespoons lime juice
Salt and freshly ground black pepper to taste

Serves 8–10

Serve this easy-to-make and healthy salad as a snack, a side dish, or as a light lunch. It is also super picnic fare.

1. Place the snow peas, peppers, onions, chilies, garlic, and couscous in a large bowl; toss to blend.
2. Pour 3 cups of the boiling water over the couscous mixture, cover tightly, and let stand at room temperature for 1 hour.
3. Add the remaining ½ cup boiling water and all the remaining ingredients to the couscous; toss together, cover, and let stand for at least 30 more minutes.
4. Season with salt and freshly ground black pepper.

Asian 3-Bean Salad

Serves 4–6

This 3-bean salad is inspired by the ones from the 1950s, but is jazzed up with Asian spices and rice vinegar.

1 (14-ounce) can garbanzo beans
1 (14-ounce) can black beans
1 (14-ounce) can red kidney beans
1 medium-sized red onion, chopped
⅓ cup chopped cilantro
4 tablespoons olive oil
3 tablespoons rice vinegar
3 cloves garlic, minced
1 teaspoon minced jalapeño
½ teaspoon lime zest
Salt and pepper to taste

1. Place all the beans in a colander. Thoroughly rinse under cool running water. Drain and set aside.
2. Stir together all the remaining ingredients and pour over beans; stir to combine.
3. Refrigerate overnight, stirring occasionally. Season with salt and pepper.

Crunchy Sprout Salad

Serves 4

Think spring! The dressing in this salad is fresh and lively, but not overpowering. This salad is also nice with a drained can of mandarin orange segments tossed in.

¼ cup rice vinegar
2 tablespoons fish or soy sauce
2 tablespoons vegetable oil
1 tablespoon sugar
2 teaspoons grated gingerroot
2 cups sprouts of your choice
6 cups baby greens (preferably an Asian mix)

1. In a large bowl whisk together the vinegar, fish sauce, vegetable oil, sugar, and gingerroot.
2. Add the sprouts, toss to coat, and let marinate for 30 minutes.
3. Add the greens and toss until well combined.

Many Peas Asian-Style Salad

1 cup sugar snap peas
½ cup snow peas
½ cup fresh green peas
2 teaspoons sesame seeds, toasted
1 tablespoon rice vinegar
1 tablespoon sesame oil
1 tablespoon brown sugar
2 teaspoons soy sauce
6 cups pea shoots or other sweet baby lettuce

Serves 4

Pea lovers rejoice—this recipe is for you. It goes without saying (even though I am), the fresher the ingredients the better. No compromising!

1. Bring a large pot of water to a boil. Add the sugar snap peas and boil for 2 minutes. Add the snow peas and green peas and boil for 1 minute more. Drain and rinse in cold water. Pat dry with paper towels.
2. In a large bowl, thoroughly combine the sesame seeds, vinegar, oil, sugar, and soy sauce. Add the peas and the greens and toss to coat.

Substituting Dried Lemongrass for Fresh

If you can't find lemongrass, substitute 1 tablespoon of dried lemongrass per stalk of fresh or several strips of peel from a lemon or lime.

Thai Pasta Salad

Serves 8–12

Salads made with pasta always used to have an Italian dressing or mayonnaise base. A great update to a concept that has been around for a long while, this salad features a spicy peanut dressing.

8 ounces dried bow tie or other bite-sized pasta
3 green onions, trimmed and thinly sliced
2 medium carrots, shredded
1½ cups thinly sliced Napa cabbage or bok choy
1½ cups thinly sliced red cabbage
1 tablespoon brown sugar
1 clove garlic, minced
2 tablespoons vegetable oil
⅓ cup rice wine vinegar
¼ teaspoon ground ginger
½ teaspoon red pepper flakes
3 tablespoons smooth peanut butter
2 tablespoons water
1 tablespoon soy sauce
1 cup bean sprouts

1. Cook the pasta according to package directions. Drain and rinse under cold water. Place the pasta in a large mixing bowl and add the green onions, carrots, and cabbage.
2. In a small mixing bowl, thoroughly combine all the remaining ingredients except the sprouts.
3. Pour the dressing over the pasta and vegetables; cover and refrigerate for at least 2 hours or overnight.
4. Just before serving, toss in the bean sprouts.

Thai Chicken Pizza

2 whole boneless, skinless chicken breasts, cut in half
1 recipe Asian or Thai Marinade (see recipes in Chapter 13)
1 unbaked pizza crust
¼–⅓ cup peanut or hot chili oil
1½ cups fontina cheese
1½ cups mozzarella cheese
4 green onions, trimmed and thinly sliced
1 medium carrot, peeled and coarsely grated
1½ cups bean sprouts
½ cup coarsely chopped dry-roasted peanuts
⅓ cup chopped cilantro leaves

Yields 1 large pizza

This is a great recipe to use up leftover Siamese Roast Chicken (see recipe on page 388). Simply chop up the leftover meat and proceed with step 3.

1. Place the chicken breasts in an ovenproof dish. Pour the marinade over the chicken, turning to coat thoroughly. Cover and refrigerate for at least 8 hours. Let the chicken return to room temperature before proceeding.
2. Preheat oven to 325 degrees. Bake the chicken for 30 to 40 minutes or until cooked through. Remove the chicken from the oven and let cool to room temperature. Shred the chicken into very small pieces; set aside.
3. Prepare the pizza dough according to package directions.
4. Brush the dough with some of the oil. Top the oil with the cheeses, leaving a ½-inch rim. Evenly spread the chicken, green onions, carrot, bean sprouts, and peanuts on top of the cheese. Drizzle a little oil over the top.
5. Bake according to package directions for the crust. Remove from oven, sprinkle with cilantro, and serve.

Grilled Steak with Peanut Sauce

Serves 6

Beef satay without the skewers! You can serve this steak with your usual steak side dishes, or it is equally good over a bed of greens tossed in a light Thai vinaigrette or a bit of the peanut sauce.

1 recipe of Thai Marinade (see recipes in Chapter 13)
1 (2-pound) flank steak, trimmed
1 recipe of Peanut Dipping Sauce (see recipes in Chapter 14)

1. Quickly rinse the steak under cold water and pat dry. Place the steak in a large Ziplock bag along with the marinade. Turn the meat until it is well coated with the marinade on all sides. Refrigerate overnight. (Let the steak return to room temperature before cooking.)
2. Preheat a broiler or grill. Cook the steak, turning once and basting with the remaining marinade, until done to your preference
3. Remove the meat from the grill, cover it with foil, and let it rest for 5 minutes to let some of the juices reabsorb. To serve, thinly slice the steak across the grain. Pass the peanut sauce separately.

Asian Marinara Sauce

Yields approx. 2 cups

Tired of the same old spaghetti sauce? Give this marinara sauce a try. Serve it over any pasta you would top with an Italian-style sauce or try it over rice noodles.

2 tablespoons vegetable oil
1 medium onion, chopped
1 (1-inch) piece of ginger, peeled and minced
1–3 serrano chilies, seeded and minced
1 cup water
1 pound chopped canned tomatoes with the juice
1 teaspoon salt
1 teaspoon sugar

1. In a large saucepan, heat the oil over medium heat.
2. Add the onion and ginger and sauté for 2 minutes.
3. Add the chilies and continue cooking 1 minute more.
4. Stir in the water, tomatoes, salt, and sugar. Reduce heat to low and simmer for at least 30 minutes.

Thai-Style Grilled Pork Chops

1 garlic clove, minced
⅓ cup fish sauce
2 tablespoons cream sherry
3 tablespoons rice vinegar
2 teaspoons brown sugar
2 teaspoons minced gingerroot
2 (1-inch-thick) pork chops

Serves 2

The sugar and the sherry in this marinade help the chops develop a nicely charred crust. But pay attention while you are grilling. These same ingredients can cause brief fire flare-ups.

1. In a small saucepan, over medium heat, bring the garlic, fish sauce, sherry, vinegar, brown sugar, and gingerroot to a boil. Remove from heat and allow to cool to room temperature. (You can also put the marinade in the refrigerator to cool it.)
2. Place the pork chops in a plastic bag and pour in the marinade, making sure to coat both sides of the chops. Let the chops marinate at room temperature for 15 minutes.
3. Pour the marinade into a small saucepan and bring to a simmer over medium-low heat. Cook for 5 minutes.
4. Grill the chops on a hot grill for 5 to 6 minutes per side for medium.
5. Serve the chops with the marinade drizzled over the top.

Southeast Asian Burgers

Serves 4

These burgers are great topped with Pickled Chinese Cabbage (see recipe on page 518).

1 clove garlic, minced
3 tablespoons bread crumbs
1 pound ground beef or ground turkey
¼ cup chopped cilantro
¼ cup chopped basil
¼ cup chopped mint
2 tablespoons lime juice
1 teaspoon sugar (optional)
3 shakes Tabasco

1. In a medium-sized mixing bowl, combine all the remaining ingredients.
2. Using your hands, gently mix the ingredients together and form 4 patties. Season each patty with salt and pepper.
3. Grill the patties to your liking, about 5 minutes per side for medium.

Serving Marinades

If you are going to use a marinade as a sauce, make sure to bring it to a boil after the marinating foods have been removed. Otherwise, reusing the marinade can make you sick (e.g., food poisoning).

Grilled Lobster Tails with a Lemongrass Smoke

6 (4–6 ounce) lobster tails
Olive oil
Cracked black pepper
3–4 whole lemongrass stalks, bruised
Salt to taste

Serves 6

These lobster tails are simply the best. The sweet lobster meat is lightly perfumed with a lemony, smoky aroma—and that's it! No masking what Mother Nature did such a great job creating.

1. To prepare the lobster tails, lay each tail flat-side down (shell up). Using a sharp knife, cut through the shell and halfway through the meat lengthwise. Use your fingers to pull the meat away from the membranes and the inner shell, then invert the meat until it sits on top of the shell instead of being surrounded by it.
2. Brush the lobster generously with olive oil and sprinkle with black pepper. Place the lemongrass stalks in a Tuscan herb grill.
3. Heat grill to medium-high heat. Place the herb grill on the main grill grate and place the lobster tails on top, meat side up. Close the lid of the grill and cook for 7 to 8 minutes. (The shells should be bright red and the meat quite firm.)
4. Turn the lobster tails over and continue cooking for 2 to 3 minutes.
5. Sprinkle with salt and serve.

What is a Tuscan Herb Grill?

A Tuscan herb grill is a flat, hinged grate that looks similar to a screen. The 2 sides fit closely together and hold fresh herbs, such as fennel or basil, which smoke during the grilling process, imparting a smoky, herbal note to grilled meats or fish.

Thai-Flavored Green Beans

Serves 6–8

The shrimp paste in this recipe adds a slightly salty flavor that is impossible to pinpoint unless you saw the cook add it to the pot. Your dinner guests will beg for your secret ingredient. Don't tell.

2 pounds French or regular green beans, trimmed and cut into bite-sized pieces
1 rounded tablespoon shrimp paste
2 tablespoons vegetable oil
3 tablespoons unsalted butter
2 teaspoons minced garlic
½ cup chopped cilantro

1. In a pot large enough to hold all of the beans, steam them until tender-crisp.
2. Drain the beans, reserving cooking liquid. Cover the beans with foil to keep warm.
3. In a small bowl, whisk together the shrimp paste and vegetable oil.
4. In a large skillet, melt the butter over medium-high heat. Add the garlic and sauté until golden. Stir in the shrimp paste mixture and 1 tablespoon of the reserved cooking liquid.
5. Add the reserved green beans, stirring to coat. Cook until heated through.
6. Remove the pan from the heat and toss in the cilantro.

Southeast Asian Asparagus

Serves 4

You can serve this hot or at room temperature. If you choose to serve it at room temperature, stir in the sesame seeds just before serving, otherwise they get a little mushy.

1 tablespoon sesame oil
1 pound asparagus, trimmed and cut into 2-inch pieces
1 teaspoon fish sauce
1 teaspoon toasted sesame seeds
⅛ cup toasted peanuts

1. Heat the sesame oil in a large skillet over medium-high heat. Add the asparagus and sauté for 3 minutes.
2. Add the fish sauce, sesame seeds, and peanuts. Sauté for 2 more minutes or until the asparagus is done to your liking.

Asian Ratatouille

2 Japanese eggplants (about 1 pound), cut into ½-inch cubes
½ teaspoon salt
3 tablespoons sesame oil
2 ribs of celery, sliced
1 onion, slivered
1 red bell pepper, cored, seeded, and julienned
3 tablespoons vegetable oil
2 small zucchini, halved lengthwise and sliced
1 cup sliced mushrooms
¾ cup vegetable stock
2 tablespoons soy sauce
1 tablespoon dry sherry
1 tablespoon cornstarch
1 teaspoon minced garlic
1 teaspoon minced ginger
2 teaspoons Plum Dipping Sauce (see recipe on page 311)
1 tablespoon chopped cilantro

Serves 6–8

The similarity between this Asian version and the French classic is evident. But instead of seasoning the dish with herbs de Provence, this ratatouille gets its zip from ginger, plum sauce, and soy.

1. Place the eggplant in a colander and sprinkle with the salt. Let rest for 30 minutes.
2. In a large ovenproof pot, heat the sesame oil on medium. Add the celery, onion, and red bell pepper; sauté for 5 minutes. Remove the vegetables from the pan and set aside.
3. Add the vegetable oil to the pot. Sauté the zucchini, mushrooms, and eggplant for 5 minutes. Stir in the celery, onion, and bell pepper and set aside.
4. In a small mixing bowl, whisk together the stock, soy sauce, sherry, and cornstarch. Pour over the vegetables and stir to combine.
5. Bake, covered, in a 350-degree oven for 40 minutes.
6. Stir in the garlic, ginger, and plum sauce. Cover and continue to bake for an additional 10 minutes.

Pickled Chinese Cabbage

Yields 3 pounds

An Asian sauerkraut—no more, no less.

4 cups water
6 cups rice vinegar
1 tablespoon chopped garlic
1 tablespoon chopped cilantro
2 large shallots or 1 medium onion, chopped
3 pounds Chinese cabbage, cored, halved, and thinly sliced
Salt and white pepper

1. Place all of the ingredients except the cabbage in a large stew pot and bring to a boil. Reduce heat and simmer for 5 minutes.
2. Bring the cooking liquid back to a boil and stir in the cabbage. Cover and cook the cabbage for 3 to 5 minutes.
3. Remove the pot from heat and let cool to room temperature. Season to taste with salt and white pepper.
4. Refrigerate for at least 8 hours before serving.

Crazy Coconut Pie

Yields 1 (10-inch) pie

I've had this recipe since I was a kid, yet it remains a favorite. Somehow the batter separates to form a crust, a custard filling, and a golden coconut top. (Yes, I can still eat the whole thing by myself.)

¾ stick of butter, melted
4 eggs
2 cups milk
½ cup flour
¾ cup sugar
1½ teaspoons vanilla
1 cup sweetened shredded coconut

1. Preheat oven to 350 degrees. Grease and flour a 10-inch pie plate.
2. Place all of the ingredients in a blender and blend for 1 minute. Pour the batter into the prepared pan.
3. Bake for 45 minutes or until golden on top.

Lime Butter Cake

3 cups cake flour
3 teaspoons baking powder
¼ teaspoon salt
2 sticks unsalted butter
1½ cups sugar
4 eggs, lightly beaten
1 cup milk
Grated peel of 1 lime
3 tablespoons lime juice
Powdered sugar (optional)

1. Preheat oven to 325 degrees.
2. Sift together the cake flour, baking powder, and salt 3 times; set aside.
3. In the bowl of an electric mixer, beat the butter until creamy.
4. Gradually add in the sugar, then beat at medium speed for 5 minutes, scraping down the sides of the bowl every so often.
5. Add the beaten eggs slowly and continue to beat for 5 more minutes. (The mixture will be thick and double in volume.)
6. Using a rubber spatula, gradually fold in ¼ of the flour mixture into the batter. Then fold in ⅓ of the milk. Repeat this process until all of the flour and the milk have been incorporated. (You will add flour last.)
7. Fold in the lime peel and lime juice.
8. Pour the batter into a greased molded cake pan, smoothing the surface and slightly building up the sides.
9. Bake the cake for 45 to 55 minutes or until the top is golden and the sides are beginning to pull away from the pan.
10. Remove from the oven and let cool for 1 to 2 minutes. Carefully unmold.
11. Let cool to room temperature. Dust with powdered sugar or serve with Ginger Anglaise Sauce (see recipe on page 474).

Yields 1 (12-inch) cake

This cake is so moist and flavorful, I simply dust it with powdered sugar. If you want to frost it, go with something light and not too sweet. A crème anglaise or vanilla ice cream goes nicely with it, too.

Meringues with Tropical Fruit

Yields approx. 24

My friend, Leslie Kowitz, hosted an afternoon tea a while back, which included a plethora of teas and sweets. My favorite was a meringue shell filled with berries. Here it is with a tropical twist.

Butter at room temperature to prepare baking dishes
6 egg whites
2 cups superfine sugar
2 cups heavy cream, whipped
2 cups mixed fresh tropical fruit, cut into bite-sized pieces

1. Preheat oven to 200 degrees. Butter pieces of parchment paper cut to line 2 baking sheets.
2. Place the egg whites in a cold bowl. Beat until soft peaks form. Add the sugar and continue to beat until stiff.
3. Using a pastry bag, pipe 3- to 4-inch circles of meringue onto the prepared baking sheets.
4. Bake for 90 to 120 minutes or until they are dry, taking care not to let the meringues turn color. If the meringues aren't dry after 2 hours of baking, turn the oven off and let the meringues sit in the oven overnight.
5. Allow the meringues to cool completely. Fill a pastry bag with the whipped heavy cream. Pipe cream into the center of the meringues. Top with tropical fruit and serve.

Chapter 27
Regional Cuisines

Singapore Shellfish Soup

Serves 6–8

Singapore sits at the southern end of the Malay Peninsula, surrounded by the Strait of Malacca, the South China Sea, and the Java Sea. No wonder seafood is a Singaporean mainstay.

2 tablespoons vegetable oil, divided
1 pound large raw shrimp, peeled, shells reserved
1 pound mussels, cleaned and debearded
3 stalks lemongrass, outer layers removed, inner core thinly sliced
3 serrano chilies, seeded and chopped
2 cloves garlic, minced
1 (1-inch) piece ginger, peeled and chopped
4 small shallots, peeled and sliced
1 tablespoon anchovy paste
1 teaspoon turmeric
1 tablespoon ground coriander
1 (14-ounce) can coconut milk
1–2 tablespoons fish sauce
1 7-ounce package of rice noodles, soaked in hot water until soft
1 tablespoon lime zest
6 large scallops, sliced horizontally into 2–3 pieces, depending on their size
1 cup bean sprouts
¼ cup chopped cilantro
Lime wedges

(recipe continues on the next page)

Singapore Shellfish Soup (continued)

1. In a medium-sized saucepan heat 1 tablespoon of the oil over medium-high heat and fry the shrimp shells until pink.
2. Add 3 cups of water to the pan and bring to a boil; reduce the heat and simmer for 30 minutes. Strain the shells from the broth, then boil the broth until it is reduced to 2 cups.
3. In a large skillet, bring ½ cup of water to a boil. Add the mussels, cover, and let steam until opened, about 5 minutes. Discard any mussels that have not opened. Strain the cooking liquid and reserve. Shell all but about ⅓ of the mussels; set the mussels aside.
4. Place the lemongrass, chilies, garlic, ginger, shallots, anchovy paste, and 2 tablespoons of water in a food processor. Process to form a thick paste, adding more water if needed.
5. Heat the remaining vegetable oil in a large soup pot over medium heat. Add the lemongrass paste and fry, stirring continuously, until lightly browned, about 10 minutes. Stir in the turmeric and ground coriander and cook for 1 minute more.
6. Add the shrimp broth and mussel cooking liquid to the pot, stirring to dissolve the paste. Bring to a boil, reduce heat, and simmer for 10 to 15 minutes.
7. Add the coconut milk and fish sauce; return to a boil. Add the noodles and lime zest; simmer for 2 minutes. Add the shrimp and simmer for 2 minutes more. Add the scallop slices. After 30 seconds or so, add the shelled mussels and bean sprouts. Gently stir to combine.
8. To serve, ladle the soup into deep soup bowls. Garnish with the mussels in their shells, sprinkle with chopped cilantro and the juice from a lime wedge over the top of each bowl.

Roasted Duck, Melon, and Mango Salad

Serves 4–6

You can roast the duck yourself, or order either roast duck or duck confit from a gourmet shop. You can also substitute chicken if you prefer. Feel free to try other fruits in this salad, too.

1 teaspoon soy sauce
2 teaspoons fine sugar
1 teaspoon oyster sauce
1 tablespoon plus 2 teaspoons vegetable oil
½ roast duck, meat removed and shredded
3 tablespoons water
½ teaspoon granulated salt
1 teaspoon sugar
½ teaspoon sesame oil
1 teaspoon ketchup
1 teaspoon bottled chili sauce
1½ teaspoons cornstarch
1½ teaspoons apricot jam
1 cup cubed honeydew melon
1 cup cubed cantaloupe
½ large cucumber, seeded and sliced
1 cup cubed jicama
1 mango, cut into bite-sized pieces
1 pear, cut into bite-sized pieces
3 tablespoons ground peanuts
2 tablespoons toasted sesame seeds

1. In a medium-sized mixing bowl, combine the soy sauce, fine sugar, oyster sauce, and 1 tablespoon of the vegetable oil. Add the shredded duck to the bowl and toss to coat; set aside.
2. In a small bowl, whisk together the 3 tablespoons of water, salt, 1 teaspoon of sugar, sesame oil, ketchup, chili sauce, and cornstarch; set aside.
3. In a small saucepan, heat the remaining vegetable oil over medium heat. Add the sauce mixture to the pan and cook until it thickens. Stir in the apricot jam and remove the pan from the heat. Cool the sauce in the refrigerator. Stir before using.
4. Mound the duck in the center of a large serving platter. Arrange the fruits and vegetables around the duck. Spoon the sauce over the duck, fruits, and vegetables. Sprinkle the salad with chopped peanuts and sesame seeds. Serve at once.

Duck Confit

Duck confit is a lusciously moist and intensely flavored treat. The duck is cured in spices and then slowly braised in its own fat. It is delicious and surprisingly not greasy!

Spice-Poached Chicken

1 whole star anise
½ teaspoon whole black peppercorns
½ teaspoon whole cloves
1 (2-inch) cinnamon stick
1 cardamom pod
¼ teaspoon dried tangerine peel (dried orange peel can be substituted)
5 cups water
¼ cup light soy sauce
2 tablespoons sugar
4–6 boneless, skinless chicken breasts

Serves 4–6

I like to use this chicken as a base for chicken salad. The subtle spices impart a terrific flavor that turns a standby into a stand-up! Serve the chicken salad on a whole-grain roll with lettuce and apple slices.

1. Place the star anise, peppercorns, cloves, cinnamon stick, cardamom pod, tangerine peel, and water in a stew pot. Bring the mixture to a boil over high heat. Let boil until the poaching liquid is reduced to 4 cups.
2. Stir in the soy sauce and the sugar. Return the liquid to a boil.
3. Add the chicken breasts and reduce to a simmer. Poach the breasts until done, about 20 minutes.

Tangerines and Mandarin Oranges

Tangerines and mandarin oranges are the same thing! The name just tells you where they were grown. If they are from the United States, they are tangerines. If not, they're called mandarins.

Tea-Smoked Chicken

Serves 6–8

Make sure your stove's ventilation hood works before you start this recipe. The smoke stays mostly in the wok while the chicken is cooking, but it comes out in a big poof when you remove the lid.

6–8 boneless, skinless chicken breasts
½ teaspoon salt
2 teaspoons rice wine
½ cup green tea leaves
½ cup brown sugar
½ cup cooked rice
1 teaspoon sesame oil

1. Quickly rinse the chicken breasts under cold water and pat dry. Sprinkle with the salt and rice wine. Set aside in the refrigerator for 30 minutes.
2. Meanwhile, prepare the wok: Line the bottom with a sheet of aluminum foil. Place the tea leaves, brown sugar, and rice in the bottom of the wok and toss to combine. Put a wire grill rack on the wok.
3. Heat the wok over medium-high heat. Put the chicken on the rack and cover with a tight-fitting lid. Turn off the heat after smoke begins to emit from the wok, but leave it on the burner for 10 minutes or until the chicken is cooked through.
4. Brush the chicken with the sesame oil. Serve at once.

Thai Asian Fusion

Blending Chinese ingredients with local spices creates a type of fusion cooking that is unique to Singapore, called Nonya. These dishes are a specialty of "Hawker Centers," open-air centers with fast-food street stalls selling everything from satay to stir-fried noodles to spicy crab. Don't miss them if you travel to Singapore.

Pork Medallions in a Clay Pot

2 tablespoons oyster sauce
2 tablespoons light soy sauce
2 tablespoons sweet (dark) soy sauce
1 tablespoon Black Bean Paste (see recipe on page 296)
1 teaspoon sesame oil
1 teaspoon rice wine
½ teaspoon ground black pepper
1 clove garlic, minced
1 tablespoon cornstarch
2 pork tenderloins, trimmed and cut into ½-inch slices
2 tablespoons vegetable oil
1 tablespoon Tamarind Concentrate (see recipe on page 304)
1 cup water

Serves 4

Soy sauce, black bean paste, sesame oil, and rice wine are all traditional Chinese ingredients. The Chinese use clay pots over an open heat source as a type of oven, an appliance still not used much in Asia.

1. Prepare the marinade by combining the oyster sauce, light and dark soy sauces, Black Bean Paste, sesame oil, rice wine, black pepper, garlic, and cornstarch in a medium bowl.
2. Add the pork slices to the bowl of marinade and toss to coat thoroughly. Cover the pork and let marinate at room temperature for 30 minutes.
3. Heat the vegetable oil in a wok over medium-high heat. Add the marinated pork and stir-fry for 3 to 4 minutes.
4. Transfer the pork to a clay pot or other ovenproof braising vessel.
5. Stir together the tamarind and water; pour over the pork.
6. Bake the pork in a 350-degree oven for 1½ hours, until very tender.

Singapore Shrimp

Serves 4

This recipe is a mish-mash of cultures—Chinese, Thai, and Indian—a bit like Singapore herself. Somehow these flavors work well together, creating a beautiful and exotic meal.

2 tablespoons vegetable oil
1 cup sliced domestic mushrooms
¼ cup green onion slices
1 clove garlic, minced
1 teaspoon minced ginger
2 teaspoons hoisin sauce
2 teaspoons oyster sauce
2 teaspoons Red Curry Paste (see recipes in Chapter 13)
¼ teaspoon Chinese 5-spice powder
1 can coconut milk
Salt and pepper to taste
1½ pounds cooked shrimp

1. In a wok or large sauté pan, heat the vegetable oil on medium-high.
2. Add the mushrooms, green onions, garlic, and ginger; stir-fry for 2 to 3 minutes.
3. Stir together the hoisin sauce, oyster sauce, and curry paste, and 5-spice powder until well combined. Add the mixture to the wok.
4. Stir in the coconut milk and adjust seasoning to taste with the salt and pepper. Add the shrimp and bring to a simmer. Cook for 1 to 2 minutes until the shrimp are heated through.

5-Spiced Vegetables

½ cup orange juice
1 tablespoon cornstarch
½–¾ teaspoon Chinese 5-spice powder
¼ teaspoon crushed red pepper flakes
2 tablespoons soy sauce
2 teaspoons honey
1 tablespoon vegetable oil
1 pound mushrooms, sliced
1 cup carrot slices
1 small onion, halved and thinly sliced
1–2 cloves garlic, minced
3 cups broccoli florets

Serves 4

Here the 5 flavors of Asia—salty, hot, sweet, sour, and bitter—are found in the sauce. Add a little more honey if you prefer a sweeter sauce and fewer red pepper flakes if you don't want as much heat.

1. In a small bowl, combine the orange juice, cornstarch, 5-spice powder, red pepper flakes, soy sauce, and honey; set aside.
2. Heat the vegetable oil in a wok or skillet over medium-high heat. Add the mushrooms, carrots, onion, and garlic. Stir-fry for approximately 4 minutes.
3. Add the broccoli and continue cooking another 2 to 4 minutes.
4. Stir in the sauce. Cook until the vegetables are done to your liking and the sauce is thick, approximately 2 minutes.
5. Serve over rice noodles, pasta, or rice.

Peninsula Sweet Potatoes

Serves 4

To really give your Thanksgiving guests something to talk about, try serving this version of sweet potatoes.

1 pound sweet potatoes or yams of varying varieties, peeled and cut into bite-sized pieces
1 bay leaf
1 teaspoon sugar
¼ teaspoon salt
1 (14-ounce) can coconut milk

1. Place the sweet potato pieces in a large saucepan. Add just enough water to cover them, and bring to a boil. Add the bay leaf and cook until the potatoes are soft. Remove the bay leaf and discard.
2. Stir in the sugar and salt. After the sugar has dissolved, remove the pan from the heat and stir in the coconut milk. Adjust the seasonings by adding salt and/or sugar if necessary. Adjust the consistency by adding more water and/or coconut milk.

Beef Cambogee

Serves 4–6

Meat and potatoes, Cambodian style. As the meat and potatoes simmer in the curry, they become tender and deeply flavored. The peanuts and bean sprouts add snap.

5 cups Red Curry Cambogee (recipe on page 536)
1 pound sirloin, trimmed, and cut into bite-sized pieces
2–3 medium-sized russet potatoes, peeled and cut into bite-sized pieces
½ cup chopped peanuts
2 cups bean sprouts

1. In a large saucepan, bring the curry sauce to a simmer.
2. Add the meat and potatoes and simmer until done to your liking, about 20 to 30 minutes.
3. Garnish with the peanuts and bean sprouts.

Hot Noodles with Tofu

½ pound Chinese wheat noodles
Vegetable oil for frying
½ pound firm tofu, cut into 1-inch cubes
½ pound dried tofu, soaked in hot water for 15 minutes and cut into 1-inch cubes
3 tablespoons sesame oil
3 tablespoons minced ginger
½ teaspoon yellow asafetida powder
1 bunch choy sum, chopped into 1-inch pieces
3 tablespoons soy sauce
3 tablespoons sambal oelek
3 tablespoons lemon juice
2 cups mung bean shoots or bean sprouts

Serves 4

To serve this dish, mound the noodles on the center of four plates. Generously top with fresh shoots or sprouts.

1. Cook the noodles al dente according to package directions. Rinse under cold water and drain; set aside.
2. Heat about 2 inches of vegetable oil in a wok or large skillet over medium high heat. Add the firm tofu cubes and deep-fry until golden. Using a slotted spoon, remove the tofu cubes to paper towels to drain; set aside.
3. Add the dried tofu pieces and deep-fry them until they blister. Remove and drain on paper towels; set aside.
4. In another wok or skillet heat the sesame oil over high heat. Add the ginger and stir-fry 1 minute.
5. Add the asafetida and choy sum, and stir-fry until soft.
6. Stir in the soy sauce, sambal oelek, and lemon juice. Add the noodles and tofu pieces. Stir-fry until hot, about 2 minutes more.

Singapore Noodles

Serves 2–3

Do you have 5 minutes and some leftover chicken, beef, pork, shrimp, or a combination thereof? If so, this is the meal for you. It's satisfying, it's easy, and it's foolproof!

2 tablespoons vegetable oil
4 cloves garlic, minced
2 tablespoons minced ginger
2 cups cooked meat or shrimp in bite-sized pieces
2 green onions, trimmed and thinly sliced
1–2 teaspoons red pepper flakes
¼ cup oyster sauce
3 tablespoons curry powder
2 teaspoons soy sauce
1 package rice sticks, soaked in hot water until soft and drained

1. Heat the vegetable oil in a wok or large skillet over medium-high heat. Add the garlic and the ginger. Stir-fry until soft.
2. Add the cooked meat or shrimp, green onion, and red pepper flakes to the wok; stir-fry until hot.
3. Stir in the oyster sauce, curry powder, and soy sauce. Add the rice noodles and toss. Serve immediately.

Oyster Mushroom Soup

Serves 4

Oyster mushrooms are fan-shaped mushrooms with a mild flavor and a tender bite. In this Cambodian-style soup they add texture to a complex, yet simple-to-make broth.

4 cups vegetable broth
1 tablespoon Tabasco
2–3 serrano chilies
½ stalk lemongrass, outer leaves removed, inner core finely chopped
3 (2-inch-long, ½-inch wide) pieces lime zest
1 teaspoon sugar
2 tablespoons lemon juice
½ pound oyster mushrooms, cleaned and separated if large

1. In a large saucepan, bring the vegetable broth and the Tabasco to a boil. Meanwhile, crush the chilies with a mallet to break them slightly open: A good whack will do it.
2. Add all of the remaining ingredients to the boiling broth, reduce the heat, and simmer until the mushrooms are cooked to your liking. Remove the chilies before serving.

Sweet Cambodian Broth with Pork and Eggs

4 cups water
5 tablespoons soy sauce
½ teaspoon freshly ground black pepper
½ teaspoon salt
1 cup sugar
1 cup fish sauce
6–8 hard-boiled eggs
1 large pork tenderloin, cut into bite-sized cubes
1 cup thinly sliced bamboo shoots
Rice, cooked according to package directions

1. Bring the water to a boil in a large saucepan. Add the soy sauce, black pepper, salt, sugar, fish sauce, and hard-boiled eggs; simmer for 15 minutes.
2. Add the cubed pork and the bamboo shoots and simmer for an additional 30 minutes.
3. Reduce the heat to low, cover, and let simmer for 2 to 3 hours. Adjust seasonings to taste.
4. To serve, mound some rice in the bottom of soup bowls. Ladle soup over the rice.

Serves 4–6

When I say sweet, I mean sweet. As the sugar cooks, it gives a syrupy consistency to this very traditional dish. Luckily the sweetness is counteracted somewhat by a good amount of salty ingredients.

Cambodian-Style Pan-Fried Chicken and Mushrooms

Serves 4–6

Spoon the seasoned mushrooms and a bit of the pan drippings over the chicken. Serve noodles on the side.

6 ounces dried Chinese mushrooms
2 tablespoons vegetable oil
4 cloves garlic, crushed
½ teaspoon grated ginger
1½ pounds chicken breasts and legs
1 cup water
2 teaspoons sugar

1. Place the dried mushrooms in a bowl, cover with boiling water, and let soak for 30 minutes. Drain the mushrooms and rinse under cold water; drain again and squeeze dry. Remove any tough stems. Cut the mushrooms into bite-sized pieces; set aside.
2. Place the vegetable oil in a wok or large skillet over medium-high heat. Add the garlic and the ginger and stir-fry briefly.
3. Add the chicken and fry until the skin turns golden.
4. Stir in the water and the sugar. Add the mushrooms.
5. Reduce the heat to low, cover, and cook until the chicken is tender, about 30 minutes.

Cambodian Beef with Lime Sauce

1 tablespoon sugar
2 teaspoons freshly ground black pepper, divided
2 tablespoons soy sauce
5–7 cloves garlic, crushed
1½ pounds sirloin, trimmed and cut into bite-sized cubes
2 tablespoons lime juice
1 teaspoon water
2 tablespoons vegetable oil

Serves 4

This simple marinade is so good that even though the lime sauce is a breeze, the meat is equally good without it. If you don't have any beef on hand, use pork tenderloin instead.

1. In a bowl large enough to hold the beef, combine the sugar, 1 teaspoon of black pepper, soy sauce, and garlic. Add the beef and toss to coat. Cover and let marinate for 30 minutes.
2. In a small serving dish, combine the remaining black pepper, the lime juice, and the water; set aside.
3. In a large sauté pan, heat the vegetable oil over medium-high heat. Add the beef cubes and sauté for 4 minutes for medium-rare.
4. This dish may be served either as an appetizer or a main dish. For the appetizer, mound the beef on a plate lined with lettuce leaves with the lime sauce on the side. Use toothpicks or small forks to dip the beef into the lime sauce. For a main dish, toss the beef with the lime sauce to taste. Serve with Jasmine rice.

Red Curry Cambogee

Yields approx. 4½ cups

This Cambodian sauce is a hotter version of the Lemongrass Curry Sauce. It makes a great base for beef dishes.

4 dried Thai bird chilies, stemmed and seeded
1 cup boiling water
4 tablespoons sweet paprika
2 tablespoons vegetable oil
4 cups Lemongrass Curry Sauce (recipe follows)

1. Break the dried chilies into pieces and place them in a small bowl. Cover with the boiling water and let sit until soft, about 15 minutes.
2. Place the chilies, their steeping water, and the paprika in a blender. Process to form a thin paste.
3. Heat the vegetable oil over medium-high heat in a wok. Add the chili paste and stir-fry until it begins to darken. Remove from heat and set aside.
4. Place the Lemongrass Curry Sauce in a medium-sized saucepan. Stir in half of the chili paste and bring to a boil. Reduce the heat and let simmer for 5 to 10 minutes. Check the flavor of the sauce, adding more chili paste if needed.

Lemongrass Curry Sauce

Yields approx. 4 cups

Thailand's influence on Cambodian cuisine is evident in this sauce. Try it over fish or chicken with a side of Jasmine rice.

⅓ cup chopped lemongrass, inner core only
4–5 cloves garlic, chopped
1 teaspoon minced ginger
1 teaspoon turmeric
1 jalapeño chili, stemmed and seeded
3 small shallots, coarsely chopped
3 (14-ounce) cans coconut milk
3 (2-inch-long, ½-inch wide) pieces lime peel
¼ teaspoon salt

1. Place the lemongrass, garlic, ginger, turmeric, chili, and shallots in a food processor; process to form a paste.
2. Bring the coconut milk to a boil and add the lemongrass paste, lime peel, and salt. Reduce heat and let simmer for 30 to 45 minutes. Remove the lime peel.

Sweet-and-Sour Vegetables

1 cup sliced carrots
1 large green pepper, seeded and cut into bite-sized pieces
1 onion, sliced
2 cloves garlic, crushed
1 teaspoon grated ginger
1 cup water, divided
4 cups broccoli
6 green onions, trimmed and cut into 1-inch lengths
1 cup unsweetened pineapple juice
¼ cup rice vinegar
2 tablespoons soy sauce
⅓ cup brown sugar
2 tablespoons cornstarch
1 cup fresh pineapple chunks

Serves 6

A medley of vegetables, this dish is heavily influenced by Cambodia's northern neighbor, China. You can serve these as an accompaniment or as a main dish over rice.

1. Place the carrots, onion, green pepper, garlic, and ginger in a large saucepan with ½ cup of the water. Bring the water to a boil and let cook for 5 minutes, stirring frequently.
2. Add the broccoli, green onions, and the remaining ½ cup of water. Bring the water to a boil; reduce the heat, cover, and let simmer for 5 minutes.
3. Meanwhile, in a small bowl, thoroughly combine the pineapple juice, rice vinegar, soy sauce, brown sugar, and cornstarch.
4. Add the pineapple juice mixture and the pineapple chunks to the wok. Increase the heat to medium and cook, stirring constantly, until the sauce thickens.

Minted Vegetables

Serves 6

Nothing fancy, just a burst of minty freshness with each bite.

2 teaspoons vegetable oil, divided
4 medium carrots, peeled and cut into thin slices
1 medium onion, cut into 1-inch pieces
1 red bell pepper, seeded and cut into 1-inch pieces
3 cups broccoli pieces
3 cups thinly sliced red cabbage
½ cup vegetable broth
Salt and pepper to taste
3–4 tablespoons chopped mint

1. In a large skillet, heat 1 teaspoon of vegetable oil over medium-high heat. Add the carrot slices, onion, and bell pepper; sauté for 5 minutes.
2. Add the remaining teaspoon of oil, the broccoli, the cabbage, and the vegetable broth. Continue to sauté until the vegetables are done to your liking, about 10 minutes for tender-crisp.
3. Season to taste with salt and pepper. Stir in the chopped mint.

Shrimp "Pâté"

1¼ cups minced shrimp
½ teaspoon salt
1 teaspoon sugar
¼ teaspoon white pepper
1 red chili, seeded and finely minced (optional)
2 tablespoons vegetable oil
8 (4-inch) pieces sugarcane
Sweet-and-sour or other favorite dipping sauce

1. Preheat oven to 375 degrees.
2. Place the shrimp, salt, sugar, white pepper, and chili in a food processor; process until smooth.
3. Drizzle in 1 to 2 tablespoons of the vegetable oil. Process the shrimp mixture until it reaches the consistency necessary to make a meatball, using more or less oil.
4. Divide the shrimp mixture into 4 equal parts.
5. Using your hands, mold a "shrimp ball" around the center of each of the sugarcane pieces.
6. Place the "skewers" on a baking sheet and roast for approximately 20 minutes. If you prefer them a bit more browned, broil them (after they are done baking) until the desired color is reached.
7. To serve, spoon some of the sweet-and-sour sauce into the middle of 4 plates. Place the sugarcane "skewer" on top of the sauce.

Serves 4

Although not really a pâté in the traditional sense, you can still see the French influences in this dish. The ground shrimp is made into an almost mousse-like concoction that is slow-roasted—perfect with a glass of Chablis.

Vietnamese Pork Sticks

Serves 6

This Vietnamese recipe is a great appetizer to serve alongside rice paper spring rolls. The add-ons are basically the same—lettuce leaves for holding the canapé, herbs and dipping sauces for additional flavor.

For the pork:

1 pound lean ground pork
6 large water chestnuts, minced
1 clove garlic, minced
1 green onion, trimmed and minced
1 tablespoon soy sauce
2 teaspoons vegetable oil
1¼ teaspoons lemon juice
1 (½-inch) piece ginger, peeled and minced
¼ teaspoon sugar
¼ teaspoon Chinese hot chili oil
⅛ teaspoon salt
12 bamboo skewers, soaked in water
12 Boston or leaf lettuce leaves
½ cup chopped cilantro
½ cup chopped mint
½ cup chopped basil

For the dipping sauce:

½ cup soy sauce
5 tablespoons lemon juice
3 tablespoons water
2 garlic cloves, minced
1 (1-inch) piece ginger, minced
2 teaspoons sugar
1 teaspoon oyster sauce
Pinch of cayenne pepper

(recipe continues on the next page)

Vietnamese Pork Sticks (continued)

1. To prepare the pork: In a large bowl, use your hands to thoroughly combine the ground pork, water chestnuts, garlic, green onion, soy sauce, vegetable oil, lemon juice, ginger, sugar, chili oil, and salt.
2. Divide the mixture into 12 portions. Shape each portion into a cylinder about 3 inches by 1 inch. Carefully insert a bamboo skewer through each cylinder lengthwise. Set aside.
3. Place the lettuce leaves, cilantro, mint, and basil in 4 separate serving bowls. Refrigerate until ready to serve.
4. To prepare the dipping sauce: In a small saucepan combine all the sauce ingredients. Bring the mixture to a boil over medium-high heat. Reduce heat and simmer for 5 minutes. Remove the sauce from the heat and let cool.
5. Prepare a charcoal or gas grill. Place the skewers in a grill basket, making sure they are firmly held but not squashed. Grill the skewers until the pork is cooked through and the outside is crispy, about 10 to 15 minutes, turning the basket frequently.
6. To serve, pour each guest some of the dipping sauce into a small individual bowl. Place the bowls of cilantro, mint, and basil in the middle of the table. Place 2 lettuce leaves and 2 pork skewers on each guest's plate.
7. To assemble, have each guest slide the pork from the skewer onto a lettuce leaf. Sprinkle the pork with some of the herbs to taste. Roll the lettuce around the pork and dip in the sauce.

Happy Pancakes

Serves 4

Another example of French/Vietnamese fusion. The pancake is actually a version of a French crepe. The topping, on the other hand, is Vietnamese all the way.

1 cup rice flour
1½ cups water
2 eggs, lightly beaten
¼ teaspoon salt
1 teaspoon sugar
1 tablespoon vegetable oil
½ cup finely sliced straw mushrooms, rinsed and patted dry
3 ounces cooked salad shrimp, rinsed and patted dry
½ cup bean sprouts
¼ cup mixed, chopped herbs (mint, cilantro, basil, etc.)
Chili dipping sauce

1. In a medium-sized bowl, whisk together the rice flour, water, eggs, salt, and sugar. Set aside and let the batter rest for 10 minutes.
2. Strain the batter through a mesh sieve to remove any lumps.
3. Add the vegetable oil to a large sauté or omelet pan. Heat on high until very hot, but not smoking.
4. Pour the batter into the hot pan, swirling it so that it coats the bottom of the pan evenly. Sprinkle the mushrooms over the batter. Cover and let cook for 1 minute.
5. Sprinkle the shrimp and bean sprouts evenly over the pancake. Continue cooking until the bottom is crispy and browned.
6. To serve, cut the pancake into quarters. Sprinkle with the chopped herbs. Pass a favorite dipping sauce separately.

Honeyed Chicken

2 tablespoons honey
2 tablespoons fish sauce
2 tablespoons soy sauce
½ teaspoon Chinese 5-spice powder
2 tablespoons vegetable oil
1 medium onion, peeled and cut into wedges
1 pound boneless, skinless chicken breasts, cut into bite-sized pieces
3–4 cloves garlic, thinly sliced
1 (1-inch) piece ginger, peeled and minced

Serves 3–4

This is a version of a sweet-and-sour chicken without the bell peppers, fried batter, or red food coloring! The glaze is multidimensional in its flavor profile, and no batter means a healthier dish.

1. Combine the honey, fish sauce, soy sauce, and 5-spice powder in a small bowl; set aside.
2. Heat the oil in a wok on medium-high. Add the onion and cook until it just begins to brown.
3. Add the chicken; stir-fry for 3 to 4 minutes.
4. Add the garlic and ginger, and continue stir-frying for 30 more seconds.
5. Stir in the honey mixture and let cook for 3 to 4 minutes, until the chicken is glazed and done to your liking.

Vietnamese Oxtail Soup

Serves 6–8

Don't be afraid of eating tails! These inexpensive pieces of meat are extremely tender and flavorful when braised in this fashion. If you can't find oxtails, beef or veal shanks would be a great substitute.

2 medium onions
1 tablespoon vegetable oil
5 pounds meaty oxtails
4 (½-inch) pieces ginger, peeled
2 medium carrots, peeled and julienned
1 small cinnamon stick
1 whole star anise
1 tablespoon whole black peppercorns
2 garlic cloves, peeled and crushed
1 green onion, trimmed and thinly sliced
3 tablespoons fish sauce
Freshly ground black pepper to taste
½ pound bean sprouts
¼ cup chopped cilantro
4 serrano chilies, seeded and thinly sliced
2 limes, cut into wedges
1 (7-ounce) package rice sticks, soaked in hot water until soft and drained

(recipe continues on the next page)

Vietnamese Oxtail Soup (continued)

1. Cut 1 of the onions into ¼-inch slices. Heat the vegetable oil in a medium-sized sauté pan over medium-high heat. Add the onion slices and sauté until they just begin to brown. Drain the oil from the browned onion and set aside.
2. Slice the remaining onion into paper-thin slices. Cover with plastic wrap and set aside.
3. Rinse the oxtails in cold water and place them in a stock pot. Cover the tails with cold water and bring to a boil. Reduce the heat and skim any residue that has come to the surface. Let simmer for 15 minutes.
4. Add the browned onions, ginger, carrots, cinnamon, star anise, peppercorns, and garlic. Return the stock to a simmer and cook for 6 to 8 hours, adding water if necessary.
5. When the broth is done, skim off any additional residue. Remove the oxtails from the pot and let cool until easy to handle. Remove the meat from the bones. Arrange the meat on a platter and garnish it with the sliced green onions. Discard the bones.
6. Strain the broth and return to the stove. Add the fish sauce and black pepper to taste. Keep warm.
7. On a second platter, arrange the bean sprouts, chopped cilantro, sliced chilies, and lime wedges.
8. Bring a pot of water to a boil. Plunge the softened rice noodles in the water to heat. Drain.
9. To serve, place a portion of the noodles in each bowl. Set a tureen of the broth on the table along with the platter of oxtail meat and the platter of accompaniments. Let your guests serve themselves.

Fruit in Sherried Syrup

Serves 4–6

This simple syrup can be made ahead of time and stored in the refrigerator for up to a week! Try it in some hot or iced tea!

2 tablespoons sugar
4 tablespoons water
2 tablespoons dry sherry
2 teaspoons lemon juice
1 orange, peeled and segmented
2 cups fresh pineapple chunks
1½ cups kiwi slices

1. In a small saucepan over high heat, boil the sugar and the water until syrupy. Remove from the heat and let cool to room temperature. Stir in the lemon juice and sherry; set aside.
2. In a serving bowl, combine the orange segments, the pineapple chunks, and the kiwi. Pour the syrup over the fruit and toss to combine. Refrigerate for at least 1 hour before serving.

Banana Brown Rice Pudding

Serves 4–6

This satisfying dessert requires no baking! It is also lacking eggs and cream, so it takes on the texture of porridge more than of custard. The banana and the fruit cocktail give the pudding flavor and structure.

1 medium banana, sliced
1 (15-ounce) can fruit cocktail, drained
¼ cup water
2 tablespoons honey
1 teaspoon vanilla extract
½ teaspoon cinnamon
½ teaspoon nutmeg
1 cup skim milk
1½ cups cooked brown rice

1. In a medium-sized saucepan, combine the banana, fruit cocktail, water, honey, vanilla, cinnamon, and nutmeg. Bring to a boil over medium-high heat. Reduce the heat and simmer for 10 minutes or until the bananas are tender.
2. Stir in the milk and the rice. Return the mixture to a boil, reduce heat again, and simmer for 10 more minutes. Serve warm.

Vietnamese Bananas

3 tablespoons shredded coconut (unsweetened)
3 tablespoons butter
3 tablespoons brown sugar
1 tablespoon grated ginger
Grated zest of 1 orange
6 bananas, peeled and sliced in half lengthwise
4 tablespoons lime juice
6 tablespoons orange liqueur
3 teaspoons toasted sesame seeds

Serves 6

This dessert is a take-off on Bananas Foster, the simple yet spectacular tableside dessert made famous in the 1960s and the 1970s along with cherries jubilee!

1. Heat a small nonstick pan over high heat. Add the coconut and cook, stirring constantly, until golden brown. Remove the coconut from the pan and set aside.
2. In a large sauté pan, melt the butter over medium-high heat. Stir in the brown sugar, the ginger, and orange zest. Place the bananas in the pan, cut-side down, and cook for 1 to 2 minutes or until the sauce starts to become sticky. Turn the bananas over to coat in the sauce. Place the bananas on a heated serving platter and cover with aluminum foil.
3. Return the pan to the heat and thoroughly stir in the lime juice and the orange liqueur. Using a long-handled match, ignite the sauce. Allow the flames to die down and then pour the sauce over the bananas.
4. Sprinkle the bananas with the toasted coconut and the sesame seeds. Serve immediately.

Basic Vietnamese Chili Sauce

Yields approx. ¼ cup

This Vietnamese chili sauce differs from most Thai hot sauces with its use of dried chilies instead of fresh, yielding a smokier, somewhat softer flavor. Brown sugar also has a mellowing effect.

2 dried red chilies, stemmed, seeded, and soaked in hot water until soft
2 cloves garlic, minced
½ teaspoon brown sugar
2 tablespoons fish sauce
1 tablespoon rice wine vinegar
1 tablespoon lemon juice

Using a mortar and pestle, grind together the dried chilies and the garlic to form a rough paste. Stir in the sugar until well incorporated. Stir in the remaining ingredients.

Chilied Coconut Dipping Sauce

Yields approx. ⅓ cup

This Vietnamese dipping sauce goes especially well with shrimp and fish.

¼ cup fresh coconut juice
1 teaspoon rice wine vinegar
1 teaspoon sugar
1 serrano chili, seeded and minced
2 cloves garlic, minced
1 tablespoon lime juice
2 tablespoons fish sauce

1. Bring the coconut juice, rice wine vinegar, and sugar to a boil in a small saucepan. Remove from heat and allow the mixture to cool to room temperature.
2. Stir in the remaining ingredients.

Tropical Fruits with Cinnamon and Lime

Zest and juice of 6 limes
3 tablespoons honey
½ teaspoon sesame oil
½–1 teaspoon cinnamon
Pinch of salt
6 cups of tropical fruits, such as mango, papaya, bananas, melons, star fruit, kiwi, etc., (anything really) cut into bite-sized pieces

Serves 6–12

Typical in many Asian fruit concoctions, salt is added to this cinnamon-lime sauce to balance sweetness. If you can't adjust your Western palate to this juxtaposition of flavors, just leave out the salt.

1. Combine the lime zest and all but about ⅓ of the lime juice in a small bowl. Slowly drizzle in the honey, whisking to form a smooth mixture. Whisk in the sesame oil, cinnamon, and salt. Adjust flavor to your liking with more lime juice if necessary.
2. Place the fruit in a large serving bowl. Pour the cinnamon-lime dressing over the fruit, toss to combine, and let rest in the refrigerator for 15 minutes before serving.

Potato Samosas

Yields 20 samosas

Samosas are a good introduction to Indian cuisine, because although they are filled with unusual spices, their main ingredient is potato—a very comforting food no matter how it's prepared.

For the crust:

1½ cups all-purpose flour
½ teaspoon salt
4 tablespoons butter, at room temperature
Ice water
Vegetable oil for deep frying

For the filling:

1¼ pounds russet potatoes, peeled
1 tablespoon ghee (see note) or oil
2 teaspoons mustard seeds
½ teaspoon turmeric
½ teaspoon chili powder
¼ pound sweet peas, thawed if frozen
1 teaspoon salt
2 jalapeños, seeded and thinly sliced
3 tablespoons chopped mint
Lemon juice to taste

1. To make the pastry crust: In a large bowl, sift together the flour and the salt. Using a pastry cutter, cut the butter into the flour mixture.
2. Add the ice water, 1 tablespoon at a time, until a firm dough is achieved. You will probably use 5 to 6 tablespoons of water total. Knead the dough for approximately 5 minutes or until it is smooth and elastic. Place the dough in an oiled bowl, cover with plastic wrap, and set it aside while making the potato filling.

(recipe continues on the next page)

Potato Samosas (continued)

3. To make the filling: Bring a large pan of water to a boil. Add the potatoes and cook until quite tender. Drain the potatoes and allow them to cool until they are easy to handle. Cut them into a small dice; set aside.
4. In a large skillet, heat the ghee over medium-high heat. Add the mustard seeds and sauté until the seeds begin to pop. Stir in the turmeric and the chili powder; cook for 15 seconds. Stir in the potatoes, peas, salt, and jalapeño slices. (It is okay if the potatoes and the peas get a little smashed.) Remove from heat, stir in the mint and lemon juice to taste, and set aside.
5. Roll the pastry until it is quite thin (1/8-inch thick). Cut approximately ten 6-inch circles from the dough. Cut each circle in half. Place a heaping tablespoon of filling in the center of each half circle. Dampen the edges of the dough with cold water, fold the dough over on itself to form a triangle, and seal firmly.
6. To fry, add approximately 3 inches of vegetable oil to a large saucepan. Heat the oil over high heat until very hot, but not smoking. Add the samosas to the hot oil a few at a time and deep-fry until golden brown. Using a slotted spoon, remove the samosas to a stack of paper towels to drain.
7. Serve the samosas with Tamarind Dipping Sauce (see recipe on page 274).

Ghee

Ghee is another name for clarified butter. It is simple to make. Simply melt a quantity of unsalted butter in a heavy saucepan. Bring it to a boil and let it simmer for 15 to 20 minutes or until the solid milk particles rise to the top and begin to brown. Remove the butter from the heat and strain it through cheesecloth. Ghee may be stored at room temperature for up to 1 week in an airtight container.

Chapati

Serves 6–8

Chapati is a simple griddle bread with a Muslim heritage.

3 cups whole-wheat flour
1½ teaspoons salt
1 tablespoon ghee or oil
1 cup lukewarm water

1. In a large mixing bowl, stir together 2½ cups of flour and the salt. Add the ghee and, using your fingers, rub it into the flour and salt mixture.
2. Add the lukewarm water and mix to form a dough. Knead the dough until it is smooth and elastic, about 10 minutes. (Don't skimp on the kneading; it is what makes the bread tender.)
3. Form the dough into a ball and place it in a small, oiled bowl. Cover tightly with plastic wrap and let it rest at room temperature for at least 1 hour.
4. Divide the dough into golf ball–sized pieces. Using a flour-covered rolling pin, roll each ball out on a flour-covered surface to approximately 6 to 8 inches in diameter and ⅛-inch thick.
5. Heat a large skillet or griddle over medium heat. Place a piece of dough on the hot surface. Using a towel or the edge of a spoon, carefully press down around the edges of the bread. (This will allow air pockets to form in the bread.) Cook for 1 minute. Carefully turn the chapati over and continue cooking for 1 more minute. Chapatis should be lightly browned and pliable, not crisp. Remove the bread to a basket and cover with a towel. Repeat until all of the rounds are cooked.

Asian Bread

Unlike in Thailand and most other Southeast Asian countries, bread is an integral part of the Indian diet. Most are not leavened and are made in individual servings, not in loaves.

Mulligatawny Soup

3 pounds chicken wings
4 whole cloves
2 medium onions, peeled
3 cloves garlic, peeled
1 jalapeño, seeded and sliced
1 (1½-inch) cinnamon stick
2 teaspoons whole peppercorns
5 cardamom pods, bruised
2 tablespoons ground coriander
1 tablespoon ground cumin
2 teaspoons salt
1 tablespoon vegetable oil
8–12 fresh curry leaves
6 cups chicken broth
1 (14-ounce) can coconut milk
Lemon juice to taste
4–5 cups cooked rice

Serves 8–10

I don't think you can find an Indian restaurant in the United States that doesn't serve this famous soup. It was first developed about 200 years ago in Madras and comes in vegetarian and meat versions.

1. Place the chicken wings in a large soup pot. Cover the chicken with cold water.
2. Stick the cloves into 1 of the onions and place the onion in the pot with the chicken.
3. Add the garlic, jalapeño, cinnamon stick, peppercorns, cardamom, coriander, cumin, and salt; bring the mixture to a boil, reduce to a simmer, and cook for 2 to 3 hours.
4. Let the stock come to room temperature. Remove the chicken pieces from the broth and cut the meat from the bones. Set aside the meat.
5. Strain the broth.
6. Thinly slice the remaining onion.
7. In a large sauté pan, heat the oil over medium-high heat. Add the onion slices and sauté until translucent. Add the curry leaves and the broth. Bring to a simmer and let cook for 5 minutes.
8. Add enough water to the coconut milk to make 3 cups of liquid. Add this and the reserved meat to the broth. Heat the soup, but do not let it boil. Season to taste with additional salt and a squeeze of lemon juice.
9. To serve, place approximately ½ cup of cooked rice in the bottom of each bowl. Ladle the soup over the rice.

Tandoori Chicken

Serves 4

Without a tandoori oven, you can't really make an authentic tandoori dish. The clay used in making the ovens gives a smoky flavor that can't be duplicated. Still, this recipe creates an acceptable variation.

4 skinless chicken breasts
4 skinless chicken legs
½ teaspoon saffron threads
½ cup plain yogurt
1 tablespoon grated ginger
2 small garlic cloves, minced
2 teaspoons salt
⅛ teaspoon chili powder
2 teaspoons paprika
1½ teaspoons Garam Masala *(see recipe on page 559)*
2 tablespoons ghee, melted

1. Using a small, sharp knife, make 3 to 4 (¼-inch-deep) slits in each piece of chicken. Set aside in a bowl large enough to hold all of the pieces.
2. Place the saffron in a small sauté pan over medium heat and toast for approximately 30 seconds. Place the saffron on a small plate and allow it to cool and crumble.
3. Stir the saffron into the yogurt.
4. Grind together the ginger, garlic, salt, chili pepper, paprika, and garam masala. Stir the spice mixture into the yogurt.
5. Pour the yogurt over the chicken, making sure that all of the pieces are coated. Cover and marinate overnight, turning the pieces in the marinade every so often.
6. Preheat the oven to 450 degrees.
7. Add the ghee to a roasting pan large enough to hold all of the chicken pieces. Add the chicken, breast side down. Spoon some of the ghee over the pieces. Roast for 10 minutes. Turn the pieces over, baste again, and continue roasting for 5 minutes. Turn them again and roast for an additional 5 minutes. Turn 1 last time (breasts should be up); baste and cook until done, about 5 more minutes.

Punjab Fish

4–6 firm-fleshed fish fillets, approximately 1-inch thick
Lemon juice
1 teaspoon salt
1 teaspoon black pepper
1 teaspoon turmeric
2–3 tablespoons vegetable oil
1 medium onion, thinly sliced
1 clove garlic, chopped
1 (1-inch) piece ginger, peeled and minced
2 serrano chilies, seeded and minced
2 tablespoons almond slivers
2 teaspoons cumin
2 teaspoons cardamom
1/4 teaspoon cinnamon
1/8 teaspoon ground cloves
2 tablespoons boiling water
1/4 teaspoon saffron strands, toasted and crushed
1/2 cup plain yogurt

Serves 4–6

Punjab, meaning "Five Rivers," is a state located in northwestern India. It is known as a land of high spirits and prosperity due to its fertile soil and many rivers.

1. Rinse the fish with cold water and pat dry. Rub the fish with lemon juice.
2. Combine the salt, pepper, and turmeric; sprinkle over the fish.
3. Heat 1 to 2 tablespoons of vegetable oil in a large frying pan over high heat. Brown the fish quickly on each side. Remove the fish to a plate, cover, and set aside.
4. Add the onion to the same pan and sauté until translucent and just beginning to brown.
5. Place the cooked onion in a food processor along with the garlic, ginger, chilies, and almonds. Process to form a paste, adding a bit of water if necessary. Add the cumin, cardamom, cinnamon, and clove; process to thoroughly blend.
6. If necessary, add additional vegetable oil to the frying pan to make about 2 tablespoons. Heat the oil over medium. Add the spice mixture and cook, stirring constantly, for about 2 minutes. Swirl a bit of water in the food processor to remove any remaining spices and pour it into the pan; stir to combine.
7. Pour 2 tablespoons of boiling water into a small cup. Add the toasted saffron and stir to combine. Pour the saffron water into the frying pan.
8. Stir in the yogurt. Bring to a simmer and let the sauce cook for 5 minutes.
9. Add the fish to the sauce, turning to coat. Cover and let simmer for approximately 10 minutes or until the fish is done to your liking.

Indian-Scented Cauliflower

Serves 2–4

This cauliflower is scented with an Indian spice mixture that seeps into every little crack and crevice, perfuming every bite. You will never look at cauliflower the same way again.

3 tablespoons vegetable oil
1 teaspoon mustard seeds
1 clove garlic, minced
1 (2-inch) piece ginger, peeled and minced
½ teaspoon turmeric
½ medium to large head of cauliflower, separated into florets and cut into pieces
1 teaspoon salt
3 tablespoons water
½ teaspoon Garam Masala (see recipe on page 559)

1. In a saucepan large enough to easily hold the cauliflower, heat the vegetable oil over medium-high heat. Add the mustard seeds and fry until they pop. Add the garlic and the ginger; stirring constantly, cook until the garlic just begins to brown.
2. Stir in the turmeric. Add the cauliflower pieces and toss to coat with the spice mixture.
3. Add the water, cover, and let steam for 6 to 10 minutes or until done to your liking.
4. Pour off any excess water and sprinkle with the garam masala.

Cardamom Cookies

4 ounces ghee
½ cup fine sugar
1 cup fine semolina
3 tablespoons all-purpose flour
1 ½ teaspoons ground cardamom

1. Preheat oven to 300 degrees.
2. In a large mixing bowl, cream together the ghee and the sugar until light and fluffy.
3. Sift together the semolina, all-purpose flour, and cardamom.
4. Stir the dry ingredients into the ghee mixture; mix well.
5. Let the dough stand in a cool place for 30 minutes.
6. Form balls using approximately 1 tablespoon of dough for each. Place on an ungreased cookie sheet and flatten each ball slightly.
7. Bake for approximately 30 minutes or until pale brown.
8. Cool on a wire rack. Store in an airtight container.

Yields 2 dozen cookies

These cookies are reminiscent of shortbread in terms of texture and ingredients, but they are perfumed with a bit of ground cardamom. They're simply delicious with tea.

Cardamom

The cardamom plant is a relative of ginger and grows in most tropical climates throughout the world. Cardamom pods have a very sweet-spicy smell and taste, similar to cinnamon. The spice refers to the seeds, which can be bought whole or ground.

Almond "Tea"

Serves 4–6

Not really a tea at all, this refreshing drink hits the spot on a sweltering day. The milk gives it a bit of creaminess, but the water makes it refreshing. It's also a great addition to milkshakes or smoothies.

3 ounces blanched almonds
2 ounces pumpkin seeds
½ teaspoon ground cardamom
3 cups water
2 cups milk
¼–½ cup sugar

1. Process the almonds, pumpkin seeds, cardamom, and half of the water in a blender or food processor until the solids are finely ground.
2. Strain the almond water through cheesecloth (or a clean Handi Wipe) into a container. Using the back of a spoon, press the solids to remove as much moisture as possible.
3. Return the almond mixture to the blender and add the remaining water. Process until thoroughly combined.
4. Strain this liquid into the container.
5. Stir the milk into the almond water. Add sugar to taste.
6. Serve over crushed ice.

Cucumber Raita

Yields approx. 4 cups

What is an Indian meal without the cooling effects and delicious taste of a raita? Milk products, in this case yogurt, counteract spicy foods by coating your mouth with fat.

2 seedless cucumbers, peeled and cut into a small dice
1 teaspoon salt
1½ cups plain yogurt
1–2 green onions, trimmed and thinly sliced
2 tablespoons fresh mint
Lemon juice to taste

1. Place the diced cucumbers in a colander. Sprinkle with salt and let sit in the sink for 15 minutes to drain. Rinse the cucumber under cold water and drain again.
2. Combine the cucumber, yogurt, green onions, mint, and lemon juice to taste.
3. Cover and refrigerate for at least 30 minutes. Check seasoning, adding additional salt and/or lemon juice if necessary.

Tamarind Dipping Sauce

3 tablespoons tamarind pulp
1 cup hot water
1 teaspoon salt
2 teaspoons brown sugar
1 teaspoon ground cumin
½ teaspoon ground fennel
2 teaspoons grated ginger
Lemon juice to taste

1. Place the tamarind pulp in a small bowl. Pour boiling water over the pulp and let soak until soft, about 15 minutes.
2. Break up the pulp and then strain the tamarind water through a fine-mesh sieve, using the back of a spoon to push the pulp through, but leaving the tough fibers.
3. Stir in the remaining ingredients and let the tamarind sauce sit for at least 15 minutes before serving.

Makes about 1¼ cups

I love this dipping sauce. I spoon it over everything—samosas, papadam, all sorts of Indian breads, over rice, etc., etc. I promise you, once you try it you'll be hooked, too.

Garam Masala

4 tablespoons coriander seeds
2 tablespoons cumin seeds
1 tablespoon whole black peppercorns
2 teaspoons cardamom seeds
2 small cinnamon sticks, broken into pieces
1 teaspoon whole cloves

1. In a small heavy sauté pan, individually dry roast each spice over medium-high heat until they begin to release their aroma.
2. Allow the spices to cool to room temperature and then place them in a spice grinder and process to form a fairly fine powder.
3. Store in an airtight container.

Makes approx. ⅓ cup

The Indian spice mix you can't do without! If you always have a bit of this mixture on hand, you are just a step away from great Indian cuisine. I promise. (Garam masala is also available in specialty stores.)

Mango Chutney

Makes approx. 5–6 cups

In addition to serving this condiment with Indian food, I use it to top broiled salmon, as a spread for scones, to mix with white rice, or for whatever takes my fancy.

2 large green mangoes, peeled and sliced
4 ounces dried apricots or cherries
½ ounce golden raisins
1 tablespoon chopped ginger
1 tablespoon minced garlic
1–2 red chili peppers, seeded and minced
2 cups sugar
1 cup water
2 cups white vinegar
3 teaspoons salt
1 teaspoon cumin
½ teaspoon black mustard seeds
2 teaspoons Garam Masala (see recipe on page 559)

1. Place all of the ingredients in a heavy-bottomed saucepan. Bring to a simmer over medium heat, stirring until the sugar dissolves. Simmer for 30 minutes or until thick.
2. Seal in airtight jars.

Appendices

Appendix A

Glossary of Asian Ingredients

Appendix B

Glossary of Thai Flavors and Ingredients

Appendix C

Thai Resources

Appendix A

Glossary of Asian Ingredients

agar-agar: Made from seaweed, it takes the place of gelatin in Asian cooking. Agar and gelatin can be substituted for each other in recipes—just remember that agar-agar has different setting properties, requiring less time to set the same amount of liquid.

bean curd: Bean curd is made from curdled soy milk in a process that has a great deal in common with making cheese. Tofu, the name by which bean curd is commonly known, is a Japanese modification of the Chinese word for bean curd, *doufu.* Bean curd comes in a number of different textures, from firm to soft, depending on how firmly the curd is pressed. There is also fermented tofu flavored with spicy seasonings, and dried bean curd sheets and sticks.

bitter melon: A green gourd with a distinctive pockmarked skin, bitter melon has a strong chalky flavor that isn't completely removed by degorging. Bitter melon is normally paired with other strongly flavored ingredients, such as chilies.

black bean sauce and paste: Savory sauces and pastes made from dried black beans. Different varieties include hot bean sauce and yellow bean sauce.

blanch (parboil): In Chinese cooking, blanching generally refers to plunging vegetables briefly into boiling water and then draining thoroughly. Blanching helps preserve the natural color and texture of vegetables, as well as the nutrients.

bok choy: A large cabbage with dark green leaves that is available in both western and Asian supermarkets, bok choy is used in soups, stir-fries, and braised dishes. The thicker stalks require a longer cooking time than the more delicate leaves. Shanghai or baby bok choy is a smaller variety of bok choy with a sweeter flavor and more delicate texture.

chili pepper: Szechwan cuisine wouldn't be the same without these small, hot peppers. Chili peppers comes in a number of varieties, from jalapeno to hot habaneros. In general, the smaller the chili, the higher the heat content. Chili peppers are used to make Hot Chili Oil (page 25).

Chinese cabbage: Also known as napa cabbage or Peking cabbage, Chinese cabbage is the other main cabbage besides bok choy used in Chinese cooking. Its pale green leaves readily absorb the flavors of the food it is cooked with. Napa cabbage is used in soups, salads, stir-fries, and even eaten raw.

Chinese sausage: Thinner and redder than sausages normally found in supermarkets, Chinese sausages are made from a number of ingredients, including pork and liver. Look for them under their Chinese name, *lop cheong.*

cilantro: Also known as Chinese parsley, cilantro consists of the leaves of the coriander plant. While coriander is a popular Indian spice, the leaves feature more prominently in Chinese cooking. Use in sauces and as a garnish.

cornflour: Another term for cornstarch.

deep-fry: Cooking food by completely submerging it in hot oil. This is one of the three main techniques used in Chinese cooking.

dim sum: Literally meaning "touch your heart," dim sum is a meal consisting of numerous small appetizers or snacks that had its origins in Chinese teahouses. Dim sum may have been the inspiration for the Western and European custom of brunch.

dried lily buds: These are the dried unopened buds of day lilies. Their earthy flavor is featured in Traditional Mu Shu Pork (page 147) and Hot and Sour Soup (page 57).

dried mushrooms: Also called black mushrooms, although their color ranges from light to dark brown, these fungi are found on decaying logs and tree stumps. In Chinese cooking, dried mushrooms are favored over fresh, as the drying process enhances their flavor. They must be softened in water before use.

dried tangerine peel: Dried tangerine peel lends a citrusy aroma to simmered dishes, and can also be used in stir-fries. Soften in water before use.

fuzzy melon: Related to winter melon, fuzzy melon is roughly the size and shape of a cucumber, with a dark green skin covered in light fuzz. It is baked, stuffed, and added to soups and stir-fries. If the recipe does not require peeling the melon skin, be sure to remove the fuzz before cooking.

glutinous rice: Glutinous rice is made from short-grain rice kernels. In Chinese cooking, it is normally, although not always, reserved for sweets and desserts.

groundnut oil: Another term for peanut oil.

hoisin sauce: A thick sauce made from soybean paste, hoisin sauce is a mainstay of northern Chinese regional cuisine, and the base for many Chinese satay sauces. Seasonings such as garlic and chilies give hoisin sauce its unique sweet and savory flavor.

kecap manis: The Indonesian version of soy sauce, although it is much more flavorful. Kecap manis is made with an assortment of seasonings, including star anise and palm sugar. *Kecap* is the source of the word "ketchup."

oil velveting: A technique to tenderize meat or poultry by submerging it in hot oil very briefly, just until it changes color. It is then cooked by conventional methods such as stir-frying or deep-frying. Prior to velveting, the meat is frequently marinated with a mixture of egg white and cornstarch.

oyster sauce: A savory sauce made with boiled oysters and seasonings such as soy sauce and garlic. Oyster sauce is most commonly used in sauces and dips. For vegetarians, Lee Kum Kee offers an oyster sauce using mushrooms in place of oysters.

red cooking: This cooking technique consists of browning food, and then braising or stewing it in soy sauce for a lengthy period of time. Dark soy sauce is frequently used in red cooking.

rice flour: Made from glutinous rice, it is used in a few Chinese desserts, such as New Year's Sticky Cake (page 281).

rice vinegar: Rice vinegar is made from fermented rice. The three main types of rice vinegar used in Chinese cooking are red, white, and black. White rice vinegar comes closest in flavor to Western cider vinegar.

rice wine: A wine made with glutinous short-grained rice, Chinese rice wine is used frequently in marinades and sauces. The most famous rice wine comes from the Shaoxing region in northern China. If rice wine is unavailable, a good quality pale dry sherry can be used as a substitute.

rock sugar: A mixture of refined sugar, honey, and brown sugar, rock sugar is used in desserts and recipes where a stronger flavor than regular sugar is required.

sesame oil: A nutty-flavored oil made from toasted sesame seeds, sesame oil is used in sauces, marinades, and dips. It is frequently drizzled over food in the final stages of cooking. Sesame oil's strong flavor and low smoking point generally make it a poor choice as a cooking oil.

sesame paste: A richly flavored paste made from toasted sesame seeds. If unavailable, peanut butter can be used instead. Tahini, the Mediterranean version of sesame paste, is not a good substitute, as it is made from untoasted sesame seeds.

sesame seeds: The seeds that come from the Asian sesame plant, sesame seeds are used in desserts such as Glazed Bananas (page 280) and savory dishes such as Sesame Chicken (page 180). They are frequently toasted before use.

shoyu: The Japanese version of light soy sauce, shoyu can be used in Chinese cooking.

soy sauce, dark: A soybean-based sauce that is aged for a longer period of time than regular (light) soy sauce, dark soy sauce is commonly used in marinades and red-cooked dishes. Do not use in place of regular (light) soy sauce, as it has a very different flavor.

soy sauce, light: A soybean-based sauce that is one of the most important ingredients in Chinese cooking, light soy sauce has a lighter color, thinner texture, and saltier flavor than dark soy sauce. Japanese **shoyu** can be used as a substitute.

steaming: Cooking food by placing it over boiling water so that the steam reaches and cooks the food. This is the third most popular Chinese cooking technique.

stir-frying: Cooking food in oil at very high heat for a short period of time, while continuously stirring. It is the cooking technique most commonly associated with Chinese cuisine.

Szechwan peppercorn: Known for the biting sensation it leaves on the tongue, the Szechwan peppercorn gives Szechwan cuisine its distinctive flavor. It is actually not a peppercorn at all, but a berry from the prickly ash tree. Szechwan peppercorns are normally roasted and ground before use.

tapioca starch: A starch made from the tubers of the tapioca plant, tapioca starch is used as a thickener in Chinese cooking. Cornstarch and tapioca starch can be substituted for each other in sauce recipes, but cornstarch takes longer to thicken.

thick soy sauce: Used to lend flavor to fried rice and noodle dishes, thick soy sauce has been thickened with molasses.

water chestnuts: The name can cause confusion, since water chestnuts come from an aquatic plant and are not related to horse chestnuts, which grow on trees. Fresh water chestnuts have a sweet flavor reminiscent of banana. Canned water chestnuts can be substituted for texture but don't have the same flavor. Jicama is also used as a substitute.

white pepper: A seasoning made from ground white peppercorns. A little-known fact is that white and black pepper both come from the same plant; the main difference between them is that white pepper berries are allowed to ripen before processing. In Chinese cooking, white pepper makes a frequent appearance in soups and spicier stir-fries. Use sparingly as it has a sharp bite.

winter melon: A type of squash with an oblong shape and dark green rind similar to a watermelon. The inside flesh is white and pleasantly sweet. Winter Melon Soup (page 63) is a popular banquet soup.

wok: A bowl-shaped utensil designed to be used in cooking methods requiring high heat, such as deep-frying. A wok is the main piece of Chinese cooking equipment.

wood fungus: This fungus is also called cloud ear fungus because of its unusual shape. Like tofu, it has no flavor but absorbs the flavor of the foods it is cooked with. It is used in soups and stir-fries. Soak wood fungus in water to soften before use.

APPENDIX B
Glossary: Thai Flavors and Ingredients

BANANAS: Bananas are indigenous to Thailand, where over twenty-eight varieties are cultivated. The most common banana is the Cavendish, but don't be afraid to experiment with different varieties, especially in tropical fruit salads.

BASIL: Most commonly thought of as an Italian ingredient, basil is actually a key ingredient in cuisines from around the world. Basil comes in many varieties, including a Thai version, but any fresh basil works well in Thai cooking. Basil is quite delicate and is usually best added to dishes at the last possible moment.

BOK CHOY: Also known as Chinese cabbage, bok choy resembles Swiss chard in looks and regular green cabbage in taste. Stir-frying softens its flavor slightly.

CARDAMOM: This relative of ginger grows in most tropical environments. Its pods release a pungent, sweet-spicy flavor, somewhat similar to cinnamon.

CHILI PEPPERS: Chilies come in three basic forms: fresh, dried, and powdered. Botanists have named hundreds of different varieties, making chilies one of the most diverse plants on the planet. With that said, there are a few generalities that seem to hold true with all chilies. Chilies sweeten as they ripen, so a red chili (of the same variety) will be sweeter than a green one. And the bigger the chili pepper, the milder it usually is. So beware of chilies that come in small packages! The seeds and the veins pack the most punch, so to tone down your chili, don't use the seeds or veins.

CHILI SAUCE: Bottled chili sauce is a smooth combination of salted fish, red chilies, fish sauce, lime juice, and palm sugar. It is served with almost everything in Thailand. It comes in red and yellow varieties, and in various strengths.

CILANTRO: Cilantro is a pungent herb with a citruslike flavor, similar to parsley. It is also known as coriander.

COCONUT MILK: Coconut milk can be made fresh by grating and pressing fresh coconut meat, but the canned variety works just as well and is a lot less work! Coconut milk is not the same as coconut water, which is simply the liquid inside the coconut itself.

CORIANDER: Also known as cilantro, this herb is a cousin to parsley and is used as such. The seeds are also dried and ground and have a semisweet aroma.

CURRY: Curry powder is not a specific spice, but rather a combination of spices that vary depending on the desired effect. Some are sweet, while others are scorching hot. Basic commercial curry powders usually contain six to eight various ingredients.

CURRY LEAF: The leaves of an indigenous Southeast Asian plant that have no relation to curry powder or curry paste. The leaves do, however, release a curry-scented fragrance when crushed and are often added to various Asian dishes.

CURRY PASTE: Various combinations of spices and chilies, which can be either homemade or store-bought. They are super to keep on hand because they can be stored for long periods of time and help make quick, simple meals.

DRIED FISH: Crispy salt-preserved fish used as a snack and in soup.

DRIED SHRIMP: Tiny shrimp that are preserved in brine and then dried and used as a flavoring agent. Just a few go a long way. They are usually soaked in water for a few minutes before being added to a recipe, which both softens them and reduces their bite.

FISH SAUCE: Fish sauce or nan pla is one of the most used ingredients in Thai cuisine. It has a flavor similar to soy, although somewhat less salty. Salted, fermented fish, or shrimp gives the sauce its characteristic aroma and complex flavor. Beware—it doesn't smell very good to the Western nose, but is well worth getting used to.

FIVE-SPICE POWDER: A Chinese spice mixture that contains cinnamon, star anise, fennel, clove, ginger, peppercorns, and dried citrus peel.

GALANGAL: Galangal is a more pungent, fiery relative of ginger and is available both fresh and dried. If you can't find it, ginger is a perfectly acceptable substitute.

GARLIC: Garlic is a much-used relative of the onion with a sweet, pungent flavor. Pickled garlic is often used as a garnish.

GINGER: A rhizome that is now available in almost every supermarket, ginger adds a certain sweet-spicy component to dishes. It is available fresh, dried, crystallized, and preserved.

GUAVA: Also known as the tropical apple, the guava comes in two varieties—green and red. The green is native to Southeast Asia; the red is native to Hawaii. The fruit is especially high in vitamin C, iron, and calcium.

KAFFIR LIME: The juice, the zest, and the leaves of this thorny tropical tree are used extensively in southeast Asian cooking and impart a beautiful tropical fragrance and flavor.

LEMONGRASS: Lemongrass, or Citronella root, is an aromatic tropical grass with a flavor similar to lemon balm. It can be crushed whole or stripped of its fibrous outer leaves and chopped. Placed in a plastic bag, it will keep in the refrigerator for weeks.

LIME: A quintessential Thai ingredient; this citrus fruit is a great source of vitamin C.

MANGO: A kidney-shaped tropical fruit, mangoes are rich in vitamins A, B, and C. They are also high in sugar, sometimes 20 percent of their weight. Mangoes are used both fully ripe and green in some cases.

MINT: An herb used throughout the world to impart a refreshing, zesty aroma and flavor. Varieties include spearmint, peppermint, and lemon mint.

OYSTER SAUCE: Oyster sauce is made from oyster extracts, sugar, and other seasonings. It has a sweet-smoky flavor and is available in mild, hot, and "vegetarian" varieties.

PALM SUGAR: Palm sugar is a dark, unrefined sugar made from coconut palms. It is usually sold in blocks and must be crushed before it can be used. Dark brown sugar is a good and much easier-to-use substitute.

PAPAYA: This tropical fruit was introduced to Thailand by the Spanish after they conquered the Americas. Thai cooks use them both as a fruit and a vegetable.

RICE VINEGAR: Rice vinegar is milder and sweeter than regular white vinegar, but in a pinch white vinegar makes an acceptable substitute.

RICE WINE: Rice wine is a fermented concoction made from glutinous rice and millet and is used to add complexity and flavor. In Japan, it is known as mirin, which is a sweetish condiment used as a flavoring agent. If unavailable, dry sherry can be used as a substitute.

SHRIMP PASTE: A thick pungent paste made from salted fermented shrimp, which is often used in flavoring other curry pastes.

SOY SAUCE: Soy sauce is really not used very much in Thai cuisine. Instead, Thai cooks prefer fish sauce. However, soy can be used as a substitute for fish sauce and is specifically called for in some recipes. Soy sauce can be light or dark, which refers to flavor and color, not salt content. Tamari is a specific type of soy sauce that is strongly flavored, so use it sparingly.

SPRING ROLL WRAPPERS: Spring roll wrappers are similar to egg roll wrappers, but they are thinner and are made with only wheat flour and water. Egg roll wrappers also contain egg. When fried, spring roll wrappers are light and crisp.

STAR ANISE: The star anise is an inedible pod with a distinct licorice flavor that is infused into broths and sauces. Slightly crushing the pod helps to release its flavorful oils.

SWEET SOY SAUCE: This thick dark brown soy sauce is sweetened with palm sugar and star anise and is given piquant overtones with garlic. Sometimes the palm sugar is replaced with molasses.

TAMARIND: Tamarind is a large brown podlike fruit that contains both seeds and pulp, although the pulp is the only part used. It is usually sold in dried blocks of pulp, or in concentrates or pastes. If using pulp, soak it in hot water and then press it to release the thick sweet and sour juice. Concentrates and pastes are used straight from the jar. Tamarind has a flavor somewhat reminiscent of prunes and lemon.

TOFU: Tofu or bean curd is made from soybeans and water and is highly nutritious, due to its high plant proteins. It doesn't have much of a flavor on its own, but very quickly takes up the flavors of the dish it is in. It comes in a variety of textures ranging from soft to extra-firm. It is also available smoked.

YELLOW BEAN SAUCE: A sauce made from salted and fermented soybeans.

Appendix C

Thailand Resources

Sources for Thai Ingredients in the United States

THE SPICE HOUSE

1512 N. Wells St.
Chicago, IL
312-274-0378
Asian Spices

THE SPICE HOUSE

1048 N. Old World St.
Milwaukee, WI
414-272-0977
Asian Spices

KAM MAN FOOD PRODUCTS

200 Canal St.
New York, NY 10013
212-571-0330
Asian ingredients

DE WILDT IMPORTS

20 Compton Way
Hamilton Square, NJ 08969
800-338-3433
Asian ingredients

CASADOS FARMS

San Juan Pueblo, NM
505-852-2692
Fresh and dried chilies

DEAN & DELUCA

560 Broadway
New York, NY
800-221-7714
Asian ingredients

ETHNIC GROCER.COM

Thai produce, spices, prepared sauces, noodles, rice, and canned goods

IMPORTFOODS.COM

1-888-618-8424
Fresh Thai produce, cookware, spices, noodles, rice, sauces, and canned goods

PACIFICRIM-GOURMET.COM

Kitchenware, gourmet ingredients, garden seeds, cookbooks, and gifts

Great Thai Restaurants in the United States

Thai dining in the United States is becoming ever more popular, with storefront Thai restaurants almost as poplar as Chinese and Mexican. The following list offers a sampling of some of the best Thai restaurants in this country, all of them out of the ordinary and all of them worth a journey.

TAMARIND

80 14th St. NE
Atlanta, GA 30309
404-873-4888

THAI

3316 Greenmount Ave.
Baltimore, MD 21218
410-889-6002

BROWN SUGAR CAFÉ

129 Jersey St.
Boston, MA 02215
617-266-2928

BANGKOK 5

Rancho Mirage, California

ARUN'S

4156 N. Kedzie Ave.
Chicago, IL 60618
773-539-1909
Chef Arun Sampanthavivat

MEMA THAI CHINESE CUISINE

4-361 Kuhio Hwy.
Kapaa, HI 96746
808-823-0899

VONG

200 E. 54th St.
New York, NY
212-486-9592
Chef Jean Georges Vongerichten

NAN

4000 Chestnut St.
Philadelphia, PA
215-382-0818
Chef Kamol Phutlek

LEMONGRASS THAI

1705 NE Couch St.
Portland, OR
503-231-5780
Chef Shelley Siripatrapa

THAI HOUSE CUISINE

4225 Convoy St.
Dan Diego, CA
858-278-1800

YUKOL PLACE THAI

2380 Lombard St.
San Francisco, CA
415-922-1599

KHAN TOKE THAI HOUSE

5937 Geary Blvd.
San Francisco, CA
415-668-6654

THEP PHANOM THAI CUISINE

400 Waller St.
San Francisco, CA
415-431-2526

DUANGRAT'S

5878 Leesburg Pike
Falls Church, VA
703-820-5775

Index

C

D

E

H

I, J, K

L

M

N, O

P

Q, R

S

T

V, W, Y